Memoirs

HANS JONAS

Memoirs

Edited and Annotated by CHRISTIAN WIESE

Translated from the German by KRISHNA WINSTON

BRANDEIS UNIVERSITY PRESS

Waltham, Massachusetts

Published by University Press of New England

Hanover and London

BRANDEIS UNIVERSITY PRESS
Published by University Press of New England,
One Court Street, Lebanon, NH 03766
www.upne.com
© 2008 by Brandeis University Press
Originally published in German as Hans Jonas, *Erinnerungen*,
© 2003 by Insel Verlag, Frankfurt am Main and Leipzig
Printed in the United States of America

5   4   3   2   1

Library of Congress Cataloging-in-Publication Data
Jonas, Hans, 1903–1993.
[Erinnerungen. English]
Memoirs / Hans Jonas. — [1st ed.].
p.   cm. — (The Tauber Institute for the Study of European Jewry series)
Includes bibliographical references and index.
ISBN-10: 1-58465-639-5 (cloth : alk. paper)
ISBN-13: 978-1-58465-639-5 (cloth : alk. paper)
1. Jonas, Hans, 1903–1993. I. Title.
B3279.J664A313 2008
193 — dc22   2008007651
[B]

This book was translated from the German by Krishna Winston
with the exception of chapter 14, which was translated by Ammon Allred.

This translation was made possible through
the generous support of Eleonore Jonas.

g green
press
INITIATIVE

University Press of New England is a member of the Green Press Initiative.
The paper used in this book meets their minimum requirement for recycled paper.

CONTENTS

Foreword *by Rachel Salamander vii*
Introductory Remarks *by Lore Jonas xv*

Illustrations follow page 142

FOREWORD
Rachel Salamander

❦

One thing is clear: this is the book the good Lord had in mind when he made you.
— Hannah Arendt, upon reading a chapter in *The Imperative of Responsibility*

When Hans Jonas's book *The Imperative of Responsibility* appeared in Germany in the fall of 1979, even his publisher, Siegfried Unseld, had no way of knowing that he was bringing out a work of philosophy that would become something of a best seller. Probably no twentieth-century work by an academic philosopher has enjoyed such rapid and wide dissemination in the German-speaking countries as this "attempt at formulating an ethics for technological civilization." No one was more surprised by this success than Hans Jonas himself. In the 1930s he had published a significant study of gnosticism in late antiquity, yet he was known only to readers with a particular interest in that subject. Now in postwar West Germany Jonas achieved a fame enjoyed by none of the other German-Jewish philosophers of his generation who had fled Hitler to countries in the West — including such eminent philosophers as Günther Anders, Hannah Arendt, Max Horkheimer, Alfred Schütz, and Leo Strauss. Jonas became a media celebrity, the star attraction at every conference on the world's prospects. Interviewers clamored for time with him, and during the 1980s no Catholic or Protestant academy worth its salt would plan a program that did not include him as a participant.

Seldom has a book appeared at such a propitious moment. Jonas's topic resonated with the spirit of the times, which, after the Club of Rome's *Limits to Growth* and the oil crisis of the early 1970s, was attuned to the environment. Postwar optimism had given way to skepticism toward progress and an unblinking awareness of the dangers posed by constant expansion in the scientific and technical realm. The project of modernism — liberation of human beings through ever-increasing control over nature, that utopia of all avant-garde thinking since the beginning of the modern era — had lost its power to persuade. Hans Jonas countered the new fatalism with his defense of the normality of human life. In his thinking, schooled on Plato and Kant, he focused on identifying the questions and answers to be obtained from a rational approach to the immense knowledge and the unprecedented and potentially overwhelming power of the natural sciences. Rejecting both technophobia and unquestioning faith in science, Jonas placed his trust in a middle way. His ethics of responsibility was based on working out rationally all the possible outcomes of a given technological innovation or a new form of experimental research. His unpretentious manner in public, his rejection of rhetorical fireworks and attention-getting ploys, stands in welcome contrast to the sterile sensationalism we have witnessed recently in debates over genetic engineering. Amid the current din, we miss the calm voice of Hans Jonas, who, without whipping up panic, would call attention to inhumane aspects of the latest scientific research.

Hans Jonas was almost eighty when we first met in Munich. He drew one's attention less by his appearance than by his riveting way of speaking. Not a tall man — in fact, we were about the same height — Jonas was clearly an intellectual giant, and he spoke with such eloquence that his words could be printed almost verbatim. Even half a century of living abroad and writing and teaching in other languages had not impaired his German at all. On the contrary, in his slightly Rhenish diction he had preserved a piece of Germany that one hardly encounters nowadays. It vanished along with the highly educated middle-class Jews who went into exile or were exterminated by the Nazis. A comment Jonas made in the mid-1980s revealed to me that he felt cut off from changes in the German language and from developments in the German Federal Republic. He said he was considering canceling his longtime subscription to the weekly newspaper *Die Zeit* because he kept stumbling over new expressions and topics he did not really understand.

After years of abstinence, Jonas returned to the German language when he set out at seventy to write *The Imperative of Responsibility*. In the late 1930s, as an instructor at the Hebrew University in Jerusalem, he had composed his lectures in Hebrew, a time-consuming undertaking. Then, as a professor of philosophy in Canada and the United States, he had become proficient at writing in English, although he still spoke with a heavy German accent. Now he acknowledged that his mother tongue enabled him to articulate things as he really wanted to. Because at his "advanced age" time was becoming a precious commodity, he decided, in spite of all that had transpired in the meantime, to write the book in German. But in the preface he anticipates any possible criticism of the book's language by announcing that he intends to treat "a highly contemporary topic" not in a contemporary style but in one that might even be called "old-fashioned." The overwhelming response the book elicited proved him right. As an old man he finally received in Germany the recognition and the honor he deserved.

Our paths crossed in 1983, when Hans Jonas was offered the first Eric Voegelin guest professorship at the University of Munich. The circumstances of our meeting were propitious. My partner, Stephan Sattler, had studied with Eric Voegelin, a non-Jewish professor of political science who had emigrated to the United States in 1938 but later taught in Munich between 1958 and 1969. Stephan was well acquainted with the scholarly debates between Jonas and Voegelin over gnosticism in the ancient and modern worlds. After attending one of Hans Jonas's lectures at the end of February, Stephan and his brother Florian arranged to meet Hans and Lore Jonas in a restaurant in Schwabing, near the university. As Stephan told me, the Jonases wanted to know all about me. A day later they stopped by the bookstore to see me. Fortunately I had worked my way the previous summer through both volumes of Jonas's *Gnosticism and the Spirit of Late Antiquity*. Hans Jonas could not get over his amazement that someone outside academia would take a serious interest in intellectual movements from late antiquity, let alone "such a young woman," as he put it.

The friendship between Stephan and Hans Jonas began with their despair over Plotinus. Stephan was working on a study of Plotinus and was only too happy to discuss it with Jonas, who had never finished his own chapter on that thinker. The philosopher was delighted that when he recited Homer in Greek, Stephan was able to chime in. And indeed, almost always when we came together with Jonas, he would recite wonderful poems for us or read aloud meaningful passages from literary works. Like all Germans raised in cultivated circles before the war, this young man from a good Jewish family had known the poetry of Goethe and Schiller through and through, and Heine's likewise. In his last years, Jonas fascinated us on many an evening with the treasures of German culture stored in his memory.

Stephan and I loved to hear his stories. His memories conjured up a world of long ago. In Hans Jonas were resurrected the great minds of the educated German-Jewish elite who had been scattered to all points of the compass and had been forced to survive far from their home and their inherited culture, while their absence from Germany from that time on meant a terrible loss. As one of their last representatives, Hans Jonas offered a brilliant example of what had been driven out of Germany. Like most of the contemporaries of whom he spoke to us, he came from a largely assimilated family that still maintained ties to the Orthodox tradition but did not hesitate to show patriotism. His father, a respected textile manufacturer in Mönchengladbach, belonged to the Central Association of German Citizens of the Jewish Faith, whereas after 1918 Hans cast his lot with the Zionists. That decision would save his life. His father died "just in time" in 1938, but his mother was murdered in Auschwitz in 1942. Hans Jonas did not learn of her death until after the war. It would remain a wound that never healed.

As a Zionist, Hans had seen the handwriting on the wall and left Germany in 1933, going to Palestine by way of England. In Palestine he met others who shared his fate — at the Hebrew University, Gershom Scholem and Martin Buber, and, roaming the streets of Jerusalem, the poet Else Lasker-Schüler. He joined a literary circle; he found it much easier to compose German texts in the style of Thomas Mann or Goethe for the weekly meetings than to write his lectures in Hebrew. This intellectual gentlemen's circle was highly distinguished, with members such as Gershom Scholem; the physicist Shmuel Sambursky from Königsberg; the journalist George Lichtheim, whose father, Richard Lichtheim, had been a force in the early years of Zionism; the classicist Hans Lewy; and the Egyptologist Hans-Jakob Polotsky. These men competed to see who could imitate most successfully the style of famous German writers. The group dubbed itself "Pilegesh," a word composed from the first initials of the members' names that meant "concubine." The circle dissolved after several members married and were expected to stay home with their wives.

A number of factors account for Jonas's emigration to North America. The two chairs for professors of philosophy at the Hebrew University were already taken. Jonas also found that conveying his ideas in Hebrew was not getting any easier, and the political situation was becoming increasingly hostile. After five years as a soldier in the British army during the Second World War, Hans Jonas was called up again in 1948–49 for the Israeli War of Independence. By then he had had enough of war. In 1949 he accepted a visiting professorship at McGill University in Montreal, and moved the following year to Carleton University in Ottawa. At last he was closer to New York, where Karl Löwith, a person he greatly admired and considered the most gifted of Heidegger's students, was living and teaching. Hannah Arendt, his dear friend from their student days, also lived in New York. In 1955 Jonas was finally offered a teaching position at the New School for Social Research in Manhattan. There he enjoyed a collegial relationship, albeit not always free of tension, with another philosopher, Alfred Schütz. Schütz was committed to Husserl's phenomenology, while Jonas had been deeply influenced by Heidegger's revolt against Husserl; thus the major controversies that had raged in German philosophy during the 1920s continued on the banks of the Hudson. At the New School Jonas enjoyed a fulfilling life as a scholar and teacher, retiring in 1976.

In the 1950s, Hans Jonas and Hannah Arendt became close again. That was possible only because each of them liked the other's spouse so much. After the terrible blowup that occurred in 1963 between Jonas and Arendt when Arendt published *Eichmann in Jerusalem*, a quarrel that resulted in a break of several years' duration, Lore Jonas intervened to restore the friendship. After all, the two philosophers had known each other ever since they had both studied in Marburg with the New Testament scholar Rudolf Bultmann and with Martin Heidegger. Hans Jonas had been impressed by the courage of the young Arendt, who went to see Bultmann before taking his seminar on Saint Paul and made it absolutely clear that he should not try to convert her to Christianity. She was and would remain a Jew. Hans Jonas saw her as the prototype of a German "defiant Jew." It caused him immense emotional distress when he became the first to know about the love affair between Hannah Arendt and his revered "Herr Professor" Heidegger.

Whenever Hans Jonas touched on the subject of Heidegger, he expressed his profound disappointment in Heidegger as a human being. In 1924, Jonas had left Husserl in Freiburg and gone to Marburg to study with Heidegger, the rising star in philosophy. Almost everyone interested in philosophy in those days fell under his spell, including many Jews: Günther Anders, Herbert Marcuse, Jeanne Hersch, and Emmanuel Lévinas. Even later, few managed to escape from that spell. Hans Jonas was one of the few. Although he put Heidegger's "existentialism" to productive use in his book on gnosticism, this young man who had turned to philosophy with such enthusiasm precisely because he assumed that "dedication to the truth ennobled the soul" could not understand his teacher Heidegger's shameful alliance with the Nazis. "A philosopher should not have been taken in by that Nazi business," Jonas thought, least of all one of the "greatest philosophers of our time." Jonas saw this betrayal as a "catastrophe for philosophy" itself. He meant not only the infamous inaugural address Heidegger delivered when he was made rector of the University of Freiburg; he also could not forgive Heidegger's behavior toward his teacher, Husserl, whom Heidegger maligned as a Jew and forbade to enter and use the university library. Jonas emphasized the political danger posed in tumultuous times by a philosophy that "hurled" the individual fatefully into the current moment.

In 1945, when Hans Jonas first set foot on German soil again, he knew there was one person he "could not visit": Heidegger. Upon leaving Germany in 1933, he had sworn to himself that he would return only as a soldier in a victorious army. And so it was. He returned as "a Jew conscious of his dignity," proudly wearing the uniform of a British officer. For five years he had fought Hitler as a volunteer in the Jewish Brigade. With the British troops he had made his way to Germany through Italy and Austria. The person he sought out immediately was Karl Jaspers. Through the entire war Jaspers had remained in Heidelberg at his Jewish wife's side. Both of them had always kept poison handy, "in case worse comes to worst." Jonas described the reunion with great feeling. He had rung their bell during the "sacred midday rest period," when Jaspers was not to be disturbed. Frau Jaspers opened the door and without the slightest hesitation immediately took him to her husband, whose exclamation, "It is our fault that we are still alive!" Hans Jonas repeated with a sob.

Next he went to see Rudolf Bultmann in Marburg, and his publisher Ruprecht in Göttingen, who immediately insisted that he should write the conclusion to the second volume of his book on gnosticism. Only much later did a meeting with Heidegger come about. Again Jonas's hopes were dashed. He had expected Heidegger to say something "by way of apology." Nothing came. After twenty minutes Jonas got up and left.

More and more Stephan and I felt it was incumbent on us to preserve this body of precious memories and share it with the world. Hans Jonas did not think highly of a philosopher's portraying himself in an autobiography. Nonetheless, in the summer of 1983 I persuaded him to speak at the bookstore. First I had to dispel some of his doubts as to whether his experiences would be of any interest to the public. It was a hot day, and the room was filled to bursting, but the audience hung on his every word. Jonas spoke without notes, yet everything sounded as if it had been carefully formulated in advance. Suddenly he realized that beyond the two of us there was a German audience eager to hear his life story.

The Jonases came to Germany every year after that, usually in June. (Lore Jonas still makes the trip.) We spent a good deal of time together, taking excursions into the Upper Bavarian countryside, usually stopping for lunch at country inns that served cèpes, a type of mushroom Hans Jonas adored and could not get in America. During these outings I realized that he still had a childlike capacity for amazement, as if he were seeing things for the first time. His comment "You don't say—really? really?" made every conversation exciting. We introduced the Jonases to our friends and families, and went to see them whenever we were in New York. They lived half an hour by train outside the city, in New Rochelle, where they had one of those wood-frame houses with a nice lawn that are typical of the area. Nearby lived several mathematicians or scientists who taught in New York or at the Hastings Institute, and with whom Jonas carried on lively discussions. Upon entering the Jonas's white house, one felt transported to another place and time. The rooms were invitingly furnished with splendid Biedermeier pieces; the library shelves were filled for the most part with works of German and Jewish intellectual history. It was easy to forget that one was in America. On the second floor hung lovely drawings done by Hans Jonas when he was a young art student. We met the Jonas children and were present when the family celebrated important birthdays and a very special occasion — the conferral of the Peace Prize of the German Publishing Industry in 1987. We had become friends of the family. Hans Jonas once described the situation thus: we had come to them "like two stray young dogs" with whom they had fallen in love.

We never ran out of things to talk about. Everything became a topic of discussion, above all the problem that preoccupied Hans Jonas during his last years: dealing with modern life. As in his book, he was preoccupied with the question of how to formulate an ethics appropriate to an age of runaway technology. Human beings had to take responsibility for their fragile environment, with the very future of the world at stake. "Man is the only being known to us that can take responsibility. Because he can do so, he is responsible." This imperative ("Ability brings with it obligation") accompanies me every day of my life. In the bookshop I have put up a poster, a wonderful portrait of Hans Jonas, with this dictum as a caption; it is read and commented on admiringly by many people.

But our conversations also dealt with less earthshaking topics, for instance our own happiness. Hans Jonas repeatedly stressed that Stephan and I should legalize our long-term relationship. At some point we could no longer evade his probing questions, so we tied the knot in June 1990, with Hans and Lore Jonas as surrogate parents. Along with my brother, Hans served as a witness. The chuppah or wedding canopy was put up in the Jonases' cherry orchard in New Rochelle. Speaking at the wedding dinner, repeatedly overcome with tears of emotion, Hans Jonas invoked the high points and low points of the German-Jewish relationship.

We had spent our most intense hours together in September 1989. I had persuaded Hans Jonas to tell, one more time, in one fell swoop, his life story, of which we had heard many versions over the years. I wanted to record it on tape. Once Lore had consented, nothing more stood in the way. The Jonases were staying as usual at the Hotel Biederstein in Munich, not far from the Englischer Garten. Over a period of two weeks, we met every day in the adjoining lounges on the hotel's ground floor. Stephan and I took turns asking Hans questions about his life, which in the meantime had become part of ours. Each session lasted no more than an hour and a half. Hans was already suffering from emphysema, but he did not want to give up cigarettes. At regular intervals he would light up, though he sensibly took only a few puffs, then put out the cigarette and trimmed off the smoked end with a little scissors that he kept in the cigarette pack for this purpose. Lore plied us with cookies and tea or coffee. Sometimes we allowed ourselves a swig of brandy from the silver flask that Hans always had on him. Our conversations filled thirty-three tapes. It would have been impossible to convert them into a book in Jonas's style had it not been for his polished speaking style. Upon reading the transcript, we knew we had exactly what we needed. Our questions turned out to be superfluous; we could let Jonas speak for himself.

When I was organizing a discussion series under the heading "The End of the Century" for May and June 1992, Lore Jonas helped me persuade Hans to give his last major public address. At eighty-nine, he had doubts about his own stamina, but his speech, "Looking Backward and Forward at the End of the Century," earned him standing ovations in the packed Prince Regent Theater in Munich. That speech has meanwhile been published in book form.

INTRODUCTORY REMARKS
Lore Jonas

Upon being asked to write an introduction to this book, I found myself wondering what I could possibly add to Hans Jonas's own words. Eventually I decided I should try to convey a sense of the character of this man, whose life I shared for more than fifty years.

If curiosity lies at the root of all philosophy, as the ancients asserted, my husband possessed this gift to an unusual degree. I am tempted to say that he was naïve — in a way that made it possible for him to look at things in a new light, as if no one had ever looked at them before. Occasionally this trait caused others to rebuke him for not citing earlier thinkers. In response he would invoke his friend Gershom Scholem's witticism: "Thinking for yourself is good for you."

He gazed upon the world with fresh, perennially astonished eyes, and was as excited by his grandson's first brave attempts at walking at a year and a half as by a magnificent sunset seen from our garden or the works of the great poets, many of which he could recite from memory even at an advanced age.

He was a proud and loving father to his three children, Ayalah, Jonathan, and Gabrielle.

Hans had received an education in the grand humanistic tradition that was typical of his generation, and is almost unknown today. He could quote Homer in Greek and Cicero in Latin, learned Hebrew in secondary school, and was fond of the Prophets. He learned English in his late forties, and in America that became his medium of communication; native speakers of English attest that he achieved considerable mastery in that idiom. Not until his seventies, when he wrote *The Imperative of Responsibility*, did he return to his mother tongue.

If other men could charm one with their good looks or manners, he could charm one with his speech. I still recall the first time I invited him to dinner; it was in Palestine in the late 1930s. The meal included olives, and he held up an olive and delivered a paean to the olive that began with the anointing of Homer's Greek heroes, went on to the use of olive oil by the high priests of the Old Testament, and eventually arrived at Goethe's *West-Eastern Divan*.

Between 1940 and 1945 he served in the British army. He wanted to join the armed struggle against Hitler. During his military service, when he was far from any libraries, he thought about *life* — for obvious reasons, given the ever-present danger of being wounded or killed — and that sparked his interest in the natural sciences. While he was in the field, I sent him, at his request, seminal scientific works by such authors as Charles Darwin, Aldous Huxley, John Haldane, and many others — whatever I could lay my hands on in Palestine.

He first recorded his thoughts about science in his "didactic letters" from the field, which he later developed into the book *Organism and Freedom*, which in later editions bore the title *The Phenomenon of Life*. His love for the natural sciences and his knowledge of them deepened in America, where he spent much of his time in the company of scientists and mathematicians. There were quite a few of the latter in New Rochelle, where we took up residence in 1955. They were mathematicians from Göttingen who had moved to New Rochelle on the urging of Richard Courant, the former head of the University of Göttingen Mathematics Department. He had left Germany in 1933 and wanted to be able to have discussions with his mathematical colleagues even on weekends.

Then came the Hastings Center, where Hans Jonas was made a fellow in 1969 and where he befriended both humanists and scientists who came together there, discussed ethical questions, and, amazingly enough, listened to one another.

He was an enthusiastic and impassioned teacher. One of his earlier students, Howard McConnell, recalled his experience with Hans at Carleton University in Ottawa this way: "Some of my most wonderful memories are connected with Hans Jonas. In his courses, philosophy became a lively and fascinating subject. He told us that we were participating in the eternal search for the answer to the great moral and cosmic questions that had occupied thinkers from Thales on, and that each generation had to confront anew."

In my husband's work I can make out three phases: he called his study *Gnosticism and the Spirit of Late Antiquity* his "beginner's piece" — a historical work. In *Organism and Freedom* he turned his attention to the present, and in *The Imperative of Responsibility* he articulated his concerns about the future. At the time he was seventy-five, yet no lessening of his powers could be detected, and it was lovely to see the feistiness of his earlier years giving way to a more conciliatory attitude, while the urgency of the problems he was treating demanded greater effort on his part.

It is well known that he had the best teachers one could possibly have in the 1920s in Germany — Edmund Husserl, Martin Heidegger, and Rudolf Bultmann. That experience set a standard that he never wearied of striving to meet, yet also never allowed him to be satisfied. In a poem he wrote in English on the occasion of his eighty-fifth birthday (he did write poetry at times), the line occurs, "You and I know I did sometimes, not always my best. / Now is the time for the long, long rest."

He had no fear of death, but held the view that he expressed in "The Burden and Blessing of Mortality": "As far as each one of us is concerned, the knowledge that we are here for but a short while, and that a non-negotiable limit is imposed on the time we may expect to have, may well be necessary as an incentive to count our days and to live them in such a way that they count for something." I believe that is what he did.

PART 1

Experiences & Encounters

CHAPTER 1

Youth in Mönchengladbach during Wartime

One of the formative experiences of my youth was the outbreak of the First World War. At the time I was eleven, a pupil at the university-preparatory *Gymnasium* — I believe I was in my ninth year of school and had already received certain impressions of what was going on in the world. In my younger years there had already been wars you could read about in the papers — for instance, the Balkan wars that preceded the World War. In 1912–13 the Greeks, Bulgarians, and Serbs went to war against the Turks, and, once they'd defeated them, turned on each other; the Bulgarians went at it with the Greeks, Serbs, and Romanians. At any rate, war dominated the news. And then came another major event that grabbed our imagination even more powerfully than the fighting far off in Turkey: it was the sinking of the *Titanic*, that enormous ship that set out for its first Atlantic crossing, struck an iceberg, and sank, with great loss of life. I still recall vividly what a shock this tragedy caused; I pored over the newspaper, and the adults in my family and everyone else talked about it endlessly. My general impression was that our own lives were very boring. When something of significance happened, it was always far away, and other people had the advantage of experiencing it close up, whether it was the soldiers and the civilian populations in the Balkans or those passengers out in the middle of the ocean. But to me it was a sad fate to have been born into a period and a world where everything was in tip-top order and the only real excitement was to be found in history books and occasionally also in the paper.

The best and most wonderful, the heroic and the edifying experiences had all occurred in the past — for instance in the days of the ancient Greeks and Romans, also in the German and European past, in the Napoleonic Era. I'd been introduced to the Greek myths, and had read the Homeric epics in particular. The Trojan War was as much part of a young person's frame of reference as the Germanic sagas and myths. But antiquity had other things to offer as well, for instance the Battle of Marathon, the struggle of the Greeks against the Persians, the victory of freedom over slavery, the great Punic War. I assume I read about that war later — I no longer recall exactly where our study of history at the *Gymnasium* began. Gustav

Schwab's *Die schönsten Sagen des klassischen Altertums* (The Most Beautiful Myths of Classical Antiquity) made a much more lasting impression on me than the biblical stories I encountered in religion class, though I eventually discovered the Bible for myself and came to appreciate these stories. At first my biblical knowledge was more of a mechanical nature — about Adam and Eve and the serpent, and the Flood, Noah's Ark, and then the patriarchs Abraham, Isaac, and Jacob, but especially Joseph and his brothers and the history of Kings Solomon and David. I believe, however, that in my youth it was the Greek and the German myths that had a far greater hold on my imagination. In those days children's books were richly illustrated, and I can still see certain images vividly, for instance a depiction of the Greeks fighting before the gates of Troy or, from the German myths, the gods Baldur, Thor, and Wotan, and the Fenris wolf.

My awareness of world events necessarily began on 1 August 1914, when my own country suddenly found itself at war. With a child's typical foolishness, I felt that at last something was happening. Up to then I'd lived a charmed life — in a country that had known nothing but peace for decades, that was flourishing economically, and as a child in a comfortably situated family, where the father was a respected manufacturer and a recognized member of the Jewish community, where the family could travel to the North Sea for the summer holidays, with enormous steamer trunks — and thought things would continue this way forever. Every year you were a little closer to the goal of being grown up. Maybe you wouldn't do exactly the same thing as your father, but essentially everything would remain the same — in the outside world and in the secure way you were embedded in that world. I certainly had such a feeling, because I still remember, with some shame, the regret I felt at being denied the experience of living in an age of greatness, in which a person could display heroism, in which there were victories, perhaps also defeats, but at least something important was happening, something I could experience directly or even play a role in, and of course it would be a hero's role, maybe even a sacrificial role — I didn't assume I would escape unscathed. What mattered was that something be happening.

We were at home when the Austrian heir to the throne was assassinated in Sarajevo. Over the next four weeks the situation became increasingly critical, and finally the first of August arrived, when — not unexpectedly — war broke out. My first encounter with wartime came on a hot August day: trains serving as troop transports sped by from the east, and there were also units on foot. The railroads couldn't handle the entire mobilization and the massing of troops on the western front. The infantry units marching through Mönchengladbach were billeted in private houses. We had three soldiers who came from the Province of Brandenburg. I don't know how far they'd come on foot. They'd probably traveled most of the distance by train and had to cover only the last stretch — from Mönchengladbach, near the Dutch border, to Liège — on foot. That was the first military destination along the segment of the front close to our hometown. There was tremendous hustle and bustle. But that afternoon I set out as usual for the town swimming pool, where I'd recently passed my freestyle swimming test. When I got there, the entire area around the pool had been turned into a reception camp for the troops passing through, and the pool director, when he saw me arriving with my bathing things under my arm, asked, "What are you doing here?" "I want to go swimming!" At that he gave me a big slap in the face. "Beat it! Can't you see we have more important things to do here!" That was the beginning of the war. The director was in a tizzy with so much to do all of a sudden, and I was in the way. I also remember the soldiers who spent the night with us. They were members of the infantry, enormous fellows from Brandenburg, who tended to each other's blistered feet. One was a private first class to whom we gave our best room, and not until later did it come out that during his short stay he'd started something with our beautiful nanny. She placed great hopes on this relationship, which weren't fulfilled. Later she suffered a nervous breakdown when he finally wrote to say that he had no intention of seeing her again. I don't know whether he told her he was married. At any rate, he broke off with her by mail. The whole business was one of the consequences of those first days of war.

Well, after that life went on as usual, which meant school. I assume we hadn't gone away for the holidays that year; at least I don't recall any trip. We were all at home when the war broke out. My father immediately went to Cologne, to the main procurement office for our region, and submitted his bid for tent material and other textiles that might be needed by the military. And he was really one of the first to get there, and came home, as I learned later, with huge contracts. Not only were all 120 or so mechanical looms in our factory working at full capacity, but other textile plants in Mönchengladbach were also hard at work filling his orders. So business was booming, and on the front lines, too, everything was going splendidly. Liège fell, and we heard the rumble of cannon in the distance when "Big Bertha" went into action, a 22-centimeter howitzer, a secret weapon Krupp had developed. It got its name from Alfred Krupp's wife, Berta. It was the heaviest artillery piece ever made and deployed. With the tremendous thrust of this howitzer, whose shells came down almost perpendicularly and with great accuracy, the enormous reinforced concrete bunkers fortifying Liège were breached. Belgium wasn't entirely unprepared; Liège's bunkers had been constructed according to the most modern principles, but Big Bertha pulverized them. And victory followed upon victory.

One episode shows how intense patriotic sentiment was during those first weeks of war, including among the Jews. My eldest cousin in Mönchengladbach was Erich Haas, the son of Aunt Berta, my father's eldest sister — after emigrating, he practiced as a psychoanalyst in Birmingham. At the outbreak of war, he was in the last year of *Gymnasium*, and because the victories were coming thick and fast, he was terribly worried that the war might be over before he had a chance to serve. Under normal circumstances he would have taken his final exams first and then been called up. But secondary-school pupils who were almost eighteen were given the opportunity to receive the so-called emergency diploma and volunteer. My cousin Erich, who'd been rather sickly during his school years and once had even been sent to a sanatorium for something, was determined not to pass up this opportunity. I think he didn't quite meet the age requirement, but in any case he and his father were seriously worried that if he volunteered he wouldn't be taken, since there was a huge surplus of young volunteers. So his father went to Cologne with Erich, who somehow managed to have the military physical. To sway the sergeant overseeing the process in their favor, my uncle, Adolf Haas, slipped him a gold piece, whereupon Erich was declared fit for service. That's how he got into the army, where he served for four years without suffering any ill effects. So in those days people used bribery to get into the army, whereas later bribery was used by people who wanted to stay out.

There are two explanations, by the way, for the above-average voluntary participation of Jews in the First World War. First, the Jews were eager not to appear as shirkers but to prove that they were loyal citizens.[1] But there was another explanation, much more prosaic, and that was that the Jews belonged to a social class in which it was customary to volunteer for military service, which was not the case with the working class. In certain educated circles, both the notion of patriotism and that of volunteer service were somehow more strongly rooted than among the working masses, who precisely because of their class didn't thrust themselves to the fore but felt they could wait until their turn came. Most of the Jews belonged to the middle class, which was ideologically most receptive to patriotism; hence their overrepresentation among the volunteers.[2]

So while the patriotic fever of 1914 gripped us as well, only my mother, who was a gentle soul, mourned in advance all the dead, wounded, and maimed, and everything connected with the war. Not out of any theoretical or principled pacifism but simply out of compassion, out of overflowing humanity: "It's dreadful, just dreadful!" Of course she also wanted German weapons to prove victorious, but at the same time she bemoaned the fact that wars took place at all. My father, meanwhile, was more naïve in this respect, and shared with 99.9 percent of the German population great enthusiasm for the war: the Germans would stand the test, and he was also convinced that destiny had actually called on Germany to play a special role in Europe. According to the official version, however, Germany was fighting a defensive war: we are encircled, we are waging war against a mighty enemy alliance that has been planning to attack us for a long time, and all we are doing is defending ourselves. Yet from the outset there were hopes for victory that extended far beyond mere defense. This is nothing new I'm saying; I daresay every history book notes that the idea that we'd been attacked and "encircled" was accompanied by childish notions such as I've summarized here—thank God this dreary, boring era of peace is over at last, and we can show who and what we are. "He who has many enemies has much honor, but we must save our skins." Third, it looked as though wonderful laurels were ours for the seizing. At first the victory bulletins piled up, but then they stopped coming, and suddenly all was silent. After four weeks, the advance was halted. It didn't reach Paris. Then came the defeat on the Marne.

Now, in my family there was one person who never participated in the general intoxication—Uncle Leo, my mother's somewhat older brother, still unmarried at the time, a doctor in Düsseldorf and one of the most intelligent and wisest people I've had the good fortune to know. During the weeks just before and after war broke out, his views differed from the others' in two respects: first, he was convinced that if England was against us, we couldn't win. In certain European circles there was great respect for England, and he was one of those who felt that if England was on the other side, the war was already as good as lost. Second, he took a very practical step. He said to himself that from now on the German press couldn't be fully trusted, that its reporting was bound to give a one-sided picture. Because he wanted to stay informed, he subscribed during the entire war to a Swiss paper — which was allowed in Germany. In this way he received news reports from a neutral country, and he knew that events had taken a major turn for the worse on the Marne; not only had the German advance been stopped, but something had gone very wrong, forcing the army to retreat. And this confirmed his original skepticism. But no one else saw it this way.

Uncle Leo was the only son of Chief Rabbi Jakob Horowitz of Krefeld, originally from Cracow, who'd attended the rabbinical seminary in Breslau and later come to the West.[3] A highly educated man, who considered himself a liberal Jew. Nonetheless his house kept kosher, of course. My mother had managed his household from a young age, for her mother — my maternal grandmother, whom I never knew, because she died long before my mother's marriage and my birth — had trained her as a young girl to keep house for her father — a rabbi's household. My mother suffered greatly in this role, not just from the chores themselves, but above all from the necessity of maintaining appearances. She knew perfectly well that her father didn't believe in the dietary laws, but they had to be observed strictly because of his position. For that reason she promised herself, "When I marry and have a house of my own, we won't keep this kind of kitchen and observe these laws." But it was a long time before she married. She was already in her mid-twenties, which was considered very late in those days, and was still Röschen Horowitz, still taking care of her widowed father's household. Finally her brother, my Uncle Leo, who was studying medicine at the University of Bonn, met a certain Otto Jonas, a fellow student. He was my father's younger brother. My father — as the eldest of ten children in a small Westphalian country town called Borken, where the family company had been in existence since 1815 — had to go into the business early, and thus took on a sort of paternal role toward his younger siblings. It was his duty, or so he felt, and he fulfilled it faithfully, to make it possible for his younger brothers to do what he'd longed to do himself, namely study at the university. Furthermore, he had three sisters who had to be properly provided for, because at that time you couldn't marry off a daughter well if she didn't have a dowry. He himself had to leave school after the eleventh grade to work in the family business; he couldn't even finish secondary school. It was the great sorrow of his life that he had to sacrifice his dream of higher education for the sake of the family and the firm, in which he eventually became the boss. His younger brothers, my various uncles, had a somewhat ambivalent relationship to him, as is usually the case when you're deeply indebted to someone who also occupies a position of authority. Of the three brothers who went to the university, two became lawyers and the third a doctor. Another brother went into business and left the country. The next-eldest brother became second in command in the company and managed the factory.

It was only toward the end of the century, around 1896, I think, that the company moved from Borken to Mönchengladbach, where the mechanization of the textile industry was in full swing at the time, and a skilled workforce as well as excellent transportation resources were available. Krefeld, where my mother grew up, was also a textile-manufacturing center, by the way, but producing a finer product than Gladbach, in the sense that silk is finer than cotton. Krefeld was the Lyon of the Rhineland, while Mönchengladbach was its Manchester. In Mönchengladbach they produced "Genoa corduroy," that ribbed fabric often used for work clothes. In addition, many textiles were manufactured for the colonial market, especially the ugly printed cotton material known as "Gladbach shoddy," in which, however, there was a thriving trade. Our family firm didn't deal in cotton but in linen and damask. These materials occupied a position between cotton and silk, so to speak.

Later my father described to me a visit to Bonn, where his youngest brother, Otto, whom he loved the most and considered the most gifted of his siblings, was at the university. Otto took him around and showed him the university and the medical school — and my father had tears in his eyes. In other words: "This is the world I've had to renounce." But something else happened. When Otto Jonas and Leo Horowitz, who'd developed something of a friendship, spoke about their families, it turned out that Leo Horowitz had a younger sister. And Otto, who was seventeen years younger than my father, remarked, "I have an older brother who still hasn't married. He's put off marriage to take care of the rest of us. Because our father was too old already, he assumed that responsibility." In fact my father had more or less forbidden himself to marry until he'd married off his three sisters and made sure his brothers' expensive university studies were finished. Altogether he'd had nine siblings, one of whom had died as a child. As a result, I had five uncles and three aunts on the Jonas side, while on my mother's side I had only the one uncle, about whom I'll have more to say later. So Leo Horowitz and Otto Jonas looked at each other: "We should introduce them." "Yes, what a good idea!" And thus it came about that Gustav Jonas, from Borken in Westphalia, a resident for the last few years of Gladbach on the lower Rhine because of the company's move there, appeared as a suitor in Krefeld and met my mother. They then married, in 1900, I think, for the first son, my older brother, was born in 1901.

So Röschen Horowitz became Frau Gustav Jonas, and they made a remarkable couple. My father was a stocky, robust, short-legged man with a powerful torso and broad shoulders, and a large head with a handsome brow, but he was broad, inclined toward corpulence, with sturdy legs that could move at quite a pace. He'd grown up in Spartan conditions, and all his life he remained modest in his demands, but he enjoyed his food, and could take real delight in a good roast, a nice meal. He was very intelligent, knew his classics, owned an excellent library, but hadn't had time to immerse himself in it, but rather put all his energy into the business. Nevertheless he greatly valued education. In contrast to us children, who took on a Rhenish accent, simply as a result of our surroundings, my father spoke pure High German — free of Jewish expressions, by the way, let alone Yiddishisms. The word "goy" never crossed our lips. We were familiar with words like "meshugge" or "chutzpah," but we never used either one. I can't recall my parents ever saying of anyone that he had great chutzpah. I don't even know whether they disapproved of such language; it was simply not considered suitable, and in our house an educated German, free of dialect, was spoken. It wasn't even a question of not wanting to be identified as Jewish — no, there simply wasn't any temptation, for neither my father nor my mother had learned Yiddish at home. They belonged to the old German-Jewish population that had lived in the country for generations, and in their hometown of Borken the Jonas family considered themselves superior to those members of the community who might speak some Yiddish at home. That was why these community members had given the Jonases the mocking title of "the Hohenzollerns of Borken." This nickname expressed a mixture of respect and mockery that wasn't entirely friendly. The Jonases were viewed as arrogant because they rejected the ways of the majority of their fellow Jews. Thus they didn't marry in Borken but looked farther afield to find their partners, for instance to Eschweiler. Everything my father said about his youth and his extended family pointed beyond Borken.[4]

But marriages to non-Jews were completely out of the question — Lord preserve us! It wasn't until the First World War that one of my father's brothers, Uncle Max, entered into a mixed marriage.[5] He'd gone to Italy as a businessman and had set up a factory, in partnership with someone, that made straw hats. When war broke out, he was drafted, but wasn't sent to the front.

He was already middle-aged. When he was finally demobilized at the end of the war — he'd been stationed in Silesia just before that — he brought home a Christian fiancée, from a very good family. And he took it upon himself to inform all his brothers and sisters that he was engaged to a Christian. At the time — that was in 1918, so I was fifteen by then — I heard with my own ears one of my aunts — it was Aunt Elfriede from Lechenich near Cologne, married to Uncle Hermann Simon but a Jonas by birth — say something you normally expect to encounter only in fiction: "Our dear Papa will turn over in his grave!" That was her comment. Can you believe it? But I swear I heard it myself. Then this poor fiancée had to run the gauntlet of the entire Jonas family. When she reached that particular aunt, Elfriede urged her to consider becoming Jewish. Whereupon the fiancée gave a reply that likewise would normally occur only in literature: "I'm not the kind of person who changes her religion like a dress!" And that was that. She remained a Christian, he a Jew. She was a good wife and emigrated with him to Bolivia. To me she was simply Aunt Klara, but when she first appeared on the scene it caused huge consternation in the family.

To come back to my father: he was a very conscientious, hardworking man who never spared himself. He took pleasure in the simple things of life. The fact that he liked to eat doesn't mean that he expected delicacies. I don't know, for instance, whether he ever ate oysters. Probably not, because he'd been raised Orthodox. In his parents' house the Jewish customs were observed very strictly, and that stayed with him. True, he didn't usually go to temple on Shabbat except on the high holy days. I also think I recall him working at the factory for a half day on Saturdays. But for as long as I went to the synagogue with him on Yom Kippur or Rosh Hashanah or other holy days, I could tell that he took it very seriously, and he participated wholeheartedly. He fasted strictly for Yom Kippur. My mother, the rabbi's daughter, saw to it, however, that our household was less Jewish than his own inclinations would have dictated. He often told me that before he married he kept strictly kosher on business trips — he traveled a lot for the company, visiting clients as far away as Hamburg and Berlin. This observance of the dietary laws meant that in small towns he often had to get by for days or weeks on boiled eggs, potatoes, and milk products, going without meat altogether. In some towns there were Jewish inns or hotels, but for the most part he had to stay in ordinary hotels. More than once it happened that he would order a meal of eggs, potatoes, and butter in a hotel's restaurant, and someone would come over from another table and compliment him on the sacrifices he was willing to make for his faith. Once he had his own household, ironically, my mother did away with keeping kosher. Still, pork never appeared on our table. We bought our meat from the Jewish butcher, of course — beef, chicken, or veal. But the stern prohibition on eating meat and milk products at the same meal wasn't observed in our house. There's a whole set of laws I simply never learned. Nevertheless we owned two complete sets of dishes and flatware, which we referred to at home as *milchig* and *fleischig*. In other regions or other families the terms were *Milchding* and *Fleischding*. We didn't use those terms. But although the distinction was still preserved for kitchen utensils, the differentiation between foods wasn't taken very seriously. When we traveled, we stayed at non-Jewish hotels on the North Sea or in the Eifel region and ate what was placed before us. Wherever possible, of course, we avoided eating pork roast or ham. I don't think I ever tasted ham as a child. Instead we ate smoked meat — Neuenahr smoked meat, which was a form of beef, like the smoked beef for which the Graubünden region in Switzerland is famous. But no ham. Certain things were just not done in our house: you didn't eat anything from the pig.[6]

My parents' personalities were as different as you can imagine. My father displayed a certain robustness — starting with his physical appearance. To me he was always the epitome of masculine strength, even though he was short, something I didn't notice as a child. He had a rather authoritarian manner, and because of his position as the eldest of the siblings had probably become used to playing the dominant role in the family. Strangely enough, despite his sternness, he was tremendously softhearted. He not only exercised authority but also had a positively choleric temperament. When something really angered him, he would fly into a rage. The veins in his forehead would swell, his hair would stand on end, and he could be incredibly furious. When the storm passed, however, it was over and done with. His rages never lasted more than a few seconds, and he didn't bear a grudge. He got relief by blowing off steam. Sometimes his rage was so extreme that my mother was afraid he would have a heart attack. She would say, "For God's sake, don't get so upset!" But he would calm down just as fast, and then everything would be all right.

My mother, however, didn't find relief this way, and things would gnaw at her for a long time. In many respects she was the opposite of my father. First of all, she was slim, and kept her girlish figure as long as I knew her. Delicate, with an enchanting grace in her movements, a long, narrow face with a prominent nose — to her sorrow, for in this period of assimilation and antisemitism, such a nose was a burden because a person felt, at least subjectively, that a large nose was characteristically Jewish. But she had a very lovely profile. In our house we had an alabaster bust, something classical, the sort of thing you often found in a respectable bourgeois home. Perhaps it was a copy of a bust of Diana, with a classic profile. And I was always convinced, the way children can be, that it portrayed my mother. The sculptor had merely made the nose a little straighter and a little less prominent. My mother was very musical, like her own mother, who came from a cultivated Silesian family and at a very young age had a passion for performing music. My father, on the other hand, was completely unmusical. He was always off-key when he sang the simple Hebrew songs on Friday evening or chanted the Haggadah at Passover. I never heard him sing properly, even the national anthem. He had a great appreciation for fine literature, knew poems by heart, and sometimes recited them, too. But when it came to music, he was hopeless, which meant he simply couldn't enjoy something that meant so much to my mother. Since he was a loving person, my father of course did everything he could to accommodate my mother's musical preferences. When the wartime contracts brought in large profits, our most important major acquisition was a Blüthner grand piano, which replaced the spinet we'd had up to then.

My dear mother found life painful, and not because of the unanswered questions but because of all the pain and suffering in the world, all the poverty and misery. She felt enormous compassion, and tried to help as much as she could. My father, who worked hard and wanted to hang on to what he earned, sometimes had to hold her back. My mother's response was to secretly set aside some of her household money so she could give it to someone in need. One time she confided this to me, and explained, "Your father's a very kind man, yet he thinks I overdo it. But for me this is a necessity." She often sent money to relatives who'd stayed in the East, in Galicia, and wrote to her begging for help, or to an aunt or cousin who had a son who'd gone astray, was causing his mother great sorrow, and would probably end up in jail if he failed to pay his debts. That was something she couldn't let happen — so she sent money. When it was a matter of larger sums, my father had to know about it, of course. That in turn limited her ability to help people out with smaller amounts, since she'd already taken too much advantage of my father's charity.

As far as I can tell — parents don't discuss such matters with their children — my father and mother were also very different in their sexuality. Since my father was a sensual person in his physical being and his enjoyment of certain pleasures, I imagine he also enjoyed the sexual aspect of love more, whereas my mother was probably inhibited about such things. On the other hand, my mother valued tenderness, whereas my father, as a result of his upbringing, was unused to showing his feelings. I can still see them sitting on the sofa: my mother nestled against him, and he somewhat awkwardly putting his arm around her, patting her on the shoulder, and saying, "There, there, it's all right." He didn't know how to behave, because he came from a family in which you didn't give way to your feelings, but were ambitious and hardworking and practiced great self-discipline in your emotional life. His mother must have been a woman of great cultivation, though, who carried her Schiller and her Goethe around with her, so to speak. That becomes apparent from a letter my father kept. Since there was no classics-oriented *Gymnasium* in Borken, he was sent to live with relatives—in Eschweiler, I think, also a town on the lower Rhine—to go to school. He was such a good student that after the ninth grade he was promptly allowed to skip a level. On this occasion, his mother, who still found time to read, even though she'd borne ten children, sent him a letter that could easily have been written by Goethe's mother. A letter from a highly educated woman, in beautiful German prose, in which she congratulates and praises him, but then—I still remember this passage—also admonishes him: "See to it that you not get above yourself and become prideful. God has given you these gifts, and I am happy to see you applying them properly. But do not become too proud of yourself." It was a wonderful letter, which he showed me one time. The family was educated, but feelings of the kind my mother displayed were foreign to it. My father and my uncles as well were all highly intelligent and successful in their professions, but somehow, by comparison with my mother and her brother, Leo, they were somewhat more primitive in their instincts and probably also in the goals they set themselves in life. I myself have inherited some of this strength of will, this sensual nature with a penchant for action, but I think that for the most part I'm a Horowitz.

As for my Silesian relatives, by the way, my mother had an aunt or great-aunt who has become well known in Germany—Friederike Kempner, also called "the Silesian nightingale." A wealthy woman who lived on an estate in Silesia and dealt with humanity's plight in poetry, writing mawkish, sentimental, involuntarily comical poems about this situation or that.[7] She became famous, and when she published a collection of her poems, the members of her family were so embarrassed that they bought up the entire printing. When she heard that the work was out of print, it spurred her on so much that she issued a larger edition, which in turn caused a Berlin theater critic and journalist who happened to have the same last name to endure so much ridicule that he was forced to change his name, and from then on called himself Kerr — Alfred Kerr! I can recall one poem, for example, that was allegedly written by her but is more likely a parody of her work: "In the heart of nature's trove / Grows a lovely poplar grove / To the right are trees, to the left are trees / And in the gap, a gap, if you please / And behind that flows a brook — just look!" Probably someone attributed this poem to her to make fun of her actual poems. But poems like "The Animal Tamer" are characteristic of her approach: in the poem the tamer's daughter appears onstage with an enormous snake, until one day, before the eyes of the audience, she's consumed by the boa constrictor. Her first name is Johanna. "Though she is dead," the poem concludes, "still she is whole."[8] How comforting! Later, when I was in Jerusalem and got to know the book collector Gershom Scholem quite well and learned that, in addition to the Kabbalah, he took an interest in literary oddities, I told him, "I have a literary oddity in my own family, Friederike Kempner, an aunt or great-aunt." He replied, "She's a relative of yours? Get me one of her books — I'd love to have it in my collection!" I then wrote to my mother from Jerusalem — this was after the Nazis came to power: "When my friend Scholem heard that we have an Aunt Friederike, he was tremendously interested. Do we have any of her books at home? Do you still have one? He would very much like to have it sent here. I'd like to give it to him as a present." And I put it this way: "A book by your crazy aunt Friederike." My mother wrote back in a reproving tone, something she hardly ever did: no, she didn't have a book anymore, and didn't want me to use the phrase "crazy aunt Friederike," either. "In my childhood I visited her on her estate several times. She was a noble lady who did many good things, and it is not right to make fun of her." And in the end I learned that she really was a noble lady, who'd succeeded, for example, in getting solitary confinement abolished. She found this practice absolutely inhumane and campaigned against it with leaflets — written in a poetic style, partly in verse, partly in prose.[9] When she refused to give up, she was finally granted an audience with Kaiser Wilhelm I, and solitary confinement disappeared from the penal practice of the Second Reich.

My mother was similarly compassionate. She even had the unusual characteristic of being more drawn to the misery in the world than to beauty, and she tended to believe that a person was intended to suffer more than be happy. Indeed, it's an old question: What, when you add it all up, is greater in the world — the sum of unhappiness or the sum of happiness — and I'm sure my mother was right when she assumed the former. My father probably thought less about such questions; for him, the main thing was that the people in the realm under his control should thrive — he put all his energy into making sure that was the case. He was a family man, and I know that several times he paid out large sums when business went sour for members of our immediate or extended family and they were threatened with bankruptcy. In general, he thought that success was there for the taking in this world — if you only tried hard enough. He also tended to be optimistic, for example during the war, when, in contrast to my mother, not to mention her brother, whom I'll get to soon, he went on believing for a long time that Germany would be victorious. But when it came to personal matters, he was also optimistic, whereas in my mother the tendency toward pessimism always had the upper hand. That certainly had to do with an incredibly hard experience she went through. My older brother was diagnosed as a child with an illness that proved incurable, despite all the efforts, over many years, by doctors, including some very famous ones. It was progressive calcification of the joints. That was no doubt terrible for both my parents, but especially for my mother. She accepted the idea that for the rest of her life she would have to live for, and with, this boy, because it was clear that he would always need help, and more and more so. But then he died at fourteen and a half, after an accident that proved fatal because his spine had become so rigid that he couldn't break his fall. It was around the time of the Battle of Verdun, in March or April 1916, that he slipped on the floor in his room, and the fall resulted in a concussion that led to his death. After that, my mother succumbed to depression and spent a whole year lying listlessly on the sofa. And that happened at a time when a housewife and mother had to be very much at her post to take care of the family, especially her two growing sons. It was her brother, Leo, who finally urged her energetically to pull herself together and return to the world; she shouldn't give herself over so completely to her grief. She then threw herself into music for comfort. Later on a good and tender relationship developed between my mother and me, but during those years I actually didn't miss her that much. My older brother died a month before my thirteenth birthday, and when I had my bar mitzvah in 1916, I was getting to the age when you would rather be left alone by your parents, and feel no need to have a motherly eye watching over you. As a result, unlike my other brother, who was three years younger than I, I didn't suffer from having my mother absent from my life during that year.

I recall my bar mitzvah very clearly, because it was overshadowed by death. It was supposed to be a joint celebration for my brother and me. When my brother had reached the right age, he was probably in a hospital or a sanatorium undergoing treatment. The event had to be postponed so often that it was decided we would have it together. We also went to bar-mitzvah instruction together. When he then died so suddenly, it made for a very sad bar mitzvah, a house in mourning trying to celebrate. Of course every member of the extended family in Gladbach was invited. We not only went to the synagogue but also had a festive dinner at home that evening, and poems were read aloud. In particular my cousin Lisl Haas, five years older than I, recited a rather long poem, in which she alluded to all sorts of comical or remarkable things from my life; she was the younger sister of that Erich Haas who'd bribed his way into the army so as not to miss out on the heroic era, and who heard of Ludwig's death when he was at the front (I still remember him taking my mother in his arms on his next furlough and saying, "I'm so sorry about Ludwig"). Lisl was a highly intelligent woman, and my favorite among my female relatives.

Around this time it was already becoming clear that the high hopes people had held for the war weren't going to be fulfilled, and a somber mood was settling over the country. In any case, enthusiasm for the war was dwindling as the general suffering increased. The exuberance of the first two years gave way to its opposite when victories ceased, terrible losses occurred, and complete paralysis set in on the battlefields, marked only by mutual slaughter but no movement. No end was in sight, and people were hungry. There were shortages of everything, but especially of food. Civilians were reduced to subsistence rations, and would go out into the countryside to try to procure eggs or a bit of butter on the black market. The mood was getting worse by the day. Somehow the will to stay the course was still alive, especially since the government continued to insist that we would pull through and win in the end if we didn't cave in. But often you would see processions of women on the streets of our very Catholic region, middle-aged and elderly women setting out on some pilgrimage, and you heard over and over again the litanies, "Hail Mary, full of grace, pray for us sinners now and in the hour of our death, amen. Blessed art thou among women, and blessed is the fruit of thy womb, Jesus, amen." The women were walking to pray for an end to the war, in response to the country's terrible sufferings.

The first time I heard that something was wrong with Germany's war objectives, I was shocked. The older *Gymnasium* students were sent out to sell war bonds, which were being issued more and more frequently as the war continued. We were supposed to visit private houses and businesses and persuade people to sign up for these bonds. On one such errand, I called on a Jewish small businessman, a man who obviously didn't belong to the original German-Jewish community but had emigrated from the East. He spoke German, but not like someone born in Germany. I assume he came from Poland. I've also forgotten what kind of shop he had, a butcher shop or some small business, at any rate very modest. But everyone was supposed to make some kind of sacrifice for the war effort. So I came to him not because he was Jewish but because I'd been assigned certain streets in this part of town. I told him that my school had sent me; I probably had identification of some sort on me, and I explained to him how important it was that we support our troops with another war bond. At that he said to me in his broken German, "Nix from me, nix from me!" When I asked, "Why not?" he drew a coin out of his pocket, showed me one side, and said, "What bird are you seeing here?" I replied, "An eagle." "So what kind of bird is eagle?" I fell into his trap, and replied, "A bird of prey." Says he, "Right, bird of prey. All they want is grab, all they want is land, for that you get nix money from me." I was thinking hard as I made my way home. What he'd said made sense to me, and I wasn't entirely unprepared; I'd simply never heard this message in such bleak, unadorned words. That was around 1917, when in school they were still explaining the war objectives as follows: "First we need the ore basin of Briey and Longwy, so we can expand our industrial area, and of course we have to take new land for settlement in the East." So the boundaries of an enlarged Germany were being drawn, perhaps not quite as ambitiously as in the first two years of the war, but still with the expectation of certain nonnegotiable territorial gains. And this at a time when the German cause was already lost, when clearly no real victory could be expected, when the parties involved should have been working toward a settlement. But none of those in charge of the war effort dared to admit this to their own people.

My own patriotism, which always supported the German position, began to fray by the time I was in the *Untersecunda*, or tenth grade, at the latest. Our Latin teacher, old Professor Ernst Brasse, who had taught us since the sixth grade, had introduced the practice of asking each day at the beginning of class, "What's the news from the front?" And then someone would raise his hand and report something from the latest dispatches. A brief discussion would follow, and then the actual lesson would begin. On one particular day my classmate Karl Porzelt raised his hand and said, "An English troop transport has been torpedoed in the Channel." "Yes," replied Brasse, a nice man but a superpatriot, a pan-German,[10] "yes, excellent news. Let's hope many were drowned." At this moment something revolted inside me. Without thinking, I raised my hand — we had to ask permission to speak — and stammered, "Is it really acceptable to wish for that?" Good old Brasse stared at me for a moment in perplexity, and then said, "Oh, I see, you mean it isn't Christian?" Whereupon I answered, "I mean not *humane*." At that he blushed. He realized he was getting tangled up. I'll never forget the sight of him blushing. He then said, "Yes, Jonas, you're absolutely right; it's really terrible, but one simply becomes tough and cruel, and that's a necessity, because, you see, if they come over here to the theater of war and are posted to the front, they'll be shooting at our boys — who'll have to pay with their lives. So it really is better if we get the enemy first, rather than the other way around!" Which is, of course, an irrefutable argument. But this somehow marked a turning point for me. At recess afterward a few other students came up to me and said with a bit of a smile, "That was a hilarious exchange between you and Brasse." I was the only Jewish student — and then his comment, "Oh, you mean it isn't Christian?"

The reversal in the war situation didn't have much impact on my father's business, but our food supply was affected, especially because my mother paid no attention to anything for a year and left everything in the hands of the maids. My father spent vast sums to hoard food from the black market, buying up canned goods or whatever was available to put them in the pantry, yet we never had enough to eat. Later it was discovered that while my mother was out of commission the maids were carrying on a brisk business in edibles — the police even came to the house. And we were hungry, or at least undernourished, which affected my younger brother terribly. He had awful rashes during the last years of the war and was somehow delayed in his physical development, too.

During this time I began not only to read a lot but also to paint. I took painting lessons from the most prominent artist in Mönchengladbach, Karl Cohnen, who'd studied at the Düsseldorf Academy of Art and was a good painter, also an excellent portraitist. He produced a nice little oeuvre in oils, none of which has survived, alas. Later I became very interested in graphic art and was actually quite good at drawing. For a while I even gave serious consideration to becoming a painter, but then realized that I wouldn't produce anything really noteworthy after all. Besides, I was more and more drawn to philosophy, to the realm of ideas as opposed to the realm of visual images. Still, a love for the fine arts has stayed with me all my life. I also studied art history at the university — it was one of my two minor subjects, and I think I'm quite knowledgeable about certain periods and can tell at a glance which artist painted a given work. I may have had my first painting lesson at thirteen, before my bar mitzvah in 1916, and I continued with lessons through the end of the war, so it was at least two years, probably longer. At the studio of the painter, with whom I spent the afternoon once a week, I made the acquaintance of Mönchengladbach's Bohemians, among them the remarkable poet Heinrich Lersch, a son of the town's working class. He was a boilermaker and had his own smithy, but at the same time was a gifted poet, self-taught, who became well known in Germany as a proletarian poet. A small fellow with a weather-beaten face, he sometimes read his poems aloud at the studio. These weren't scheduled events; when a group was present, he would pull out a piece, hot off the anvil, so to speak, and read it aloud. At the beginning of the war he'd become a German celebrity overnight, for he greeted the war with a poem that made its way through the entire country. It began with the words, "Let me go, Mother, let me go," and after every stanza came the refrain, "Germany must live, even if we must die. Let me go, Mother, let me go."[11] After that he published a volume of patriotic poems, inspired by the war, under the title *Heart! May thy blood flare up!* That was the first line of one of his poems.[12] Well, his work matured, and the poems he read aloud during the next few years to the audience in Cohnen's studio changed in character, especially at the time of the unprecedented, increasingly meaningless battle of Verdun, which dragged on for months and resulted in huge losses for the Germans, as well as for the French. And then Lersch came in one day and read a poem with the title "Verdun," a poem filled with terrible pessimism, brought on by this nightmare, this utterly meaningless mutual slaughter.[13] So I had no need to wait for that little Jewish man who refused to sign up for war bonds. But this was something different: Lersch didn't criticize Germany's policy but simply gave expression to the horror and meaninglessness of the war.

My love for lyric poetry and for reciting poems actually manifested itself early on. I recall, as if it were yesterday, that a teacher from my *Gymnasium* visited my house to ask whether I would recite a poem in the auditorium for a celebration — before the entire school. And he explained, "I'm asking you because you recite poetry so well." This poem was some dreadful contemporary piece celebrating the success of a German submarine in the war against England. There was one line whose impact was unmistakable. The poem describes how this U-boat catches sight of an enemy ship in the distance—in those days the U-boats had to sail above the surface for the most part, and could remain under water only for limited periods—and then comes the exclamation, "The U-boat sinks!" A general murmur ran through the auditorium: "Oh, my God, the U-boat!" What was meant was that the U-boat was submerging, but for the sake of the rhyme it had to "sink."

So my relationship with poetry began early. I had no trouble learning by heart the poems I liked, and I enjoyed reciting them. They didn't have to be bombastic poems about ships sinking, either. Of course I knew all the famous Schiller poems by heart—"The Song of the Bell" and "The Diver." During this time I also read prose by Theodor Storm, Adalbert Stifter, and Stefan Zweig, and Thomas Mann's early short stories, and I was crazy about Franz Werfel, whom I considered the greatest poet of all times, something I now see differently. I loved Heinrich Heine, and learned a few poems by Eduard Mörike by heart that have stayed with me. Starting with the November revolution in Germany, the Expressionist poets, who'd been appreciated previously largely by an elite audience, became widely known. I especially remember an anthology compiled by Kurt Pinthus with the title *Menschheitsdämmerung* (Dawn of Humanity),[14] the first edition of which was given to me at some point, with an inscription from a girl who was in love with me, a girl I'd met in dancing class. At the time, around 1919–20, I was enrolled by my parents in dancing class in Rheydt, between Gladbach and Odenkirchen, though I had no interest in going. These lessons were attended by Jewish boys and girls only, by the way. Poetry was much more important to me. In addition to Franz Werfel, there were also Walter Hasenclever and Johannes R. Becher and a Jewish poet who enjoyed a brief, meteoric career—Ivan Goll. He'd written a great Jewish poem several pages long that I knew by heart from beginning to end and recited at meetings of Jewish youth organizations in the Rhineland.[15] In those days young people were starting to travel around to such gatherings, where the spirit of Martin Buber exerted a powerful influence.[16]

CHAPTER 2

Dreams of Glory

THE ROAD TO ZIONISM

My war-wary uncle Leo, along with my mother the most remarkable of the Horowitzes, was a wise, extraordinarily intelligent man with a strong interest in science. He'd studied medicine, specializing in gastroenterology, but his practice in Düsseldorf proved not all that successful, because he lacked the requisite "bedside manner." Given his skeptical nature, someone who came to him with a complaint might be told, "This is something medicine doesn't know much about yet. I can prescribe something for you, but you have a problem we're not very familiar with, and can't be sure of getting under control." Patients preferred doctors who cheered them up and gave them confidence, while he was profoundly aware of how much medicine didn't know, and he didn't keep this insight to himself. Still, he managed, finally even getting married, and certainly his income was adequate. With his talents, he could have played a larger role, but strangely enough, his ambition was directed less toward fame than toward acquiring knowledge and understanding. For instance, right after the war, in the spring of 1919, I think, around the time an expedition was setting out from England to observe a total eclipse of the sun in Brazil, suddenly banner headlines appeared, declaring Albert Einstein a new genius on the world stage; it turned out that Uncle Leo had been studying Einstein's theory of relativity since 1913, never saying a word. He knew the theory inside out. His wife, my Aunt Dora, said, "Lötzchen" (her nickname for her husband Leo) "is terrible. I can't leave a scrap of paper lying around the house without finding it completely covered with formulas." He took up mathematics for the pure pleasure of it and studied scholarly publications on Einstein's theories simply because they interested him. When he died at ninety-two in Santiago, Chile, where he spent his old age with his daughter, who'd emigrated there, I wrote a long letter of condolence to my cousin, expressing what made Uncle Leo so special and offering a kind of confession as to what he'd meant to me. One of my statements was "He had a high opinion of reason, but a low opinion of its distribution among human beings."

Before Uncle Leo married—very late—he would come from Düsseldorf every weekend and spend at least one night with us in Gladbach, so
as to be with his only sister and her family. He took a great interest in me
as I was growing up, but didn't try to lecture me or influence me; instead
he talked with me and paid close attention to whatever I had on my mind.
On one of his visits he found me reading Felix Dahn's massive potboiler, *A
Battle for Rome*, a novel set in the time of the Ostrogoths and Byzantium.[1]
"Do you find this period interesting?" he asked. I said, "Yes." "Then next
time I'll bring you something you might read instead of this, or in addition." The next time he brought a heavy tome, printed with two columns on
each page, Edward Gibbon's *Decline and Fall of the Roman Empire*.[2] "Have a
look," he said. "You'll really enjoy the spirit and style of this book." That was
his way: he steered me from Dahn to Gibbon, an admirer of Voltaire—and
by means of such interventions influenced my intellectual development.
His first contribution consisted of telling stories, which he invented himself
and continued from week to week. Perhaps he drew on literary sources, but
he came up with most of the material himself. Later he engaged me in intellectual discussions. Strangely enough, he was fascinated for a while by the
history of witchcraft trials—this tied in with his interest in enlightenment,
he said. Perhaps the best way to describe him would be to say that intellectually he was at home in the eighteenth century, the age of reason. He
wanted to understand how the witch trials had come about in the first place,
and what had finally ended them. Apparently a fairly major study of this
subject appeared around that time.[3] One day he said the following to me:
"You know, Hans, during my study of the witch trials I came to see that people who bring rational arguments to bear against something by no means
always convince other people. In fact, that never happens. The situation is
quite different. Certain views die out only because younger people tend to
listen to those who are more enlightened, more rational, not to the others.
People in the same generation never convince each other. Nor should we
assume that those who recognized that the witch trials were ridiculous were
necessarily the better-educated, more intelligent people. No, those who
saw the witch trials as justified often had extraordinarily complicated and
learned reasons for doing so. Of course it was all nonsense, but the sheer
brainpower devoted to that nonsense was certainly equal to, if not superior
to, that of those taking the rational position. But then younger people come
along who don't believe in the old magical thinking anymore. New views
gain acceptance, but not because the arguments supporting them are more

convincing." Later on, I saw this interpretation confirmed in other examples, for instance in the resistance of those medieval thinkers who believed in the Ptolemaic system so absolutely that Copernicus's arguments couldn't sway them. And remember the famous situation that arose in Venice in 1610, quite some time after Copernicus, when Galileo challenged his adversary, the Aristotelian Ludovico delle Colombe, to look through his telescope and see the moons of Jupiter and other phenomena that would prove him right — but Ludovico simply refused to look.

So Uncle Leo had a great deal to teach me. There was only one thing I didn't take over from him, namely his suspicion of all ideologies. Instead, I soon found myself powerfully drawn to an ideology, and it wasn't socialism or Marxism but Zionism. Uncle Leo wasn't opposed to Zionism; he simply distrusted every ideology. That became particularly apparent during the revolution of November 1918. He understood perfectly well that the monarchy was finished and new political ideas were due to have their turn. But because he abhorred belief in any doctrine of salvation, he approached what he saw as the Marxist illusion or romantic notion with the same skepticism with which he'd viewed the imperial dream of German hegemony and the nationalist romanticism of the Kaiser era. Filled with this wise skepticism, he made no attempt to convert or even instruct others. When the business with Rosa Luxemburg and the Spartacus uprising began, he merely remarked, "This is no way to go about it. You can't turn the world upside down simply on the basis of a formula." He rejected Zionism in the same dispassionate way. "Yes, I certainly understand. But if you think this will really solve all the Jews' problems, you're mistaken, I'm quite sure." I fear he turned out to be right. But at the time I didn't want to hear any such thing, of course.

My Zionist phase began, at the latest, after the end of the First World War, when I was in my last two years of school. My father was dismayed. With the exception of a cousin in Lechenich, I was the only Zionist in the family. After the proclamation of a German republic, at a time when young people's allegiances were generally divided between the right and the left wing, it would have been perfectly natural if I'd become an enthusiastic Social Democrat or perhaps had discovered Marxism, which was in the air after the Spartacus uprising and the murder of Rosa Luxemburg and Karl Liebknecht. On one side were figures like Friedrich Ebert and Gustav Noske; on the other the Kapp putsch took place, and fronts were hardening on the left and the right. But meanwhile I'd long since stumbled onto something else, for in the course of my voracious reading in my later years in school, a time when, in addition to the assigned reading, you pick out books of your own, I'd discovered my Jewishness.

Of course it had long been obvious to my fellow students that I was a Jew. Except for a brief period when there was another Jewish student in my class, I was the only one. I had friends at school with whom I was on very good terms. But I was aware that I was a Jew, and the others were, too, for some incidents had occurred. I'd inherited my father's quick temper, and as a schoolboy I was a holy terror, at least when the occasion called for it and someone made a remark that riled me. If you think back to the time before the Nazis, there was a kind of everyday antisemitism that found expression in petty teasing and aggression of the sort that's common among boys. But when a joke was made at the expense of Jews, I would be overcome with blind rage. Everything would literally go black before my eyes, probably from the blood rushing to my head, and I would hurl myself at the offending person. Differences in size and strength meant nothing—which made a terrifying impression. I discovered that even the strongest boys would back off. I still remember Karl Porzelt, the son of the city council president, whose seat was next to mine, saying to our classmates, "Watch out for Jonas. If anyone makes a careless remark, he won't let it pass." So they were forewarned about my anger. That was something that stayed with me later. But one time I found myself up against such superior strength that I came away the loser. That was during my period in Wolfenbüttel, which I'll talk about later, when I was doing my training in agriculture in preparation for emigrating to Palestine. We were a good-size group, and the young men in the surrounding area knew that Jews were working nearby. One day, after quitting time, I was walking down the street by myself when a group of boys passed me, one of whom made an antisemitic remark. At that I was flooded with Maccabean rage, and I fell upon the boy and almost knocked him down. But when the others joined in, one of them hit me so hard that I had a black eye for days, and I was knocked to the ground. Then the others went on their way. Still, as they were leaving I had the satisfaction of hearing one of them say to the one who'd started it all, "Why did you have to do that, you idiot? If you hadn't been wearing your new suit, I wouldn't have pitched in to help you, and you would've ended up on the ground." So because of his new suit, I was the one who got knocked down. Those were my fits of rage, but always connected with my Jewishness. All through school I was aware that I belonged to a minority and that we couldn't take anything lying down; we would never be completely accepted. This defiant pride has stayed with me all my life.

The sense of being an outsider was reinforced by every suggestion of hostility toward Jews, even when it took a fairly mild form. At home we did speak of Jewish problems, by the way, especially antisemitism. My father thought antisemitism would dwindle over time; certainly there would be relapses, but on the whole history was on our side because tolerance was increasing and fanaticism and the significance of religious differences were gradually fading. He had the optimism that had been part of the ideology of emancipation and the dreams associated with it since the days of Moses Mendelssohn, the confidence that, despite unpleasantnesses that had cropped up in the meantime, ultimately everything pointed toward improvement. I can recall the moment when Rathenau was murdered—I was studying in Berlin at the time. "Let's shoot down Walter Rathenau, that godforsaken Jewish sow" was the slogan that had become popular before the assassination.[4] I wrote an outraged letter to my parents, expressing my shock and indignation at the murder and arguing that it proved that we Jews weren't welcome in Germany. This was the kind of thing the hatred directed against us could lead to. I still remember my father's reply. He said I shouldn't discount the huge sympathy strike that workers had staged to protest Rathenau's murder, and the widespread disapproval of the murder among the general population. Unfortunately my father was wrong, but his letter illustrates his characteristic reaction. As terrible as this event was, and as indubitably as antisemitism had played a decisive role in it, he said, the overall picture wasn't nearly as grim as my portrayal of it—the response from republicans and leftist Social Democrats suggested the opposite. Basically my father always tended to see things in a positive light, and for him the answer to the Jewish problem was that you simply had to wait for better days, which would come eventually, even if not in our lifetime. So for him the Jewish problem was reduced to antisemitism, which still existed but would eventually disappear.

Yet he certainly encountered antisemitism on his business trips, in other situations, and in society. After all, antisemitism was a fact of life, an attitude that was always there, even when it didn't assume violent, aggressive forms. In general, the Jewish community in Mönchengladbach, which consisted of about three hundred families, or 1,200 people (with other communities nearby in Rheydt and Odenkirchen), was prosperous and quite well integrated. There was a Jewish elementary school, but there was nothing to prevent children from attending the public school, which is what I did. Outside the synagogue, purely Jewish cultural events took place only in Zionist circles. We children were occasionally invited to visit our non-Jewish neighbors, so I experienced Christmas, complete with a Christmas tree, for instance. For my parents it was a different story. The non-Jewish acquaintances my parents invited to their house never reciprocated, and in other respects, too, strict racial separation was maintained. Just one example: there were social clubs in Mönchengladbach for the Catholic and Protestant manufacturers and local dignitaries, including the academics—the Casino society for Catholics, Rest and Recuperation for Protestants, and the Association, which was the Jews' organization. This separation existed without overt hostility, but the lines were unmistakably drawn. Much later, at a reception held at the Rest and Recuperation clubhouse when I was made an honorary citizen of Mönchengladbach, my cousin Erich Haas asked me, "Were you aware that our Uncle Jonas belonged to this club?" "Impossible," I replied. "It had no Jewish members." "No, Uncle Jonas, Jonas Benjamin Jonas of Mönchengladbach, was a member of Rest and Recuperation for fifty years. The only one." He served on the city council, and thus was invited to join. He did join, nominally. But I doubt that he ever made much use of his membership.

This Jonas Benjamin Jonas was an uncle of my father's, a younger brother of Herz Jonas, my grandfather, who was alive only during my earliest years. My grandfather was born in the 1830s and was the son of Benjamin Jonas, the founder of the B. Jonas Company, Linen Weavers. As I mentioned before, his wife was already dead when I was born, and he himself died in 1907. At that point he was no longer active in the company but was retired, living in a handsome villa in Mönchengladbach. Now, his younger brother, Jonas Benjamin Jonas, also had a great influence on me, though in a very different way from Uncle Leo. The latter was the man of reason, the intellectual, the scholar, whereas Jonas Benjamin Jonas was the embodiment of religious faith, a truly devout man who made the Jewish faith the centerpiece of his life. When I knew him, he'd been widowed for a long time, and he'd never had children. At one point he'd owned a leather business in Gladbach, with its own cesspit, I assume. Later he withdrew from the business and lived very comfortably as a retiree. Among his fellow citizens he'd earned great respect at a young age, first in the Jewish community, then in the community at large. For decades he served on the city council, to which he was reelected time after time. He received the Order of the Crown, Third

Class, or one of those Prussian awards, and for forty years he was a leader of the Jewish congregation, either elected or on an honorary basis. From him I learned what a genuinely religious life is like. First, he strictly adhered to all the observances and laws, and second, he really prayed. During Sukkot he spent seven days living in the rear courtyard of his house, where the sukkah, covered only with leaves, was set up. He was in the synagogue from morning till evening, but the rest of the time he sat out there, keeping warm with a little kerosene stove, because it was already late in the year. In the synagogue, which was the only one in Gladbach, by the way,[5] he was a model to all members of the community, who, even if they didn't follow his example, revered and respected him. And that despite the fact that by far the majority of the community was liberal! For his sake, so as not to offend him, they kept the Orthodox service, in Hebrew and with the traditional ritual; only the sermon was in German. There was also no organ, since they knew that this would greatly displease old Herr Jonas. Instead we had a cantor from Poland, a handsome young man who sang magnificently. On Yom Kippur, Jonas Benjamin Jonas wore white death garments, like all pious folk. He considered it mandatory not only to fast all day and to spend the whole day in the synagogue but also to stand for most of that time, sitting down only occasionally. As the years passed, the others praying in the synagogue worried about him more and more: "How will Herr Jonas manage?" Finally they implored him at least to sit down, so as not to distract the others from the Yom Kippur service by making them nervous. And then comes the moment in the liturgy when you're expected to throw yourself to the ground, and the old man was shaking like a leaf and had to be helped up. There was something saintly about him. I still recall that at Yom Kippur Great-uncle Jonas Benjamin Jonas, who was growing paler and paler, with the eyes of the entire community upon him, was always called upon to read the Haftarah for the Mincha prayer — namely the Book of Jonah!

As a boy I began to develop rebellious and critical thoughts that included religion, and I asked, "Uncle Jonas, how do you manage at Yom Kippur? I don't understand. How can a person really pray all day and think only of God? Your thoughts must wander. You can't keep them fixed on God all the time!" He replied, "Oh, certainly, that's only human. Of course other thoughts come to mind and you lose your concentration. But I've found a method for making myself pay full attention to the prayer and to the meaning of Yom Kippur." And then he showed me something I've never found confirmed elsewhere, though I've asked many Jews about it. Apparently this method was his own invention. He said, "When I catch my mind wandering, I press hard on one fingernail. And what happens?" I said, "It turns white." Then he said, "Yes, it turns white. And that reminds me of death, that we must all die and will then stand before God. And that focuses me again." That was a great moment, an unforgettable one, and tears still come to my eyes as I'm telling this. That was my great-uncle, Jonas Benjamin Jonas, who died at the age of ninety-two or ninety-three in the late autumn of 1932, two months before the Nazis came to power, six years before the Mönchengladbach synagogue was burned down and then razed.[6] He was the most significant Jewish figure in my youth, the quintessential image of piety, a piety of the heart. He was no great Jewish scholar. I doubt he'd studied the Talmud. The West German Jews from Westphalia were highly observant, but not learned. They didn't make Judaism the object of study, as was the case in the yeshivas of the East. In the eyes of a learned "Eastern Jew" he was an *am ha-aretz*, uneducated as far as Jewish learning is concerned, something you can acquire and maintain only through unremitting study. But this kind of learning wasn't part of Jewish culture in northwestern Germany, and I think it was no different in southern Germany.[7] Observe faithfully that which is decreed: that was the watchword. Of course people knew the Bible, which was read, after all, at the Shabbat services, also the Chumash (the Pentateuch), and the Prophets, and the Haftarah read after the Torah. In addition to my parents, who were very conscious of being Jewish, it was above all the simple form of piety exemplified by Jonas Benjamin Jonas that influenced me. When I was going off to the university and paid him a visit to say good-bye, he sent me on my way with the words "Remain a good Jew!"

In addition to such influences, it was above all reading about the Jewish tradition that inspired me to concern myself with Judaism, which in turn reinforced my Zionism. First I went through a phase in which I found Indian philosophy and the general history of religion exciting, especially Far Eastern religions, and I read a little Lao Tse and Buddha in German translation. Then, as a raw youth, I was of course fascinated by Nietzsche's *Thus Spoke Zarathustra*, a work I view today as one of his least worthwhile. But more and more, Judaism held my attention. In those days my thoughts and feelings were shaped by three subjects I was reading up on. First I stumbled on the Prophets of Israel, not because they were assigned in religion classes but because I'd discovered them in the course of reading works in the so-called School of Religious History, founded by scholars such as Julius Wellhausen,

Hermann Gunkel, Hugo Gressmann, and others.[8] This movement within Protestant theology—primarily focused on the Old Testament, but from a scholarly, philological perspective—published a new translation with commentary, which I read with the greatest enthusiasm;[9] it was brought out by the Göttingen publisher Vandenhoeck & Ruprecht, which would later play a role in my own life. In this work I discovered the Prophets of Israel in their historical context. It wasn't simply a question of the Holy Scripture and a more or less timeless revelation of divine truth but of something that had taken place in historical time, involving figures of flesh and blood, who sent forth their word into the world out of a sense of inner necessity and with full personal commitment. Their voice spoke powerfully to me, and made Israel's legacy come alive for me in a way that no service or religious instruction had been able to do.[10] This reading resulted in my first scholarly paper, a handwritten treatise of at least sixty pages on the ethics of the Prophets. I still recall that later, when I was a student in Berlin, I showed it to a woman friend who was very much taken with it. When I emigrated in 1933, I left the manuscript at home, and it later disappeared, to my chagrin. It was written with the enthusiasm and immaturity of a sixteen-year-old, yet with scholarly ambitions. It reflected my own reading of the Bible but was also influenced by the findings of the School of Religious History.

During this period I was reading the Prophets through the lens of modern historical scholarship, but to my mind inspiration and historical reality weren't mutually exclusive: what the Prophets articulated was for me the word of God, but in human language. I should add that by the time I began reading it in this new translation I no longer believed in the Bible, but had already gone through a phase in which I subjected everything to rational analysis, and thus tended to consider the whole business obsolete. So I had no childish belief to be destroyed; on the contrary, studying the books of the Prophets in the version produced by the historical-critical* school actually gave me a positive relationship to the Bible. It was from the realistic, historically oriented portrayal by these Protestant biblical scholars, not from a doctrinaire, ahistorical view of the Bible as revelation, that I learned to see the contents of the Bible as something to take seriously in the here-and-now. Precisely the historical aspect made the Bible come alive for me. It was then that I came to the recognition that has shaped my entire life: that the word of God can be uttered only by human mouths. The voice atop Sinai that the entire people heard amid the thunder, the message that Moses received and then formulated in words, but especially what the Prophets heard — their utterances always begin with the words, "Thus spoke Yahweh" — and the way in which they proclaimed the message now became for me the modality in which the divine finds expression on earth: in the inspiration of the moment, when God's elect hear his voice and spread word of his will. Yet they're not saying something the masses want to hear, but instead are announcing, at great risk to themselves, something no one wants to hear, something bound to shock everyone. They're uttering something that's new and usually disturbing rather than edifying, not a Sunday sermon but something that interrupts the flow of things, upsetting assumptions, shaking people out of their stubborn or unthinking, heartless behavior toward their fellow human beings. Only later, after the great misfortune had occurred, and comfort and encouragement became necessary, did the prophet's task change; then his word was needed to lift up people's spirits. But up to then he was the unpopular one, the ecstatic speaker filled with the divine spirit, who proclaimed exactly the opposite of what people expected. That was different from our preachers in the synagogue or the priest in church nowadays. Those were the true mouthpieces for the word of God. What fascinated me at the time, aside from what the Prophets had to say about politics, war, power, social injustice, and oppression of the weak, were the circumstances under which their proclamations took place. There's the famous, unforgettable scene that shows how books originated and were preserved — the story in which Jeremiah decides to capture in writing all the words he's received from the Lord through the years. He dictates them to Baruch, his friend and scribe, and sends the scroll to the winter palace of King Jehoiakim in Jerusalem. Thereupon Baruch reads Jeremiah's speeches aloud to the king, who is standing next to a brazier filled with glowing briquettes to keep warm, as well as to the retinue gathered around him. And each time he reaches the end of a section, the king takes a penknife, slices off the section, and throws it into the coals, until the entire scroll has been destroyed by fire, without the king's taking fright at Jeremiah's words. At that Baruch returns to Jeremiah, who is living in hiding, and tells him what's happened, whereupon God commands Jeremiah to dictate everything again — and that is how we came to have the Book of Jeremiah [Jeremiah 36]. Such tales made a great impression on me — I was proud to be descended from this prophetic tradition, felt its hold over me, and was fascinated by the way revelation comes, that is, by the circuitous route through a person's inner ear. Prophecy doesn't originate in a voice that rings out for all to hear but rather in a person's soul, his inner ear, and only rarely is it the eye, as in the vision that summoned Isaiah [Isaiah 6]. But usually it's words that the Prophets hear, like Jeremiah, for instance, who doesn't feel equal to the task, yet also feels obliged to proclaim what he's heard, or Amos with his magnificent utterance, "The lion roars; who is not afraid? The Lord speaks; who can but prophesy?" [Amos 3:8]. Anyone who heard that couldn't help proclaiming it; to me, that was the essence of revelation.

So my reading material on the one hand was the Prophets, God's elect. In addition, as a result of reading Martin Buber's *Three Speeches on Judaism* and *The Legend of the Baal-Shem*,[11] which I found marvelous, I discovered modern Judaism as the new bearer of this divine mission. My third source was someone who at first glance has nothing to do with the Old Testament, with Judaism, or with the Jewish calling, namely Immanuel Kant, whom I'd already read as a schoolboy. I no longer know how Kant fell into my hands, and of all things his *Groundwork for the Metaphysics of Morals*—I assume it was the ambitious title that attracted me. At the time, the *Critique of Pure Reason* was way beyond my comprehension. But the *Groundwork for the Metaphysics of Morals*—ultimately, Kantian ethics is derived from the spirit of the Bible, and there's no doubt that the categorical imperative and the word from Sinai are related somehow. At any rate I sensed a relationship.[12] It was probably Uncle Leo who brought me this work in a little Reclam paperback, when he noticed that my interests were turning in that direction. The *Groundwork for the Metaphysics of Morals* begins with a thundering proclamation that I've never forgotten: "Everywhere nothing can be conceived of in the world, or outside of it, either, that could be considered good without reservation, excepting a good will."[13] That was the bread that nourished me in those days, and the years between the November revolution of 1918 and my final secondary-school examinations in the spring of 1921 became the crucial period in which my intellectual direction was determined.

While socialism held an enormous moral as well as intellectual appeal for many in my generation, Martin Buber led me to Zionism. True, he was not the initial cause of my becoming a Zionist. It began with the heightened sense of Jewishness that I've just described, to which was added the keener awareness of politics sparked by the events of the day, and third, I was deeply affected by the virulence of the new antisemitism, which assumed a hostile and aggressive character in response to the fall of the monarchy, the German defeat, the establishment of the Weimar Republic, and the Spartacus uprising in Berlin, with Jews playing an active role on the radical left.[14]

It was no longer merely a matter of Jews being caricatured a little, humili-ated, mocked, or kept at arm's length; this was actual, overt hostility. I real-ized that we were no longer welcome, that we were being made scapegoats for the defeat and the revolutionary chaos, were being blamed for the "stab in the back." Even I found it not entirely appropriate that it should be a Jew, Hugo Preuss, who drafted the constitution of the Weimar Republic: "That's something the Germans should do; we shouldn't put ourselves in such an exposed position."[15] In short, I was developing a sense of Jewish nation-alism, according to which we weren't merely German citizens of the Jew-ish faith but members of an ethnic group that could certainly hold its own when it came to knowledge of German culture — even then I knew Goethe and the other classical writers better than the majority of my classmates — but who didn't really belong. This sense of difference, together with pride, and the conviction that the arguments put forward earlier by the emancipa-tion and assimilation movement had failed, led me to Zionism.[16]

When I embraced Zionism, I had the most terrible confrontations with my father. An avowed Jew who never hid that fact, he'd served for years as the chairman of the Gladbach-Rheydt-Odenkirchen chapter of the Cen-tralverein, the Central Association of German Citizens of the Jewish Faith. Three thriving Jewish communities. Any Jew in this region who belonged to a Jewish organization in addition to his local congregation was in the C.V.[17] Politically my father was close to the German Democratic Party; for a manufacturer, the Social Democratic Party was out of the question, and the Stresemann party was too far to the right for him. When I was old enough to vote, I also voted for the Democratic Party. In that respect I remained true to my father's example. But when it came to my Zionism, he was beside himself: Why did it have to be *his* son, the only one among the Jewish youth in Gladbach, Rheydt, and Odenkirchen, who fell prey to this madness and argued for founding a state of our own in Palestine and settling there! We had horrendous battles. At the same time I fell under the spell of German Expressionism and was an enthusiastic reader and reciter of Franz Werfel, among others. There's a poem by him titled "Father and Son" that has the following line: "Grim looks exchanged at midday meal / clash like steel, armed to fight. . . ."[18] That was the situation at our house, and my mother trembled. At the lunch table, one word often led to another, and my mother sat there, perhaps crying — I don't recall exactly — but definitely trembling, while my father, whom I've already described as hot-tempered, exploded, and I wasn't much better. But on the other hand my father was a softhearted and loving man, and once he saw that I wasn't going to be budged from my decision, and in the meantime a local Zionist chapter had been founded, he asked me, "So tell me, Hans, how did you even find out that something like Zionism existed?" And I said, "I'll tell you exactly how: from reading *In the German Reich*." That was the newsletter put out by the C.V.,[19] whose contents consisted primarily of a chronicle of antisemitism and a strategy to combat it by means of education, protests, and lawsuits. There were also reports on the struggle against Zionist delusions. This reading, I said to my father, had convinced me of the truth of the Zionist message. And my father was magnanimous enough to concede, "Well, in that case there's nothing more I can say."

By the time I was in my next-to-last year at school, it had become clear to me that it wasn't enough to believe in the Zionist cause; there was a practical mission to carry out. That implied political action, striving to put the Zionist ideal into practice, the first step being to win hearts and minds. Suddenly word spread — it must have been around 1919 or 1920 — that a neurologist from Vallendar in the Rhineland was going to establish a practice in town, a Dr. Sally Löb, said to be a Zionist. The moving van was still parked in front of his building when I was already there, offering my services. And as his furniture was being unloaded, we discussed establishing a Zionist chapter for Mönchengladbach and Rheydt. It began with meetings in his apartment, with several people participating. It's interesting, by the way, to mention who was there — no one from the Jewish upper class, of course. I was the black sheep in the Jewish community. "So how do you suppose the son of Gustav Jonas got caught up in this madness?" The hatred for Sally Löb was so pronounced that, as I heard one day, at a gathering of the upper-crust Jews — on Schillerstrasse, across from his apartment, where the young Zionist chapter met — someone said, "Now let's all go to the window and spit across the street!" That was just a joke, of course, but it conveys a sense of the spirit, the mood prevailing among assimilated, comfortably situated Jews in Gladbach. Aside from me, the group included several people about my age from the lower classes. Small businesspeople, often also Jews who'd originally come from the East, which meant the kind of people you didn't mix with socially, people who weren't entirely acceptable. Needless to say, my father was very unhappy that I'd betrayed my class this way and was aligning myself with a lower social group as a result of my Zionist views. Even later on, it was hopeless to try to raise money for the Zionist cause among the upper-class Jews of Mönchengladbach. I still remember hearing a man from the Jewish *haute volée* of Rheydt (he was the younger brother of Else Benjamin, with whom I was hopelessly in love for years) declare, after the Jewish boycott on 1 April 1933, when I gave a speech on emigration problems at a gathering of Jewish young people, "We German Jews don't intend to emigrate!" He dismissed the idea out of hand because at the time Zionism was still considered a betrayal of Germanness. My mother told me later that Jewish ladies had stopped her on the street and said, "Your son was right; he was a real prophet." But that didn't occur until after the Nuremberg Laws had come along, and other forms of persecution. The Jews of Gladbach were simply too well off to see the reality of their situation.

If I recall correctly, our local chapter had no more than ten members. There were only two adult couples among them, one of which deserves particular mention, for the wife was a born Berger, the sister of Julius Berger, the well-known Zionist leader.[20] She'd moved to Gladbach when she married. She came to the meetings with her husband. Then there was a daughter of the head teacher, Fröhlich, married to a man from the lower classes. The rest were a few young people and me. We met about once a month. I myself had more frequent meetings with Löb. An important factor for me was that he belonged to the Cartel of Jewish Organizations (KJV), the umbrella organization for Zionist student organizations at German universities — not to be confused with the Cartel Convention of Jewish Corporations (K.C.),[21] to which assimilated Jews belonged, including the vast majority of students.

During my Mönchengladbach Zionist period, delegates would come from time to time from the headquarters of the Zionist Organization for Germany (ZVfD) in Berlin to give speeches and also to raise money. Of course, at home we all had a little blue canister from the Jewish National Fund; in it we collected money to support Jewish settlement in Palestine. The money went toward the purchase of land or reforestation.[22] And for my graduation, at my request, my father donated money to have twelve trees planted in Palestine. I kept the documentation for a long time. As this gift indicates, things were patched up with my father after all. The rising tide of antisemitism enabled him to understand my thinking more and more, and to see the positive side of Zionism. One thing continued to trouble him, however. He said, "If a new Jewish society is built in Palestine, the land of our fathers, religion should be an indispensable component." Now, Zionism was actually a secular movement within Judaism. Theodor Herzl's *The Jewish State*,[23] but also the much-quoted Zionist writings of Leon Pinsker,[24]

Ahad Ha-Am,[25] and others had an entirely secular orientation. They respected the Jewish religious heritage as a national tradition about which one should certainly be informed, just as every good German should know the *Song of the Nibelung.* But they didn't assume that being a Jew necessarily included faith, or that the Jewish people's identity was inseparable from adherence to the Mosaic religion. That was something my father couldn't swallow. Although he himself no longer led a religious life, he commented, "If you go back to Palestine, you have to take all that seriously again; otherwise I don't see the point of claiming we lead an exceptional existence."

Not until later, when I was studying in Berlin, did I have contact with Jews from Eastern Europe. But the following incident gave me a little preview: I heard that Georg Landauer, one of the leading figures in Zionism,[26] whom I later came to know well in Jerusalem, wanted to come to the Rhineland from Berlin. In contrast to most German Zionists, he represented the working-class Zionism that wasn't so prominent in our Mönchengladbach chapter — I think his group was Hapoel-Hazair.[27] Landauer, an educated and intelligent man from an assimilated German-Jewish family, was one of the few German Zionists who belonged to this branch. At the time I traveled to Cologne to meet him. There he'd opened a temporary office, where he met with refugees from Eastern Europe who were passing through. They'd fled to the West as a result of the Russian Revolution and the subsequent pogroms, and were emigrating to America or Palestine. There I saw for the first time a Jew coming directly from the East, but not an orthodox Jew with payos but a leftist. I still remember that Landauer let him cool his heels for a bit before asking, "So what do you want?" The man said, "I want to go to Palestine." "So what do you want to do there?" "I want to work." Landauer then advised him and helped him get papers, a recommendation, or also financing. Here was someone who didn't want to emigrate to America or stay in Germany but wanted to go straight to Palestine. He wasn't shilly-shallying, whereas I was going to the university and in my Zionist student association was meeting people who talked about Palestine and the future Jewish community there but only in the rarest cases were actually preparing to emigrate.

In those days, by the way, no one in our Zionist group gave any thought to the Arab population. What we said was, "We'll buy the land from them — after all, we'll pay well, far more than anyone else would be prepared to pay for those swamps." We thought the Arabs in Palestine would somehow still be able to live there.[28] No one really gave much thought to the situation until the Hebron massacre occurred in 1929.[29] Before the Arabs reacted with violence to the Balfour Declaration and the Jewish immigration, with the land purchases it set in motion, we loftily ignored their existence. To my shame, I must admit that I, too, didn't give the matter much thought. I even had strange, militaristic dreams. People tend to fantasize about playing important roles, what the Americans call "dreams of glory": there was a series of cartoons under this heading in the *New Yorker*, showing young people or adolescents imagining their future as filled with great deeds. My first "dream of glory" involved becoming a doctor and discovering a cure for my brother's disease. But the dream didn't stop there: "If my brother's healthy, like Castor and Pollux the two of us can accomplish great feats." First I had to heal him, but then we would amaze the world—and how? I would invent something that would enable human beings to fly into space, and we—my brother and I—would be the first cosmonauts, doing research in space and returning to earth! I developed this scenario while my brother was still alive. I often lay awake at night sobbing for my brother, because I could see he was getting sicker and sicker. But once he was restored to complete health through my efforts, my brother and I (but I think in my dreams I was the main inventor) would be the first to venture into space. I'd learned enough physics by then to know that in a vacuum propellers would be of no use; there was only one means of moving forward, and that was propulsion—the rocket principle. But my idea was that we wouldn't shoot straight up but would accelerate gradually, leaving the ground like an airplane and then circling the earth in spirals—faster and faster until eventually we would reach an orbit from which we would be hurled into space. I still recall picturing us flying for days and weeks alone in a capsule, subject to increasingly terrible psychic pressures and deprivations, until finally we'd return to earth from space with a sense of being saved. Those were my dreams, the first dreams of glory.

In the period after the First World War, when paramilitary organizations like the Stahlhelm and the Nazis sprang up in Germany (which people didn't take seriously at first), but also the aggressively antisemitic Free Corps, I expected that we Jews would be subjected to actual physical violence. Then I pictured us, after being trained to shoot and equipped with weapons, barricading ourselves in our houses and resisting the armed attacks of these enemies of the Jews. It was a dream, but at least it involved resistance, not being defenseless. At the same time, it was a matter of earning respect. As my Zionism developed, I immediately realized that this strategy would at best work only for a short time; in reality what mattered was to emigrate to Palestine. My last dream of glory — because I soon became enough of a realist to dispense with such dreams — involved my fighting my way through a hostile Europe, then crossing to Asia Minor over the Bosphorus and reaching Palestine at the head of a Jewish army that had formed in the various regions of the Galut and accompanied by women and children. In this dream I saw myself as the leader of this band of desperate Jews, saving their skins after terrible persecution and now reaching the land of their fathers, and I was quite amazed when I read a few years later that this had also been the dream of Ferdinand Lasalle in his youth! The very same dream — that as the leader of an armed Jewish horde he would conquer Palestine for a Jewish state.[30] Similarly I was pleasantly surprised to discover, much later — actually just a few years ago — that Sigmund Freud's hero in his youth was Hannibal, just as he had been my great hero when I was in school: because he was the great "Semitic" general who had given the "Aryans" a good thrashing, who'd shown them that you can't just push the "Semites" around.[31] To be sure, I'm being very candid about these associations — I have no idea whether they'll really show me to posterity in a good light.

CHAPTER 3

Between Philosophy and Zion

FREIBURG – BERLIN – WOLFENBÜTTEL

From the beginning it was settled for my father: "Hans is going to the university." Not for a moment did he consider having me work for the family business. "That would be a waste!" He himself had had the ambition, the desire, and the brains to go on to higher education, and now he wanted his talented son Hans to fulfill that dream. Whether I went into a field with good earning potential didn't matter. The company would always produce enough income to support someone who lacked earning power—a philosopher, for instance. That was something I shouldn't worry about—Gustav Jonas could afford to have a son who studied philosophy and perhaps became an adjunct lecturer. In those days, an adjunct lecturer had to either have a private fortune or marry a wealthy woman. The thought that I would go to the university gave my father special satisfaction. And the purer the field, that is, the farther removed from any vulgar considerations of earning money, something lawyers and doctors did, the better. His thinking was a holdover from an old Jewish tradition according to which a learned son was the best. It had earlier been the aspiration of a prosperous Jewish businessman to have his daughter marry a *talmid chacham*, someone who devoted himself to theology and would be supported by his father-in-law. That brought distinction to the family. "Earning money—that's something we already know how to do." So some of this tradition, but especially his own missed opportunity to get a university education, motivated my father, and also his great love for me, a great fatherly tenderness. Thus he encouraged me to study whatever I wanted and for as long as I wanted. And I took full advantage of his generosity, for I started in 1921 and didn't receive my Ph.D. until 1928. That makes seven years that I spent at German universities.

Actually it had become clear to me in my last years of secondary school that I wanted to study philosophy, art history, and religion. Religion for me included Judaica as well as the world religions—something along the lines of a comparative history of religion. I chose Freiburg because it had the reputation of being a very lovely city, but especially because I'd heard that the famous philosopher Edmund Husserl taught there. If you ask why I didn't go to Heidelberg or Marburg instead, I can only reply with the Jewish saying, "Am I a bird, that I can be in two places at once?" I wanted to study under Husserl, so that meant I couldn't go to Heidelberg. Marburg wasn't even in the running, since Paul Natorp was already retired and Hermann Cohen had died in 1918. Had he still been alive, Marburg would have offered a serious alternative.[1] And Heidelberg was an entirely different matter; the so-called Crêpes de Chine were there — Alfred Weber, Friedrich Gundolf, and so on. The rich Jewish girls from Berlin studied in Heidelberg, but philosophy wasn't taken all that seriously. Heinrich Rickert was already retired, and Karl Jaspers, who'd started out in psychology, was just beginning to earn a reputation in philosophy. Even later on, although he was an impressive figure, an unusually fascinating and stimulating thinker, he never became as original a philosopher as Heidegger, or as powerful a thinker as Husserl. No — for me Husserl and the southern Black Forest were the deciding factors.

It was clear from the outset that I would join the Freiburg Zionist students' association. The name of this association was Ivria, the Hebraic association.[2] My father was so sure that I still needed looking after that on one of his business trips he arranged everything for me in Freiburg. I don't know whether the city was even on his route, but he had customers in Alsatia. In Freiburg he had a business associate who put him in touch with a Dr. Levy, whose son was studying medicine at the university and was the chairman of Ivria. My father more or less placed me under his protection. He also rented a furnished room for me, what today we would call a student pad, in a respectable house with a retired doctor and his wife. Thus when I got to Freiburg, my father had long since prepared the ground and didn't have to worry about me. I recall that the younger Levy, who later went to Palestine as a doctor, asked me mockingly how I could have allowed my father to find me lodgings in Freiburg and make inquiries as to who would be the most suitable company for me.

At the university I enrolled in as many courses as was humanly possible in one's first semester. The most important was Husserl's introductory lecture course on the history of modern philosophy. The course began with Descartes, included the English empiricists, Wolff, and Leibniz, but ended before Kant. Husserl, already far advanced in age, was the founder of a new method in philosophy, the famous phenomenology,[3] so he taught the history of modern philosophy. Once he'd laid out how far a thinker like John

Locke, David Hume, or George Berkeley had progressed in the examination of consciousness or epistemology and what problems he hadn't been able to solve, he never failed to conclude with this statement, "Not until phenomenology came along did it become clear how these problems had to be attacked."[4] In his view, every philosopher since Descartes had come to grief at a point that only phenomenology could get past. I also did a lot of reading, above all Husserl's famous logical studies, a truly magnificent accomplishment.[5] His ideas on a phenomenological philosophy were already classics, and not easy to get through. Frau Husserl sat in on all his lectures, by the way, and watched with an eagle eye to make sure the students were paying attention. With her sitting there, you had to listen hard and take notes, and if she caught you doodling, she would report it. As a first-semester student I was not admitted to Husserl's seminar, so instead I enrolled in the beginners' seminar offered by the young instructor Martin Heidegger. That's how I found my way in my very first semester to Heidegger. Of course he was much more challenging than Husserl, but also a brilliant teacher. As God and chance would have it, the topic was Aristotle's *De anima* or *Peri psyche*,[6] and the first question, when I went to sign up with Heidegger, was "Do you know Greek?" I responded, "Yes." "That's fine, then." That was my first encounter with Heidegger—a fateful encounter, as it turned out. It was clear that Husserl was an old master, but his thinking was essentially completed, and he thought he possessed the one infallible method philosophy had to follow if it was ever to get to the truth. He approached every question the same way, and in that sense offered more instruction than excitement. Heidegger, on the other hand, whose lectures I couldn't follow very well at the time, was very comprehensible in his seminar and, being a good teacher, knew how to draw the students out. He would have the students read a sentence from the text, and then he would ask, "How do you interpret this? What's Aristotle saying here? What does this word mean?" That was excellent, and accessible even for me.

Heidegger's lecture course treated Augustine's *Confessions*, if I recall correctly.[7] He came into the auditorium with a huge tome under his arm and had the Latin text open in front of him while he lectured. I remember grasping next to nothing of his interpretation, but I had a compelling sense that something immensely important was at stake and that he was grappling with the material in the most serious way. This sparked something in me. At the time I wrote a letter in which I spoke of Heidegger and this experience, and how incredibly difficult it was. I could follow his explanation for a while, but would then lose the thread and no longer be sure what he meant. But what I never lost was the sense that this was incredibly important, even if I didn't understand it.

Around this time I had my first encounter with Karl Löwith; he was way ahead of me and already writing his dissertation. One time he gave a guest lecture in Heidegger's course that rivaled Heidegger in incomprehensibility but made the same impression of profundity. Löwith, who'd been shot in the lung during the World War,[8] spoke softly, but in a brooding style like Heidegger's. I still remember how the latter listened to him with great attentiveness and respect, and then commented on his lecture. All of this was beyond my comprehension, but something about it pierced my soul, to be specific the conviction that this was philosophy in the making — my ear was witnessing the philosophical process while my consciousness was witnessing the philosophical results. I should emphasize that Heidegger's profundity was deeply creative, and you couldn't suspect him for a moment of putting on a show. When I say that I didn't understand a word, that's a slight exaggeration, of course, for occasionally I did grasp something. But altogether I felt as if I were up against a mystery, though convinced it was worth the effort to become an initiate. In that instinctive feeling I wasn't alone; the other students likewise fell under the spell of his suggestive language, though I'm not sure they understood much more than I. But in those days the impression was becoming widespread that this was of great moment. Even before *Being and Time* Heidegger had acquired a sort of crypto-fame, and among those in the know word had got around that here a philosopher was striking out in a new direction: "This is where you have to come to learn philosophy!"

In Freiburg there was another philosopher in addition to Husserl and Heidegger — Jonas Cohn, a good man but no great philosopher. He suffered from standing in Husserl's shadow, but he suffered still more from his name, which he was too proud to change, even though it marked him as a Jew and invoked associations with a Jewishness of which his mind didn't show a trace.[9] His son, who was a little older than I and also took his seminar, had changed his name to "Gottschalk." I assume that was his mother's last name, for it's a Jewish name, too — but at least not Cohn! I spoiled my relationship with Jonas Cohn from the very beginning, for at the time I was naïve enough to think that when you were asked a question you should tell the truth. A completely mistaken idea! I went to see Jonas Cohn because I wanted to take his seminar on the Platonic dialogue *Theaitetos*. He received me kindly and asked, "And what brings you to Freiburg?" "Edmund Husserl," I replied. After those two words, I saw, to my astonishment and dismay, a slight quiver pass over his face, and his friendly manner vanished. He didn't exactly turn mean, but I noticed immediately that there was no sign of his earlier kindliness, and my participation in his seminar subsequently turned out to be quite unfortunate. Whenever I raised my hand and said something, I could tell from his expression that my presence was fundamentally unwelcome to him. I realized later that I shouldn't have said that, but at the time I thought it was obvious that you would come to Freiburg because of Husserl's philosophy. He was the famous man, while no one had ever claimed that Jonas Cohn was a famous philosopher.

That Husserl was a Jew played no role, by the way, least of all for him. The following story shows that especially well. A few years later, after I'd been in Wolfenbüttel for an interlude that I'll get to later, when I returned to Freiburg I'd already made friends with Günther Stern. I'd noticed him during my first semester but hadn't dared to approach him—I'd merely admired him from afar. I knew who he was and thought he was splendid. He was a year older and had therefore begun his university studies a year before me. He was also the son of William Stern, the famous professor in Hamburg, and was clearly a brilliant young man, so much so that I felt very timid in his presence. William Stern and Edmund Husserl knew each other, so Günther Stern was a frequent guest in Husserl's house. I really got to know him in Berlin, where we both took a seminar with Eduard Spranger on Kant's *Critique of Pure Reason*. After a meeting of the seminar in which I'd contributed to the discussion, Günther Stern spoke to me and paid me some compliment on what I'd said. And thus our friendship began. It was in Freiburg in 1923 that we then became close friends. One day he told me jokingly that Husserl had warned him against me. He'd discovered that I was in the Ivria, the Jewish student association, and in his view membership in such an organization was synonymous with Orthodoxy. So I was a strictly observant Jew, and that was incompatible with philosophy. As a philosopher one couldn't commit oneself to a specific belief. Stern should be careful not to let himself be infected. So that was Husserl's impression of Zionism. It shows how far his understanding of things Jewish went, and how naïve he was. It wasn't enough that he, as a baptized Protestant, wanted to know nothing about his own Jewishness; he also thought that anyone who stuck by his Jewish faith couldn't be a philosopher—strangely enough, it had never occurred to him that his own adopted religion, Christianity, might be incompatible with philosophy.[10]

This same Husserl showed in other ways, too, that when it came to matters of public life and politics he was basically unsophisticated, and in that sense typical of the German professoriate. He didn't come from Germany, by the way, but from Prossnitz in Moravia, where he was known as "crazy Uncle Edmund" — this I heard much later in New York, at a reception organized by our friend Ludwig Kahn, a noted German professor at Columbia. There I ran into a political science professor who also came from Moravia. This professor was working on a study of Thomas Hobbes, and in the card catalogue of Harvard's Widener Library he'd stumbled on an entire section devoted to Edmund Husserl. He asked me, "Does the name mean anything to you?" When I said it did, he remarked, "In my house people always talked about 'crazy Uncle Edmund' who'd become a philosophy professor somewhere in Germany. People never had a very high opinion of him, and also never heard much about him. So I was amazed to discover that half the drawer was filled with titles by and on Husserl. He must be a thinker of some importance." I said to myself, "This was a man who stood German philosophy on its head; entire journals are devoted to working out the implications of his philosophy; countless philosophers use his ideas as the basis for their life's work, and here we have a great-nephew of his asking whether 'crazy Uncle Edmund' ever amounted to anything in philosophy!"

But as another telling story shows, Husserl had indeed become the quintessential German professor. At the time an American named Marvin Farber was studying with him; Farber later became the editor of the *Journal of Phenomenology* and Husserl's mouthpiece, as it were, in America.[11] Since Husserl was aware that this would be Farber's calling, he made him his protégé, so much so that eventually Farber had the run of Husserl's house. Farber's brother, who was studying medicine in Freiburg, was tall and athletic, a trained boxer. Once the two Farbers and Husserl were crossing the bridge over the Dreisam River when a student fraternity member jostled them, growling antisemitic slurs. Farber's brother grabbed him and threw him into the river. Around Whitsuntide, all the students in Freiburg would plan an excursion for the holidays, such as a long hike through the Black Forest or a trip to Lake Constance or into Switzerland. The Farber brothers, however, decided to go to Paris. When Husserl heard of their plan, he said, "You want go to that disreputable city?" To him, the patriotic German, Paris was the city of the enemy and the Treaty of Versailles. That kind of attitude was typical of the stodgy German professor.[12]

Initially I spent only one summer semester in Freiburg, which was lovely. But you couldn't study Judaica there, and that was something that meant a great deal to me. For such studies there was only one place in Germany — the Hochschule für die Wissenschaft des Judentums [Institute for the Study of Judaism] in Berlin, an institution noted for its high intellectual standards.[13] In the nineteenth century the liberal Jewish population then coming into its own wanted to be up on the latest theoretical advances, and that meant organizing the study of Judaism in the spirit of modern philological and historical scholarship, as opposed to the traditional approach used in the yeshiva. So I enrolled for the 1921–22 winter semester at both the University of Berlin and the Institute for the Study of Judaism, where a number of splendid people were teaching, among them Leo Baeck and Ismar Elbogen. This was the only time in my life when I did some study of the Talmud.[14] In addition, I signed up for lecture courses and seminars with Harry Torczyner, a scholar well known among experts for his modern Jewish biblical exegesis. But the professor who came to mean the most to me personally was Julius Guttmann. He specialized in medieval Jewish philosophy, especially that of the Spanish-Arabic epoch, when Muslims and Jews lived together quite harmoniously, so that Jewish life was able to develop unimpeded. In addition to Arab Aristotelian philosophy, a Jewish Aristotelianism came into being, whose most important figure was Maimonides. I still remember a course I took with Guttmann on Judah Halevi's *Sefer Hakuzari* — a work of historical fiction depicting a formal debate involving Jews, Christians, and Muslims at the court of the Chazaric ruler in southern Russia that the author used as a literary device to prove the philosophical superiority of Judaism.[15] Guttmann, whom I often visited later on in Jerusalem, had the true philosopher's spirit. He was a lovable man and a true scholar. He wasn't creative in philosophy himself, but he was a respected Jewish Kantian who applied modern philosophy to the interpretation of the medieval Jewish philosophers.[16]

At the University of Berlin I continued with my study of philosophy, especially with Eduard Spranger, a man of fine intellect, if not of the stature of Husserl and Heidegger. In the department of Protestant theology there were very good Old Testament scholars, notably Hugo Gressmann and Ernst Sellin,[17] whose lectures and seminars I attended. I also heard Ernst Troeltsch lecture, and of course the respected historian of classical antiquity Eduard Meyer, who, however, was antisemitic. I took Greek history with him and audited his lecture course on the post-Alexandrian period, in which he discussed the Maccabean revolt, among other subjects; I still recall how negatively he portrayed the Maccabees in contrast to the Hellenistic Syrians. He described the young Hasmonean state as a kind of robber state, created by means of highway robbery on a sort of grand scale.[18] Later I heard a delightful anecdote about Meyer from Eugen Täubler, by the way. Täubler was also a historian, his area of expertise being Roman history. He was a Prussian Jew, but at the same time a Jewish nationalist. Later he emigrated to America and taught ancient history at Hebrew Union College in Cincinnati.[19] For a while he'd been Meyer's assistant, and it was clear to him that this antisemite was also a decent man. He harbored a dislike for the Jewish element in world history, but he treated Täubler absolutely properly and decently. One day Täubler said to Eduard Meyer, "Herr Geheimrat, I've just come upon something that will interest you." Then he told him about an incident in Carthaginian history that he'd found in his reading: a Roman delegation had arrived with demands that angered the Carthaginians so much that they killed the members of the delegation and nailed their corpses to the gates of Carthage. Eduard Meyer responded, "Yes, yes, typical Semitic cruelty. A noteworthy story." At that Täubler continued, "Sorry, Herr Geheimrat, I realize now I made a mistake. It wasn't Carthage at all but a delegation sent by the Lombard cities to Barbarossa, and he nailed them to the city gates of Milan." Whether the story is true, I don't know. But that's how Täubler told it to me. He'd managed to lay the perfect trap for Eduard Meyer.

In those days Berlin was a magnificent city and metropolis, even though it was repeatedly shaken by unrest, conflict, poverty, and political movements representing every extreme. There was a lot going on, which wasn't always agreeable but was enormously exciting. My financial support from home made it possible for me to live in a decent furnished apartment in the Tiergarten district, and life was good. But psychologically I wasn't prepared at all for the phenomenon of Berlin, as a comical incident will illustrate. One time, when I was out walking through the city with my cousin Erich Haas, who was studying medicine there, I remarked to him, "I must say, the people-watching is fabulous here—all these folks out strolling on the Kurfürstendamm. Look at those chic ladies!" And he said, "Hans, those are whores!" I was thunderstruck. I'd been thinking they were elegant ladies showing off their attractive attire, though the skirts were rather short, even for the current style, something you'd never see in Mönchengladbach or Freiburg, and they had fur trim around their necklines and hats. I was thinking, "This is the elegant world"—and had to be set straight by my cousin.

Political life in Berlin was breathtaking during that period. My three semesters there—from the 1921–22 winter semester to the spring of 1923—were a wild time. The murder of Walter Rathenau happened in the summer of 1922, after which hundreds of thousands of Social Democrats took to the streets in protest and a general strike was called. Everywhere the effects of the lost war made themselves felt—the public transportation didn't always work, so you could end up walking vast distances. It was cold, and the street lighting was poor. Clearly hunger and poverty were widespread, but you could also sense the energy and freshness of new political ideas and experiments. At the university, though, a reactionary wind was blowing, and our professors were unmistakably loyal to the deposed monarchy. They condemned the imposition of the Treaty of Versailles and rejected all leftist notions. In the Zionist circles I moved in, the Treaty of Versailles was of no interest, however. We had the sense that it didn't really apply to us but only to the German people. It was clear, of course, to everyone that it was an unreasonable treaty and that the reparations in particular had caused the inflation and the economic conditions from which we were all suffering. But the only aspect of the Versailles Treaty that really interested us was that the 1917 Balfour Declaration had more or less become part of the New World Order and of the basis for the League of Nations, which was established in the aftermath of the First World War. The League formally entrusted England with administering Palestine as a mandate, and gave England the authority to create a Jewish national homeland, while preserving the rights of the native population. That was essentially enshrined in international law. In that respect we approved of the Treaty of Versailles, not for what it did to Germany but for legalizing a unilateral political pledge England had made to the Jews during the war. We were naturally pro-English, because England had opened the gates of Palestine to us.

My private and social life revolved entirely around the Zionist student body, and I spent almost all my time in my fraternity, Maccabea. I think there were four different fraternities in Berlin—Maccabea; Hasmonea, a rowing club for Jewish students, who rowed on the Spree and the Havel and whom we called the "muscle Jews," while the Maccabeans were more the "intellectual Jews"; and Blau-Weiss, a Jewish hiking group strongly influenced by the example of the German Wandervogel movement.[20] I had essentially no contact with non-Jewish students—in Berlin there was such a large, diverse Jewish world that you could stay within it without feeling confined at all. The strong Jewish presence of course gave rise to overt anti-semitism, including within the student body, which hadn't been the case in Freiburg. In addition to this Jewish milieu and the university, Berlin offered an extraordinarily varied and innovative theatrical life, beyond anything I ever experienced elsewhere. You would go to the Schauspielhaus or the Volksbühne or to another of the theaters where modern directors were put-ting on their highly creative productions, directors such as Erwin Piscator. It was splendid, and as a student you could get tickets quite cheaply if you were willing to sit way up in the balcony or even stand for hours. These were real cultural experiences. In the Berlin of this period, with all its utopian, political, and ideological groups, a cultural life on the highest level of sophis-tication had sprung up, characterized by experimentation and modernity. And there were many modern plays written by left-wing intellectuals, plays such as Ernst Toller's *Masse Mensch*,[21] and others similarly propagandis-tic in nature. On the other hand, you could also see immensely interesting Shakespeare productions or a production like Max Reinhardt's version of Jacques Offenbach's *Orpheus in the Underworld*, performed in the Grosses Schauspielhaus on New Year's Eve, in 1921–22 or 1922–23. It was one of the most beautiful productions I've ever experienced — with Max Pannenberg, Eugen Klopfer, and Käthe Dorsch. I saw Fritz Kortner and all the other major German actors and actresses. You could say that the place was crazy, but it was perhaps one of the most fertile periods in German cultural life, a period when everything — like Expressionism — that had played more of a dissident role earlier now came into its own as a result of the revolution.

Within my Zionist milieu, as a philosopher I was actually an anomaly. Most of my fraternity brothers were studying medicine or law, others eco-nomics. But there was one other philosopher, a few years older than I, who began working on his dissertation shortly after we met: Leo Strauss. We were as different as could be, but we discovered each other. It interested him greatly that a young philosopher had turned up among his fraternity broth-ers, and we became friends. He had a first-class philosophical mind, and he was one of the distinctive characters among the younger generation of philosophers, a man who early struck out on his own. He was never a Hei-degger disciple like me, most of whose studies took place under Heidegger's aegis, but he'd encountered Heidegger in Freiburg and had been immedi-ately convinced that he was probably the most important philosopher of our time. Strauss came from the village of Kirchhain in the state of Hesse, not far from Marburg. His father was a genuine rural Jew. Although he didn't farm on a commercial scale, he dealt in grain and kept cows and poultry for the family's use. I visited Strauss at his home once and met his father—his mother was dead. The farm where Leo had grown up had a large barn in which the grain was stored. His family had been Orthodox, and it had cost Leo intense spiritual pain to tear himself away from his traditional upbringing. It hadn't been easy for him to make philosophy his guide, to free himself, that is, from all preexisting dogmatic assumptions when it came to the ultimate questions bearing on God and the world. This freedom, which was essential to being a philosopher and incompatible with adherence to a specific religion or revelation or god, this intellectual necessity of becoming an atheist in order to be a philosopher, tormented him all his life. He did make the leap, but he could never shake off the sense that he'd committed an act whose correctness could never be proved once and for all. That hurled him time and again into a fundamental state of doubt as to whether following the path of rational enlightenment, which requires the denial of established articles of faith, is consistent with the truth and beneficial to the human being. He suffered from the necessity of being an atheist. An experience we had as émigrés made this clear to me. When I got to England in 1933, he was there, too, and we saw each other quite often. Leo Strauss was living in London at the time with his young wife and her little son from her first marriage. On a fall day — it must have been in 1934—we went for a walk in Hyde Park. We'd walked along in silence for quite a while. Suddenly he turned to me and said, "I feel terrible." I said, "Me too." And why? It was Yom Kippur, the day of atonement, and both of us were not in the synagogue but were walking through Hyde Park. That was telling. For him much more than for me, for in my case relinquishing our traditional faith had been much easier, having already been accomplished by my parents; I'd grown up in a climate in which you could think freely about such things. But for Strauss it was a source of torment. "I've done the equivalent of committing murder or breaking a loyalty oath or a sinning against something." This "I feel terrible" came straight from his soul. Yet this topic didn't dominate our friendly discussions. He was a committed Zionist like me, and understood Zionism as a secular movement that wasn't tied to preservation of the Jewish religion.[22] But above all, we had real philosophic discussions; he was one of my sharpest and most profound interlocutors during those years. After he left Berlin, we saw each other only at greater intervals. Since he received little financial support from home and had to finish his studies quickly, he went to Hamburg and wrote his dissertation under Ernst Cassirer, receiving his degree in 1921. He chose to write on some neo-Kantian topic, taking what he considered to be a rather easy way out.[23] For a while he worked at the Free Jewish Lehrhaus in Frankfurt, until in 1925 he found a position at the Akademie für die Wissenschaft des Judentums [Academy for the Study of Judaism] in Berlin. There he was part of the editorial team for the jubilee edition of Mendelssohn's writings, overseen by Ismar Elbogen and Fritz Bamberger. In 1933 all that came to an abrupt end, of course.[24] Our friendship continued in exile—Strauss was living in France and England from 1932 on, before he emigrated to the United States.

My most exciting experiences and encounters during my time in Berlin took place in conjunction with the Zionist movement. An interesting situation arose in 1924, when a merger was initiated between the Cartel of Jewish Student Associations and Blau-Weiss. The styles of these two organizations—the student associations modeled on the German fraternities and the hiking association inspired by the Wandervogel movement— were very different, but somehow both sides felt the need to work together. I joined Blau-Weiss to provide a sort of liaison with the KJV, participated in its ambitious hikes and sang the hiking songs, which, as I see it today, were never authentic German folk songs but belonged to a pool of pseudoarchaic German song inspired by the youth movement. Take, for instance, the song "We are the vultures' black-winged horde / Heia ho ho! / Aiming at tyrants our flashing sword / Heia ho ho!" I'm convinced that in the sixteenth-century peasants' revolts the followers of the knight Florian Geyer never sang such a song; rather this was a creation of a later age. Yet at the time we were all convinced that these were old German uprising and mercenary songs. Why most of the members enjoyed the music so much can be explained only by reference to the organization's origin in the Wandervogel movement.[25] The members wanted to have something of their own, and Jewish tradition didn't offer any such songs—Hebraic synagogue songs were simply incompatible with a sturdy hiking culture, and the Yiddish fighting songs from the Eastern European Yiddish-socialist movement expressed the wrong political sentiments.[26]

Eventually a large meeting took place in Berlin, bringing together representatives from the Cartel of Jewish Associations, all the universities, and the leadership of Blau-Weiss. "Leadership" in this case implied an organization almost fascist in structure, for Mussolini's leadership principle held a certain attraction in those days for this nationalist Jewish youth movement and its fanatical followers. In our student movement, on the other hand, we were all critical, independent thinkers, all university educated, who'd come to Zionism on our own and were trying to acquire an understanding of Jewish history. In short, these two very different partners were supposed to be brought together at the conference, and I'd been assigned the task by the KJV of introducing the motion for this to happen.

My fraternity brother Ernst Simon, who came from a completely assimilated family but had found his way back to Judaism and had turned in his thinking to a religious Zionism,[27] gave a rousing speech against the merger. It was one of the best oratorical performances I've ever heard, and it threatened for a while to bring the whole event to a catastrophic conclusion, until the speech was skillfully parried by Blau-Weiss. Simon inveighed against the new heathenism represented by Blau-Weiss and admonished us to be Jewish, upholding the great Jewish tradition, while he characterized Blau-Weiss's romanticism as a phenomenon of assimilation and an untenable position. It was a masterful speech. Among those in attendance was also Gershom Scholem, who interrupted the speaker with shouted comments, vehemently opposing the fusion, although actually he had no right to speak—he was already a confessed Zionist but belonged to neither of the two organizations that were supposed to merge. So here I saw him for the first time—waving his huge hands and loudly interrupting the proceedings in an attempt to protect us academic Zionists from entering into this fateful merger that would only exacerbate the "dejewification tendencies" and the alienation of modern assimilated Jews. At the time I didn't actually meet him, merely observed him from a distance. His appearance, his way of speaking, of shouting, of gesticulating had something at once impressive and grotesque about it. But there was no doubt he bore the stamp of an exceptionally independent thinker, of an original and deeply spiritual personality.[28]

If you ask about the figures who had a decisive influence on us Berlin Zionists, Martin Buber and Franz Rosenzweig must be mentioned. Many of us were profoundly impressed by Buber and shared his interest in Hasidism.[29] As the editor of the journal *Der Jude* [The Jew] and, together with Viktor von Weizsäcker, editor of the journal *Die Kreatur* [The Creature], he was a personality known to both the non-Jewish and the Jewish public. At the same time he proclaimed a powerfully Jewish message, which was, though by no means Orthodox or Conservative, positively and enthusiastically Jewish. Rosenzweig, on the other hand, was a much more esoteric figure, whose work *Der Stern der Erlösung* [The Star of Salvation] was considered a book you had to take seriously,[30] though I myself hadn't read it, any more than I'd read Ernst Bloch's *Spirit of Utopia*.[31] What was known about Franz Rosenzweig was above all that he'd inspired the establishment of the Lehrhaus in Frankfurt and, along with Buber, was the driving intellectual force there.[32] People also knew about his illness — that his paralysis was progressive and that he could already hardly speak, yet continued to exercise an enormous influence, though that was still limited to very small circles. A person like Leo Strauss took the figure of Rosenzweig very seriously,[33] yet even I, who on the basis of my Jewish and philosophical orientation should have done so, didn't find it all that necessary. I merely registered the fact that together with Buber he was involved in the odd undertaking of preparing a new translation of the Hebrew Bible into German. Odd because the Germany that was intended to receive this translation as a gift was taking an increasingly hostile attitude toward the Jews. The whole thing was almost a tragicomedy; just when the project was almost finished, the end came for German Jewry. Even before that I had a prophetic sense that German Jewry had no future, and accordingly there was no pressing need to translate the Bible into German again — the whole thing struck me as anachronistic. While Buber and Rosenzweig were proceeding on the assumption that German Jewry continued to have a mission, I tended to share the view of Felix Theilhaber and others who predicted the disappearance of German Jewry, though not as a result of violence but rather as a result of assimilation, a falling birthrate, and intermarriage.[34] I should add that to this day I find Buber's and Rosenzweig's idea of retranslating the Bible an interesting but ultimately highly questionable experiment, with little legitimacy or meaning. And I didn't always agree with their decisions when it came to adapting German to the sound of the original Hebrew. But my chief objection was that I saw the future of Jewry as being located somewhere else entirely.[35]

Despite the great distance between them and us, we in the KJV also took an interest in the significance of Eastern European Jews for Zionism. It's unfortunately true that German Jews became aware of this population only when it needed our help. Relatively early, aid organizations had been established in Germany to assist the Jews fleeing from the ghettos and oppression in czarist Russia, and to buy them tickets for passage to America on ships of the Hamburg–America Line. From the point of view of the successful, assimilated German Jews, these Jews from the East weren't especially welcome in Germany. If they stayed, especially in the larger cities, and particularly in Berlin, where quite a large Eastern European Jewish population had settled in the Scheunenviertel, it was feared that this Jewish element would attract unfavorable attention because it was so foreign. People had as little liking for the Yiddish language, which they called a "jargon" and viewed as a distortion of German, as for the immigrants' exotic clothing and behavior. In short, Eastern Jews were considered inferior, and German Jews were willing to help them move on, partly for their own sake, partly out of Jewish solidarity, but also in order to get rid of them.[36] The young Jews raised in Germany had hardly any contact with them, and the children of Eastern European Jews seldom joined our fraternity. So there was hardly any personal interaction. Nonetheless, a second kind of encounter with Eastern Jewry became important specifically for the Zionists and thus also for me: during the First World War, the German Zionists ran into Eastern Jews in the territory known as the Eastern High Command. Sammy Gronemann and others came home with accounts of ethnic Jews who considered themselves Jewish in a way entirely different from that of German Jews.[37] In the occupied territories with huge Jewish settlements, Jewish members of the German armed forces, themselves in the Herzl mold — culturally a mixture of Viennese, French, and liberal — discovered, with shock yet also excitement, that in Eastern Europe there was an ethnic Jewish population with its own customs, art, songs, and literature, and a political movement that was partly Zionist, partly socialist. In short, this was a Jewry with which we still had little personal contact, but of whose importance for the settlement of Palestine we became more and more convinced, for we couldn't help recognizing that the main impetus for creating a new Jewish communal life in Palestine would come not from us academic types in Western and Central Europe but from the Jewish masses in Eastern Europe. To that extent the Eastern Jews were a major factor in our Zionist thinking. This didn't mean, as I said before, that we often came together with Eastern European Jewish groups in Berlin, but we realized that our Zionism was far more abstract than the full-blooded and culturally rich longing for, and fixation on, Zion to be found in the Eastern population.

I had at least as little contact with the largely anti-Zionist upper-middle-class Jews of Berlin as with the Eastern Jews. To the end, the Zionists remained a minority among German Jews, so much so that when I threw in my lot with Zionism I essentially cut myself off from those circles. There was, however, some cooperation between Zionists and non-Zionists: in

1921, the Keren Hayesod [Jewish National Fund] was established to serve as a nonpartisan organization to support settlement in Palestine, with prominent non-Zionists also working toward the purchase and settlement of land in Palestine. This international organization, which owed its existence in part to an initiative of Chaim Weizmann's, also had a German branch, led by Kurt Blumenfeld, with the extraordinarily important mission of bringing together the well-heeled, assimilated, and culturally dominant German Jews, most of whom had always been anti-Zionist, with the Zionist wing, at least for practical purposes. I myself played a modest role in this undertaking. The meetings of Keren Hayesod were very dignified, with famous personalities as speakers. Since you couldn't attend without a personal invitation, it was an honor to be among the guests. At such meetings the Jewish student associations always provided marshals. One day I was assigned to serve as a marshal at quite a large gathering where Albert Einstein was scheduled to speak in favor of Palestinian settlement. As I was standing in the vestibule, receiving the guests and checking their invitations, a man entered who had salt-and-pepper hair billowing somewhat unkemptly but impressively around his head. On such occasions, everyone of course wore a black suit. His shoulders were dusted with dandruff flakes. It was Albert Einstein. I welcomed him and first guided him to a table near the entrance and asked him to sign the book laid out there. I still recall his asking, "What's this? Oh, it must be the guest book." And he signed his name with his characteristic political innocence, not suspecting that his signature here was intended less as an entry in a guest book than as important evidence of his identification with the Palestine project.[38]

In addition to my Zionist activities and my studies, my time in Berlin was also notable as a phase when I absorbed a great deal of the literary and intellectual happenings of the day. All of us in my Zionist or philosophical and academic circles had of course read Thomas Mann's *Magic Mountain*. Each of us could quote from this work when appropriate or make allusions that others would recognize immediately. In this novel and in *Joseph and His Brothers* you can often find more import than in the entire phenomenological school, with the exception of Husserl himself. One page of Thomas Mann offers more profound insights than entire treatises on the constitution of the objective world through intentional acts of consciousness. A great writer! Of course I also read the left-wing *Weltbühne* [World Stage], though usually with distaste; as a Zionist, you couldn't very well approve of the role Kurt Tucholsky arrogated to himself as a referee on German politics and culture. We felt there were certain German controversies we should stay out of, rather than setting ourselves up as judges and spokesmen. One literary work that overwhelmed me, however, was Karl Kraus's *The Last Days of Mankind*—a great document written during the First World War, probably the most significant antiwar protest in the German language, the equivalent of Henri Barbusse in France.[39] My friend Gerhard Nebel was a great admirer of Karl Kraus, while I was put off by certain one-sided judgments, exaggerations, and also a maddening self-righteousness and arrogance. What I found most distasteful—though I recognized that he'd converted not out of opportunism but because he'd actually been attracted by Catholicism for a while—was his traitorous relationship to Judaism and his manifestation of a sort of Jewish self-hatred.[40] But *The Last Days of Mankind*—that was a magnificent work, one I read from cover to cover, despite the local Viennese allusions that I, not being Viennese, couldn't understand. I also found some of Kraus's pieces in *The Torch* marvelous. I still remember the one about a Negro in Vienna.[41] But I also remember poems. He was certainly no great poet, but some of his poems were wonderful, as only the work of a truly important mind can be—for instance the one about Immanuel Kant's treatise *On Eternal Peace*. Kant writes, not in the treatise itself but in an afterword or a later gloss, that the sight of the sorry course of human events shouldn't mislead us into hoping that words can do much to change things, yet duty calls us to point the way to something better for the distant future, "and with selfless benevolence," for there's no chance we'll experience these times ourselves. A mixture of pessimism, recognition of the sad state of the world, especially in international politics, and a completely unselfish hope that we may be able to contribute something after all, so that our descendants will at least have the possibility of inheriting a better world. So in the middle of the First World War, Karl Kraus wrote this poem, which goes as follows, and which I count among the great, unforgettable poems of the time:

> No eye ever read, flooded with tears
> Words like Kant's, in all the years.
> By God, no heavenly comfort can outdo
> The sacred hopes this epitaph promises you.
> This grave marks a noble renunciation:
> "Dark falls on me, may light flood the Creation!"
> For all the becoming that humans destroy

The Immortal dies, full of thanks and of joy.
His farewell brightens the darkening day
That for you the sun may chase clouds away.
Through today's and these earthly gates infernal
He dreams his way trustingly to peace eternal.
He speaks it, and the world is true once more,
And God's heart opens to me amid the scourge of war.
This truth is proclaimed: if faith thwarts damnation,
You all shall enjoy the promised salvation.
O shun perdition, in the spirit place trust
That shows you the path that traverse you must!
What a mankind! What a shepherd so dear!
Woe to him whom the renunciant cannot steer!
Woe, if in Germany's madness the world slept unaware
Of the last German miracle that defied despair.
A dwarf stretched to touch the stars on high,
His earthly realm but Königsberg, yet he reached so high.
Above any monarch's castle and madness
This subject of the universe rose, spreading gladness.
His word has more strength than sword or power,
And his pledge liberates us from dungeon and tower.
To his blessed heart's transforming dawn
Yields the shame of man's sword against other men drawn.
Through the flames of war, let these words stand:
"On Eternal Peace" by Immanuel Kant![42]

After my first four semesters—one spent in Freiburg and three in Berlin—I felt it was time to get serious about that portion of my life goals that was connected with my emigration to Palestine. There was a Hachshara organization that arranged training on livestock and fruit-and-vegetable farms for young Jews who wanted to prepare for going to Palestine, where they might change professions and work in agriculture. Usually there were several trainees in a group. Among my fraternity brothers, I was the only one to sign up for the Hachshara, and in 1923, between March and October, I was sent with other German Jews to Wolfenbüttel, where we were assigned to Richard Grabenhorst, who lived at 3 Kälberanger. This area had no farmers with large amounts of acreage under cultivation, but rather truck farmers who grew some grain on the side and raised a few animals, especially pigs, to be slaughtered for domestic use and turned into enough smoked ham and sausages to see the family through the winter. But Grabenhorst's main farming activity centered on the orchard, the vegetable plantations, extensive strawberry fields, asparagus beds, and berry bushes. The workday began early, long before breakfast, even before daylight during asparagus season. And during the strawberry harvest you slid along the beds every week on burlap sacks, picking the ripe berries. My boss often perched high in the cherry trees with me and, while we picked, philosophized with me about the meaning of life and such matters, about which even the most simple man ponders, though he may enjoy consulting a trained philosopher to achieve greater clarity. For me the work was very hard, for I wasn't accustomed at all to this kind of physical effort. But I learned just about everything that could be learned, such as how to guide the horse-drawn plow and make a straight furrow. My pay consisted of a bit of pocket money and room and board. I had a tiny room under the eaves, actually more of a garret, with only a bed and a chair. I worked about fourteen hours a day, sank into bed, and fell immediately into the deepest sleep.

Richard Grabenhorst was a tall man who'd served during the war in the Goslar Rifle Battalion, an elite infantry unit. Two things have stuck in my mind from his tales of his wartime experiences. One time he used the expression, "When you're hungry, sausage without bread will do instead." When I laughed, he said, "That isn't nearly as funny as it sounds. In the long run, sausage without bread doesn't agree with you. That's really something you eat only when you have no choice. During the campaign in Romania, we advanced so fast that our food supplies couldn't keep up. Since Romania had a rich agriculture, wherever we stopped for the night we'd simply slaughter a pig and roast the fresh meat. After a while we all had terrible stomachaches. You can't live on meat alone. Bread's a necessity. So it's really only in an emergency that sausage tastes good without bread." Another time we were out in the field and he saw a storm gathering in the distance. There was heat lightning, and we heard thunder. At that he said, "We'd best go home now." So we took our equipment, the horse and the plow, and hurried back to the barnyard. I ventured to ask why he was so nervous, because I found it odd in such a giant of a man. At that he said, "Should I tell you? I've been this way ever since the war. It reminds me too much of artillery fire. Since the war I've been scared of thunderstorms."

The Hachshara was a boon to the farmers in the area, because it gave them help for free. It was known that we were Jews, for no one else would be so crazy as to work under such conditions. My boss boasted to the other farmers about his Jews, at which many said, "I'd love to get a Jew like that, too." When the people from the Hachshara organization asked for trainee positions again, they received a whole slew of offers. We were soon known around town and throughout the countryside, and were considered one of the oddities of the time. But for the most part we were received respectfully and enjoyed a certain admiration. People appreciated us for being eager and inexpensive workers, though untrained. The only luxurious aspect was the food. We were fed much better than would have been possible in town in those days. I still remember the sausage and ham that people put on their bread — that wasn't available anywhere else. And our appetite was insatiable.

The farmer I worked for asked me lots of questions, of course, and when he heard that my father was a manufacturer, he shook his head and said, "Why do you have to do such hard labor here when you have a father who pays for you to go to the university?" I tried to explain it to him, but he must have thought, "Well, there are all sorts of creatures in God's garden, so there are some who instead of being grateful for living so comfortably are foolish enough to do hard labor for us and then take off for Palestine." But in parting he advised me to go back to philosophy, and said, "You've held up your end, Hans, and worked well, but this really isn't the right thing for you." And I had to agree. I'd stuck it out and was glad I'd done the work and got to know others in the group. There were also girls among us, and some of the boys were real muscle men — I was amazed at the kind of "muscle Jews" I met there. True, I was the only one to come from the university, and in Wolfenbüttel I realized that whatever became of my Palestine plans, it would be a waste if I went into farming; I really could accomplish more with my head than with my arms.

CHAPTER 4

Marburg

From Wolfenbüttel I returned to Freiburg for the winter semester, and spent the 1923–24 academic year at the university. Günther Stern was there, writing his dissertation under Husserl, and I also met Rudolf Carnap and Max Horkheimer. The latter attended Husserl's seminar for a semester and, to my amazement, kept bringing in Hegelian philosophy, which didn't really belong there. But since Heidegger had been offered a chair at Marburg in the meantime and all his students had migrated with him, I soon saw that I would have to change universities as well. So I asked Gerhard Nebel, whom I knew from my first semester at Freiburg, what had been going on while I was away, what lecture courses Heidegger had given, and what was planned for the coming semester. I remember his telling me about a seminar on *De ente et essentia*, in which this treatise of Thomas Aquinas and a commentary by the later scholastic Cajetanus were read in Latin and discussed for an entire semester.[1] After hearing this, I sat down to study the treatise on my own, so as not to be behind. Then in the fall of 1924 I moved to Marburg. I found I had no trouble joining the discussions under way there, but the Heidegger cult among the philosophy students was hard to take. Its chief characteristic was a kind of bigoted arrogance, with members of the group almost going so far as to claim a monopoly on divine truth. This wasn't philosophy; it was more like a sect, almost a new religion, which I found profoundly repellent. Many of these young Heidegger worshippers, who'd come great distances, even from as far away as Königsberg, were Jews. That can't have been a coincidence, though I have no explanation for it. But I assume the attraction wasn't mutual. I don't know whether Heidegger felt entirely comfortable with all these Jews swarming around him, but actually he was completely apolitical. In that sense, what he later asserted in self-defense was accurate.[2] He didn't have a political bone in his body, didn't think about his political options, but was simply captivated by the national renewal movement. I'll have more to say on this subject later.

At any rate what was developing in Marburg in those days wasn't healthy, more a phenomenon like the relationship of the faithful to the Lubavitcher rebbe, as if Heidegger were a zaddik, a miracle rabbi, or a guru. Even Hannah Arendt, who would soon enter into a relationship with Heidegger far more intimate than that of any of the others caught up in this hero worship, preserved enough objectivity to find all the veneration unpleasant. We two, who'd quickly discovered each other, shook our heads over this arrogant, exclusive adulation of Heidegger.

There was one other skeptic who refused to participate in this circus: Walter Bröcker. He was an intelligent student, and Heidegger had a soft spot in his heart for him, so much so that he made allowances for Bröcker that he wouldn't have made for anyone else. Bröcker, you see, didn't know Greek, and also didn't think it was necessary to learn. How anyone could study Aristotle with Heidegger without knowing a word of Greek still baffles me. But Bröcker pulled it off. When I saw Heidegger again decades later, under curious circumstances, we were exchanging memories, and he told me what had happened when Bröcker took his orals — like me, he'd spent many years getting his degree. Heidegger placed before him a passage from the *Metaphysics* that he was supposed to interpret. "And then," Heidegger said, "Bröcker kicked me under the table. I'd completely forgotten that he didn't know Greek and I shouldn't have given him that text. So I whipped it off the table and gave him something else." Bröcker went on to become a respected professor in Kiel. After the war he wanted to lure me there as a colleague, but I turned down all offers from German universities, including a much more attractive one from Marburg. Well, I was on excellent terms with Bröcker; he steered clear of the whole sect business and was a smart, calm, sober person, yet also had a good sense of humor. He always stayed in touch with Heidegger, since he had far less reason than I to break with him. When Heidegger died, Günther Anders asked Bröcker in a letter whether he'd gone to the funeral in Messkirch. Bröcker replied, "No, I didn't go to Heidegger's Catholic-Christian burial. As an old Nietzschean and atheist I wouldn't have fit in." Bröcker and I shared a passion that we both had to give up at the same time, in the interest of making progress in our studies: chess. We often played each other; it was almost a vice. But one night — it was between one and two in the morning — we suddenly looked at each other and said, "This can't go on. We'll never get our dissertations done if we keep this up." And from one minute to the next we stopped playing chess and after that never played again.

So we took our studies very seriously. And to be able to keep up in a Heidegger course or seminar, you had to do a ton of work, so you were stingy with your time. Nonetheless, in Marburg I had two close friendships. While Bröcker's personality was somewhat cool, and he seldom spoke of his feelings or anything personal, I had a genuinely warm relationship with Gerhard Nebel. Nebel also came home with me to Mönchengladbach several times. He adored my mother. But my most momentous encounter in Marburg was with Hannah Arendt, whom I met in 1924—at the time she was eighteen. Of course I noticed her at once—who wouldn't have? That's not the point. Aside from the fact that we liked each other immediately, what brought us together was that we were the only Jews in Rudolf Bultmann's seminar on the New Testament. The seminar was packed, of course, with Protestant theologians and certified goyim, while we two, who to begin with were philosophers, not theologians, but above all Jews, not Christians, really didn't belong there. Hannah was very aware of being Jewish, without really knowing anything about Judaism—she was what is called an *am ha-aretz*. But she was also a "defiant Jew," and, as she told me, she'd introduced herself to Bultmann as follows: at the beginning of the semester every student had to go to the professor's office hours for permission to enroll in his seminar. Hannah explained to him who she was and said she was just starting her study of philosophy, and Bultmann told her he was very glad to have her. Hannah then continued, "But I'd like to make one thing clear from the beginning: I won't put up with antisemitic comments!" Thereupon Bultmann, the inimitable Oldenburger, replied quietly, "Fräulein Arendt, I think if anything like that should come up, you and I together will be able to handle it." Wonderful—the way this young Jewish woman articulated her combative position in advance with the professor! She then became a terrific student of Bultmann's. I actually studied with Bultmann much more seriously than she did, but she had such an intense interest in the New Testament that she spent several semesters studying with him, visited him again after the war, and always showed him respect.

Our position as outsiders in Bultmann's seminar immediately created a bond between us. I needn't go on at length about what a fascinating, attractive, enchanting person she was, what an exceptional being. You didn't have to be particularly perceptive to recognize that—it was plain as day in her eyes and in her expression. Besides, she was so attractive, and apparently she liked me, too. We quickly became close. We were such good friends that one time, when my father visited me in Marburg and met Hannah, he interpreted our relationship as something different from what it was, and through a business contact in Königsberg made inquiries about the Arendt family, which of course was promptly reported to Hannah's mother. Hannah told me this with great amusement—by the way, my father received a very positive report. But when I speak of the long and loving relationship between us, it's important to stress that it was never physical. I've often been asked why that was so, because there's ample evidence that Hannah was attractive to men, and the fact that I'm receptive to women has also been sufficiently demonstrated. And yet—it was different with us. I'll have more to say about this later. In the beginning we regularly had lunch at the same restaurant. As students we usually took one meal a day in a restaurant and provided for ourselves the rest of the time in our lodgings. After the first two or three meals, Hannah said, "I'd like to propose a deal." She came from a good bourgeois home and was well brought up. "I'd like the privilege of lighting up while you're still eating." She made use of this privilege for the rest of her life, for she was a heavy smoker, and I was a slow eater.

It was also understood that I would protect her. Hannah had her vulnerable side and felt in need of protection against impertinent male advances. I recall an incident that occurred when we were at our usual table in the restaurant: a student from one of the dueling fraternities got up from his table, came over to us, stood at attention, clicked his heels, introduced himself, and said to Hannah, "Will you permit me to join you?" Hannah looked at me with terrified eyes, and I said, "No." Whereupon he clicked his heels again, bowed, and withdrew. Hannah said, "Thank you so much!" We talked a great deal, for she needed someone to confide in. That's one factor that kept our relationship from becoming erotic; you couldn't be a confidant and a lover at the same time. That was what I became, and I took my role so seriously that there were some things I didn't share even with Lore, my wife, as long as Hannah was alive, for I told myself I'd heard about them under the seal of confidentiality. Over the years, she also discovered certain vulnerabilities in me—for instance that in some respects I was more sensitive than she. She often said to my wife, for example when it was a question of reports on the Nazi period, especially about the concentration camps: "This is nothing for Hans to hear." She was what would be called in English *tough*. She had a robust constitution and could look the horrors of the world in the face in a way she couldn't expect of me. She knew that things that were profoundly disturbing could throw me off balance and that I had to be protected a bit.

During that time in Marburg we saw each other every day. We met for classes, went out to eat together, and I also came by to see her. Since she had not much money, she lived in a rather chilly attic room. There she'd discovered a little mouse, and had trained it to come out at a certain time of day to be fed. Though there was a whole cohort of students from Königsberg in Marburg, with some of whom she was on good terms, Hannah was very much alone. I was a close friend, but the only person who was really close to her was someone she couldn't go to see, and that was Martin Heidegger. I heard from Hannah's own mouth how her affair with Heidegger had begun. That's one of the secrets I've carried around with me for decades, a secret that can finally be talked about, after all this time.[3] For the 1924–25 winter semester, Hannah had come to Marburg as a brand-new philosophy student. She came — like so many Jewish students from Königsberg — because of Heidegger, drawn by his strange magnetism. Hannah confided the following to me: at some point during this first semester she had to see Heidegger during office hours, for something having to do with her studies. It was late in the day, and in his office it was growing dim, for he hadn't turned on the light. When they'd finished what they had to discuss and Hannah got up to leave, Heidegger saw her to the door. At that moment something unexpected happened; in Hannah's words, "Suddenly he went down on his knees before me. And I bent down, and from below he reached up his arms toward me, and I took his head in my hands, and he kissed me, and I kissed him." That was how it started. It wasn't the usual beginning for a professor's seduction of a student, nor was it lust for adventure on the part of a student out to seduce a professor; the whole thing was very dramatic, taking place on an emotional plane that gave the relationship an absolutely exceptional quality from the very beginning. Heidegger had had his eye on her. She was by no means the only one; as I learned only later, he took an interest in a woman student from time to time, and I never heard of one who resisted. But these affairs were entirely different — they certainly didn't begin with his falling to his knees, and surely none of them lasted a lifetime. This moment marked the beginning of something from which both parties never freed themselves. Later, when someone asked me after a reading whether I could explain why Hannah Arendt had forgiven Heidegger for his antisemitism so quickly after the war, I said, "I can put my answer in one word: love. And love can forgive a great deal."

My wife can attest that as long as Hannah was alive I never told her this story, and usually you tell your wife everything. But because Hannah had honored me by describing this most secret experience, I felt obligated to keep silent and spoke of it only quite a while after her death. "Suddenly he went down on his knees before me." Whether she'd already felt attracted to him before this happened, I don't know. If anyone had thoughts of a sexual relationship, it was probably Heidegger. Of course she was under Heidegger's spell, as we all were; as I picture it, she saw him as a fascinating thinker and teacher, but I doubt there would have been any thought of love or even a special relationship on her part. But I can't say anything definitive about that — Hannah and I never discussed it. She shared this incident with me not long after it occurred — even before that winter was over, I was in the know. How this came about is one of my most intimate memories. One day I was visiting Hannah in her room because she was sick and had a bit of a fever. She had to stay in bed, and I came to keep her company. And while I was sitting by her bed, something happened that's almost unavoidable when two people of the opposite sex are fond of each other. Hannah was beautiful, and I wasn't too bad-looking myself. So we kissed, and I held her in my arms a bit. She was lying in bed in her nightgown, and I was perched on the edge of the bed — but then I got up to go. It was a good-bye that besides tenderness had a distinctly erotic component and could be understood as an incipient shift in our friendship toward something more than platonic. But at the time I was decent or delicate enough not to want to take advantage of the situation. So it was actually only a tender good-bye. As I was on my way out, however, wishing her a speedy recovery and heading for the door, she called out suddenly, "Hans!" I turned around. "Hans, come back here. Sit down. This won't do. I must tell you something." So I went back, sat down on a chair by her bed, and she told me about her relationship with Heidegger. From that moment on, there could be no question of a sexual relationship between Hannah and me. She became taboo for me. That was what she'd meant to accomplish — she confided in me to prevent me from harboring any hopes. She liked me, and no doubt a love relationship could have developed if Heidegger hadn't been between us. But neither was it the case that from then on I viewed this as a yearned-for but thwarted possibility. Instead, any such thoughts were completely banished, and not once in our friendship — of course we hugged and kissed when we greeted each other or said good-bye — did I feel the slightest temptation to push it beyond the limit that had been set. Because she'd been forced to tell me something she wouldn't have shared with me otherwise, so as to prevent our friendship from being destroyed, I became her complete confidant. That formed the basis of a lifelong friendship.

Between 1925 and 1933 I laid the foundation for my first major scholarly work, *Gnosis und spätantiker Geist* [Gnosticism and the Spirit of Late Antiquity], which developed out of my dissertation. I want to say just a little about it, since I've already dealt with this subject more thoroughly elsewhere.[4] Any discussion of my philosophy should begin not with gnosticism but with my efforts to establish a philosophical biology. My work on gnosticism was just my journeyman's project, an application of Heidegger's philosophy, especially of existential analysis, with its particular interpretive methodology and its understanding of human existence, to a specific body of historical material, in this case gnosticism in late antiquity. It was an interesting attempt, and a unique one, not previously undertaken, because no philosopher had become interested in this phenomenon up to then. So I produced something original that represented an actual contribution to the scholarship on late antiquity. I wouldn't go so far as to say, however, that an independent Jonas philosophy manifested itself here; instead I took what I'd learned and applied it so as to cast a new light on, and through, a certain historical subject and interpret it in a way that had become possible only as a result of Heidegger's existential analysis. Let me explain briefly how the project came about. One day in Bultmann's New Testament seminar I'd signed up to give a report on the concept of recognition of God, the *gnosis theou* in the Gospel according to John. While working on this project, I began to explore (partly encouraged by Bultmann's own interest in gnosticism) the farther reaches of this part of religious history as it related to this conceptual world. Suddenly I realized that my topic extended well beyond the specific realm of the New Testament, and my seminar report turned into a monster, which Bultmann found so impressive, however, that he urged me to make it the subject of my dissertation. When I objected that I didn't intend to become a New Testament scholar, he said, "Let me talk this over with Heidegger!" Thus it became clear that I could write my dissertation under Heidegger on the phenomenon of gnosticism. It was not unusual, by the way, for a dissertation written under Heidegger's supervision to draw heavily on original sources, for the discussion in his seminars always focused on primary texts. Heidegger's teaching of philosophy had a historical orientation, yet it didn't deal with the history of philosophy; he took the sources seriously as pretexts to engage in philosophical reflection. Heidegger's uniquely penetrating and stimulating brand of textual interpretation was very special. Thus my need to engage in intensive study of the original texts didn't deviate from what was usually required for a dissertation written under Heidegger.

Whether Heidegger had any interest in my research I never found out. He seldom said much. From time to time he let me report to him on my progress, but the initiative always had to come from me. Such reporting usually took place during our summer vacation. Once or twice I visited Heidegger in Todtnauberg in the Black Forest and told him what I'd accomplished and what direction my work was taking. He would nod and say, "Fine, that sounds very good. Keep up the good work. You seem to be on the right track." Basically he had little to say on the topic, because I knew far more about it than he, and he left it up to his friend Rudolf Bultmann to make sure my research was solid. But no doubt my approach appealed to him as a philosopher. It was self-evident that a Heidegger student would look at a philosophical text through a Heideggerian lens. But it surely pleased him and filled him with a certain satisfaction that I wanted to apply the Heidegger method to a phenomenon like gnosticism, something so untamed and fundamentally alien to philosophical thought, and to coax out of it a meaning that could be elicited only by means of such an approach. Even so, I doubt this resulted in his being much interested in gnosticism. At the time, by the way, I saw gnosticism as an early equivalent of Heideggerian thought, but not the other way around. Only much later, when I'd weaned myself from Heidegger worship, did it occur to me that not only were some of Heidegger's views of existence anticipated by the gnostics but Heidegger's thinking itself also represented a sort of present-day gnostic phenomenon.[5]

In the fall of 1928 I submitted my completed dissertation to Heidegger — all handwritten and bristling with Greek and Latin quotations. The second reader for the Philosophy Department, a sort of glorified high-school teacher, responded negatively; he couldn't make head or tail of my work. Heidegger paid him no mind, but wrote an evaluation that completely invalidated the other reader's. But month after month passed before he did so, and during that time I heard nothing from Heidegger. I was waiting for the verdict of my teacher and judge, or at least a word, some echo. I'd returned to Marburg that winter, after having been away for an interlude. Once I'd earned enough certificates for attending lecture courses and had found my dissertation topic, I'd gone off to Heidelberg and later also Bonn and Frankfurt. I didn't want to and didn't dare to hang around Marburg anymore — that could fry your brain. So now I was back in Marburg, waiting to hear from Heidegger. One evening I went to a concert, and was already in my seat when Heidegger showed up and had to squeeze past me to reach his seat in the same row. As he did so, he remarked, "Your dissertation is excellent." And continued down the row. So that was how he treated a candidate in suspense, and I think it didn't trouble him in the slightest that a student had been waiting in fear and trembling to hear how something he'd spent years working on would be received. My oral defense took place on 29 February 1928, for it was a leap year; accordingly, the anniversary comes only once every four years. When I'd been informed of the outcome, I went to the post office and send two telegrams, worded exactly the same — one to my parents and one to Hannah Arendt in Königsberg: "Doctorate awarded summa cum laude." And I remember that a student who'd looked over my shoulder as I was handing in the form commented, "I'm green with envy!" That same afternoon a telegram came from Königsberg: "Summis cum gratulationibus. Hannah." After that, on special occasions we always congratulated each other in Latin. In the fall of 1974, on the fiftieth anniversary of the beginning of our friendship, I sent her a telegram in Latin from Israel — the only completely original Latin text I'd ever composed: "Amicissimae quinquagenta annorum amicus semper dedictus. Hans."

I've written about Martin Heidegger as a teacher in my essay "Wissenschaft als persönliches Erlebnis" [Scholarship as Personal Experience],[6] but I can't talk about him as a person, since I had next to no personal contact with him. That may have been different for Gadamer and Löwith. But I did spend the night one time in his hut in Todtnauberg. He had a sort of bunk in which a visitor could sleep. Heidegger loved being up there, and was very relaxed. He might take you hiking with him. But I never went skiing with him, unlike many of his other students. During that visit to Heidegger's hut, I had my only conversation with him about Zionism. I'd just come from Basel, where the sixteenth Zionist congress had taken place in the summer of 1929. When I mentioned the congress, he asked me to explain in a few words what Zionism was. He had no idea, and said, "Zionist congress — what goes on there? I suppose the whole thing takes place in a big tent?" To which I replied, "No, there's a conference center where the participants stay, a hotel." So he had very primitive notions, picturing a Zionist congress as some kind of campout. He had no idea what such a political gathering was like! Yet in addition to the Zionist congress there were also socialist congresses and all sorts of other political conventions. But Heidegger was oblivious to such things. I also can't say whether it had even entered his consciousness that one of his students supported a movement that aimed to move the Jews from Germany to Palestine. He probably never considered that in theory this would have meant that his school, made up largely of Jewish philosophers, could dissolve as a result of emigration. Still, I was the only Zionist among his students. At least to my knowledge no one else among the Jewish Heidegger disciples was a supporter of Zionism — on the contrary. I did run into some of them later in Palestine, but they didn't choose to go at a time when you still had a choice. Probably Heidegger thought there just happened to be such dreamers among the Jews, and his student Hans, on whose dissertation he'd conferred the highest praise a teacher could give a student, namely summa cum laude, was one of those dreamers and would eventually go off to Palestine. So a Heidegger student would establish himself in Palestine and perhaps spread his teachings there. The thought that his standing in Germany might suffer as a result of so many Jews leaving or being forced to leave apparently didn't occur to him. Heidegger was in no way prepared for such a thing. I should mention, too, that here and there he even helped Jewish students of his. For instance, Paul Oskar Kristellar later said in New York that he had nothing against Heidegger because when he emigrated to Italy, Heidegger sent letters of recommendation that helped him find a position there.[7] No — Heidegger wasn't a personal antisemite. Presumably it felt a little uncanny to him that so many of his students were Jewish, but more in the sense that it was somewhat one-sided, that there weren't enough others who were more like him. The only discussion of antisemitism in his immediate surroundings came up when word got out that his wife had belonged to the nationalist youth movement. Perhaps she nagged him occasionally, saying, "Martin, why do you act deaf and dumb? Why are you constantly surrounded by young Jews?" There were rumors that Elfride Heidegger had antisemitic leanings, but I can't say how people knew this. It was true she had every reason to be jealous of a certain Jewish woman, for at some point she must have heard about her husband's affair and surely didn't have friendly feelings about that.

A noticeable feature of the circle that swirled around Heidegger in Marburg during the years when I was writing my dissertation — about twelve to fifteen philosophers, among them, in addition to Hannah Arendt, Gerhard Nebel, and me, Karl Löwith, Hans-Georg Gadamer, Gerhard Krüger, and Günther Stern — was that we were all apolitical. Günther Stern was the exception; he'd written his dissertation under Husserl, and was now studying with Heidegger and coming under his philosophical influence, but politically he was developing into a leftist social critic. That alone would have alienated him from Heidegger, who had nothing to say about the burning problems in contemporary society and politics.[8] To me, socialism never seemed like a viable alternative, because it didn't make rational sense to me. When I was younger, at the time of the Russian Revolution, socialism held a certain fascination for me, so that after the November revolution in Germany I was trying to picture how a socialist republic might look in Germany. But I can't say I ever went through a prolonged phase in which I thought that history required a violent revolution, the total overthrow of society and the dictatorship of the proletariat. Obviously the goals of the Social Democrats appealed to me more than those of Gustav Stresemann's German People's Party and the German nationalists. If I'd had the choice, of course I would have voted social democratic. As it was, I voted for the German Democratic Party, and was a liberal or left-leaning liberal. Of much greater concern to me was the fate of the Jews. Perhaps that narrowed my vision, or I wasn't looking for the formula that would solve the problems of the world but was concentrating on one problem, namely that the Jewish existence in the Galut — in a human, psychological, and political sense — was untenable in the long run and had to be overcome by means of the Zionist solution. This sense of purpose largely satisfied my need for involvement in politics, and the growth of antisemitism and the rise of the Hitler movement in Germany could only reinforce my commitment.

Hannah Arendt was no exception when it came to being apolitical, and this although she'd grown up in a politically minded household. Her mother had been an early socialist and an admirer of Rosa Luxemburg.[9] Thus Hannah had all the prerequisites for becoming involved in politics — as a socialist. But as she saw it, philosophy had such power over her thinking and her existence that this entire realm was excluded. A comparable example might be the early Christians, who turned their backs on the world or went into the desert to escape the world and to seek to perfect themselves in direct contact with God — that was philosophy for Hannah Arendt. It was an intellectual and spiritual realm that removed one from the hustle and bustle of ordinary life. It took the inescapable Hitler phenomenon — as well as the influence of her husband, Günther Stern — to force her to confront politics; not until reality burst in the rudest fashion into this isolated and dust-free existence did the political sphere open up to her.[10] She'd regarded my own political commitment to Zionism with amused tolerance, as a lovable weakness on the part of her good friend Hans: "Let the child have his plaything. He's crazy about Zionism, and men need their toys." The wider world, including the Jewish world, didn't interest her — taking a political interest in Judaism would have been as foreign to her as caring about the fate of the working class or the German nation, or any other concerns of the day. That was unworthy of a philosopher, whose thinking took place on another plane entirely. My dissertation topic, gnosticism, was potentially a thousand times more political than Hannah Arendt's, the concept of love in Augustine.[11] It's impossible to imagine how removed from the world you could be in Marburg, paying no attention whatsoever to current events. A fateful situation.

When I came to Heidelberg after receiving my doctorate, things were different. Sociology was still flourishing, and you couldn't be a student of Max Weber's or Karl Mannheim's without being interested, at least in principle, in the realities of the social and political world. So my horizon widened during this period, and I discovered sociology, especially Max Weber's study *The Protestant Ethic and the Spirit of Capitalism*,[12] which at the time was completely transforming our view of the modern world. But I can't claim I ever became a Max Weber expert. I was particularly fascinated by his collected essays on the sociology of religion, in which he also discusses ancient Judaism,[13] whereas his theory on scholarship as value-free, which struck me as philosophically inadequate, never really impressed me. Still, questions of social or political philosophy suddenly acquired importance for me in Heidelberg, since I belonged there to the circle around Karl Mannheim, who placed certain hopes in me and was glad to have attracted a philosopher who might become a spokesman for his sociology of knowledge. I participated assiduously for one or two semesters, and in 1929 attended — as a newly minted Ph.D. — the international sociology conference in Zurich. At this conference, where I presented a paper,[14] there was considerable controversy, the more so because Mannheim's Heidelberg colleague Alfred Weber laced into Mannheim in public, having been annoyed for a long time by the teacher training Mannheim had been conducting under his very nose.[15] But this was my only guest performance in the field of sociology, undertaken out of fondness for Mannheim, whom I considered an important thinker at the time. As a person I always found him lovable, but as for his scholarship, which he himself considered immensely significant, I soon came to have doubts.

During this period, I wasn't looking for a position as a professor's assistant, but was living as an independent scholar. That was something a son of Gustav Jonas could afford — to continue to live at one university or another. My first task was revising my dissertation for publication, so what I needed

most of all was a good library and an intellectually stimulating environment. I alternated among Heidelberg, Paris, Frankfurt, and Cologne; I
was in Cologne during the winter of 1932–33 when Hitler came to power. I
spent the winter of 1928–29 in Paris, rewarding myself a bit for receiving my
degree. I wanted to study at the Sorbonne, but above all familiarize myself
with Paris — that "disreputable city," as Husserl had called it. In my pension
at 10 Rue de la Sorbonne, I met Hans Yorck von Wartenburg, who occupied the room next to mine. I'd heard his uncle's name mentioned at the
beginning of my studies, when the correspondence between Wilhelm Dilthey and Count Paul Yorck von Wartenburg had appeared.[16] In its day, this
correspondence was greeted as a great revelation, because it showed that
the most original and significant of Dilthey's ideas, especially his hermeneutics, were actually inspired by Count Yorck von Wartenburg, a highly
cultivated man from the Silesian town of Klein Oels. This discovery struck
like a bomb. Someone called it "the greatest posthumous embarrassment
in the history of philosophy." So I made friends with the aforementioned
count's nephew, who was a little younger than I and still at the university.
Our relationship didn't extend beyond our shared time in Paris, but during this period we had many conversations. I owe to him an important
insight into literature. He told me about his childhood, the atmosphere in
his home. His father had grown up in the tradition of intense literary education and intellectual activity that was apparently customary in the Yorck
family. One day, when he came home from school, Hans said, his father had
asked him, "What did you learn today? What did you do in German class?"
"We discussed Goethe's poem 'The Fisherman.'" "All right; do you know it
by heart?" "Yes, yes, I do." When his father called on him to recite the poem,
he began, "Das Wasser rauscht, das Wasser schwoll, ein Fischer sass mit
seiner Angel ruhevoll. . . ." At that his father said, "Wait, son, that's not how
it should sound!" He next recited the poem, very slowly, and only then did
the boy realize what the poem was all about. "Since that time," Yorck von
Wartenburg said, "I consider this poem one of the most precious, immortal
treasures of the German language." Hans Yorck von Wartenburg was a sensitive young man who confided many personal things to me. On the wall of
his rented room hung two pictures that he'd apparently brought with him
to Paris. One of them showed his ancestor, Count Yorck von Wartenburg
von Tauroggen, who'd concluded the famous treaty of Tauroggen, in which,
after Napoleon's retreat from Moscow, Prussia suddenly went over to the
Russians. The beginning of Germany's liberation — an old engraving. The

other—imagine!—was *Napoleon Bonaparte on the Bridge at Arcoli*, one of the great images of the young general. It turned out that the young count was an ardent admirer of Napoleon. And now his ancestor and his ancestor's great adversary hung side by side in his room!

During my years as an émigré I now and then found myself wondering, "What can have become of Hans Yorck von Wartenburg? How did he conduct himself? How did he make it through the Nazi period?" I knew that his older brother, Paul Yorck von Wartenburg, had been involved in the conspiracy to assassinate Hitler on 20 July 1944 and had been executed. Only much later did I find out what had become of Hans. In her book *Die Stärke der Stille* [The Strength of Silence], Paul Yorck von Wartenburg's widow Marion mentions that her young brother-in-law was killed in Poland in the very first days of World War II.[17] Apparently he was his mother's favorite, and she was inconsolable. He was one of the many victims of this terrible war.

In the years before Hitler's seizure of power I essentially aspired to find a position as a university lecturer. Only by writing the second dissertation required for a professorship, the *Habilitation*, and launching an academic career could I have made myself completely independent of my parents' financial support. I spoke with Karl Jaspers one time about his sponsoring me, but he turned me down; presumably there were others with whom he had a much closer philosophical or personal relationship. So I had no one to mentor me. Husserl was already too old, and in any case would probably not have advocated for someone who'd left him to go over to Heidegger. Heidegger himself was not very forthcoming in this respect. In 1928, by the way, when Husserl retired, he'd returned to his old stamping grounds in Freiburg. In any case, I couldn't qualify officially for a professorship until I'd written the second dissertation. Because I was still revising my dissertation for publication, it was unclear where my dissertation would stop and my *Habilitation* would begin, since I wanted to continue working on the same topic. Yet because it was an unwritten law that the *Habilitation* had to have a completely different subject, during my last years in Germany, from mid-1928 to January 1933, I was confused as to what I should really be working on. Essentially I had to look for a new topic. But in the end, world events made this question moot, for after Hitler's seizure of power it was clear that the *Habilitation* was not to be.

CHAPTER 5

Emigration, Refuge, and Friends in Jerusalem

I became aware of the Nazi threat only gradually, as Hitler began to achieve his first electoral victories in the wake of the Great Depression of 1929. Everyone saw what was happening, yet "one" — for this applied not only to me but unfortunately also to many German intellectuals — continued to harbor a certain contempt for Hitler and all he represented, including the mob character of the National Socialist movement — the storm troopers [*Sturmabteilung*, SA], the Goebbels rallies, the sea of flags. Few recognized the dangerousness of the phenomenon.[1] You could sense that National Socialist thinking was spreading, yet I considered it more probable that we would end up with a right-wing conservative and reactionary government than that these fellows would actually come to power. By the end of 1932, however, I had no doubt that the Nazis would get into the government at some point. If such a large percentage of the German people kept voting for them, and in increasing numbers, I thought, it was unavoidable, according to the democratic parliamentary principle, that their turn would come eventually and they would have to show what they were capable of. On the evening of 30 January, or perhaps it was 31 January, 1933 a great costume ball took place in Mönchengladbach's Kaiser Friedrich Hall — it was Carnival time. I went because Carnival was celebrated independent of all religious, party, and class differences, and by then I'd developed an appreciation for the freedom a mask gives you to approach and dance with pretty girls. And while we were celebrating there, drinking and dancing, word spread through the hall that Hitler had just been named chancellor. I still recall coming home and saying to my mother, "Thank God. It's finally happened. This is the only way we'll get rid of this plague. In a few months they'll have cooked their goose. They had to get into office at some point, and since they're madmen, they'll be done for in short order." At the time I spoke of several months. I couldn't have been more mistaken in my prediction. And I soon realized just how wrong I'd been. The way the Nazis seized one powerful position after another, elbowed Alfred Hugenberg and Franz von Papen aside, and monopolized and secured their power caused me to change my mind. Above all, what happened on 1 April made it clear to me that no matter how long this ordeal lasted, no self-respecting Jew could stay in this country. I wasn't even thinking of a threat to our physical existence, for the plan of exterminating all of us didn't exist yet. At the time none of us had read *Mein Kampf*. Only Günther Stern said years later, "I was one of those who'd read *Mein Kampf* and recognized then how great the danger was." But since I never heard him say anything of the sort, I have my doubts as to whether I can believe him — perhaps his memory was playing tricks on him. I, at any rate, considered it absolutely beneath my dignity to read anything of that sort. No one who thought himself intellectually respectable would stoop so low as to subject himself to that kind of garbage. That, of course, was a mistake. But when I saw the SA troops posted outside Jewish stores, law offices, and doctors' apartments, and the signs saying "Jew," "Don't buy from Jews," "Boycott Jews," and "Jewish Boycott Day,"[2] I decided to leave Germany and — of course — go to Palestine. I made the decision on 1 April and didn't need to act on it right away because in those days you could still emigrate legally and even take a certain amount of your own money with you — though not a large amount. So I applied for an immigration certificate for Palestine, specifically a so-called capitalist's certificate or thousand-pound certificate. Applications for these were handled separately from the immigration quota. Anyone who could prove that he had one thousand Palestinian pounds, or the equivalent of one thousand British pounds (around twelve thousand reichsmark at the prevailing exchange rate) received a transfer permit from the National Socialist government. The Nazi authorities actually preferred Palestine as an emigration destination for Jews; to receive permission to transfer the same sum for emigration to America was far more difficult. If a person had nothing on his record, that is, if he wasn't subject to political persecution, he could transfer the money directly to a foreign bank. Equipped with the certificate and with the famous thousand pounds, I headed to England, because the first volume of my gnosticism book was just going to press in Göttingen and I still had to put the finishing touches on one or two chapters.[3] I wanted to be closer to Germany for the back-and-forth of the editing process, but above all to live in a place where library conditions were as superb as they were in London, so that any necessary further research on sources could be taken care of under the best possible circumstances. By contrast I could anticipate that adjusting to conditions in Palestine would probably make heavy demands on my attention, and I would have to get used to doing everything in Hebrew; but above all I didn't know what books the library at the University of Jerusalem would have in its collection. So I went to England for a year and a half and oversaw the printing of my book from there. That was in 1934. During that time I didn't set foot on German soil again — I took care of everything by post. I did travel to Holland once, where I met someone from Gladbach, and I went to Paris, too, where I saw Hannah and Günther Stern, who were living there as émigrés, and before I set out for Palestine I had a rendezvous with my parents in Switzerland. I didn't return to Germany until July 1945.[4]

I have a very distinct memory of the day I left Germany. It was an absolutely beautiful late summer day at the end of August, and my parents and I strolled back and forth in the garden. Everything was ready: I had my train ticket and papers, my suitcases were packed, and the arrangements had been made for my furniture to be shipped to Palestine around the time when I would be going there from England. As we walked in the garden — our last time together — suddenly, as if on signal, we all broke out in the most heartrending sobs. Up to then not a tear had been shed over all the things that were happening, including my decision to emigrate, but now that the moment had come and the last half hour, the last ten minutes were upon us, we cried our eyes out. And I secretly vowed never to return except as a soldier in a conquering army. I've already mentioned that my imagination had a certain military cast, and I thought that precisely because they were considered to be softies, cowards, and weaklings, Jews could wash away such affronts to their honor only with blood. And here, aside from the threat to our economic welfare that the boycott of Jewish businesses unmistakably portended, and aside from the impending ghettoization that events pointed to, I was overcome by the sense that my own honor had been damaged, that our honor as human beings was being injured by the denial of our civil rights and the other legal harassment to which we Jews were increasingly being subjected at the hands of the state. I instinctively felt that all this could be set right only by our taking up arms. The answer had to be a military one, something we weren't capable of at the moment, but which had to come sooner or later. Joined to this specific Jewish and personal motivation was a more general insight or premonition: that for the world, too, for Germany and Europe, this plague could be eliminated only by means of war. Probably from that moment on, and certainly as soon as I got to England, I saw ever more clearly that in the last analysis either National Socialism would determine Europe's fate, or a European war was inevitable. And during my early years as an émigré in England and Palestine, I recognized that the longer this war was put off, the more difficult it would be, and that timely military intervention could perhaps put an end to this horror before it got much worse — for instance when the Germans reoccupied the Rhineland in 1936. And there were many such occasions when a firm stance on the part of the Western powers or the other European powers, including the Soviet Union, could perhaps have averted the whole tragedy. When the war began at last, there was thus no question but that I would volunteer immediately, though I was already no longer sure that the war could be won. But at the very least, I thought, you had to go down fighting. I was one of those who longed for the war to come and were convinced that the sooner it came the better, that it could be won with fewer casualties and with greater certainty. When the time finally arrived, I was glad that England hadn't shied away again, but at the same time I thought, "By now the Germans have gained superiority. They're much better prepared. And if it were only a question of whom the god of war rewards and punishes, actually the Germans would have to win, because they've really gone to all the trouble of preparing for war, while the others have blown smoke rings and failed to get ready." To me, Chamberlain and his policy of appeasement was a nightmare, a catastrophe. Instead I placed my faith in Winston Churchill, and was already a fan of his at a time when he was generally despised in England. My only hope was that someday he would prevail. In that respect I really was right. I made several historical predictions that turned out to be accurate, but I was also incredibly mistaken about some things — for instance when I thought that the Hitler magic would have run its course in six months. On several details I did hit the bull's-eye, for example when America had already joined the war and the initiative had shifted to the Allies after the Nazis' capitulation at Stalingrad in 1943. The question was where an Allied invasion would take place, and I immediately thought of North Africa: Algeria, Morocco — that was where the first American landings would occur. And I still recall that I was in a military camp when I heard the news of the invasion, and I called up Jerusalem or Haifa to say, "Well? Didn't I tell you so?"

But back to that leave-taking in our summer-warmed garden, and to my family. My parents had a multitude of compelling reasons for deciding not to leave with me. I'd talked it over with my father: "Couldn't you sell the business? Couldn't you convert the factory into money, manage to find a buyer while there's still time, and get out? Or how about setting up a textile factory in Palestine?" But my father explained that he couldn't do it. It turned out later that he was already a sick man. He was old, and eventually died of cancer in 1938. But even if he'd been in better physical shape, it would hardly have been possible for him to take such a step. Building up a textile company from scratch in Palestine, liquidating the family firm under the circumstances prevailing in Germany at the time, that was something Jews weren't accustomed to, and it could have been accomplished only with ridiculous losses. But of course it would also have been the right thing, certainly better than staying in Germany or being killed later on. We talked about it, and my father said, "I'll send as much money to you in Palestine as I can." He managed to do that several times — with increasingly great losses. Only a fraction of the amount that was to be transferred from Germany was ever paid out in Palestine. The Nazis raked off their share more and more shamelessly. Nonetheless, for quite a while support arrived from home. But unfortunately not my parents themselves. One time they did come to visit me in Palestine. In 1936 we spent Passover together in Jerusalem. My father and mother arrived by ship from Marseille or Trieste, stayed for about three weeks, and went home again. My father was already walking with difficulty, trembling and using a cane. The illness had taken root in him, but he was deeply moved at seeing his son again and having seen the land of his fathers and attended a seder in Jerusalem. The seder took place at the house of my cousin Heinz Simon, the son of my father's sister Elfriede from Lechenich. He was also living in Jerusalem, and his parents had come to visit on the same ship as mine. Both sets of parents returned to Germany — the Simons to a terrible fate, for they were later deported, and, as I mentioned, my father would die in 1938, and my mother was murdered a few years later. They would have been able to get out, but they didn't have immigration certificates. At the time they could still have procured one; the sooner you did so — which meant the more money you had to support an application to enter Palestine or some other country — the better your chances. The longer you waited, the harder it became, and the people who still managed to get out at the end did so with about ten marks to their name, or empty-handed.[5]

After my father's death, my mother lived for a while with my Uncle Leo. He'd married an enchanting and very gifted but sickly woman, and had been widowed in the meantime. His children were considerably younger than I. His son — Hans Horowitz — had become a businessman; he emigrated to Holland. There his fate eventually caught up with him, and he was deported to the East. His daughter, Lotte, on the other hand, who while still a girl had already gone to Lisbon to work as a governess and had learned

Portuguese, married a young man from Düsseldorf. They emigrated and settled in Santiago, Chile. Uncle Leo, in front of whose house SA storm troopers had also stood on 1 April 1933, gave up his medical practice and moved to Mönchengladbach, where he took my mother in. But then his daughter got him to come to Santiago just before the war broke out, and there he stayed, living to a ripe old age with his daughter, his grandchildren, and his great-grandchildren. After the war I reestablished contact with him, and we carried on a correspondence.

My mother stayed on alone in Germany, and because she couldn't get out, she suffered a terrible fate. It was my brother who, without being to blame for it, actually caused this unspeakable misfortune. He was three years younger than I and had always been a worry to us. He certainly did his best to work, but could never hold a job, until finally in Palestine he was able to eke out a modest living, working as a hotel doorman and in similar positions. I don't want to say more about this, except that after he'd failed to find work or any way of staying afloat after emigrating initially to France and Italy, and had been feeling miserably unhappy and lonely, he returned to our parents' house, the nest where he'd always sought refuge when things didn't work out for him. During the Night of Broken Glass, 9 November 1938, he was picked up and sent to Dachau. My father had died in January of that year. My mother had an emigration certificate for Palestine, as well as her ticket for the ship; and the so-called lift, the enormous wooden crate filled with everything she would need to furnish an apartment and equip a household, was already in Hamburg, ready to be loaded onto a ship. And then my mother informed me in November 1938 that she refused to use her certificate and emigrate as long as her son was in Dachau. The Nazis had announced that no one would get out of Dachau unless he had permission to enter another country and could leave Germany within a week of being released from the concentration camp. My mother asked me to have the certificate reissued by the Palestine mandate government in the name of Georg Jonas. I had no choice but to comply. My brother reached Palestine in January 1939, and lived there from then on. I immediately undertook the necessary steps to obtain an immigration certificate for my mother, but that had become difficult for two reasons. First of all, after the issuance of the so-called White Book, the British had become more cautious and were strictly limiting the number of Jewish immigrants admitted to Palestine — at precisely the time when certificates were most urgently needed. But the British had their reasons, which were by no means anti-Jewish or antisemitic, but were connected with the Arabs' active uprising against the Zionist program in Palestine. The clashes were very bloody.[6] At the time I was already actively involved in the Haganah's resistance to the Arab attacks on Jewish settlements, and the British, who had major interests throughout the Arab world, allowed their policy, which was administered by the Colonial and Foreign offices, to be determined by these factors. Limiting Jewish immigration was part of that policy. Another complication was that I'd essentially shot my wad, because it was only the financial capital with which I'd immigrated that had made it possible for me to request the certificate for my mother — she'd come under the special quota, which was handled separately from the general quota. But once she passed the certificate on to her son, my privilege as a thousand-pound immigrant was exhausted, so now I had to go through the normal application process. And there was no way to predict when my mother's number would come up. Of course I did everything I could to speed up the process, including such illegal measures as bribing officials, which proved useless, or meeting with people who said they could obtain an entry visa in Persia or Cuba or somewhere else, for the right price. Either these agents really believed they could accomplish something, or they were exploiting the desperation of people in Palestine who were looking for some way, any way, for their relatives to emigrate. Twice I paid rather considerable sums to people who promised to pull off something in country X or Y. I never heard from them again. But on 1 September 1939, when England declared war, for which I was very glad, all possibility of helping my mother was gone. For a while longer I was able to correspond with her by way of Holland. You wrote to an intermediary in Holland — in this case my cousin Hans Horowitz. I sent letters to him, and he mailed them in a new envelope to my mother. The German invasion of Holland in May 1940, however, put an end to this form of communication, which could be carried on only through neutral countries, and I no longer had any direct link. Later, when I was already in the British army, I received word through the Red Cross that my mother was in Łódź, in the Litzmannstadt ghetto, as it was called at the time. That was the last I heard. I didn't find out about her death until I came back to Gladbach after 1945. Yes, it's a grim story, the great sorrow of my life. This wound has never healed — my mother's fate. I've never got over it, as my children know. It was terrible — the fits of uncontrollable sobbing that overcame me at certain moments, when the conversation turned to something that reminded me, or when we saw a film. There's no way to get over something like that. My mother was the most loving person you could imagine. And Uncle Leo, my revered and beloved Uncle Leo, wrote to me from Lima after the war: "In this unspeakable war, I lost the two people who were most precious to me — my sister and my son."

Otherwise, aside from my worry about my mother, my life in Jerusalem was happy. It was a marvelous place I found myself in when I arrived in 1935 at Passover, this land of my fathers, where friends were waiting for me. That I arrived at Passover was pure chance, dictated by the schedule of the Messagerie Maritime's departures from Marseille to Jaffa, by way of Alexandria. In Alexandria the ship even had a two-day stopover, and I used the opportunity to look up Bettina Strauss, Leo Strauss's sister, and my old friend Gerhard Nebel, with whom I'd studied under Heidegger. With him I traveled to Cairo for a day. Well, so now I arrived in Palestine. At the harbor — of course Jaffa didn't have a proper harbor, only an open roadstead, where you disembarked onto a smaller boat — George Lichtheim was there to greet me, a young friend who felt obligated to me, and whom I also liked very much. He was considerably younger than I, by about ten years, the son of Richard Lichtheim, a highly respected German Zionist leader from the first generation of Herzl disciples, a man who'd played an outstanding role in the formative years of German Zionism. He was a genuine Herzl Zionist, free of aspirations to religious renewal or other mystical or socialist embellishments. Nothing of the sort. What counted for him was quite simply the Jews' national cause, the Jews' restoration as a sovereign nation in Palestine. But eventually he left the mainstream of German Zionism, which politically followed a bourgeois, moderate course, and took a turn to the right, becoming a follower of Vladimir Jabotinsky and the so-called revisionism, which was actually at home in Poland and Russia.[7] At any rate, when I was becoming a Zionist, Richard Lichtheim had a great influence on me, for he was the author of a paper published by the Zionist Union of Germany in which the Zionist program was masterfully laid out in classic German prose, with marvelous clarity.[8] In addition, during the First World War Richard Lichtheim had played a tremendously important role in the history of Zionism. All this is relevant to my personal memories only insofar as I want to mention that he had an absolutely stunning wife, who came from Constantinople. During the war Lichtheim had lived in Istanbul entirely officially as the representative of the World Zionist Organization in Turkey, functioning as a sort of ambassador. He was the representative of Zionism in Turkey, and that was a key position in a way, because Turkey ruled over Palestine until 9 December 1917, when the British under General Edmund Allenby marched into Jerusalem. From that moment on, when England assumed the leading role in the Palestine issue, Lichtheim no longer had a function in Turkey. But he'd had the foresight to convert the Zionist Organization's financial holdings into gold, which saved them from the general debacle that befell the Central Powers.[9] When he returned to Berlin after the end of the war, he brought with him a wife from Istanbul's Sephardic community whose mother tongue was not Ladino but Greek. There was a community in Istanbul whose lingua franca was Greek. Whether Ladino was ever spoken in her household, I never found out. Irene Lichtheim was really an incredibly beautiful woman. They had two children, a son, whom they called George, and a daughter called Miriam. Both tall, slender greyhounds, who had a highbred and aristocratic air about them.

George had a brilliant analytical mind and was an excellent speaker and writer. He was a Marxist — in contrast to his father, who was a distinguished member of the upper middle class and therefore in the fortunate position of never having had to work for a living; he could afford the luxury of being an unpaid Zionist statesman, a statesman of the newly forming Jewish state. To be sure, George was an armchair Marxist, a person who found Marxist theory convincing, who sided with the working class and even assented to the dictatorship of the proletariat, although anything remotely bloodthirsty, violence in any form, was anathema to him. But he approved of everything he thought necessary to bring about the victory of socialism.[10] I, on the other hand, came from industry. True, I'd seen in our factory what it was like to be a factory worker. I knew working-class types. So I asked him one time: "George, tell me: you talk about the plight of the working class, you've studied Marx and Engels. Have you ever been inside a factory? In an industrial setting?" He replied, "No, never!" "That's something you should experience, so you can learn something about the working class, to which you want to devote yourself and all your energy." To that he said, "I don't need to. All you need to know can be found in the statistics." And that was typical of him — this disarming, cynical, self-satirizing openness. All his insights grew out of abstractions. He had no knowledge at all of the people who embodied the lot of the proletariat. George was an extraordinarily intelligent person, but otherwise not well equipped for life, because in his human relationships — especially those with the opposite sex — he had problems and, let me put it this way, suffered from an excess of skepticism and irony when it came to the natural instincts. He lived at a certain remove from the world, which he observed but with which he couldn't establish a down-to-earth relationship. Thus he fell in love time and again with women who were bound to be inaccessible. This inaccessibility was practically a prerequisite. He had a great many love affairs, but none of them brought fulfillment. That was somehow part of his personality. His sister, Miriam, whom I got to know in Jerusalem, where she was studying with Hans Jakob Polotsky, the great Egyptologist and Coptic scholar, became an excellent and internationally recognized Egyptologist in her own right.[11] But she never married, either. She was always a "spinster," from birth, you might say, and I could hardly picture her with a husband — it wasn't her style. And she remained true to that style.

I'd met George Lichtheim in London, when I was living in a pension there during my first years as an émigré. The pension was run by Annie Rosenbluth, the wife of Felix Rosenblüth, a Zionist leader of Richard Lichtheim's generation. The entire family of Felix Rosenblüth, who later changed his name to Pinchas Rosen and became Israel's first minister of justice, belonged to the leadership of German Zionism, but he was probably the most significant figure in the family.[12] He was married to an extraordinarily attractive, intelligent, and charming woman, who, to his misfortune, was anti-Zionist. She found Zionism completely wrongheaded and refused to go along to Palestine when her husband moved there at the beginning of the thirties. When she had to emigrate in 1933, she didn't go to Palestine to join her husband — they weren't divorced, but lived apart — but instead took her two growing children to London. Stopping over in Mönchengladbach, by the way, where she spent the night with us at 9 Mozartstrasse, for I'd made friends with her and had a huge crush on her. I was rather in love with her, let's put it that way. She was an enchanting and charming woman — but tough as nails. So, for instance, in her relationship with her husband she refused to give in and stuck to her point of view, which was "No, not Palestine!" In London she ran a pension in Golders Green. Karl Mannheim lived there for a time, as did other prominent personalities among the intellectual émigrés who came to London, such as Adolf Löwenstein and others. And George Lichtheim frequented the place as a friend of the family. That's where I got to know him. I also visited his mother, on whom I lavished attention, since I had a thing for feminine beauty. And a beautiful woman in her middle years must find it very pleasant to have such a young man pay court to her. To be sure, she was first and foremost a mother and made use of my admiration as follows: she invited me to tea one afternoon and gave me to understand that she wanted me to make friends with her son, George. She told me, "I know he's much younger than you. But I also know he worships you. He's mentioned you to me, and you appeal to him. And I know he very much needs a friend. He's a lonely boy, and it would mean a great deal to him if you were willing to become his friend." So I responded, out of love for Irene Lichtheim first of all, whom I worshipped, not with any erotic intentions but simply as a beautiful and also intelligent and sensitive woman: "Gladly, with pleasure!" So the friendship between George and me came about at his mother's behest. But I soon discovered I'd found an extraordinary young friend. We spent a lot of time together in London, before he set out for Palestine, half a year before me. And he was the one who was waiting for me when I disembarked in Jaffa.

As far as I recall, I went straight from Tel Aviv to Jerusalem, where I was already expected. I arrived in Jerusalem the day before Passover and promptly announced my presence to my fellow Zionist and later friend Hans Lewy. He wasn't a member of KJV, not a fraternity brother, so we didn't use the intimate form of address. But he'd been active in Blau-Weiss, so he was an old Zionist like me, in fact going back to his school days. He was a classicist, had studied under Werner Jäger, Ulrich von Wilamowitz-Möllendorf, and Eduard Norden, the great classical philologist in Berlin, and he'd come to Jerusalem with a position at the Hebrew University lined up. In the meantime he'd read my gnosticism book, which had made its way to Jerusalem before me and had smoothed my entry into this circle of intellectuals. Lewy had written to me in advance and offered to put me up for the first few days until I found my own place. So I stayed with Hans Lewy at the start. Shortly thereafter I paid a visit to Hugo Bergman, the philosophy professor at the Hebrew University, who came from Prague and had studied with Franz Brentano, a predecessor of Husserl's.[13] Bergman, who was also familiar with my book, received me with great respect. Someone else who was expecting me was Hans Jakob Polotsky, whom I'd never met, but who came from Göttingen and had been one of the chief editors of the Coptic Manichaica. These papyrus finds of the first third of the twentieth century included a corpus of Manichean texts, among them writings of Mani himself, the originals of which were lost for good, but which now became available in Coptic translation. These texts were in the Prussian State Library in Berlin. And when the Prussian Academy of Arts and Sciences was planning to issue an edition, the already somewhat older German expert on Coptic, a certain Carl Schmidt (referred to for short as "Coptic Schmidt," to distinguish him from other Schmidts) engaged the new bright light in Coptic studies, Hans Jakob Polotsky, as his chief collaborator.[14] Polotsky made a name for himself with his work on these Coptic Manichean writings. But his fame also rested on his excellent introduction to Manicheanism, in which he discussed the doctrine itself, not merely philological matters.[15] But in 1934, while I was in London, Polotsky was still in Göttingen, and was one of the first to see a copy of a book by Hans Jonas, straight from the publisher. Of course he had no idea who this Hans Jonas was. Polotsky belonged not to the world of German academic philosophy but to the rather obscure field of Egyptology, in which one doesn't usually hear about current discussions in philosophy. It was in Göttingen that his professor, whose assistant he probably was, showed him this book: "Here, this has just been delivered." And they looked at each other, wondering, "Could Hans Jonas be a Jew?" And then the professor said to him, "Oh, that's easy enough to find out." He picked up the telephone and called Vandenhoeck & Ruprecht and asked about Hans Jonas: "Is he Jewish?" Whereupon he received the answer, "Yes, he's a Jew, but an absolutely upstanding one." So I was certified as an upstanding Jew by my publisher.

Well, Polotsky, who then read the book, apparently with admiration, was eager to meet me. He soon stopped in to see Hans Lewy, with whom he was friends, since in the meantime he'd also received a teaching appointment at the Hebrew University, in Egyptology, and asked to make my acquaintance. He said to me, "After reading your book, I pictured you very differently." "So how did you picture me?" "The way one imagines a Talmudic student, a yeshiva bocher. Completely self-absorbed." What astonished him was the youthful air I projected in those days, and which stayed with me for a long time, to my own sorrow, because I was always taken for younger than I was, and that somewhat diminished the respect people showed me. It seemed like forever that my friends called me by the diminutive "Hänschen." It annoyed me to be so boyish at a time when I really should have been considered a man. Polotsky, on the other hand, seemed very manly: he had an incredibly deep, powerful bass voice and a face that Hans Sambursky described in his poem "Portrait of a Philologist":

> He holds his tongue. His wish to stay unscathed
> hangs heavy on him like a weight
> that then reveals itself in his deep, mellow voice
> when speak he does, though very late.

His face, so like an owl's, so sharp,
lit up by dark eyes' brilliant glance
rests atop his body's massive column,
the image of his intellect's substance.

He lacks but one thing: a thick beard,
black and wrapped around his face,
he'd seem an emperor, a judge
from some distant, still mysterious place.

By contrast, I had a child's face. Years later, to jump ahead for a moment, after we'd lived through a world war and I was being reunited with long-lost friends, when I visited Karl Jaspers in Heidelberg, I also ran into Dolf Sternberger, who told me the following story: "You know, your name came up in the meantime. It was 1943, I think, when I was giving a lecture in Paris, where there actually was a German cultural life under German occupation." (I must add here that Dolf Sternberger stayed in Germany all through the war with his Jewish wife and succeeded in saving her.) "After the lecture, Ernst Jünger, who was living in the Hotel George V in Paris, where the German military administration had its Paris headquarters, gave a reception for me. I came into the hall and saw someone in an airman's uniform sitting on a sofa, his legs splayed; I don't know whether it was an airman third class or an airman first class—at any rate, not an officer. And he looked at me so expectantly that I went up to him and said, 'We must have met before. You look very familiar.' So he says to me, 'Of course, it was at Hänschen Jonas's place in Heidelberg that we met.'" It was my friend Gerhard Nebel, who'd visited me at some point in Heidelberg and had met Dolf Sternberger through me. My reason for telling this story is just the "Hänschen" part.

But back to Jerusalem. So Polotsky said to me, "That's not how I pictured you at all." He was very pleased me meet me, and that was the beginning of the Polotsky-Jonas-Lewy friendship—"PIL." We immediately formed a club, which met regularly and took its name from the first letters of our last names. PIL is the Hebrew word for elephant, and we adopted the elephant as our emblem. To this day there are all sorts of elephant figurines in our house in New Rochelle, in memory of what we created back then. Soon others joined the club: George Lichtheim, the physicist Hans (Shmuel) Sambursky, and unavoidably also Gershom Scholem. When the latter was taken in as a regular member, he said, "The club's name has to reflect that." We asked him what he considered a suitable variation on PIL, and he already had a name in mind: "Pilegesh"—a Hebrew word that in the Bible designated a concubine.

Gershom Scholem was also one of those who'd been expecting my arrival in Jerusalem. I'd met him a few years earlier during a trip to England with my mother, before the Hitler period. In my later years as a student and in my time as a young scholar in Germany, my mother and I were very close, and we took quite a few trips together, since my father no longer liked to travel. We got along splendidly. It was really an enchanting relationship between a mother and her grown-up but still unattached son. I've forgotten how the meeting with Scholem came about. I knew that he was visiting London from Palestine, and someone, Martin Buber, I think, had come up with the idea that it would be a wonderful opportunity for us to get together, since I was going to London anyway, and Scholem happened to be there.

So my mother and I met Scholem. He paid a visit to us at our hotel, where he was seeing me as well as Rosa Jonas for the first time. We talked, and he was immediately very interested in my plans. This was after I received my doctorate but long before the completion of the first volume of the gnosticism book—perhaps around 1930. And he was the only one, so far as I recall, whom I really kept posted about my progress on the book, who read the introduction and the first chapter in draft form and wrote to me, full of praise. After that I sent him each chapter as it was written, and he was immensely enthusiastic about the book and wrote an excellent recommendation, which proved very useful to me later on. Among other things, he wrote that he'd followed the genesis of this work with growing interest, and with every chapter that I sent him his impression had become even more positive. He'd seen it more and more as a work that deserved his full approbation and his respect. I still recall the following sentence: "With each chapter my admiration for the work and its originality increased."

Martin Buber, to whom I owe this acquaintance, was among the first to praise my book when it appeared, though I didn't even have it sent to him. At the time—in 1934—he was still in Germany. Since he was a great book collector and reader, he must have purchased the book as soon as it came out, for that same year, before I went to Palestine, I received in London a highly encouraging letter from him, in which he wrote that he'd read my book with the greatest interest. Then came the sentence, "I consider this to be one of the most important works of intellectual history of our time." The actual wording. I still have that letter in my possession.[16] During this period a letter also arrived from Oswald Spengler, to whom I *had* sent the book. I'd called his attention to a particular paragraph in the introduction, in which I paid him the tribute he deserved, saying that he, although not a specialist in this period, had recognized with brilliant intuition certain of its features that had never been done justice in the historical and especially also the church-historical scholarship on this era. In the second volume of his *Decline of the West — Problems of Arabian Culture*,[17] which I'd devoured, he attributed the cultural features of the Near East that found expression in the gnostics' speculations to a nascent new culture, which he called the "Arabian culture" because it later culminated in Islam, and which he characterized as a "magical culture," in distinction to the Faustian culture of the Germanic West. Independently of these concepts, he'd recognized that this was not simply the fading of antiquity but something new that was taking shape during this era. That was also the basic motif of my interpretation of gnosticism; I wanted to demonstrate that here a new consciousness was breaking through, a consciousness that displayed decisive differences vis-à-vis that of antiquity and classical civilization. So I articulated my great respect for him, and received a letter from him in Munich in which he thanked me for the book and said, "This is one of the most important periods in world history. Yet it has never been sufficiently recognized and studied. What I said about it no one has understood except you. Yours, Oswald Spengler." That was the highest compliment he could have paid me.

So a certain fame had preceded me to Jerusalem, and a circle of friends quickly formed. An important trait these friends shared was that they were all unmarried — they'd never been married, or they had just been divorced, or they were separated from their spouses; in Sambursky's case, the reasons were mournful: his wife was mentally ill and confined to an institution. I do believe he divorced her later. Scholem's first marriage had just broken up. (It was Hugo Bergman who later married Scholem's ex-wife, Escha.) The fact that we were unattached was useful, because the men in our group had plenty of free time. We had no wives waiting at home to demand that we devote the Sabbath afternoon to them instead of engaging in endless talk with other men. Over the years, as one man after another married or remarried, it turned out to have a detrimental effect on the group. Initially we met at least once a week, on the afternoon of Shabbat. I saw Hans Lewy daily, however, because we ate lunch together, usually at his place, where someone cooked for him, but for a while also at my place, where my landlady, Frau Erlanger, cooked for us. Hans Lewy was my closest, most trusted friend. Hans Jakob Polotsky, on the other hand, was a person who didn't let anyone get too close to him. The sort of comradeship in which two people could share everything with each other didn't suit him. As for Scholem, he had much too wide a circle of friends and acquaintances to form a closer connection with someone. I must say that the intellectual climate in Jerusalem was splendid during those years. We were all people at the height of our powers and our intellectual development. Each of us was interesting in his own way, and we were all different. And we got along wonderfully. That we also had a lot of fun was documented by the poems that came out of our group, many of them from the pen of Hans Sambur. sky, poems that offered many a humorous portrait. A series of these poems was devoted to Scholem, whose personality and field of research provided a particularly fruitful subject for our poetic attempts, as the following three examples will show.

TO SCHOLEM (15 January 1940)
Oh, fisher in the muck of darkling waters,
You interpret distant stammering as form,
Transform a whirling, whipping wave of words
Into sense-filled sentences well structured and long,
Expending thus the intellect's precious hoard
On matters of a lower order, true.
You should rise up from Zohar's swirling bleak and blackish fog
Into the realm of true and healthful light
Before the Frankists' rotting, poisonous fruits
Accomplish their dark deed and do you in.

THE CROOKED GIANT (G.S.) (September 1943)
When he speaks masterfully, in a voice
That brooks no contradiction and boldly scales
The mountain, determined that no other's choice
To follow him shall succeed, not matter how he rails,

He'll seize the dwarf and bat him to and fro
Till all audacity gone, the fellow says "enough!"
While others, looking on, enjoy each throw,
When suddenly a thoughtless word and rough

Short-circuit-like renders him mute.
He moves his mouth like an insentient beast,
Speaking with muscles that utter not a toot,
As if life had no value in the least.

His eyes now flicker, seethe like burning charcoal,
Spreading the glow slowly round and round,
Not healthy and not hale and whole,
As once a Frankist may have made a sound,

Appearing there and finding it appalling,
This oft-played scene that daily he must repeat,
And suddenly he sends the spectators all sprawling
By showing knowledge, the initiate's private feat.

THE PROFESSOR OF MYSTICISM (November 1947)
Life with its many contradictions
Even his brain found hard to grasp,
So incomprehensible that by comparison
The absurdities and conflicts of the past,

Of obscure spirits from the Middle Ages
Seemed almost rational. He sniffed out sense
In every muddle, recovered rejected pages
Of ancient heritage, however dense,

And there found peace. For these bewitched ideas
Were softer than the harshness of being,
Gave him a refuge, the company of seers,
A cloister. When to corrupted texts he's fleeing

And from them lifting meaning like a crust,
In those distant, worldforsaken zones
He feels well sheltered, knowing just

That life's unfathomed mysteries never
Are plumbed by the most pious drones
Or occult heresies' excesses — ever.

Aside from the humorous moments when we recited such poems to each other, we could carry on endless discussions — on any and all subjects. Of course certain topics required particular expertise, and these brought Scholem, Polotsky, and me together — for instance when knowledge of the cabbalistic and gnostic world of late antiquity was called for. Sambursky, however, was a physicist, a highly cultivated man who knew something about many other subjects as well. Hans Lewy, the classicist, was also an expert in late

Greco-Roman antiquity. His major work, which unfortunately remained incomplete when he died of a heart attack toward the end of the war, was a study of the so-called *Oracola Chaldaica*, a pseudoepigraphic collection of writings for religious edification, allegedly Chaldean oracles from the second or third century of the Christian era.[18]

In short, we all had something to say, and didn't hold back. There was never a dull moment or a lack of material, not to mention the current events on which we commented in our conversations. And all that in German! Here we were, having come together in Jerusalem, the holy city, in Palestine, with its Jewish settlements, the place that had been chosen by Zionism as the site for a rebirth of the Jewish people as a nation. Except for me and George Lichtheim, who was soon admitted to this circle, all the others were connected with the Hebrew University and very good in Hebrew — though to different degrees — especially Scholem and Sambursky. But in our private conversations we stuck to German — not because of any bond with the Germanic, but simply because it was the language that came naturally to us, the language in which we could express ourselves best. Even as zealous a Zionist and Judaist as Scholem never asserted that we really ought to speak Hebrew. We were completely impervious to the stupid contention that because Germany was infamous and our greatest enemy we shouldn't be allowed to speak German. If you think it through, those who had sworn on their honor never to speak German again, even in private, were essentially handing Hitler a monopoly over the German language, something he didn't deserve; they were rejecting a heritage to which they had every right, that is, to express themselves in their own language.

I myself had a terrible time with Hebrew, even though I wasn't that badly prepared. During my last years in secondary school I'd already begun learning modern Hebrew and had continued during my time at the university — but the way you learn a foreign language if all you do is read and learn the grammar. To get from there to writing lectures on gnosticism in Hebrew was a huge step. When I finally obtained a part-time teaching appointment at the Hebrew University — they had no opening for a professor, but there were enough people there who felt I had something to contribute — preparing one lecture cost me an entire week: half a day for planning the content and the rest for getting it into Hebrew. I took lessons again and had a linguistic coach, a highly paid expert in Hebrew stylistics, who worked with me on the preparation of my lectures, that is to say, corrected the Hebrew. In 1938 I gave my first public speech in Hebrew, for this was the year of

Edmund Husserl's death. Word of his death reached Jerusalem immediately, of course, and it was felt that a memorial address should be delivered at the Hebrew University, where there was a Husserl student, after all — Hans Jonas. So I took on the assignment of delivering the eulogy at the academic memorial service for Edmund Husserl. Never have I slaved, suffered, and struggled so much over a one-hour speech as I did before this appearance. My topic was "Husserl and the Problem of Ontology," but the task I'd set myself was to give an account of his entire philosophy.[19]

I didn't have to depend, by the way, on receiving a regular salary, and managed very well with the money I'd invested, for there was no more inexpensive place to live at the time than Palestine. I was a well-heeled young man with six pounds a month at my disposal, while my future wife, Lore, who was working as a maid, had to make do with two or three pounds. It was customary to live modestly and primitively. Quite a few people had furniture that consisted of empty orange crates. In Jerusalem we were content with little. Hans Lewy received a proper professor's salary, of course, as did Polotsky and Scholem, but that, too, wasn't lavish. George Lichtheim soon found a suitable position with the English-language daily in Jerusalem, the *Palestine Post*, later renamed the *Jerusalem Post*. So professionally he was doing quite well. He maintained a lively friendship with various important intellectuals in Jerusalem, yet he remained something of an outsider. That had to do in part with the fact that he'd not had any specialized education but was a highly gifted autodidact, who'd made himself into a very interesting personality by means of his own reading and thinking. He didn't have a solid knowledge base in any field, except perhaps when it came to the history of the Marxist movement, in particular the Marxist ideology, which he knew inside out, from intensive reading in the original sources. His private life was ruled by an unlucky star, probably from birth — I mean one hopeless relationship with a woman after another. He would fall passionately in love, but things would never take their natural course. When our friend Sambursky married for the second time, a beautiful young woman called Miriam, herself previously divorced, George Lichtheim promptly fell in love with her. She liked him, too, but the idea with which he became obsessed, that she could be the woman who would finally save him from his sexual loneliness, wasn't fulfilled. Not that this woman played a unique role in his life; this sort of thing was typical of him. We all observed this pattern with considerable sympathy. I was on good terms with Miriam Sambursky, and she told me, "I'm in a strange and embarrassing situation. I like him. I'd also really love to see him find the right woman. But I'm not available." And this was a typical situation, an archetypal situation, that he created for himself time and again. He always chose as a love object someone who couldn't belong to him. He stayed in Jerusalem all through the war and wrote on foreign policy for the *Palestine Post*. Later he had himself transferred to London as a correspondent for international affairs. He became increasingly successful as an expert on the history of Marxism, publishing books on the development of Marxist ideology, for instance on the history of the socialist and Marxist programs and parties in France, that were considered the best things written on the subject.[20] So in that respect his life was a success. Yet he remained an immensely lonely person who developed lively friendships and intellectual relationships with men but always fell unhappily in love with women. That was surely one of the reasons why he became more and more depressed. Then he suddenly concluded that his creative wellsprings had dried up. At some point he started writing a new book and found that whereas he usually wrote as if divinely inspired, now nothing usable occurred to him. That probably exacerbated his depression. But there was another element as well, something very worrisome: he had such terrible insomnia that even with increasingly high doses of sleeping pills he couldn't get a good night's sleep. As a successful freelance writer, George also received invitations. So he spent at least a year in America, part of it on the East Coast, even in New York, where he had a short-term teaching appointment at Columbia. After that he went to the West Coast, and worked for a while in San Francisco. There he met Susan Sontag, one of his last great loves, who shook him to the depths. Although she liked him, she clearly gave him no encouragement, but he was so much under her spell for a while that he even talked to me in confidence about making her a beneficiary in his will, and asked whether I would be willing to serve as his executor, which I agreed to do. Apparently he later changed his will, for when the end came, her name didn't appear in it. This must be mentioned, too, to show how such a brilliantly talented person labored under a curse and was headed straight for despair. After he returned to England, he threw himself into his last relationship with a woman. It was a return to his first love — a Russian Jew, Inna Arian, who, if I'm not mistaken, had been in school with his younger sister and with whom he'd been in love at the time. Wherever he lived, he always had with him an early photo of this beauty, whose features were not Semitic but Slavic, by the way. Still, I'm fairly sure that she was Jewish. She was the romantic figure in his life, and she reentered his life in the following way after they'd not seen each other in many, many years. She was living in England and had married in the meantime, while he was in Palestine and was starting to make his way through the world and through the minefields of friendships with women. When he ran into her again in England, she was recently widowed. She was living not in London but in Cambridge or Oxford. And of course he went there often to visit her, and she took him on as her boyfriend. Over the years he probably changed all the provisions in his will. As it turned out, she developed a terminal illness. I no longer recall the details, but he was already speaking of what her death would do to him: "Then I'll die. When she dies, it will mean my death, too." You could tell he would experience his last love sitting at her bedside and holding her hand. And he remained true to this notion after she died. In our letters and personal meetings in London or in America he often said that he couldn't stand it anymore and would do himself in. And then I made the unforgivable mistake of thinking that someone who talked that way wouldn't actually lay a hand on himself. But I was completely mistaken. He had a very nice apartment in a house where good friends of his lived. One morning they found him in bed, unconscious, with a suicide note. But they'd found him in time and had his stomach pumped out, bringing him back to life against his will. A year later he succeeded, with the tacit cooperation of friends whom he'd essentially sent away on a trip. They knew they would find him dead when they returned. He'd made them promise not to do anything to save him, and they could keep their promise only by not being there. And that's how George Lichtheim left a life in which he'd always been unhappy.[21] Many people were fond of him, but he always felt alone, lurking on the sidelines of society as an observer who never fit in. To me it was a great blow, the more so because I reproached myself for failing him. Later I learned that a friendship had sprung up between him and Jürgen Habermas, and that he'd visited Habermas several times. Frau Habermas told me: "Yes, when he was here, he said he was more and more in despair because of his insomnia, and wanted to kill himself. I said to him, 'Please don't do it in my house. I won't have it.' I simply forbade him to do it." She was convinced, by the way, that his suicidal ideation had psychological origins; it wasn't a medical condition that doomed him to commit suicide — it was simply despair, general despair over life. I never experienced another person who was just beyond help, the result of something deep inside him that made him suffer from the inability really to live.

My other friends from Jerusalem were quite normal. They were unusual personalities, but in structuring their lives they followed perfectly normal paths. All of them married, or remarried, and quite of few of them had children. That gradually dissolved our circle. There is a nice poem by Sambursky, written in June 1945, that describes how our Saturday afternoons gradually became tedious as we had less to talk about and our gatherings were less stimulating then they'd once been:

Sabbaths became a trickle then, like water
that flowed more slowly, then no longer flowed.
The later years a dim reflection only,
Vague image of earlier days, yet memory still glowed

With brilliant verbal duels and
Deft argument that seldom now unbidden came,
Yet faithful to their fellowship, those foregathered
Here still practiced all the same

Holding their tongues, a skill they never lost
In which they shone, both fertile and most clever,
And in the ring of silence and of words
The march of time was never halted, ever.

What contributed to the dissolution of our circle was the increasing involvement of the members in their own work and domestic lives. The phase in which the circle flourished was approximately between 1935 and 1945. When I came back from my military service, it still existed, and had even expanded, because quite a few new members had been recruited, and their wives had also been admitted, though usually they didn't attend, with the exception of Miriam Sambursky. Yet it was no longer what it had been. By the end of the war, our circle had passed its high point, and indeed the entire heroic period was past. For the Yishuv in Palestine a new, exciting time was beginning, and my longing, when I returned from the war, to get away from world history for a while and to escape to nice, boring surroundings was of course not fulfilled, because the birth of the young state of Israel turned out to be very stormy. But almost as a matter of course our gatherings in Jerusalem came to an end.

CHAPTER 6

Love in Times of War

꙳꙳꙳

Let's return to the period before the Second World War. While Lichtheim was working at the newspaper and my other friends were teaching at the university, I chose military service. Around Passover in 1936, during my parents' visit, the Arab uprising against the mandate government and the Jewish settlement program began. After their departure I promptly volunteered for the Haganah, the underground Jewish self-defense organization, which had a very good command staff but was poorly armed. The only weapons we used were the kind you could conceal on your body, under your clothes: handguns such as pistols and revolvers, and hand grenades. These weapons were transported from one base or house to another, by girls for the most part, because in this region, where Islamic law had such a powerful influence and was binding even on the mandate government's security forces, only a woman could conduct a body search of a woman. The men's assignment was to defend against the Arabs' nocturnal attacks on kibbutzim and the Jewish settlements scattered throughout the country. Little happened in the cities, because the Arab guerrillas hid out in the mountains or in rural refuges and carried out their attacks only at night against isolated settlements.[1] I spent many nights on the flat roofs of settlements around Jerusalem, where you woke up in the morning — even in the driest summer weather — completely drenched with dew. During my entire time in the Haganah, which extended over several years, I never found myself involved in an exchange of fire. But you always had to be prepared. We made it possible for the settlers to sleep at night and work by day. The assumption was that we city dwellers would still be able to go about our day jobs, or that they were not as important as what we were protecting at night. My ability to continue working on the second volume of the gnosticism book suffered, of course. But this was something I felt I had to do. In my training I actually didn't learn much more than to handle skillfully pistols of various makes and to hit a target, as well as to remove the pin from hand grenades and throw them. Still, being assigned a place in a specific military command structure amounted to military training in itself. But it was all illegal and secret, operating underground. In my circle I was the only one who was active in the Haganah.[2] Sambursky or Polotsky probably also did some form of service in Jerusalem, but they weren't members of the mobile Haganah, which could be sent here or there in the countryside. So as far as that went, I was the great exception in our circle. By the way, once the uprising began, the mandate government imposed a curfew on Jerusalem, for safety reasons, which lasted from seven or eight in the evening until five in the morning. That made it easier for the security forces to patrol the streets, of course, but the result was that people had to stay home in the evenings. In Polotsky's case that resulted in a marriage, because in the house where he was boarding he met a girl whom he then married. We always had the feeling that the Polotskys' marriage was a by-product of the Arab uprising and the curfew.

During this time in Jerusalem it was clear to me that the actual war would take place elsewhere. The way things were developing in Europe convinced me that either everything was moving toward war or, if it didn't come to that, every further increase in Hitler's power would raise the level of threat to us. I also feared that the settlement project in Palestine would be done for if Hitler acquired the control over Europe and beyond to which he aspired. So I was waiting for the moment when the Allies would finally stand their ground. As we know, this moment didn't come until the late summer of 1939, after Czechoslovakia had fallen. As Germany's threat to Poland grew, a decisive moment could again be discerned: Hitler would have to be stopped if this country, too, was not to fall victim to him. Apropos of these developments, George Lichtheim remarked to me in August, "When push comes to shove, England will back down again," and he knew England much better than I, for he had spent a good part of his youth there. At this point I made my first historical bet, after Scholem had emphatically seconded Lichtheim's prediction. England and France had committed themselves in a mutual-aid pact to protect and defend Poland's sovereignty and territorial integrity, if necessary. As the situation developed, my friends in Jerusalem were all predicting that at the last minute Chamberlain and Daladier would capitulate again. So I wagered with Scholem, who loved to make bets. I knew he had a terrible sweet tooth,[3] so I bet him a pound of marzipan or chocolate against a roast duck, prepared by Fania Scholem, whom he'd married in the meantime. Fania Scholem, née Freud, came from a Galician home in which modern Hebrew was spoken; she was his second wife. I met her, as Fania Freud, when I arrived in Jerusalem, and everyone told me she was a splendid girl. She wasn't especially attractive, but she had character, and a magnificent command of Hebrew. That was a huge advantage in those days. I took Hebrew lessons from her for a while. Even Scholem acknowledged her superiority in Hebrew. Several men were considered possible husbands for her, but she chose Scholem. Around the time I'm describing, they'd been married for several years, and in a sense Fania was part of the bet, because eventually she owed me that roast duck. We know who won the bet, of course, namely me: at this juncture England didn't back down after all. In the meantime I'd joined the military, but I insisted on the fulfillment of the bet. During a furlough, I was invited to the Scholems'. Yet I felt somewhat cheated out of full enjoyment of my victory, for they'd invited a considerable number of people from their circle of friends, so I didn't get a very big piece of my duck. Still, this episode involving Scholem as a wagerer and sweet tooth was captured in a humorous poem from our Pilegesh circle, written on 5 December 1939:

At Scholem's place some demons reside;
He lets a room to them on the side.
The demons owe him many praises,
For he speaks of them in lavish phrases.
And thus establishes their fame,
Which gives them a gratifying name.
Finding his sweet tooth far too costly
They've invented a solution that works mostly:
These scoundrels give him prompt reports
On all impending events and sports:
On marriages, divorces, peace, and war,
Whatever human life holds in store.
Scholem makes bets on all such news,
Knowing his opponents are bound to lose.
Thus these denizens of the shadows
Spare him unease, anger, and other sorrows.
His tongue curls in anticipation
Of a delectable marzipan ration.

But let me return to more serious subjects, which take us back a few years. In February 1937 I happened to attend a Purim ball. On my way home, I passed the Hagelberg Pension, run by German Jews in a handsome house, built by Arabs; I regularly ate lunch there. I was living with a German-Jewish family, the dentist Dr. Erlanger and his wife, who was not a German but a South African Jew. She came from a Zionist family, and her father had sent her as a young girl to visit Palestine, where she met Erlanger, who'd just immigrated — as part of the "Hitler Aliyah." They rented me a fine large room in their own Arab stone house, whose thick walls and high ceilings made it pleasantly cool in summer. The house was located on Rechov Ha-Chabashim, Abyssinian Street, not far from Rechov Ha-Neviim, Prophet Street, in the Abyssinian quarter. All the houses there belonged to Arabs, who were not Muslims, however, but Christians. These weren't Muslims who'd been converted by Christian missionaries but what was left of a Christian population that had resisted conversion during Islam's victorious surge and considered themselves superior to their Islamic neighbors. Often they were also better educated, and of course somewhat more oriented toward Europe, for as long as the Ottoman Empire existed and they constituted a minority in a Muslim-dominated society, they looked to France or other Christian powers for protection. On the basis of their education, the Christians in the Near East, above all in Lebanon but also in Palestine, thus had a stronger affinity to Europe than the other Arabs. They'd sold or rented houses to Jews, with the result that many of the Jews in Jerusalem lived in houses built by Arabs and had Arab neighbors. So the Hagelberg Pension was on the same street where I lived. As I was passing on the evening of Purim, the windows were brightly lit, and I could see that a dance was in progress. I noticed a girl in a red blouse dancing and thought, "I'm going in." I'd seen this woman once before. One day when I was walking along Prophet Street with my friend Hans Lewy, a young girl wearing a Circassian cap came toward us. She glanced at us rather shyly. Lewy formally doffed his hat, and I asked, "Who was that?" "Oh, she's in my Latin seminar at the university — a student, a Fräulein Weiner."

This was a decisive moment in my life. To understand it, and what happened afterward, I must back up and talk a bit about my emotional state at the time. Before I left Germany, I'd been very much in love, with Gertrud Fischer, a young Swabian student from Stuttgart, whom I met in 1929 in Heidelberg, after I received my Ph.D. The greatest love of my life up to that point seized hold of me under the eyes of Hannah Arendt and Günther Stern, who'd met in Heidelberg. Hannah was there because she wanted to write her dissertation under Karl Jaspers, and Günther was spending a semester there because he needed access to a university library. While I was in Paris during the winter of 1928–29, I received word one day that they'd decided to marry, and I was tremendously excited—after all, they were my best male and female friends! One day after I returned to Heidelberg for a semester in the fall of 1929, I was having lunch with them in a restaurant when a young girl came in, nodded a shy greeting in the direction of our table, where Hannah and Günther returned the greeting, and then sat down at another table. Looking completely alone, solitary, introverted, she immediately buried her nose in a book. I asked, "Oh, who's that?" And Hannah said, "A very nice girl, a certain Gertrud Fischer." Her father, Johannes Fischer, was a well-known democratic politician in Stuttgart, who'd risen from being a tradesman to become an advocate for democracy as a journalist and itinerant speaker, a disciple of Friedrich Naumann and a collaborator of Theodor Heuss, who would become the first president of the Federal Republic after the war. Gertrud Fischer was an enchanting young woman, and I was immediately smitten. During our meal I kept looking at her. When she glanced up occasionally, she had to meet my eye, and immediately turned away. And when she got up and left, I said to Hannah and Günther, "You must excuse me. See you later." And I followed her. I saw her walking along some distance ahead of me. She turned off and went over the Neckar Bridge. Then on the other side of the river she headed up the hill with the great forest. The path zigs and zags, and I followed, always keeping some space between us. Finally she stepped down off the path and seemed to be searching for something among the trees. Still on the path, I called down to her, "Is there something I can help you with? It's Advent. Let me help you." So together we gathered pine branches suitable for an Advent wreath. Then we went back down the mountain. That was the beginning of a great love affair, which went on for the next few years. Between Advent in 1929 and the beginning of 1933, I wooed her with all my might. She, however, suffered from all kinds of constraints. She was a very devout Christian, and among her Madonna-like traits was her commitment to saving a young man who had terrible psychological problems, and subjected her to the most horrible treatment. Eventually she escaped from his hold over her with the help of psychoanalysis, but that was long after I'd emigrated to Palestine and had lost track of her. In spite of her problems, we had a passionate relationship—passionate on my part, that is, and on hers submissive and increasingly loving, but always with the caveat that she wasn't free, that she couldn't turn her back on her obligation to save the soul of this dreadful man. She was studying German literature, but sensed that it wasn't the right choice for her, so she decided to become a photographer instead.

At that point I said, "Listen, I have a cousin in Gladbach, Lisl Haas, who's a professional photographer. Perhaps she'll be willing to take you on as an apprentice." So she came to Gladbach and hit it off with Lisl Haas, who offered to train her. My kind parents, bless their souls, who loved me so much, agreed to let her live with them for a year, though it wasn't easy for them, especially for my mother. First of all, Gertrud wasn't Jewish, and that was a problem for them, no matter how much they liked her. Second, she had a mild case of tuberculosis, and my parents, who'd had their fill of illness, were afraid I would marry a sickly girl. And even Lisl Haas, who was very devoted to her, always said, "I don't know whether she'll ever become a successful photographer, because her fingers are slightly damp from hot flashes. And when you pick up photographic plates" — at the time everything was still done with glass plates — "you mustn't have any moisture on your fingers. It's because of her illness." As it turned out, she eventually got over her illness completely.

In 1933 the great question that presented itself to us was whether she'd emigrate with me. She decided not to. She didn't want to leave her native land, and she didn't feel as attached to me as I did to her. We'd become lovers, but she was still in a strange, neurotic bondage to that other man, who was sadistic and tormented her emotionally, and himself and others as well. But that wasn't the main reason. The most important reason for her not wanting to go with me was her perception, probably correct, that she wouldn't fit into a Jewish environment. She was a Christian, and remained one all her life. If she'd allowed herself to be overcome by the feeling that she had to stand by me at such a time, and had forced herself to come along, she would probably have been utterly miserable. She would have felt terribly lonely amid the robustly positive and Jewish-nationalist mood that prevailed among the Jews in Palestine. But I left Germany feeling that I could never love a woman that way again. Instead I had affairs, for which plenty of opportunities presented themselves. It was a period when women would smile at me, and I had no trouble finding girlfriends, though admittedly they were almost always married. That had been the case already during my last years in Mönchengladbach. After being incredibly shy and timid for a long time, I suddenly realized the effect I had on women. One of these women simply took matters into her own hands, seduced me, and thus banished my fears — at that point I was about twenty-one. That seemed rather late to me, because friends of my own age were already boasting of their conquests and nocturnal adventures, and I envied them. My young women were always a bit older than I, with perhaps one or two children, and something drew them to this unattached younger man. In short, I had a number of such relationships before the relationship with Gertrud came and shunted everything else into the background. But once Gertrud was gone from my life, I had the feeling that I'd found true love and couldn't experience that more than once.

In 1933 we parted. Before I emigrated, we went on a hike through the Spessart region: a Jewish young man and a Christian young woman who spent the night together in hotels and presented themselves as married. One day we stopped at an inn to eat. Other hikers were seated in the dining room. At the time people went hiking instead of touring by car. There were also families with children and local people, eating or having a beer. At the table where we were seated were also several hefty men, perhaps local loggers, and they struck up songs, among them the song with that charming refrain, "When Jewish blood from the knife blade spurts / Then all will be well again." As soon as I heard that, I said, "Come on, pull out your knives. Here I am. Here's a Jew." Sudden silence. And then one of them spoke up and said, "I'm the regional commander here. You're lucky I'm the one in charge, because otherwise you'd be in trouble. You must leave my territory immediately. I'll assign someone to escort you to the border of my district and make sure you get out of here." All the guests were shaken. It was a complete moral victory for me, but incredibly dangerous, as I could tell by looking at the faces around me. I recall a couple with half-grown children who were obviously out for a hike. They didn't say a word, but they looked stricken, and were hugely embarrassed that something like this was happening. Fortunately Gertrud didn't look Aryan but had dark hair and dark eyes and could pass for a Jew. That probably saved us. Gertrud was shaking all over, realizing that she was in terrible danger. I, however, felt so provoked that I said directly to the men: "Pull out your knives. You can have Jewish blood right here if you want." These jolly fellows were apparently completely dumbfounded. The only other thing I remember is that one of them said, "It's just a folksong." I said, "That's not a folksong! That's a song attacking me and those like me!" The man who was supposed to escort us trotted along beside us like a damp poodle, not saying a word. My Gertrud and I marched off in triumph, and when he started to say something, I snapped, "I don't want to hear it." Finally he said, "Well, this is as far as I have to go." Then he began to give us directions. It was obvious that the whole thing was horribly uncomfortable for him, and he was ashamed. This incident gave me a sample of how an entire population can be stampeded into such behavior and can cooperate without realizing what it's doing. For those who witnessed the confrontation, it provided a moment of clarity. At any rate, the man who'd received the order to accompany us said good-bye apologetically and wished us the best for the rest of our journey. As soon as he was gone, Gertrud said, "That could have been a disaster." At that point I realized that I'd put her in danger in a way that was irresponsible. So that was our farewell hike in the Spessart region. Later, when I'd already moved to London, we met once more, in Zurich, before I set out for Palestine. Once she'd said that she couldn't tear herself away, I didn't pressure her. She said, "But I'll wait for you. I will wait for you." I had a whole box of letters from her, and she had one of mine. Later, when we met again after many years, she said, "All your letters burned up." But it wasn't she who'd burned them; it had happened during an air raid. Yet she'd begged me to destroy her letters, because she would have been done for if they'd ever fallen into the Nazis' hands. And even more so the photos — I had wonderful pictures of her, which she insisted that I get rid of, for heaven's sake. So at some point in Jerusalem I pulled myself together and did something that was terribly painful: I burned a whole series of magnificent photos I'd taken in the bedroom at my parents' house — she had a wonderful body, divinely beautiful. Her letters, which I'd left in a box in Jerusalem along with many of my books, went missing during some move or other.

So now when I saw Lore Weiner in Jerusalem, this young woman in the Circassian cap who greeted her professor shyly, a voice inside me spoke up, saying, "This is an experience you had to leave behind you and thought you'd never have again." It must have been because of my mother that this type of woman appealed to me: a woman whose physiognomy expressed something spiritual — the longish face, the deeply serious eyes, a slightly tragic quality and a certain shyness. So on the evening of Purim I saw this woman again as I was passing the Arab house, heard the music, and went in. Before long she was enjoying dancing with me, as I could tell from the tenderness of her touch, but she was by no means willing to let me have every dance; she danced with others if they broke in. Whenever that happened, I stood by the wall and watched. An acquaintance of mine, a young married woman, who also lived in that part of town, came up to me and said, "Jonas, pull yourself together! Don't make a fool of yourself. She's certainly charming, but don't look so miserable when she dances with someone else!" That night I didn't dance with any other woman. As soon as she was free, I'd ask her for the dance, and we danced again and again. As she

later told me, she, too, immediately felt that I was the right one. But at the
end of the evening I had a little shock. Long after midnight — around two
or three in the morning — people began to go home, and a blond young
man in glasses, very good-looking, came up to us and said, "May I entrust
this lady to you? Will you see her home?" I responded, "What gives you the
right?" And as soon as we were outside, I asked, "Who was that, and why
was he so presumptuous as to entrust you to me?" At that she said, "Oh, I'm
married to him." I said, "What?" and She nodded. "So what's your name?"
"Krause," she said, "but it doesn't mean anything." At the time there were
many so-called certificate marriages. A person who had only a visitor's visa
and wanted to circumvent the tedious immigration process could become
a permanent, legal immigrant by marrying. For that reason there were lots
of young people, mostly men, who'd arrived with an immigration certificate and were willing to marry young women eager to legalize their status.
These pseudomarriages were either dissolved later on or developed into real
marriages, in which case they were celebrated with a proper wedding. In
Lore's case, something had gone wrong with her parents' immigration, with
the result that she had only a temporary residence permit. Hans Krause, a
young man who was in the KJV — Lore's father was also a KJV member,
an old Zionist, and I'd discovered during that first evening that I'd once
spent the night in Siegfried Weiner's office in Regensburg during my Blau-
Weiss period — offered to marry Eleonore Weiner. So the man who'd had
the chutzpah to entrust her to my care was officially her husband.

After this night of dancing we saw each other from time to time, and it
was clear to me that she'd fallen in love with me. Unfortunately I still believed
that I couldn't fall in love again, so I made no effort to allow real intimacy
to develop. I realized that this was a girl you didn't trifle with. We took long
walks together, also by moonlight, in Jerusalem, which ended with my delivering her to her door and kissing her good night. But as I said, there wasn't
any real physical involvement. I held back. When I saw that she was waiting
for a serious move on my part, I told her I couldn't make a definitive, long-
term, and exclusive commitment anymore; a love such as I'd experienced in
the past was possible only once in a lifetime. Yet as Lore later confessed to
me, far from scaring her off, my statement encouraged her, for she said to
herself, "If he could feel this way once, he can feel this way again. I just have
to wait." She told me, "I didn't believe you for a minute when you said that
business about not being able to have those feelings again. Anyone who can
have such feelings doesn't lose the capacity for them." And she was right.

But then I left Palestine for several months, for in the fall of 1937 it became clear to me that I wouldn't be able to finish the second part of my gnosticism book if I continued to perform my almost nightly duty in the Haganah. So I went to spend the winter on the island of Rhodes, under Italian rule at the time. There I saw Italian troops stationed and the posturing of the arrogant fascist colonial regime. But Rhodes is a wonderful place. I lived in a pension there. The archeological institute had an excellent library for the study of classical civilization, where I managed to get a carrel. It was there, in January 1938, that word of my father's death reached me. In February I returned to Jerusalem. My friends already knew that my father had died, for it had been in the *Jüdische Rundschau*, the German Zionist paper, which was also available in Palestine, and I received their condolences. My landlady, Frau Erlanger, told me after my return that my friend Lore Weiner had married while I was away. Indeed she'd accepted a proposal, a serious one this time, from her spouse, Hans Krause — the blond Hans — and had had a proper wedding. Now she really was Frau Krause, no longer merely on paper. Under the circumstances it would be difficult to resume a relationship with her — impossible, actually. But when Frau Erlanger told me about the marriage, I blurted out, "Oh God, I let her get away. I have only myself to blame." Not long after this, Frau Erlanger, who already had a little girl, bore a second child and hired Eleonore Krause as a nanny. She'd received training in the Hadassah. Frau Erlanger, who took an extraordinarily keen interest in me and how I lived my life, now had nothing better to do than to tell Lore, "This is what Hans Jonas said when I told him you'd got married." And Lore told me later, "At that I went weak in the knees. My head began to spin, and I was afraid I was going to faint." The very thing she'd been hoping for had now come to light, thanks to Frau Erlanger's indiscretion. The fact that she was soon disappointed by her husband made it possible for us to meet again. In addition, this piece of information had empowered her in a way. Up to the outbreak of war, we met from time to time for long walks. I obediently saw her to her door, where she would take the elevator up to her floor, where her husband was waiting for her. And it could have gone on this way if war hadn't broken out and I hadn't promptly volunteered. At that she said to herself, "If he's going to war, I want to have given myself to him before he goes." Previously she hadn't allowed herself to think such a thing, but with war in the offing she wanted to become my lover after all. And that's what happened in the summer of 1940.

Not until France fell to the Nazis did the British accept us as volunteers and create the Jewish units from Palestine that we were demanding. After my physical they inducted me. From the British training camp in Sarafant, which was down on the plain between Jerusalem and Tel Aviv, I returned to Jerusalem to put my affairs in order. When I saw Lore, I said to her, "Well, the day after tomorrow I'm leaving for boot camp." She came to my room, and from then on we belonged to each other, even though her marriage remained in effect. In camp my fellow soldiers saw her picture next to my cot. One day, when we were already abroad, one of those soldiers, a kibbutznik from the Haifa area, went to Palestine on leave. That night, as he was walking through Haifa at night, because he had to wait until morning to take the milk truck back to his kibbutz, he saw a young woman on the street and spoke to her: "Aren't you Lore?" At first Lore didn't respond, but then she asked, "How — where are you from?" He said, "I saw your picture next to Hans Jonas's bed." He'd recognized her face. And then they walked and walked through the streets until about five in the morning, when the milk truck from the kibbutz arrived. This episode shows me that even then — when she was still married to another man, after all — she was already seen as connected with me. In 1943 she sued for divorce, which her husband fought, because he really loved her. Finally she persuaded him to agree to it, and we were married — in considerable haste, because I'd heard rumors that we were going to be mobilized and sent out of the country. So we couldn't wait the ritually required nine months after the divorce but gave false personal information so we could marry before I left.

So how did it come about that I made a firm commitment, when I'd told Lore that I wasn't capable of falling in love again? Up to now, whenever I was furloughed we'd seen each other. But I hadn't spoken the decisive word yet. Not yet! In 1942 we met at a place along the coast, south of Tel Aviv, in Bat Jam, I think. There we took a room in a small guesthouse. The next morning we went for a swim in the ocean. What I didn't know was that along this coast there was a dangerous undertow. No one had mentioned it, including the owners of the guesthouse. While we were swimming, I realized suddenly that I was being drawn away from the shore. I fought the current, but it was stronger than I was. I could no longer touch bottom, and I was being pulled farther and farther out into the deep water. At that I shouted to Lore, who was still in the shallow water, "Lore, go right now and get help! I can't make it back!" At that moment something life-altering occurred. With an indescribable expression of terror, she did exactly the opposite of what I'd told her. She swam out to me, grabbed my hand, and pulled me back. She put her own life in danger to save me from drowning. The message in her eyes was unmistakable: "If it must be, I'll drown with you." Later she told me that this very thought had gone through her head, and something more: "Without him, nothing means anything!" Once back on shore I at first just lay there, completely exhausted—I couldn't have held out for more than a few seconds. Then we returned to our room in the guesthouse, packed our things, and set out for Jerusalem, where I was supposed to spend the night at the Scholems'. I'd given up my room in Jerusalem, and when I was on leave always stayed with friends. When I arrived—a fairly large group had been invited for the evening—I said to Fania, "Fania, I can't join you for the party. Something bad happened to me. I have to lie down." So I lay there in bed and heard the noise from the party taking place down the corridor. I was swept by an indescribable euphoria at still being alive. I was filled with happiness, and at the same time there was a new clarity that might be expressed thus: "You fool, what are you waiting for? It's so obvious that she's the woman to share your life with. Was that what it took to open your eyes, you idiot?" On 3 September 1942 I proposed to her. I came with flowers, for it was her birthday, and I asked her, "Will you be my wife?" And what did Lore reply? "You're out of your mind!" It took me a long time to persuade her, because I'd assured her too often that I was no longer capable of making a commitment. But finally she said, "All right, but on one condition." "What's that?" "I want children." "It's a promise." Though I must say the thought of children hadn't occurred to me. And then I said, "For my part, I'd like to say that I'm not the type to get divorced." So we were engaged on her birthday, and with this mutual understanding: children, yes; divorce, no. We married in 1943 in Haifa, and fourteen days after the wedding I was sent into combat, as I'll describe later—by way of Cyprus and Egypt to Italy, not to return until 1945. This period of separation can perhaps be summed up in a poem I sent Lore from Italy—words from the field, a dream such as every soldier dreamed who was separated from his sweetheart or his wife:

I lie awake and think of you,
my spirit fills with peace,
my heart with joy,
your image fills my eye.
Tranquil in my bed I lie,
All thoughts of trouble cease.

Around me breathe the other men,
our tent weighed down with sleep.
A thousand tents between us, Love,
Asleep or awake my breath swells with sighs.
The night wind whispers in the trees,
The tent wall billows out,
your face wafts toward me on the breeze,
your body, pearly white, at ease,
in starlight shimmers on your couch.
Your heart thumps gently in my hand
that reaches for you in the dark.
My dearest one, I hear you say,
Why are your waking me this way?
I thought of you as here I lay.
Why did you wake me now?
Go back to sleep, my dearest love,
The hour is not yet come.
I, too, now that I've thought of you
will sleep this short night through
that keeps us from the light.
But now my smile will reach the stars;
There's someone at my side,
For you are with me day and night,
And I with you, so all is right,
And into sleep I glide.

I still know these lines by heart, for they express the beauty and depth of our love, which fills me with gratitude. Nothing could ever change that, even though in many respects our temperaments are very different. The differences become apparent when we look back on our lives to weigh the positives and negatives. In a conversation about these memoirs, Lore said one time, "You see everything too much as a success story, with everything taking such a good and fortunate course. In reality there was also a great deal in our life that was trying and terrifying—sometimes it wasn't even clear how we could keep going. And that hasn't really been expressed." And I responded, "I have to force myself to find a tragic note in my life and in my relationship to the world, aside from the loss of my mother and what every Jew carries with him as a result of the Holocaust. But to me, even though terrible things happen, of course, the world has never been a hostile place." In the course of my life I've experienced misfortune, but that hasn't altered my overall relationship to existence, which was fundamentally always affirming. Obviously every human being, even the most optimistic and positive, has periods of deepest unhappiness, and I, too, went through a phase in puberty when I thought about suicide. But that doesn't really count; it's part of the turmoil caused by hormonal changes, and eventually it passes. Lore, on the other hand, has a more melancholy, tragic sense of the world and herself. The kind of happy affirmation with which I view the world and that I once admitted to in my essay "The Nobility of Sight,"[4] which I'm very fond of, rests on the conviction that our existence — in spite of the terrible things that are part of life — reveals itself to our senses and inspires admiration and amazement in the observer, such that ultimately he assents to it and thereby demonstrates an internal connection between the richness of being and his sensibility. I'm not referring to any particular metaphysical concept of a divine order in the universe, but simply to the fact that the alert, receptive organism — feeling, seeing, perceiving — coincides with that which is worth seeing, receiving, and feeling, and that ultimately affirmation is implicit in any sentient and conscious existence. I've never been able to share that sense of alienation that's based on the idea that the human being is cast into this world without being asked and sees himself confronting an alien, hostile, or even absurd universe.

But Lore has this tragic sense deep within her. She suffered greatly as a girl. Once she found a revolver that her father had brought back with him from the First World War, in which he had served. One day, when she'd reached the conclusion that life wasn't worth living, and that she wasn't meeting the standards she'd set for herself, she decided to do away with herself. Fortunately the revolver jammed, but she'd already put the barrel to her temple and pressed the trigger. I mention this only to suggest the bouts of despair she went through. Since she was still a young girl, it isn't so relevant — more the equivalent of my turmoil in puberty. But when I met her, she still had a certain tragic and melancholy look in her eyes. That was one of the traits that attracted me, for the image of a woman's face was always in my mind's eye — that of my mother. And that was a tragic face, for my mother — quite apart from the fact that she later suffered a tragic fate — fundamentally had a sense of existence that was always colored by tragedy. Lore was vulnerable. In addition, her life wasn't easy. Her father was a dear man, but he hadn't made any plans that would have allowed the family to be properly provided for when they emigrated; instead he arrived in Palestine as a penniless refugee,[5] so that Lore had to break her back to help her parents survive, and was thrust from a protected existence into the rough-and-tumble reality of immigrants' life in Palestine.

And then came her love for me and the happiness of our marriage. It's clear to me that I was the one who drew the winning ticket, that living with me was certainly no picnic. Apparently I'm rather a tyrannical person. Many decisions in our life together were made in the interest of what was right and best for me, for my career, for the development of my mind, for my intellectual and human needs. After our emigration to America, which will be discussed later, the unfortunate result was that she often felt isolated, for she had to leave behind her friends in Israel. In New Rochelle, where we lived from 1955 on, her life was ruled by a man who was never properly there, but instead was either teaching in New York or sitting at home at his desk, while she raised our three children. That meant she couldn't have a profession and find fulfillment that way. Though it gave her great satisfaction to see my career flourishing, and we succeeded in having a family and creating a nice home, I'm aware that basically she was often quite lonely. I was the center of her existence, but didn't always spend enough time with her, focusing instead on my work, as is often the case with a scholar and writer. Many times, when I could have been spending evenings with her, I would sit up late at night, obsessing and struggling and sometimes also tormenting myself over my writing. The result was that I didn't give enough back to her, to whom I owed so much and without whom I would probably not have had the strength and persistence to do my work. Love, yes, but not enough company. Certainly she approved of what I wanted to accomplish, and even nagged me at times, but it was also a sacrifice. I talked myself into believing that she found happiness in supporting me this way, and actually expected it. So our love story includes the confession that I sometimes forgot that part of marriage is being together. Furthermore, it's become clear to me over the years that it can't always have been easy for Lore to be married to a person who places reason above all else, a logical thinker and debater. Something within her — despite all her admiration for me — always rebelled against my stubborn way of looking at things, of experiencing the world and my own life, only in rational terms. So she maintained her view of the world, in which dark and light are both present, whereas my own view was always sunny, at times maybe too sunny.

CHAPTER 7

A "Bellum Judaicum" in the
Truest Sense of the Word

As a boy he stared in fascination
At maps of the great battles, and his imagination
Showed plains bristling with the weapons he loved so much,
While near by, almost close enough to touch,

In coastal waters Roman triremes rock,
On board their grappling hooks point toward the dock
As victors in a clash at sea they seek the bay.
But later something tore the youth away,

Something that once saved from the world's misery
People seeking the light in higher ecstasy.
He studied with passion all the phases
Of true existence, of which Proclus sings the praises,

And wrote them down, in colors far more bright,
Than they deserved, infusing them with light.
Then came the war, dashed the man to the ground,
Leaving the *nous* behind, reality he found.

And peering round to catch the enemy in his sights,
Far from all books and scholarly delights,
He recovered the dreams he'd had once as a boy
Loading his cannon now, no longer a toy.

This poem, with the title "The Philosopher's Fate," which George Lichtheim wrote on the occasion of my fortieth birthday, expresses in a cheerful tone the serious circumstances that kept me for years from getting on with my research on gnosticism. England's declaration of war on Germany in September 1939 came as a great relief to me. I knew that now we'd at least be able to fight for our survival instead of merely watching from the sidelines as things ran their inevitable course owing to the weakness of the other side. The first thing I did was to sit down and compose an appeal, to which I gave the title "Our Part in This War: A Word to Jewish Men." It began with the words "This is our hour, this is our war." I argued that we shouldn't be content to owe our survival to the efforts and sacrifices of others, and I demanded that we make our own contribution in an unmistakable way. I spoke of what had been done to us and what threatened us, though the thought of violent extermination hadn't occurred to me yet. There were people who said, "If there's war, all Jews will be in mortal danger." But my focus was on what had already happened and what would inevitably happen if Hitler won, and I tried to make it clear that Palestine was no safe harbor, but on the contrary a post from which we could take up the struggle. So I summoned Jewish men to join in the war against Nazi Germany—not only men who'd just come to Palestine after being driven out by Hitler, but all sons of the Jewish people. Here's my manifesto, verbatim:[1]

This is our hour, this is our war. It is the hour for which we have been waiting, despair and hope in our hearts, through these deadly years; the hour when it has been granted to us, after we have borne helplessly every disgrace, every injustice, every physical deprivation and moral humiliation of our people, to look our mortal enemy in the eye at last, to meet him with weapon in hand, and to demand satisfaction; the hour of reckoning when we can claim what is owed us; the hour when we can actively participate in striking down the enemy of the world, who was ours first and will remain ours to the end.

This is the war without which this evil cannot be crushed; the war without which it would have continued to spread through the world without limit or measure, leaving us destroyed in its wake: for this reason it is our war. We have a primary right and a primary duty to wage it. We must join in the fighting because this war is being fought for us. We must wage it in our name, as Jews, for the outcome must restore our name. Our willingness to give our lives must be no less than that of the sons of those nations that have now declared war on Hitlerism. Individual dignity, national honor, and political considerations all call equally for our full participation in this war. It is our duty and must be incumbent upon any man worthy of the name.

We do not wish to speak of the feelings of the individual, feelings born of the personal experiences of these years—of the cloud hanging over us, of the feeling, burning deep within our hearts, of the grievous hurt inflicted on us, of the righteous thirst for revenge. But we do wish to speak of the reasons for which this war against Hitlerism is our people's concern, since our concerns are at stake in it, in the absolute sense of the word. If any people was provoked by Hitler, it is ours. If any people is obligated by honor and self-interest to take up the struggle and carry it forward, prepared to make the supreme sacrifice if necessary, it is our people. To an incomparably greater degree than any of the countries now allied against Hitler we have been attacked by him and threatened with total destruction. To an infinitely greater degree, we risk *everything*. For the others, one interest or another, one aspect or another of their national, cultural, or imperial existence is at issue; they are threatened in one aspect of their being on earth, however significant, whereas in our case the Nazi principle, which aspires to impose itself on the entire world, strikes at the heart of our human dignity and, at the same time, at the very possibility of our existence on earth. We are the Nazis' metaphysical enemy, their designated victim from the very first day, and we shall know no peace until either that principle or our own people is no more.

For us, therefore, it is not a part but the whole that is at issue. Directed against us is truly *total* war. For we are *negated as a category of human beings*, plain and simple, no matter what political, social, or ideological form our existence takes. No accommodation, no adaptation is possible. Our mere existence is incompatible with the existence of Nazism. Here we have a confrontation that has taken on mythological dimensions, and it can end only with the destruction of one or the other. No other people is in this situation. For all the others, some sort of accommodation — however distasteful — is at least conceivable, and was attempted for a long time: a good thing for us that the willingness to make concessions is at an end, and that the call "This far and no farther!" has finally rung out. This turn of events gives us the longed-for opportunity to enter this struggle at last.

If today there existed a Jewish state, it would have had to be the first to declare war against Hitler's Germany, following England and France. That it does not exist changes nothing in the basic fact that we must regard ourselves as at war with Germany, and does not absolve us of the duty to conduct ourselves like citizens of a state at war — i.e., to do our share at the front.

In truth we have already been engaged in this war for six years —

passively. In the year 1933 war was declared on us, and since then it
has been waged against us without pause, with ever-increasing ruth-
lessness, with an ever-expanding geographical reach, and accordingly
with growing ruin on our side. Up to this hour, it was a *one-sided* war.
We have had to stand by helplessly and bear what was done to us and
our name. Thousands of Jewish lives destroyed, thousands of Jewish hearts broken, thousands of Jewish people robbed, tortured, persecuted, driven to suicide, loaded up like cattle and hurled into the
void. Think of the refugee ships with their desperate cargo, this hellish vision of our century. Think of Shanghai. We had to watch as our
name was besmirched, our values cast down, our synagogues torched,
our Holy of Holies desecrated. Wherever we were citizens, we were
treated worse than animals, and every lout was allowed to spit on
us — we had to bear it! We saw even the defenseless souls of our children subjected to this truly satanic hatred and crushed in the bud. This
pain is branded on our souls and cannot remain silent. And no defense
was possible, not the slightest attempt at striking back! We were at the
mercy of this boundlessly impudent power, which heaped scorn on our
wretchedness.

What has been portrayed here as a human fate reveals itself collec-
tively as a national fate: during one year of horrors after another, we
saw highly civilized Jewish populations in the core lands of the Golah
[Diaspora] cast down and wiped from the face of the earth. We saw a
war of extermination declared on us wherever we existed in the world
and advancing like a juggernaut. We had to yield one position after the
other to the irreconcilable enemy. A world began to expand in which
Jewishness had no right to be, Jews had no right to live — and in which
it would not have been worthwhile for a Jew to live. The mere proximity
of the Nazi Reich began to undermine the foundations of Jewish emancipation even beyond its borders, and even the most distant Jewish
populations learned to tremble, something that will long remain with
them. All of them felt the ground beneath their feet quake. But not only
the *emancipation* of the Jews was threatened, a status that no nationalist Jew, no Zionist may relinquish; even for the *ghetto* life, a condition some already saw making a comeback, there would be no room in
this system: the retreat to the yeshiva, which mighty Rome granted to
a politically defeated Jewish population, would not be granted by victorious Hitlerism to its victims, even supposing this population were

willing to seize such an opportunity. The torched and dynamited synagogues testify to that.

Jewishness of the "Pharisee" and the "Sadducee" brand is equally impossible in a world ruled by National Socialism. No intellectual life can flourish under the heel of the Gestapo. The structure of the totalitarian state has no neutral zones where anything nonconforming might flourish; this state spares the soul as little as the body. Its antisemitism can imply only one thing: extermination — or that ultimate humiliation that is even worse.

This antisemitic principle of "domestic policy" must of necessity become an instrument of foreign policy: just as a demonic fate unfailingly drives the Hitlerian expansion into the very areas where Jewish mass settlement has taken place and thus provides a constant supply of material for the machinery of destruction — so, too, Hitlerism is compelled by the law according to which it developed to take aim at us in all facets of its world policy — and most of all in areas where we mean something. Therefore, what was said of the Golah applies also to Eretz Israel, which we had been so eager to see as an exception to that tragic law. Let us not deceive ourselves: to this enemy, a proud Jewish people must be even more unbearable than one that is cowed; and however far this enemy's influence extends, it cannot tolerate our political and national self-fulfillment, the sovereign evolution of a free Jewish people, our flourishing as human beings, drawing on our people's own strength, for that would serve as the living refutation of the Nazis' image of Jewish inferiority. In a practical political sense, too, the enemy had to bump into us here, and sooner or later Jewish Palestine, far from enjoying an exceptional status, would have had to experience the full impact of a Nazism that had become a world power.

Let no one believe, then, that this germ of our future could have flourished or even preserved itself in a world in which Nazism triumphed. Let no one succumb to the Little Palestinian delusion that a blooming Jewish oasis could long survive amid the desert of a destroyed Diaspora — *al horban hagaluth*; that Jewish freedom could raise its head in a world from which freedom was disappearing; that a self-sufficient Jewish island could maintain itself in a world ruled by hostile powers. The opposite is true, as has become evident in the course of the current unrest, in the mandate government's retreat in the face of the greater threat lurking behind it. And this was just the first hint of the shadow Hitler cast. What "Hitler in the Orient" would really mean to us can be imagined only when we contemplate the fate of the Armenians.

That is how the world in store for us looked, to the extent that it was not already a reality. A flood tide was rising that would have swept away both our Diaspora and our national existence in this land. And the most desperate aspect, the most destructive aspect of all this was the awareness that we were condemned to complete defenselessness. In the long run, no individual, no people can endure such impotence without suffering damage to the soul. The victim of abuse sooner or later becomes a pariah. Many among us were already beginning to accept the notion that this evil was all-powerful, that nothing could halt its advance. A kind of fatalism was setting in, paralyzing us. At the sight of the sinister growth of the boa constrictor, of its ability to transfix its victims with its gaze, a fatalistic certainty that this fate was inescapable was spreading, i.e., a certainty that *the death sentence imposed on us as a people could not be reversed*. It becomes difficult to breathe when the air is filled with hatred and a dull premonition of destruction.

But there were also some among us who were just waiting for their hour, who had vowed not to feel at home again in this world or to take pleasure in its beauty until fate had granted them an opportunity to fight and settle accounts. This hour has now struck. It is our great chance — a political and a moral chance at one and the same time.

Politically it means that the Jewish people, by committing its sons to the struggle, can do its part to turn aside the evil fate aimed at it, and, by visibly joining on the front lines the forces allied against Hitler, by accepting the same risks and sacrifices in order to overthrow him, can regain its right of citizenship on earth — and that means both its right to live anywhere on earth as well as its particular right to Eretz Israel. Morally this opportunity means that for the sake of our self-respect and the respect of the world we can prove that we are not pariahs, helplessly swallowing their pain, but rather men who know how to take responsibility for their lives and strike back. The honor of which National Socialism deprived us would be truly lost the moment we entertained the thought of letting other peoples defend our cause and then received at their hands the gift of our recovered equality or merely the elimination of our mortal enemy.

The appearance of Herzl in our history has the following significance: he made such a ghetto attitude impossible for us henceforth —

an attitude in which we duck our heads to let the storms of history pass over them, while we wait to see what the outcome might be for us. When Zionism proclaimed to the people of the ghetto that they were a nation, it brought that people into the world arena and obliged it to assume the risk of an *autonomous historical existence*. And the partisan position that the diasporic situation had up to now prevented us from taking in the conflicts between peoples — this remnant of paralysis when it came to acting decisively in the realm of foreign policy has been dissolved by National Socialism: with inescapable clarity it has shown us which side we are on in the larger conflict and thereby propelled us to the front where we shall stand or fall. This time no conflict of loyalty can cloud the clarity of our position as a unified national actor.

This is not the first war in modern times in which Jews are participating. But it is the first in which the Jewish people is fighting as such. Yet never *in our entire Galut history* has the Jewish people, through its sons, been able to fight as an entity on one side and in defense of its own cause in a world war. Now this situation is at hand. That is what is historically new and unique about this war. That is why this is a "bellum judaicum" in the truest sense of the word — the first since the end of our existence as a state. But in contrast to that last bellum judaicum, this one, we hope, is not a war of catastrophe but a war that will rescue us from the Jewish catastrophe; not Judah against the world, but Judah with the world against the enemy of the world.

This war is also in a figurative sense the first war of religion in modern times. This spiritual aspect transcends all political calculations on the part of the governments waging war and originates in the very definition of the two sides. Of necessity — and independently of the degree of conscious choice — this constitutes a clash between two principles, one of which, in the form of Christian-Western humanism, also represents the heritage of Israel, the other of which represents the cult of power that mocks human values, the absolute negation of that heritage. National Socialism first recognized this clash when it maligned Christianity as the Jewification of European humanity and made Christianity a target of its metaphysical antisemitism. The churches recognized this clash when they realized — for the first time — that this struggle against Judaism was an attack on their own spiritual origins, rooted in Jewish tradition. The rational humanist civilization of modern Europe, too, which has freed itself from religion yet espouses instinct control, an ethics of conscience, and respect for the human individual, is ultimately descended from that great spiritual tradition originating in revelation. Thus National Socialism, as the adversary of all these values, as *heathenism* in the most profound sense, has created the apparent paradox that a bellum christianum can at the same time be a bellum judaicum. Europe's earlier wars of religion were struggles within Christianity and did not affect us Jews; this one is the quintessential struggle against the heathen, and when reduced to its simplest terms suddenly reveals the foundations shared by our Jewish culture and that of the Christian West. Our people's ancient tradition, our still relevant contribution to the ethical formation of the human race, is summoned to the lists in this struggle. In this sense as well, which extends far beyond mere self-preservation, this war is a bellum judaicum and calls us to arms.

What form can our participation in this war take? For the individual, it must of course entail activity in all the arenas in which modern war is fought, directly and indirectly. But since here collective and absolute matters are at stake, let only the most extreme form of participation be spoken of here — military participation. It is our wish and hope that Jewish units, presenting themselves as such, will fight in the Allies' ranks, precisely in those locations where there is direct confrontation with our enemy, with the armies of the Third Reich: we want a *Jewish legion on the western front*. In several countries, Czech and Polish legions are being formed. It would redound to the Jewish people's eternal shame if we, who are more affected than either of those two peoples, did not show our flag next to theirs in the main theater of war. We expect this deed of the Jewish people, this proof of its manhood, this contribution to seizing control of its own destiny.

This legion should be an all-Jewish legion, i.e., a legion representing world Jewry. Its recruitment territory is the entire Diaspora outside the area under Hitler's domination, in particular all the places where refugees from Hitler's tyranny forgather. Unless we are sorely mistaken about the Jews' sense of honor, these refugees will be particularly receptive to this call to arms, indeed will be awaiting it with impatience, and will answer it with enthusiasm. We place hope, furthermore, in the greatest pool of Jewish people, and, since the blows of the last few years, the only one that remains intact: America.

In such an all-Jewish legion, Palestine must be represented as well. As the group of Jews most mature in a political sense, as the only one that is nationally emancipated, the Palestinian community has a higher obligation to seize the initiative and serve as an example to Jews everywhere. Palestine is not a refuge from the vicissitudes of the Golah; it is the avant-garde of the Golah. Zionism is not confined to Little Palestine. This pan-Jewish duty imposed on Palestine is an additional one for the Yishuv: it does not conflict with our duty to protect our positions here, but from a higher vantage point complements it. The natural priority that must be given to local defense is uncontested; but it is not enough for the fighting power of Jewish Palestine to be restricted to serving as a garrison when entire peoples face off. Waiting to see how things develop here must not provide a convenient excuse for the individual to place limitations on his willingness to sacrifice.

Under current conditions, the actual front lines for a country may be located at a great remove. Attending to the purely local aspect would do justice neither to Palestine's inextricable involvement in global decisions nor to its moral obligation to Jews throughout the world. It would be a failure of the true national idea, a failure on the part of Palestine to realize the true meaning of Zionism, which calls for Chaluzi-uth [pioneer existence] for Israel, wherever it may be. The fate of Palestine will also be decided on the battlefields of Europe. Only there can a new legitimation of our claim to Palestine be obtained. A Palestinian division — we can say nothing about its size — must not be absent from the all-Jewish legion in the war against Hitler. In this military kibbutz haggalujoth [gathering of Jews from the Diaspora], a Zionist core must be represented.

Seeing to the proper deployment of the Palestinian Jewish forces is the responsibility of those in charge, who can use their judgment when it comes to implementing the outcome of this appeal, which can only be on too small a scale, never on too great a one; this has nothing to do with the personal decision for the *more dangerous* assignment at which this appeal aims. The individual will hardly be in a position to judge whether the border is located ahead of or behind him; he must merely ask himself: What am I prepared to do? Ultimately his decision is a human one, not a political one. In choosing the most difficult assignment he will not let himself be deterred by the fear that there might be too many like him. It is easy to deal with too many: anyone who has volunteered for the more ambitious assignment will always accept an order to take on a more limited one. The reverse is less easy to deal with.

Let one more thing be said to clarify our inner attitude and our outward position: whatever we may hope for from the outcome of this war in the way of Jewish political gains, of advancement of goals that are dear to us—and everyone is free to harbor such hopes—this may not be made a condition of our participation. Toward whom could such a condition be asserted in any case? Our axiom is that from a purely Jewish perspective this is "our war." For that reason it is not a matter of our offering to help with someone else's cause and expecting something in return, but of doing our part in a situation in which we are implicated from the outset, in which we have no choice. A "do ut des" attitude would falsify the entire basis for this struggle as the cause of the Jewish people par excellence. We should be clear on this, and not let any doubts on this score arise among others: in fighting, we are not helping others in expectation of a reward; rather we are helping ourselves by averting our annihilation—and by restoring our honor. Our volunteering to join the struggle would only be devalued if it came with the expectation that others would reciprocate. In any case, in this war our cause is automatically at stake—and the whole world knows that. We are the party at war, and with as much justification as those at whose side we want to fight—no, with more justification. That is why it is not true that we choose to back them and join them as allies, but the other way around: their declaration of war on Hitler now gives us the opportunity to wage the war that was imposed on us a long time ago. The basis for our alliance is the prime minister's declaration that this war shall continue "till Hitlerism is destroyed." No further basis is needed. The annihilation of Hitler is a sufficient purpose—at the moment the purpose—and we can amply justify our claim to participate (not our "offer") by citing our preeminent interest in annihilating Hitler. Therefore the Jewish people as a whole has no other war objective than this, and our commitment may not be conditional; it must be unconditional. The moment we are able to participate in achieving this goal, indeed when this goal itself first became possible, is not the moment for considering other commitments, even those to our otherwise valid causes. We must go into this war without looking to left or right, without contemplating any outcome other than this one. Only then will we be able to say that the first war the Jewish people has fought in its modern history was a purely *defensive* war.

Jewish men! A generation that was old enough to be fully aware of the First World War is inoculated against going to war frivolously, against succumbing to self-deception when it comes to the horrors of war. But armed with this knowledge, to which is added knowledge of the six years of outrage we have endured at Hitler's hands, we swear that this war must be taken up by Jews and fought wherever it rages most fiercely — and where we can look our chief enemy in the eye. We need not condition our participation on the illusion that we are certain of the outcome. It is enough to know the alternative: if the Western powers prove victorious — and that we believe will be the case — Hitler will fall, and the Jewish people will again have a *prospect* of survival. If Hitler proves victorious, that means our downfall, here and everywhere else: so at least we want to go down fighting. But it is pointless, at the beginning of such a momentous historical process, to want to see beyond the immediate goal and to ask how the world may look after it is all over. As a spur to action the immediate goal is more than sufficient: the overthrow of Hitler. Let us conduct ourselves in such a way that one day our grandchildren will have no reason to be ashamed of us.

It was clear to me that since my appeal was composed in German it would reach mainly those who'd immigrated from German-speaking regions. So I began to peddle it around. First I organized a meeting; it took place [on 6 October 1939] in the apartment of a prominent figure in German Zionist circles, an older fraternity brother of mine called Gustav Krojanker. A goodly number of people attended,[2] none of whom could be expected to join the military themselves, but whose moral support and influence I needed in order to move this cause ahead. All those present were immediately persuaded that we had to try for a visible Jewish involvement in the war on the Allies' side, on the model of the so-called Jewish Legion formed by American Jewish volunteers in the First World War, which at the time — already under the aegis of the Balfour Declaration — helped conquer Palestine under the British flag.[3] In this case, however, it was a question of taking on the enemy of the world, who was also the enemy of the Jewish people and whose victory would mean our total destruction. The group agreed unanimously that we absolutely had to be present and active in the theaters of war, not somewhere on the periphery. I thought, of course, that the center of the struggle would be located in France, as in the First World War, for I was betting on the quality of the French army and the British expeditionary corps, which I hoped would mount an effective military resistance to Hitler. At the time no one could have predicted France's rapid collapse.

After I'd won over this circle, I disseminated some copies of my appeal, with the help of other Jews from Germany. It's unlikely, however, that at the time it reached many people, because it wasn't written in Hebrew. From my perspective, the most important thing was to gain access to the army, and that was where I directed my efforts for the time being. I managed to arrange a meeting with a British military commander or his adjutant, and presented our request: the creation of units in which Jews could volunteer to serve in the various branches of the service, units that would fight under British command but be identifiable as Jewish, with their own flag. I made no bones about it: "We want to be deployed to the western front." The English reaction was frosty: "We'll handle things as we see fit." Other than pleasantries I received not one encouraging word, not even the concession that our request would be forwarded to London. Alas, mine was a private initiative, with far too little authority behind it. The Jewish Agency (Sochnut), which otherwise represented international Zionism and the Yishuv to the British, wasn't involved at the time, and from that quarter, too, I received no encouragement. The agency told me, "This is a political matter, one that we'll take up with the proper offices in the correct manner at the proper time," and they weren't pleased to see this kind of thing being pushed from below and without authorization. It became clear to me that the Jewish Agency was interested exclusively in Palestinian issues and would insist on linking any Jewish fighting force with the Zionist cause. I, on the other hand, was convinced that this war went far beyond Zionist local interests. Up to then we'd been subjected to active Arab attacks, which had ceased only because after the war began the English forces in the country were reinforced so much and received so much more authority to intervene that the Arab uprising was essentially stopped in its tracks.[4] Palestine or the Middle East had now become a theater of war, or at least a potential theater of war. Actually this didn't really happen until Italy entered the war, which, as we know, didn't occur until 1940. Italy had of course colonized Libya, while Germany originally had no foothold in the Middle East. Be that as it might: it was clear that the Middle East was a potential theater of war, and even though I didn't know the Jewish Agency's plans at the time, I was certainly aware that the agency was by no means enthusiastic about putting our military strength to work far from Palestine, despite the possibility that situations could arise in which the presence of armed Jewish units might be critical. I countered all these considerations with the argument that our fate would be decided by the outcome of this war; everything we undertook locally in Palestine would be completely meaningless if Hitler won, while a victory of the Allies would also give us freedom of movement for our efforts in Palestine. To my mind, the top priority was to overthrow Hitler, an idea that not all Jews accepted. I engaged in debate with Jewish groups who said, "First of all we must make ourselves very strong in this country and see to it that we're armed when hostile forces come here." During one discussion in Tel Aviv someone raised the following objection to my position: "The Red Army is practically close enough to touch; a hop, skip, and jump from Russia's southwestern border, and it will be in Persia and on the Black Sea. But that's such an immediate danger that it may not be Hitler at all we have to fear." Such things were going through people's minds.

After we'd been turned away by the British, who were polite and amiable, Walter Gross and I requested a meeting with the French consul general in Jerusalem and presented to him our wish — I'd prepared our statement in French — to place a Jewish volunteer fighting force at the disposal of the French high command on the western front. We emphasized that while these troops would be placed under French command, they would fight under their own flag — "pour l'honneur du drapeau." The consul was polite and friendly, too, and said, "Yes, we have a channel for citizens of other countries who wish to volunteer: the Foreign Legion." I explained to him that this was precisely what we didn't want. Not the Foreign Legion, but Jewish troops fighting under their own flag! French uniform — yes, French command — yes, French officers — yes, but not in the Foreign Legion. Yet the offer of the Foreign Legion was the most he was willing to grant us, and that was where we left it. Our efforts had come to a dead end. Both the Jewish Agency and the British and French commands turned a deaf ear to our proposal. On the other hand, it was fairly clear that without the support of the Jewish Agency we couldn't do anything for the time being but stand by and observe the course of the war. Developments were not slow in coming, and the result was that in 1940 England suddenly found itself sustaining the war effort all alone.

My initiative was backed by only a small group of enthusiastic amateurs, who thought it was possible to take on and implement something like this without much organization. We flattered ourselves that this undertaking would have instant appeal to Jewish pride and Jewish capacity for self-sacrifice, and that young Jewish men who were waiting impatiently for their chance would flock to us. We'd miscalculated, however. A further problem was that no Jewish organization wanted to support us. What was taking place behind the scenes I had no way of knowing. George Lichtheim, with his superior knowledge of politics and his ironic temperament, explained to me that I was rushing into this situation like Parsifal, the "dumb fool," while the political dynamics were moving in an entirely different direction. And that was indeed the case. My friends were very impressed by my determination, but initially breathed a sigh of relief—not for my sake but for theirs—when nothing came of my efforts. When the moment was ripe, it turned out that I was the only one who volunteered, at first with the exception of Walter Gross, who, however, dropped out between September 1939 and August 1940 because his extremely decisive wife, Lola, who already had one child, quickly and intentionally got pregnant. She wanted to prevent her Walter from joining Hans Jonas in this madness.

After the collapse of France, word reached me from the Jewish Agency and the Haganah that certain agreements had been made with the British High Command, and now Palestinian volunteer units were being formed. You could go to Sarafant for a military physical exam. I went and was found fit for service. At thirty-seven I was no longer young enough for the infantry, but I was accepted into the First Palestine Anti-Aircraft Battery. At the time you could join the infantry, the artillery, the engineers, and the air force, but the latter only for service on the ground. For training as a pilot you had to go to England. The volunteer units weren't organized under one command but were scattered: the infantry units were deployed to North Africa, while the anti-aircraft batteries were set up in Haifa to defend against aerial attacks from Damascus and Beirut, where the Vichy French were now fighting on the side of the Germans. The battery in which I received my training was made up of young Jews—some of them brand-new immigrants, who'd fled Germany, Austria, and Czechoslovakia,[5] but also men from the kibbutzim, who'd been urged by the Haganah to volunteer so we could gain experience in all branches of the service as the basis for building the future Jewish army. The Jewish Zionist agencies' interest was focused primarily on the postwar period. Accordingly, the Haganah decided who would receive training in the British army and who would stay in Palestine. Lore's brother, Franz, for instance, was denied permission to volunteer, because he was needed locally. So my battery consisted on the one hand of individual volunteers, who, like me, had spontaneously decided to report for duty, and on the other hand of volunteers secretly picked by Jewish organizations. The kibbutzniks all belonged to the latter category. Among them were Sabras, born in the country and raised as farmers, sturdy boys and excellent soldiers, in whose eyes Hitler and German Jewry were part of another world. On the other side were those who felt directly affected because they came from Europe and were acutely conscious of the fate of family members who hadn't got out in time. Among them was a volunteer originally from Metz, the only academic besides me, who'd given up his position as a botanist at the Hebrew University. His name was Michael Evenari, originally Walter Schwarz, an irrigation specialist who'd made the greening of the Negev his life's work, an excellent man, a few years my junior. When it came to military matters he was much more gifted and eventually became a sergeant major — the highest noncommissioned rank. He refused to go to England for officer training because he — like me — wanted to be with the enlisted men.[6]

In the course of the war, some of those with real military talent were sent to England for officer training, and some of them didn't return until we had the Italian campaign long since behind us. Among the officer trainees was one man of whom I had a particularly high opinion and with whom I remained in contact later on: a man born in America who'd come to Palestine as a child with his Zionist parents, a corporal, who was my direct superior on Cyprus and in Italy, and then also in the War of Independence. His original name was Josef Levin, but he changed it to Josef Nevo. Eventually he became a general in the Israeli army. His example showed me the difference between someone who really has what it takes to be a military leader and someone who merely has the honest desire to be a decent soldier. I count myself one of the latter. Josef Levin, however, was the kind of person who remained cool under fire, as if he didn't fear for his life at all, and could thus give orders while in danger himself. I wanted to mention these two people, Evenari and Levin, as comrades in arms with whom I spent the entire five years. I saw both of them again afterward, and whenever we met, we fell into each other's arms. Sharing the experience of war forges unbreakable bonds. I remember running into Josche Levin, by now Nevo, after many years. He already had a great military career behind him and had been a general in the Sinai campaign of 1956 and the Six Days' War of 1967. Later he'd gone into politics and become the mayor of Herzliya. I'd seen him once in America, where he was visiting, but then we hadn't heard anything of each other for years. One day, he told me, he'd turned on the radio, and his wife had said suddenly, "That's Hans Jonas. That's his voice." I happened to be at a conference in Israel, and had mustered all my Hebrew to take part in a little panel discussion in Haifa, which was being broadcast. They then invited me to visit, and that was the beginning of a close friendship.

In our anti-aircraft battery we generally spoke Hebrew, though the soldiers from Central Europe spoke German among themselves. At first our superiors — real officers — were British. The fact that those among us who had the greatest military talent were sent to England for officer training made it possible for the British officers to be replaced more and more by Hebrew-speaking Jewish officers from Palestine. Initially we were stationed in Palestine to defend the oil refineries of Haifa, but then we were transferred to Cyprus, which was also being bombarded. The North African campaign, in which the Germans were very successful, posed a lasting threat to British supply ships in the Mediterranean, and Cyprus was an important base. On Cyprus I began to learn modern Greek, and the Greek Cypriot farmers in the wine taverns were thrilled to hear me recite Homer. It was nice on Cyprus, but I was getting impatient to be where the action was. I was one of the foolhardy ones who applied for a transfer to England, so as to participate in an invasion of Europe. Nothing came of that. Instead we accomplished something else, something very important, namely that Churchill realized the moral significance of the Jewish cause and our participation in the war, and, over the resistance of his generals, ordered that our units, scattered among the various branches of the service, be joined into a single military entity. Thus in September 1944 the *Jewish Brigade Group* officially came into existence.[7] It made a great difference whether there were Jewish units here and there, fighting in North Africa, in Tobruk or in the western desert, while the artillery was stationed only in parts of the homeland, as opposed to a special Jewish brigade. Churchill then ordered that we should receive our own insignia — blue and white with the star of David embroidered in gold. Furthermore, Churchill opened this brigade for transfer applications from other parts of the British armed forces, so that we suddenly had an influx of young Jewish soldiers from England, South Africa, Canada, Australia, and New Zealand, and were now no longer merely Palestinian but a bona fide Jewish brigade. It was amazing how many soldiers seized this opportunity to transfer in.

The Jewish Brigade Group, which included all branches of the service except the air force, was finally deployed in the last stages of the war, for we were sent to Italy. The invasion of Europe began from the south, after all. The decisive phase took place in Normandy, but first came the landing in North Africa, just as I'd wagered years earlier, and from that moment on I knew we'd get our chance, too. The brigade formed at different locations until we were all loaded onto ships, and in 1944 we first came together in southern Italy. In the meantime I'd become a specialist in automatic anti-aircraft guns, and, after receiving additional training in the mechanics and repair of these guns, assumed the position of master gunner in my battery. First we were sent to Alexandria, and from there to a large training camp on the edge of the western desert, where we were trained in field artillery. In addition to our anti-aircraft guns — Swedish Bofos guns — the most important weapon we were now equipped with was the British army's main field cannon, a 75-mm fieldpiece. In contrast to heavy artillery, this is a mobile artillery piece, relatively easy to operate, which is used on the front lines, directly behind the infantry. This retraining took several weeks, and then we were granted home leave, for it was clear we wouldn't be able to get away once we were deployed. So in quick succession every soldier received a three-day furlough. Since there was no time to write home, the first group were asked to deliver a message for their comrades: "Please tell my wife or so-and-so that I'll be arriving at such-and-such a time." That was how Lore learned that I was coming. I hadn't had a leave in a long time, for once you were outside the country leave was seldom possible. We traveled by train from Alexandria, crossed the Suez Canal at Port Said in large livestock transports, rolled north across the Sinai, and reached the railroad station in Haifa at three in the morning. From there I tramped up Mt. Carmel with my gear. At about two or three hundred meters above sea level, located on a slope, was Hadar Har Karmel, a part of Haifa that was purely Jewish. I knew that Lore had a room on the fourth floor, and when I saw a light up there, I whistled our special signal. Lore opened the window and then came down to open the front door for me. Because we knew that this would be my last leave, I'd sent word to her that she should take a room for us for two or three nights at the best, most expensive hotel on Mt. Carmel. When Lore woke up the next morning, I wasn't sleeping beside her but on the floor! During my time in the military I'd become so used to sleeping on hard boards that I couldn't sleep on a soft mattress. After Lore fell asleep I'd spread something on the floor and was sleeping on a somewhat firmer mattress — the tiles.

And then back we went — by way of Alexandria — to Italy. We landed in Taranto, the ancient city of Tarentum, located on the instep of the Italian boot. From there we made our way north. Wherever we arrived, Jews crept out of their hiding places, for word got around fast: "Jewish troops are approaching!" We'd already heard rumors about the fate of the Jews in Europe. Some attempts had been made to penetrate this secret, among them the famous mission of Enzo Sereni, the Italian Zionist, who renounced his pacifism after the defeat of France, joined the British secret service, and in May 1944 was dropped over Yugoslavia with a group of paratroopers to make contact with partisans. Sereni was captured by the Germans and later murdered in Dachau, and most of those in his group lost their lives.[8] The messages that made their way out of Eastern Europe were vague and uncertain, and how accurate they were, no one could tell. What was clear, however, was that terrible things were happening in the areas under German occupation. We'd also heard about deportations — entire regions being cleared of Jews, something that even in wartime couldn't be kept secret. But where they were moved to, and what happened to them, was largely unclear. We knew about the ghettos and also about the concentration camps, but we hadn't heard about the gas chambers. Not until we reached Italy were our eyes gradually opened, for the farther we advanced the more terrible were the things we heard. But we also learned that in many cases the Italians had hidden Jews, saved them from the Gestapo, and smuggled them from place to place. The love I already felt for Italy was transformed during this time into a love for the Italians, who distinguished themselves from all other European peoples, including the Dutch, by never falling prey to worship of the state. They'd never paid that much attention to the laws and directives issuing from Rome, for there was a deeply rooted anarchic element in their psyche. The ordinary Italian, whether a villager or a city dweller, was infinitely superior to the German in the way he refused to let the state tell him what to think about the things that really mattered in life. Even fascism, which is an Italian invention, after all, never managed to delude the population as to what a person owes a fellow human being. We heard stories that brought tears to our eyes. We met a mother and her daughter, about seventeen or eighteen at the time. Both of them — they came from Germany, and there was no father — had fled to Italy and wandered from place to place for years. Finally, when the deportations began in Italy, supervised directly by the Gestapo, they reached a village where they sought refuge, illegally, and without ration cards. On the Sunday after they arrived — they'd been taken in by a farm family — the priest said in his sermon in church, "There are a few among us who are suffering persecution. They have sought our protection, and our Christian duty commands that we protect them. No child in my congregation may speak of their presence and report it to any outsider." Those instructions were followed—people fed them and kept them hidden. It was often the parish priests who helped, while the highly placed churchmen stood by and said nothing.

At the end of the war, when the German troops in Italy capitulated on 29 April 1945, we had just fought the battle of Senio, the only larger battle in which I participated, and one that ended with our breaking through the German lines. We were advancing after the battle, and entered Bologna as liberators, greeted by girls who kissed us.

For months, indeed years, my connection with Lore, by the way, had been maintained only through letters. I wrote two kinds of letters; some I characterized as love letters, some as "didactic letters." In the latter, I began to develop my philosophy while I was serving in the field. Far from books, lacking any materials for scholarly research, I was thrown back on the question that should actually preoccupy every philosopher, namely the question as to the meaning of our existence and the existence of the world around us. So I began to wonder what it implies in ontological terms that there are organisms, and what significance the nature of organic being holds for life, including the nature of consciousness, of emotion, and of the spirit; all this I developed in letters.[9] We weren't allowed, by the way, to divulge our location in letters from the field, since that was a military secret. Nonetheless I often managed to convey this information to Lore in code. When we were in Rome (which was also no particular secret, since it had been taken by the Allies long before this), and we visited the collections of the Vatican, I sent her a picture.[10] It showed a remnant of a fresco that had once adorned some part of the Vatican, but then had been removed: Melozzo da Forlí's angel playing music. Melozzo is the artist's name, da Forlí indicates the place he came from. A harmless picture. Hugs from your loving Hans. Later we were stationed for a while not far from Ravenna, where the front ran along the little Senio River. Our headquarters were in the village of Forlí, and in one of my letters I simply reminded Lore that I'd sent her that picture of the angel from the Vatican. So she knew we were near Forlí. That's how you can sometimes fool the censors.

Finally we were bivouacked in Udine, in northern Italy. There I heard the most wonderful story to come out of the whole war. In the town marketplace, a few fellow soldiers and I, who were recognizable by our blue and white shoulder patches with the Star of David, were approached by two older Jewish women. They asked whether we spoke German, and we sat down with them in the middle of busy Udine, where it happened to be market day, and had them tell us their story. They came from Trieste, which had belonged to Austria until the end of World War I, but as a result of the Italian defeat had then become Italian. When the persecution of the Jews was already in full swing in Germany, they were still relatively safe in Trieste, for Mussolini hadn't immediately adopted Hitler's anti-Jewish policy. But eventually the threat of deportation reached Trieste as well, and they decided to move farther south. Apparently that was the watchword among Jews: the farther south you could get, into Italy proper, the safer you'd be. So they packed only hand luggage, including jewelry and cash, and set out for the station to head south. Just as they were approaching the barrier where you had to show your ticket to get onto the platform, they noticed that Gestapo agents or their Italian equivalent were standing beside the conductors. As they stood there at a loss, trying to think what they should do, they saw one of the Italian railroad officials wink at them and wave them to a spot where they could get through the barrier onto the platform without being checked. Not a word was spoken; the man had simply recognized what was happening. They got on the train, and got off in Udine, where they found an unfurnished garret, lacking even beds. There they could go into hiding at any rate, without registering with the police. In the neighborhood, however, people were aware that they had moved in. Two days and nights after their arrival, a truck pulled up to the house. Several men unloaded two bed frames with mattresses, carried them up the stairs, and knocked on their door. When the women opened the door, trembling, the men explained that His Eminence the Archbishop of Trieste had learned of their circumstances and was sending them this furniture to make their lives easier. From then on they lived in this attic room, sacrificing one piece of jewelry after another to buy food on the black market, because of course they had no ration cards. One day, when their means were almost exhausted, they learned that in another part of town a woman was selling lard on the black market. They hurried there and bought a kilo, at an outrageous price, and brought it home. After nightfall, there was a knock on their door. When they opened it fearfully, there stood the woman from whom they'd bought the lard that afternoon. She said, "Please forgive me. You bought something from me this morning. I didn't know who you were. Later someone told me, and said where you live. I don't want to take any money from you." She gave them back their money, turned, and left. The two women, who were sisters, by the way, told me this story, and then said, "And now you understand why we don't want to go to Palestine, but prefer to spend the rest of our lives among the Italians." Of course we saw it as our duty to tell all the surviving Jews we met that they had to emigrate to Palestine, and to advise them as to whom they should get in touch with to make it happen. Apparently other members of the Jewish Brigade had already conveyed this message to these ladies, and now they were giving us their reasons for wanting to stay — this lovely story. You can see why I have especially warm feelings for the Italians; I heard many such tales.[11]

CHAPTER 8

Travels through a Germany in Ruins

The farther north we advanced, after our brief stopover in Udine, the more gruesome stories we heard. The entire brigade, numbering between ten and twelve thousand soldiers, along with all its equipment—the motor pool, the artillery, and the munitions transport—crossed the Austrian Alps and at Garmisch-Partenkirchen finally found itself on German soil. In late May or early June, on the way to Ulm, before we got onto the autobahn near Augsburg, we passed a side road that suddenly filled up with Jews. In nearby Landsberg was a camp liberated by the Allies that was now being used to house displaced persons. Word had spread like wildfire that Jewish troops were approaching. People streamed out of the camp, took up positions along the highway, and cheered us as we passed. We stopped, and they embraced us and kissed the Star of David on our uniforms. They'd been liberated by the Americans, but here they were encountering armed Jews—coming as victors, not as martyrs and victims! We began to hand out our rations of corned beef, peas, coffee, chocolate—whatever we had. The brigade slowed to a crawl. After ten minutes we had to move on, for the sake of military discipline and also so as not to block traffic, and the liberated Jews ran along behind us for a while. That was our first mass encounter with survivors. The few things they could blurt out through their tears gave us our first direct confrontation with the horrors perpetrated on the Jews in Eastern Europe. There weren't any German Jews among them; most of them came from Poland and spoke Yiddish, but we had enough soldiers among us who knew Yiddish. Though we didn't have much time, we heard the first concrete details about things we'd merely been able to guess at from the rumors in Italy, and for the first time the names Auschwitz, Treblinka, and so on reached our ears.

As we traveled on by way of Karlsruhe and Pforzheim, we passed through German cities reduced to rubble, or at least saw them from the autobahn. Later on, during my travels through Germany, I saw many places that looked like ghost towns—especially Kassel, which resembled a moon landscape, full of bomb craters, ruined buildings silhouetted against the sky. This sight inspired an emotion that I hope never to experience again but also don't want to fail to mention: a sense of rejoicing, of satisfied, or at least half-satisfied, revenge. This is one of the ignoble emotions, but it gratified me to know that the terrible things that had happened here, what had been visited on our people, had at least not gone wholly unavenged. There were years when if you'd asked me to name the moment of my most intense happiness, I would have said, "That moment when I saw the German cities in ruins, as evidence of justice, of divine retribution." Now that I've experienced moments of much greater happiness, I wouldn't say that anymore — fortunately.

As we were crossing southern and southwestern Germany, I received my only "war wound." It happened one morning while I was supervising the loading of a truck, and a round fuel canister rolled off the truck and hit me in the head. It made a deep gash, and I was transported, with blood streaming down my face, to the nearest field hospital. We were already on the left bank of the Rhine, on our way to Saarbrücken. I spent a few hours in the field hospital, where I was patched up, and then, with a large white dressing around my head, through which a little blood was still seeping, was driven to Saarbrücken, where I rejoined my unit. From there we moved in a large convoy across northeastern France to Lille. In each truck an officer or noncom sat or stood next to the driver. Since I had the rank of sergeant, I sat next to our driver, while the lower-ranking soldiers rode in the back. Whenever we drove through a town, we passed cheering citizens, who saw us not as a Jewish brigade but as Allied troops. Since instead of my helmet I had a bandage around my head, I was the object of much cheering, as a soldier who had supposedly been wounded in combat. People pointed at me and applauded specially, letting me cross northern France surrounded by an undeserved nimbus of heroism. Lille was one of our rest stops, followed by Tournai in Belgium, which we soon left behind, however. And what does God do in his mysterious ways? Our final destination was Venlo, twenty kilometers from Mönchengladbach, just over the Dutch border. Venlo, which I'd known since childhood as the town you could ride to by bicycle, to have a cup of coffee or buy Dutch chocolate. From there, about a month and a half after Germany's surrender, I ventured forth on my first visit to my hometown.

On the way to Holland we'd heard numerous reports about what had gone on during the war. In the course of our travels it even happened that some of my fellow soldiers slipped away from camp one night, broke into a German house somewhere in the countryside, and killed the people inside.

That was one factor in the English command's decision not to give us occupation duties in Germany but to station us in Holland. In all there were two incidents. As we were marching through the mountains of Austria, some of our infantry soldiers managed to surround an Alpine hut where some Waffen-SS soldiers were holed up. Our fellow soldiers didn't turn their captives in immediately. Instead they tortured them all night, trying to force confessions out of them. They didn't kill them, but the captives were in pretty bad shape when they were handed over. The other incident took place somewhere in Germany during an overnight stop: some of us sneaked away and took revenge on a family—I have no idea whether they were guilty of anything in particular. It was after this that the commanders decided to station us in Holland. But we could move about freely, and of course made contact with Jewish survivors from the camps. Some of them spoke very bitterly of other survivors who'd been kapos in the concentration camps. "If I find him, and he's still alive, he's going to pay." Some of my fellow soldiers organized a sort of research bureau that systematically collected information and passed it on to a central collection point. That was how I heard the name of Paul Raffaelson, someone I'd known in my youth, a member of a Jewish family from Mönchengladbach. I didn't speak directly with the people who'd sworn to get back at this man, but people told me about him because I came from the same town. When I got to Mönchengladbach— I'll tell that story separately—I paid a visit to the English commandant. On this occasion I wasn't just Sergeant Jonas but a former citizen of the town, which had now been placed under his military control. He'd installed his command post on Mozartstrasse, in the house belonging to Hermann Aschaffenburg. It was the best house on this short street of villas, where my family had lived before the war. So my conversation with him took place just steps away from where I'd spent my youth. Two things have stuck in my memory from that meeting. One of them was that he said, "Mister Jonas" (he called me "Mister" because at that moment our relationship wasn't military), "there's one thing I can tell you: there were no Nazis here. Nobody ever was a Nazi. There was never any such a thing as a Nazi. You won't find a single person who will freely admit to being a party member or a Nazi." A very British comment, by the way. I can still hear the utter disdain in his voice. And then he asked me, "Tell me, Mr. Jonas, does the name Raffaelson mean anything to you? Was he a member of the Jewish community of Mönchengladbach?" "Oh, yes, I remember him," I replied. "Can you tell me about him?" To which I responded, "Not really." As a young man he had a rather bad reputation and got in trouble with the police before the war for some kind of fraud. "He's one of the survivors who came back, and now he's a prominent spokesman for the Jewish community here. I have my suspicions," the commandant told me. To that I replied, "I see — have you heard things?" "Yes," he said, "but I don't know whether they're true." I told him I couldn't confirm anything, but had also heard things and would check with my fellow soldiers; if I found out anything, I could let the commandant know.

But in the meantime Raffaelson learned that I was in Mönchengladbach, and invited me to lunch. He told me that up to the end he'd taken care of the grounds of our house on Mozartstrasse, and he described my father's last days: "He would sit in a chair out in the garden, since he couldn't walk very well, and he'd say, 'That bush there, that stretch of lawn needs attention.'" What he described was precisely what I'd imagined — that my father, who died in January 1938, had sat out in the garden in the summer and fall of 1937 and spoken with Raffaelson, who was earning some money as a groundskeeper. Raffaelson served me an excellent lunch, far superior to what was generally available. After his return he'd married a Christian woman. I did ask him who'd been in this or that concentration camp in Czechoslovakia, but of course I couldn't formally interrogate him. His guilt remained unresolved for me. Still, I'd enjoyed his hospitality and the best meal I'd eaten up to then in Germany, for he had special sources and could obtain delicacies. Some years later, when I was in Canada, I read a newspaper report of the execution of a Paul Raffaelson, convicted in a war crimes trial of displaying great brutality in a concentration camp. On the request of the Czech government he'd been handed over by the British occupation forces and sentenced to death by hanging. It's impossible to say whether that was just or unjust, for the kapos were fighting for their own lives, sometimes at the cost of others'. In his great essay *The Drowned and the Saved,* Primo Levi describes graphically what Jews did to other Jews.[1] When I read that account, I had to think of Raffaelson again. Apparently he'd played such a role. I still recall how odd it made me feel to think that I'd contributed to his conviction by adding to the scraps of evidence that ultimately came together to form a damning picture.

A far more painful personal experience than this encounter with a survivor whose fate eventually caught up with him was, of course, the news of my mother's death. The first time I returned to Mönchengladbach, I asked where I might find a Jewish community center. Where the synagogue had once stood was now a vacant lot. The temple had been torched during the Night of Broken Glass and then demolished. But somewhere a center had been set up where returning Jews or Jews passing through could register and receive information. There I tried to discover what had happened to my mother. The last word I'd received in Jerusalem, by way of the Red Cross, was that she was living in the ghetto in Litzmannstadt — now Łódź. When I got to the community center, it was packed with people I'd never seen before, but there was one woman who looked familiar. She heard me ask for information and mention the name Jonas. At that she said, "Oh, so you're Hans Jonas?" Then she burst into tears and said, "I was with your mother in Łódź, but she was sent on to Auschwitz in 1942." Everyone knew what that meant — Auschwitz — and that was how I learned of my mother's death. The woman who told me had survived, along with her daughter, first of all because they were strong enough to work, and second because they were young enough to be forced to perform sexual services for the SS personnel. But you couldn't ask: "How did you and your daughter manage to survive?" At any rate, this woman wept as she told me about my mother.

What was striking during this period was that people in Mönchengladbach didn't want to believe that anything had been done to the Jews. When I visited our house at 9 Mozartstrasse, the new owner said, "Oh, so you're Hans Jonas. And how's your mother? Have you heard from her?" I replied, "She was killed." "Killed? Who would have killed her? People don't do that to an old lady." "She was killed in Auschwitz." "No, that can't be true," the man said, "that can't be true. She was resettled." He simply refused to face the facts. I remember vividly how revolting I found it when he put his arm around me and said, "Come on, now! You mustn't believe everything you hear! No, I'm sure it was resettlement. And if she died, I'm terribly sorry to hear it. But what you're saying about killing and gas chambers — those are just atrocity stories." That was in the summer of 1945. In the house I saw a handsome desk that had belonged to my father, and when he asked me, "Do you want it? Do you want to take it with you?" I said, "No, no, I don't want it." And I left soon after that. I couldn't stand the man. But at least I'd been inside the house — for the last time.

Then I visited some of my Christian friends, the ones who I knew hadn't been involved in anything, who'd been bitterly opposed to the Nazi regime. The painter Kurt Beyerlein, whom I'd been especially eager to see, had unfortunately been killed two months before the end of the war. He was a year younger than I. I'd become friends with him in the last years before

Hitler, and we'd had wonderful conversations. He was a pure soul and a good painter, if not a great one. His search for spiritual truth had led him to Kierkegaard, to a sort of Protestant piety, even though he came from a Catholic background. I learned that during an air raid he'd been crushed between two train cars while locomotives and freight cars were being shunted in the freight yard. A colleague of his, Hans Lünenburg, a talented painter from an irreproachable family, told me he'd asked Kurt shortly before his death whether now that the Americans were approaching he couldn't simply slip away. But Beyerlein had answered, "Oh, it wouldn't be worth it now. All this will be over soon, and then we'll be free!" And he added, "And then Hans Jonas will come back, and we'll sit night after night in the gazebo and talk about the meaning of life." Later on his wife published his letters, and what he'd written to her during the war showed beyond a doubt what a fine person he was. So, for instance, he wrote on 29 June 1943, "The complete destruction of all the towns in our beautiful region is a fact — a fact that remains incomprehensible to me. After the destruction I have witnessed recently, I can imagine how the precious city of Cologne must look. Yes, a people that permitted the Jews' churches to be destroyed does not deserve to have its own historic churches kept intact." And in another letter from the field, written in June of that year: "Here is the significance I see in all this: the final reckoning has begun, and there is so much to do penance for. Now every night I expect Gladbach to be reduced to ashes and rubble. That in one night everything will be destroyed that it took fifty years to build up. Ah, my dearest, may you stay safe. God preserve us from this ever-growing catastrophe." In a later letter: "I assume you have heard about Cologne, too. That is truly a cause for mourning. What an enormous misfortune we have been driven into! Who will liberate us, when, and how? Before we have even a glimmer of better prospects, our suffering must increase immeasurably. I always think most people picture the terrible as taking place on the margins of events, but in fact it is at the very center, with only one outcome — death and destruction. The fiendish false ideologies still have too powerful a hold on people and give them the impression that they are borne along by positive forces," and so on. That was written in the middle of the Nazi period. "Poor, stupid German people. But not innocent. I think about when and how the citizens of Gladbach will rub their eyes, inflamed from smoke, and grub in vain though heaps of ashes for any possessions. This is something they did not anticipate when things were in high gear. But I fear the process of winding down will be slow, for the Satan they hailed so enthusiastically will not be so easy to drive away." There are incredible passages in these letters. Also about the Bible, in particular the psalms in the Old Testament. "What a people. Only the people of Israel had such a relationship with God." In the midst of it all he expressed solidarity with the Jews. Magnificent.[2]

When I asked around to find out who had seen my mother last in Mönchengladbach, someone told me I should look up Hetty Gier-Lünenburg, a sister of the painter I mentioned, since she had supposedly seen my mother the night before she was deported. So I went to visit her. One evening, she told me, her brother had come to her and said, "You must go to Frau Jonas. I've heard she's to be sent away to the East tomorrow morning. I can't go because the Gestapo is watching me" (Hans Lünenburg was viewed with great suspicion as an enemy of the Volk). Hetty provided comfort to many Jews and helped them by bringing them food, and she went to my mother and spent the last night with her. All she could do was try to comfort her a bit, and she gave her a Catholic amulet with a saint that would protect her on her journey. "Unfortunately it didn't help," she said, "but that was the best I could do." In her arms I wept for my mother, and she comforted me like a child. I still recall telling her, "That's something I can never forgive the German people for." And she replied, "No, that can't be forgiven."

There would be much to tell about my encounters with friends in Mönchengladbach during those days, but I'll limit myself to one incident. I ran into a young girl from a Catholic family who'd been just starting school when I emigrated. Her name was Brigitte, and she was eighteen now, had graduated and was living with her aunt, who'd been a friend of mine before 1933. I asked the girl what German poetry she'd learned in school, and whether she knew Conrad Ferdinand Meyer. She'd never heard the name. Yet she was living in a house with a large bookcase, and I saw an edition of Meyer's works on a shelf. So I said, "I'd like to read you something by Conrad Ferdinand Meyer." I opened a volume to a poem with the title "The Feet in the Fire." A splendid, long poem about the Huguenot period in France, dealing with religious persecution and torture. On a stormy night a messenger from the king comes to a castle somewhere in southern France and asks to be put up for the night. The lord of the castle gives him a room. The following morning, when the lord is saying good-bye, he asks the messenger, "Do you recognize me?" The other man then realizes who it is. Years earlier, during the religious persecution, he tried to pressure the man's wife into revealing where he was hiding. When she refused, he held her feet in the fire until she died. Now, without realizing it, the messenger has placed himself in the hands of his enemy, but during the night he's seen the truth in a sort of vision — of the feet in the fire. When the lord sends him on his way without doing him any harm, the messenger says, "Lord, you are a clever man and full of wisdom / And know that I am subject to the greatest king. / Farewell. May we never see each other again!" Whereupon the lord of the castle replies, "You spoke the truth! Subject to the greatest king! Today / my service to Him weighed heavily upon me. . . . You murdered fiendishly / my wife! And still you live! . . . Mine is the vengeance, sayeth the Lord." A magnificent, terrible poem! Later I visited Brigitte once in Cambridge — an English soldier in the army of occupation had fallen in love with her and taken her home with him to England. When I called her up and said, "This is Hans. Do you remember me?" she answered, "But of course — you read me the poem 'The Feet in the Fire.'" And she told me she was working as a German teacher, and all her pupils had to read that poem.

Of course I also visited Hofstrasse in Gladbach, where our factory had stood, for I was curious to see what had become of it. I found the whole large site in ruins. After my father's death the company had been Aryanized. Had it still been a working factory after the war, the provisions enacted by the Allies would have let me calculate its value and demand restitution. But there was nothing you could get out of an owner who'd been bombed into bankruptcy. A few years later, by the way, one of my students in Ottawa was a former pilot with the Canadian air force. During a gathering at my house, he asked me, "What part of Germany do you come from, Professor Jonas?" And I said, "You've probably never heard of the place: Mönchengladbach." At that he said, "Mönchengladbach? That was the target of our last bombing run, which I flew on 13 March 1945." Friends in Gladbach had told me about this raid — it had been the worst night in the whole war. So I asked him, "Do you know anything about the damage this raid caused?" And he replied, "Yes, because the day after a raid our intelligence-gathering planes always flew over and took photos to assess how effective our attack had been." So I said, "Let me show you how it looked from the ground." I went to my desk and took out a large envelope, filled with photographs that my lawyer in Gladbach had sent me to make it clear that there was nothing I could recover. The pictures of our former factory showed that all that was left was ruins, including the machine shed and the looms. "Look at this," I said. "This was once my father's factory. And thanks to your thorough work I can't receive any restitution for our property." At that the charming young man looked at me remorsefully and said, "I'm so sorry, Professor Jonas." And I told him, "Don't be sorry. On the contrary, I thank you for what you did. I would have done the same thing if I'd been an airman." That was one of those strange coincidences—a philosophy professor who's emigrated meets a student who, of all people, bombed the professor's hometown.

My dark and gloomy time in Europe lasted quite a while. The demobilization proceeded slowly, and it wasn't until November that I was put on a ship heading for Palestine. Until then I remained in Europe as a soldier. At our base in Venlo my military duties were minimal; for the most part I was furloughed and had a good deal of freedom to move around occupied Germany, but also Belgium and northern France, so long as I found my own transportation. Occasionally I had watch duty, but I had nothing to do with the interrogation of prisoners of war, for example. At the time there were special units in the American, English, and French military government handling what later came to be called denazification. I was spared this work. In those days I had no mental image of anything that might be considered a purification or renewal of Germany. The German people could go to the devil, for all I cared. I felt that the Germans' guilt was so overwhelming that the only appropriate thing for them would have been to do public penance and show general remorse. But I observed that, with the exception of my friends, the majority of Germans you ran into either refused to acknowledge what had happened or repeated ad nauseam that they hadn't been involved. Most of what Germans said was disgustingly obsequious—they wanted to curry favor with those who'd won and now ruled them, so they kept insisting, "He was terrible, that Hitler, that idiot; he led us all into misery. We had no choice but to go along." Not once did I hear anyone confess to having let himself be hoodwinked; it was all protestations of innocence and denial of the facts that were now coming to light: "No, that's simply unbelievable!"

I did quite a bit of traveling around in this humiliated, conquered, beaten Germany. These weren't duty assignments; I asked for leave, which was granted without objection. For local excursions I could use our own motor pool. But I also took longer trips, to Göttingen, Marburg, and Heidelberg. No trains were running, but if you were wearing a British uniform, you could hitch a ride with any of the Allies' troops, so I would ride in a British or American vehicle—whatever was available—from place to place. My destinations and the order in which I sought them out were determined almost exclusively by the availability of transportation. Göttingen was the first place I visited. I'd never been there, and I'd never laid eyes on any-one from my publishing house, the venerable Vandenhoeck & Ruprecht, founded in 1735. All my contact had been by letter with the head of the firm — Wilhelm Ruprecht at the time — and I'd mailed my manuscript and the corrected proofs to him. After the first volume of the gnosticism book appeared, I'd arranged with the publishing house to send the second vol-ume in sections from Jerusalem — it was supposed to carry the subtitle "Philosophical/Mystical Gnosticism," and focus on Neoplatonism and early Christian monastic mysticism, which had evolved in the Egyptian desert and was strongly influenced by gnosticism. I saw the anchorites as heirs to or Christian transformers of the gnostic spirit. The last thinker I was plan-ning to study, and on whom I'd already compiled a lot of notes, was a cer-tain Euadrius Ponticus, one of the masters of this early Christian monastic mysticism, who was unmistakably influenced by Neoplatonism but, with his ecstatic states and his instructions for ascending to the higher spheres of being, could also readily be assigned to a general gnostic context — so long as you no longer limited "gnosticism" to a specific group of early Christian heresies but understood it as designating a spiritual and existential prin-ciple, an existential category for this entire period. It was only by means of stretching the concept that I could include a man like Plotinus, who'd polemicized energetically against the gnostics, and Porphyrios, his chief disciple, in this comprehensive study of gnosticism and the spirit of late antiquity.

So I was supposed to be sending one chapter at a time from Jerusalem, and the publisher intended to keep printing them. When I moved to Pal-estine from England, they'd already begun printing the second volume. In other words, the proofs were piling up. More text had been set, but then things ground to a halt because after the Night of Broken Glass I broke off all contact with the publishing house and didn't send any further sections. Probably they were grateful to me, though they never said so, because con-tinuing the project would surely have got them in trouble. They never wrote to say that the project had been halted. It was clear to me, however, that I couldn't let anything of mine be published in Germany — nor did I want it to be. Yet during the war years I was always aware that part of my intellec-tual work was lying there in Göttingen, work to which I'd devoted years. I'd written the Origenes chapter on Rhodes and had only a handwritten copy. It was a fairly lengthy essay that could stand on its own; I'd dedicated it to Scholem at the time. Soon after the end of the war it appeared in the *Theolo-*

gische Zeitschrift, published in Switzerland and edited by Oscar Cullmann.[3] It had never been sent to Ruprecht. During the war I'd occasionally found myself wondering what had become of the printed pages and those that had only been typeset. After all, the latter amounted to thirty-two pages of expensive manual typesetting, with each page calling for six different typefaces. I wouldn't have been surprised to be told, "It's all gone, all lost." So it was with uneasy thoughts like these that I set out for Göttingen.

I remember well the part of the route that I covered in a Jeep driven by an American soldier. He drove at such breakneck speed that I thought, "Good God, here I've survived five years of war, and now I'm going to die?" But it turned out that he was an excellent driver and knew exactly what he was doing. When I reached Göttingen, I immediately checked in with the local British command, and asked to be assigned to quarters. After that I set out to find Vandenhoeck & Ruprecht. Here I must mention a dream. Since my emigration I'd had dreams that recurred insistently over the years. One of them had to do with Hitler and his behavior. In another dream I came to Göttingen in a British uniform to visit my publisher. But we were still in the middle of the war, and suddenly I said to myself, "For God's sake, this is madness; they'll recognize you right away." I'm not sure how I got to Göttingen in the dream, whether by parachute or some other daredevil means. At any rate, suddenly there I was, as a member of an enemy army, and I knew that as soon as I was recognized as a German Jew, the Nazis would arrest me. But then I told myself, "Oh, there are hordes of uniforms here. No one will notice one more person in a uniform who looks a little different. Maybe no one will realize that I'm wearing a British uniform." And then I roamed the streets, looking for Vandenhoeck & Ruprecht, but in vain. When I told this dream in Jerusalem to Hans Jakob Polotsky, who'd lived in Göttingen, he smiled and said, "Oh, that's easy. It's on Theaterstrasse. Everyone in Göttingen knows where the publishing house is." The fact that I can remember what Polotsky told me shows that the search for my half-finished, half-typeset or possibly lost manuscript preoccupied me so intensely during the war that I dreamed about it. At the same time this dream indicates that I pictured myself returning to Germany as a soldier in an anti-German army—and that's why in my dream I was so careless that I didn't even think to hide my uniform.

So now I came to the real Göttingen, and it wasn't hard at all to find the publishing house. I rang the bell—in battle dress with my insignia on my chest, which gave me the appearance of a highly decorated soldier, even though I hadn't earned the insignia by performing any acts of heroism but simply by being there. I was let in, and without giving my name, said, "I'd like to speak with Herr Wilhelm Ruprecht." When I was told that he'd died two years earlier, I asked to see his successor. A short time passed while I waited in a handsome room furnished with antiques. Then the door opened, and young Helmut Ruprecht — who was about my age — came in, looked at me quizzically, and asked, "What can I do for you?" Not obsequiously, but hesitantly and somewhat uncertainly; in that period it was understood that the head of the firm came immediately if someone in a British uniform asked to see him. At that I said, "Herr Ruprecht, I've traveled a great distance to meet you at last. My name is Hans Jonas." The effect was dramatic. "You're Hans Jonas? We've been waiting for years to see you!" What he told me next is one of the chapters of my life that deserves to be recorded for posterity. "Yes," he said, "your *Gnosticism* is one of our most important books. It wasn't until the war began that we thought it would be prudent to withdraw it from circulation" — he mentioned a year, 1940 or so — "and store the remaining inventory in a secure location." So the books had been moved to caves in the mountains somewhere. "How about the sections of volume two?" I asked. "Also in safe storage." He was referring to the proofs of the parts that had already been typeset. "And how about the parts that had been set but not yet seen by me?" "Yes, that was quite a problem for us. Every year the question would come up at an editorial meeting as to what we should do with those two sections, because we were running out of type. But every time we decided, 'No, all this will be over eventually, and then Dr. Jonas will turn up again, and we'll be able to resume the project.'" A situation like this was unusual — because of the risk and the cost, of course, but above all because it was a truly great act of loyalty.

Admittedly they hadn't been complete heroes either. At a later date longtime residents of Göttingen told me that Vandenhoeck & Ruprecht had also compromised, making concessions to the literature of the day. Without that, they might not have been able to stay in business. But they didn't compromise when it came to Hans Jonas's gnosticism book. They said, "We didn't want to expose the book to danger. And we wanted to keep the book on our list. We didn't believe the Hitler period would last." Their editorial meetings took place during the war, after all, when it was becoming clear that the Thousand-Year Reich wouldn't last for a thousand years. Helmut Ruprecht was a man of honor, a member of the Confessing Church, deeply religious, and his wife came from an even more devout special Protestant commu-

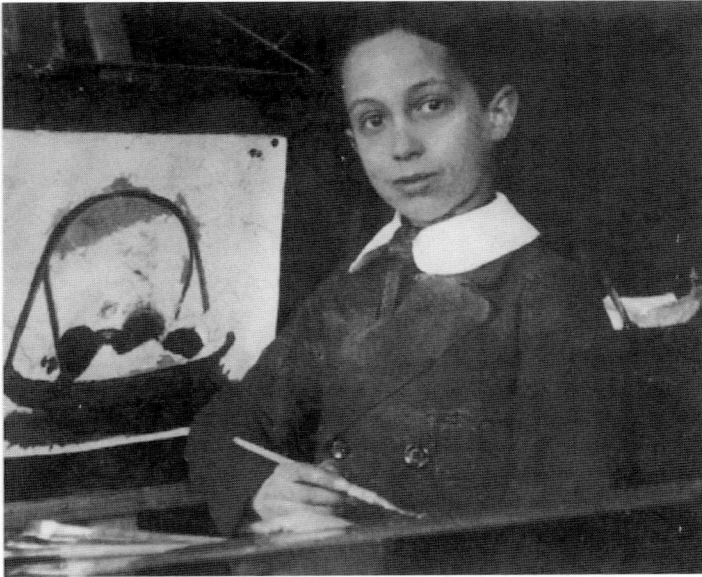

1. Hans Jonas in Mönchengladbach, 1916. (Private collection)

2. *Jonas's mother, Rosa Horowitz, in a drawing by Hans Jonas, 1923. (Private collection)*

3. *Hans Jonas, self-portrait, 1923. (Private collection)*

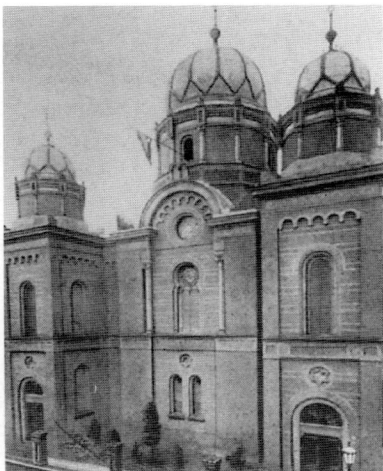

4. *The family house in Mönchengladbach. (Private collection)*

5. *The synagogue in Mönchengladbach, 15–17 Karlstrasse, today Blücherstrasse. During the 1938 pogrom, SA troops burned the structure to the ground. (Gidal Photographic Archives, Steinheim Institute)*

6. *Rabbi Jakob Horowitz, Hans Jonas's maternal grandfather. (Gidal Archives, picture no. 3143, Steinheim Institute)*

7. Hannah Arendt in 1927. (Hannah Arendt Estate)

8. Günther Stern (Anders) and Hannah Arendt around 1929. (Hannah Arendt Estate)

9. *Edmund Husserl. (Gidal Archives, picture no. 675, Steinheim Institute)*
10. *Martin Heidegger in 1933. (J. B. Metzlersche Verlagsbuchhandlung und C. E. Poeschel Verlag GmbH in Stuttgart, Germany, 1986)*

11. *Edmund Husserl and Martin Heidegger in 1921.*
(J. B. Metzlersche Verlagsbuchhandlung und C. E. Poeschel Verlag
GmbH in Stuttgart, Germany, 1986)

12. Jonas Cohn.
(Gidal Archives,
picture no. 4176,
Steinheim Institute)

13. *The German Pro-Palestine Committee in 1928. Front row,
from right: the chairman, Heinrich Count Bernstorff, Prof. Chaim
Weizmann, Carl von Schubert. To the left behind Schubert, Albert
Einstein. Between Schubert and Weizmann the secretary, Katharina
Oheimb. Behind Bernstorff to the left, the banker Oskar Wasser-
mann, and next to him Kurt Blumenfeld, president of the Zionist
Association for Germany. (The Central Zionist Archives)*

14. Hans Jonas in Mönchengladbach, 1933. (Lisl Haas)

15. *Gershom Scholem. (Gidal Archives, picture no. 872, Steinheim Institute)*

16. Richard Lichtheim
with his family.
(Gidal Archives, picture
no. 864, Steinheim
Institute)
17. George Lichtheim.
(Gidal Archives, picture
no. 796, Steinheim
Institute)

18., *The Jewish Brigade, 1944.*
(Private collection)
19. *Hans Jonas as a soldier in the*
Jewish Brigade, 1944.
(Private collection)

20. *Rudolf Bultmann. (Private collection)*

21. *Hans Jonas in Jaffa, 1946. (Private collection)*
22. *Hans Jonas in 1953. (Lisl Haas)*

23. *Hans Jonas in 1953. (Lisl Haas)*
24. *Martin Buber, Jacob Taubes, and Hans Jonas in New York, 1958.*
(Private collection)

25. *Hans Jonas and his family in New York, 1966. (Private collection)*
26. *Hans Jonas with his daughter Ayalah, June 1967. (Private collection)*

27. Hans Jonas at the New School in New York, 1968.
(Peter Moore)

28. Hannah Arendt. (Private collection of Käte and Ernst Fuerst, Ramat Ha-Sharon, Israel)

29. *Ernst Bloch. (Gidal Archives, picture no. 4080, Steinheim Institute)*

30., Hans Jonas in his New Rochelle back yard, 1980.
(Private collection)

31. *Raymond Klibansky, Hans-Georg Gadamer, and Hans Jonas in Heidelberg, 1986. (Archives of Dr. Michael Schwarz, Heidelberg)*
32. *German President Richard von Weizsäcker and Hans Jonas at the conferral of the Peace Prize of the German Publishing Industry. (Private collection)*

33. Lore and Hans Jonas in Frankfurt am Main, 1987.
(Brigitte Seelbach, Königswinter)

34. Hans Jonas and the mayor of Mönchengladbach,
Heinz Feldhege, 1988. (Udo Dewies, Mönchengladbach)

35. *Hans Jonas in 1988. (Private collection)*

nion in Saxony and East Prussia, the Herrnhuter. At one point she told me, "When the synagogues went up in flames, my mother said, 'The Lord will punish us for this. We'll all have to pay.'" At any rate, I was received with open arms and invited to the Ruprechts' house. In those days even wealthy and well-situated people like the Ruprechts, whose house was furnished beautifully with old Biedermeier pieces, were living in pinched circumstances. When Helmut Ruprecht suggested moving ahead quickly with printing my book, I had to inflict great pain on him. I said, "I just came from my hometown of Mönchengladbach and learned there what happened to my mother. Knowing this, and knowing the other things I've heard about the fate of the Jews, I can't publish with a German firm anymore." I still recall the expression of deep sorrow on his face as he said, "That's a real blow to us. We were loyal to you through all those years. Don't we have a right to expect that you'll continue to publish with us?" And I replied, "As the house of Vandenhoeck & Ruprecht — yes. But as a German publishing house — no. I can't publish in a country that murdered my mother."

In the discussions that followed someone from the technical staff was brought in, who asked, "So what do you envision happening with the book?" I said, "I don't know. It will appear somewhere, but not in Germany." To that he responded, "How would it be if a Swiss house with which we have friendly relations took over the book — Franke Brothers in Berne? The printing would have to be continued in our plant, because we started it. But they would accept a collaborative arrangement with us and presumably bring out the book under their imprint." And I said, "That's something I'd be willing to discuss." I left it there for the time being. But I made an additional arrangement with Ruprecht. It turned out that about three hundred copies were left from the original printing. Since I wanted to have these copies distributed from outside Germany, I had the volumes shipped first to a distant relative in Holland who'd survived the Nazi period. Then I negotiated with Brill in Leyden, which agreed to take over sales of the remaining copies. So after some delay, Brill handled the sales, and I received the royalties.[4]

Otherwise, this was the beginning of a personal friendship with the house of Ruprecht. I spent several days with the Ruprechts and their children, and was treated as an honored guest. Then I announced my plan of continuing southward to Marburg. Ruprecht said to me, "Aha, you're going to Marburg to visit Bultmann. I wonder if you could do me a favor. Bultmann is waiting for a book we can't send him." During the war Vandenhoeck & Ruprecht had published Rudolf Bultmann's commentaries on the

Gospel according to John.[5] If I recall correctly, the book he gave me to take to Bultmann was a new edition of the commentaries that Bultmann hadn't received, because there was no civilian mail delivery yet.

So I got to Marburg, where first I had to find Bultmann, because he'd moved in the meantime and was now living on the Schlossberg, on Calvin-Strasse, a street of lovely villas. One morning I rang the bell there, and Frau Bultmann came to the door. I didn't say a word, only looked at her. What she saw was a stranger, a British soldier wearing a beret and a khaki uniform. She stared at me for a second or two, then suddenly recognized me and exclaimed, "Herr Jonas, Herr Jonas, it's you, Herr Jonas!" The words came tumbling out amid a flood of tears; she was talking and crying at the same time. "Oh, it's so wonderful to see you! We've spoken of you so often, hoped so often that you were still alive, that you'd survived this war! It's been so terrible! We've had such dreadful experiences! It was awful. And we didn't want to win, we prayed for defeat." And then she added, "My daughter lost her husband in Russia." All this came out in a jumble, and then she said, "Come in, come in! My husband's so fond of you. He spoke of you often!" It was a highly dramatic scene, in which I didn't have to say a word. She knocked on her husband's door and said, "Rudolf, you have a visitor!"

I entered his study. He was sitting at his desk as always. He'd aged, and looked shrunken from malnutrition. His collar was much too big, his gaunt face was pale, the sleeves of his jacket hung loosely around his arms. But his face seemed peaceful. He immediately got up from his desk and hobbled over to me — he'd been born with a clubfoot — and immediately said, "Herr Jonas, Herr Jonas, welcome!" It obviously gave him great joy to see me. So we stood in the middle of his study and exchanged the first awkward greetings: "So how are you?" "I can see. You must have been a very good soldier — all those decorations." Twelve years had passed since I'd had lunch with him in his old house — I'd gone to say good-bye before emigrating. I'd sat there at table with his three growing daughters, and I recall mentioning something I'd read on the train to Marburg: about the German Association for the Blind's decision to expel its non-Aryan members. I recall, too, how his face suddenly turned as white as a sheet and he said nothing, merely shook his head. I launched into high-flown rhetoric and said, "Just think, Herr Bultmann, here they are, living in the face of eternal night, the experience that most binds human beings to one another, the fate of blindness, and that hasn't stopped them . . . ," and then I saw his face and knew that I didn't have to say anything, that he'd understood what was at issue.

So now I stood there, with the package containing the book Ruprecht had sent under my arm. And then something remarkable happened. He pointed at the package and asked, "May I hope that that's the second volume of the gnosticism book?" At that moment something changed inside me. For the first time since my return to Germany, the terrible bitterness gave way, and a sort of peace filled my heart. The evidence of this man's loving loyalty, which had outlasted the liquidation of an entire world, the most terrible catastrophes, and the destruction of Germany, and had clung to the hope that his student Jonas might yet finish his gnosticism project let me feel for the first time the possibility of reconciliation. What I needed was to recover my belief in humanity, which had been shaken and almost obliterated. What happened in this moment was the restoration of trust in a person of German origin. Since then I've revisited this scene countless times in my imagination: the two of us standing there, he still deeply moved by a completely unexpected reunion, and I for my part transfixed by my revered teacher's pale, gaunt appearance, and his inability for the moment to speak more than the emotion-laden but conventional words of greeting, and then that one sentence about the second volume of the gnosticism book.

Until 1933 we'd had the relationship of a student to his revered teacher and of a teacher to a student for whom he had a very high regard and in whom he not only placed great hope but already saw certain hopes fulfilled. But now the relationship developed into a real friendship. One day he said we could address each other as friends, and from then on, he always began his letters with "Dear Friend." Later he and his wife visited America and stayed at our house. During numerous visits to Germany I went to Marburg and was always a welcome guest at the Bultmanns'. We had splendid conversations. In 1976 I attended the memorial service for Bultmann, and flew back to America with his daughter Antje, who'd emigrated after the war and become a librarian at Syracuse University and later a professor of library science. We spoke of her father and his relationship to me. Turning to look at me, she said, "Oh, he loved you! A visit from Hans Jonas was always a great event in the Bultmann household." When the dean of the Theology Department had asked the family whom they wished to have as the principal speaker at the university's memorial service, they'd promptly replied, "Hans Jonas." Of course one of Bultmann's theological students also had to speak—the distinguished New Testament scholar Erich Dinkler talked about Bultmann's work.[6] My own contribution was titled "Is Faith Still Possible?: Memories of Rudolf Bultmann and Reflections on the

Philosophical Aspects of His Work." I paid tribute to Bultmann the man, but also commented in philosophical terms on his thesis of demythologization and, in a posthumous dialogue, explained how he, as a theologian, had come to embrace this process out of exaggerated respect for the findings of modern science and had credited science with more power to get at the truth than philosophers did. It was a paradoxical situation that a philosopher should set out to rescue a theologian from wholesale capitulation before the findings and methods of modern science, encouraging him not to let himself be too impressed by scientific truth claims when it came to metaphysical matters. This lecture expresses a great deal about Bultmann's meaning for me, but it also shows what I had to say to him in a philosophical vein.[7]

I should add that as early as 1934, when the first part of my gnosticism study appeared, Bultmann came out in favor of my work. The book was published with an introduction by him that was extraordinarily courageous, in which he indicated how much he'd learned about gnosticism from my work.[8] He'd promised this introduction to the publisher before the Nazis came to power. The occasion had been the public response to my first publication, a monograph on Augustine and the Pauline problem of freedom based on a paper I'd written for an Augustine seminar taught by Heidegger.[9] At the time Heidegger had been so impressed that he'd told Bultmann about the paper. Bultmann asked to see the manuscript and suggested to his publisher, Wilhelm Ruprecht, that he publish it in his series Studies on the Religious and Literary Aspects of the Old and New Testament. This famous series had been founded by Julius Wellhausen, and was later edited by Hermann Gunkel and then Bultmann. I'd read books in this series when I was still quite young, never dreaming that someday it would include a publication of my own. In 1907 a treatise by the Protestant theologian Hans Schmidt had appeared, a work of religious history on the Book of Jonah.[10] It was an excellent study that caught my eye in part because it dealt with my biblical namesake, but it also taught me a good deal about religious history. Not long after this Wilhelm Bousset's book *Hauptprobleme der Gnosis* [Essential Questions in Gnosticism] appeared in the same series.[11] And this was the series in which I was to be introduced to the public! But then the following happened. The first review of my Augustine book appeared in the *Theologische Literaturzeitung* [Theological Literary Gazette], and it was devastating. Hugo Koch, a respected Protestant church historian, expressed great indignation at the temerity someone had shown in writing about Augustine in an impenetrable jargon—he meant my Heideggerian language. Here the first battle over Heidegger's use of language was ignited, with me as a proxy. The review ended with this sentence: "For his defiance of the Holy Spirit of the German language the modern Jonas deserves to spend three days and three nights in the belly of a large fish." The reviewer didn't comment at all on the content, merely enumerated linguistic monstrosities like "thrownness," which cause no outrage today but in those days greatly irritated the old defenders of German academic prose.[12]

Before the publication of the Augustine monograph, Bultmann had secured the publisher's commitment to publish my longer work, which at the time existed only in a shorter dissertation version. After Koch's review appeared, Ruprecht wrote to Bultmann that he wanted to take back his promise to bring the gnosticism book out in the same series, since that seemed risky now. Bultmann wrote back to him, "If you do not have confidence in my judgment, I will resign as the series editor." That was in 1930. Because of Bultmann's stature in the theological world it caused a small scandal. "But if this will bolster your confidence or reassure you, I promise you herewith that when the book is finished I will write an introduction." Whereupon Ruprecht responded, "All right, for God's sake, if you insist." So in 1934 Bultmann kept his promise.

In Marburg I paid another visit as well. Bultmann said to me, "Didn't you also study with Julius Ebbinghaus at one time?" In fact I'd enrolled in a lecture course and a seminar given in Freiburg by the Kantian Ebbinghaus. That was after my agricultural interlude. We'd even locked horns. He was a pugnacious orthodox Kantian, who'd found his way back from Hegel to the true font of wisdom, to Kant. I couldn't help having a rather critical attitude toward him, for he had no patience with any opinion that diverged from Kant's, and he was a somewhat overbearing but extraordinarily sharp, clear, and precise interpreter of Kant's theories. "You should go and see him," Bultmann told me. "He's one of the people whose behavior was really magnificent." It so happened that a few days earlier I'd read in a German newspaper an account of a radio address by Julius Ebbinghaus in which he discussed the question of German guilt. And in words that revealed great moral fortitude. I still remember his saying that in the war Germany had sinned against the key principle of Kant's political ethics, formulated in his essay "On Eternal Peace," to the effect that nothing should be done in any war that would render it impossible to achieve peace later. Ebbinghaus argued that Germany had placed itself outside the international community of laws—quite an unpopular position at the time. He maintained that the Allies couldn't be expected to do the Germans the favor of concluding a peace treaty with them. "We've gambled away any right to a peace treaty."[13]

We greeted one another cordially, and I expressed my admiration for the strong stand he'd taken during the Nazi period, for Bultmann had told me that he'd remained uncompromising even at a time when you couldn't speak so freely. Ebbinghaus then said something I'll never forget: "Yes, Jonas, but I want to say one thing: without Kant it wouldn't have been possible for me to survive this period." It was as if a Christian had said, "Without Jesus Christ I wouldn't have been able to do it." At that I suddenly saw clearly what it means to live by one's philosophy. Such steadfastness reduces Heidegger, the far more important and original philosopher, to a nonentity. What the Kantian had grasped, and the existential philosopher hadn't, was that philosophy also imposes the obligation to live and behave in a way that can withstand public scrutiny. Later, on my trips to Marburg, I visited Ebbinghaus many times. He never dropped the role of the Kantian, still trying to teach me things I hadn't learned properly. One time, when I was invited to give a philosophical lecture in Marburg, Ebbinghaus was in the audience, ancient but as sturdy as ever, a small man who stood ramrod-straight, with blazing eyes and blistering speech. He walked Lore and me to the railroad station. From the platform, when we were already in our compartment, he said through the open window, "Jonas, what I wanted to tell you was this: if you'd paid better attention in my Kant seminar, you wouldn't have said some of the things you did in your talk yesterday." It sounded as though he thought I wasn't a hopeless case—if only I'd listen to him. He was a one-track thinker, in a certain sense limited, who never looked back once he'd chosen Kant. But in his own way he was an admirable man.

CHAPTER 9

From Israel to the New World

LAUNCHING AN ACADEMIC CAREER

In November 1945 I returned to Jerusalem, to my wife and circle of friends, and tried to resume the life I'd been leading before the war. It was incredibly hard to find a place to live, since no new houses had been built in Jerusalem in the previous five years. Lore had heard from a Dutch nurse, a Christian, that there was an unoccupied house in the Arab village of Isawiya, located in the Jewish hills above Jerusalem. With the help of an Arabic-speaking Jewish lawyer we negotiated the rent with the *muchtar*, a dignified old man with three wives. "It would be an honor to have a learned man like you in my house," the muchtar said, and at first gave me to understand that he wasn't prepared to demand rent from me. After I'd convinced him that he had to take our money, the old man agreed — and set an exorbitant price, which our lawyer fortunately managed to bring down. But when I insisted that the lease include the landlord's promise to repair the hand pump (which was needed to pump water from the cistern up to a tank on the roof, so we could take showers), he was quite offended. "You have my word," he said. "Why do you need it in writing?" And now suddenly it wasn't just a question of the hand pump but of the cistern itself. We could use it, but his family was also to have access to it. So they brought their donkeys to our cistern, and sometimes a camel as well, in the course of which it turned out that half the villagers belonged to the muchtar's family.

Under the admiring eyes of the villagers we moved with our hundreds of books into the house. I owned a Koran in Arabic, which the muchtar noted with satisfaction on his occasional visits. He also stopped by on the Jewish high holy days. On such occasions I would clap three times in the Arab fashion, whereupon Lore would bring Turkish coffee in little cups and then withdraw modestly. It was a patriarchal world. The third cup signaled the end of the visit. The muchtar's principal wife, who ruled over him and his other two wives with an iron hand, sometimes came to call on Lore. The house was very beautiful, with arched ceilings and double-thick walls, altogether different from the modern concrete structures that had been thrown up in Jerusalem before the war; they were boiling hot in summertime and ice-cold in the winter. Of course we had neither electricity nor running water. From our window we could see the hills of Judea, sometimes even the Dead Sea, which was ninety kilometers away. An olive grove surrounded the house, and during harvest time a night watchman slept in the shadow of our house to keep thieves from stealing the ripe olives. It was considered dangerous, of course, to live so far from any Jewish settlement, because people hadn't forgotten the unrest of 1938–39. A friend promised sarcastically to come to our funeral, but we were young and happy, and got along very well with our neighbors.

The end came suddenly. When the state of Israel was proclaimed in 1948 and war broke out, the muchtar came to warn us. "Our people love and admire you, but I can't stop others from coming over from the other side of the border. I'll sleep on the threshold and defend you with my life. But if I don't succeed, I'll avenge you with my blood, as I would my own son." It was clear he wanted to us to move. So we rented a truck, and almost all the villagers, men as well as women, helped us load the books as fast as possible. We didn't have much time. One of the muchtar's sons offered to ride along on the running board, so we wouldn't be shot at as we drove through the Arab part of Jerusalem. I declined the offer. With heavy heart, we finished loading the truck, said good-bye to our life in Isawiya, and finally reached the famous Mandelbaum Gate, which would separate Jews and Arabs for a long time to come. We found a new place to live in Rechavia, on Alfasi Street.[1]

The year 1948 demanded an existential decision of us. After the war I hadn't managed to get a firm footing in Jerusalem. I did find temporary teaching appointments at the university, but no chair in philosophy was in sight. For quite a while I taught history and philosophy for the British Council, but once the British mandate was dissolved, this option disappeared. An additional factor was that because I'd served five years in the British army and had artillery training, I was drafted into the War of Independence, this time by the Israeli army. The birth of our daughter Ayalah, the intense uncertainty as to when I would ever be able to get back to my intellectual work, the death of Lore's brother, who'd fallen near Jenin in June 1948 as the commander of a Jewish unit,[2] and the fear that the Arabs would never come to terms with the state of Israel—all these factors made me think hard about our situation. I wrote to Leo Strauss, already living in the United States, and asked if he could help me get out of Israel, at least for the time being, so I could pursue my research in peace in Canada or the United

States and move in the direction of an academic career. I soon received an invitation from the Lady Davis Foundation, offering me a year's fellowship of five thousand dollars for teaching and research in Montreal.

In the summer of 1949 I finally got my discharge from the Israeli army. After a short stay in Switzerland, we took a ship from Marseille to Canada with our almost one-year-old daughter, and again found ourselves in a country where I knew no one, on a new continent. This was entirely different from returning to Europe from Israel. We were received with wonderful warmth and cordiality, and found the Canadians to be people who viewed immigrants not as interlopers but as welcome additions who would help populate their vast country. When we disembarked in Quebec, a train was waiting by the dock to take passengers on to Montreal. After we got settled in our compartment, we saw women walking up and down outside the train, calling out, "Are there any mothers with babies?" Through the window they handed in bottles of milk, packages of diapers, and other useful items, which made the long train trip much easier. I still recall how delighted Lore was by such considerateness. When we reached the station in Montreal, Samuel Risk was waiting for us with his wife and eight-year-old daughter. They'd been there for an hour or two. Sam Risk was the secretary of Samuel Bronfman, the chairman of the Association of Friends of the Hebrew University, and in this capacity he'd been delegated to come and pick us up. The Risks took charge of us very sweetly and drove us to the summer cottage that a Jewish teacher had placed at our disposal while he was on vacation.[3]

In Montreal we received a good deal of sympathy for our fate as emigrants. In the Jewish community I also enjoyed a special aura as a resistance fighter recently released from the Israeli army, a man who'd laid his life on the line for the rebirth of Israel in the Holy Land. Right from the start there were people who took a great interest in us. I met Lady Davis, who wanted to meet all the recipients of grants from her foundation—by no means exclusively Jews. We had far less fleeting contact with Samuel Bronfman, one of Canada's richest people. He'd earned his fortune, as his name ("brandy distiller") suggested, by becoming the whiskey king of Canada. Today his company, Seagram, is one of the major whiskey manufacturers on the American continent. During Prohibition, smuggling whiskey into the United States from Canada was extremely lucrative, and Bronfman's company made a killing. By the time I arrived, the company had also acquired some of the oil fields that were just being opened to exploration.

Samuel Bronfman, usually referred to as "Mr. Sam," was quite a likeable fellow. No doubt he'd been a ruthless businessman and had allied himself with organized crime during Prohibition. Though I never heard any details, there were rumors that the Bronfmans had been involved in all kinds of dealings, some of them bloody. But by now, thanks to their wealth, they belonged to the upper crust and were acquiring legitimacy through major philanthropic activity.[4] That's certainly not typically Jewish, but rather part of the American nouveau-riche phenomenon. The example of John D. Rockefeller, who eventually donated so much money that entire universities could live off their endowments, shows that you can't always make that much money and keep your hands clean. Without the generosity of these "robber barons," who sanitized their ill-gotten gains by donating them for charitable or cultural purposes, the Metropolitan Museum, the Metropolitan Opera, and so many other cultural institutions would have been unthinkable. This is part of the socioeconomic reality of America, and we encountered it for the first time in Canada in the person of Samuel Bronfman.

We were invited right away to the Bronfman mansion, where a butler opened the door. To all outward appearances, everything was very elegant. Samuel Bronfman was extraordinarily generous, donating large sums, primarily to Jewish causes. He was immensely active in the Zionist movement, and had played a major role in the development of the Hebrew University of Jerusalem, where several buildings are named after him. At the same time, he was quite uneducated and crude, almost vulgar. We'd been invited to lunch, along with the Risks and a few other friends. After the meal, following the American custom, the men and women separated, the gentlemen going into another room to smoke. No sooner were the men alone than Bronfman said, "Now we're going to tell some dirty jokes, and I want everyone to join in." That was something I'd never experienced—and among Jews, too! These nouveaux riches were no doubt hardworking and clever when it came to business, but their intellects were undeveloped. Their educational ambitions were focused on their children, who were supposed to receive a first-class education. Thus a Bronfman son, Edgar, later the president of the World Jewish Congress, was at Yale, one of America's top universities. He had to pass a particular exam that would determine whether he could continue his studies, and among the subjects he would be tested on was philosophy. In return for the nice welcome Bronfman had arranged for me in Montreal, he expected me to do something for him, and asked me whether I could prepare his son for the philosophy exam, something

I agreed to, of course. Bronfman remunerated me handsomely, and thus Edgar M. Bronfman, who was an eager and intelligent young man, became my private pupil for a while and passed his exam with flying colors. In this way I contributed in a sense to his becoming one of the leading figures in the American Jewish community.[5]

So our life in Canada began in Montreal. It soon turned out that my wife was pregnant; she must have conceived either in Paris or on the crossing from Le Havre. This state of affairs of course made it more urgent for me to find an academic job, something the Lady Davis Foundation couldn't do for me. I had to take the matter in hand myself.[6] But I did receive help from my new Canadian benefactors, among whom was a man named Siegel who owned a large shoe store in Montreal. In Jerusalem his son had enjoyed the hospitality of my friend Ernst Simon for a while, so he felt particularly indebted to recent arrivals from Palestine. He went to a great deal of trouble to find something for us, first inviting me to have lunch at a club—I think it was the B'nai Brith Lodge—with a professor from McGill University. Montreal had another university, the francophone Catholic Université de Montréal, while McGill was essentially the intellectual bulwark of the English-speaking population of Quebec Province. McGill had a special role in the academic world of eastern Canada, where French speakers were in the majority but were on the whole less well educated. Out in the country, on the sprawling plain outside Quebec, McGill had turned a former air-force training camp into a campus. For the large number of somewhat older married students, who'd spent many years in the war and under Canadian law now had a right to government-financed higher education, the barracks had been divided up into small apartments. Other buildings housed laboratories and classrooms. This Dawson College was a temporary institution, intended to be shut down once it had fulfilled its mission of offering the veterans a chance to earn a degree.

The man whom the shoe salesman Siegel invited to lunch was a professor of chemistry and the director of Dawson College. I had a good conversation with him, and he liked me very much. What probably appealed to him most was that I could teach philosophy, so we shook hands then and there, and said, "It's a deal." Apparently he had the power to strike such deals on the spot, and when I got home from this lunch, I could tell Lore where we would be for the winter. We spent the latter part of the summer outside Montreal in a lakeside cottage.

As the year drew to a close and it started to get cold, we moved to the

Dawson campus. That was the beginning of a really lovely time. Everyone welcomed us warmly. Word got around quickly that a little girl from the hot land of Palestine had landed in the middle of the Canadian winter. Young women immediately came to see Lore and said, "Your little girl needs a snowsuit," and they gave her one of those thickly padded garments, which another child had just outgrown. We all received presents to help outfit us for the winter. We were housed in one of the barracks that had been converted to living quarters. Since I was a professor, not a student, we were assigned two apartments with a connecting door. So I had a somewhat privileged status, but living with the married students enabled us to gain insight into the mentality, way of life, habits, and psychology of the Canadians, which were quite different from the Americans', which we came to know later.[7] But above all, the attitude toward life, the political views, and also the form of Christianity were different from Europe's. For instance, except in Roman Catholic Quebec the dominant influence of large religious denominations was absent. The students were Presbyterians or Baptists for the most part, or belonged to other, smaller denominations. Many young families with small children lived on campus, and as soon as word got around that Lore was pregnant, we were offered all sorts of help.

At Dawson College I taught an introduction to philosophy, and even though my English wasn't the best, the students were enthusiastic — I didn't quite know why. But Lore reported to me that one of the women had told her that the students called me "the best teacher on campus." I also got along very well with my colleagues, especially the scientists. I received many invitations to dinner or faculty parties. We felt at home. And we had a once-in-a-lifetime experience: a Canadian winter. You must remember that we hadn't come directly from Central or northern Europe, but had spent the last fifteen years of our lives in a country that doesn't have a real winter. For Lore a cold winter with a frozen pond was a dim memory from childhood. I'd gone through wartime winters in Europe, but the Canadian winter was unlike anything I'd experienced. Snow began to fall, and once there was snow on the ground, it didn't melt. Week after week, month after month snowplows had to clear the streets, roads, and paths, and the snowbanks got higher and higher. The snow crunched underfoot, and the nights were long and bitter cold. Dawson College was located on a plain, so the wind whistled across the campus. At night we often saw the northern lights blazing. That was something I'd only read about and seen pictures of. This was the real thing, because eastern Canada is relatively close to the magnetic North

Pole. It was a glorious sight. We loved this harsh winter. One colleague or another would ask, "So, what do you think of our winter?" and I would say, "It's wonderful!" "Wonderful? You can have my share, then!" They were so surprised to hear that we found it beautiful. Later I came around to their view. The first time it's wonderful, but by the second time you begin to sigh at how long the winter is and how short spring and summer are. And the longer you stay in Canada, the less you enjoy winter, or even begin to dread it.[8]

I recall a winter trip to Montreal. Dawson College was located about fifty or sixty kilometers east of the city, and there was a bus I always took when I needed to go into town. One day I went to Montreal to see Raymond Klibansky, an expert in ancient Greek philosophy whom I knew from Heidelberg; he was teaching at McGill. He was an ambitious young man, a disciple of the poet Stefan George, whom he modeled himself on in the way he wore his hair and in his whole demeanor. An able scholar, he was also a real go-getter, and when I'd met him in Heidelberg he'd already been working on a Latin edition of the writings of Meister Eckhart and Nikolaus von Kues, commissioned by the Heidelberg Academy.[9] After Hitler's seizure of power Klibansky was ousted as editor, of course. He'd emigrated fairly early to Canada, where he'd been offered a chair at McGill.[10] Although we'd never been friends, we were in the same field and had in common the fate of being refugees from Hitler's Germany, so it was perfectly natural for me to look him up and exchange memories of our time in Heidelberg. When I called him, he said, "Why don't you come to the Faculty Club for tea." So on the appointed day I set out on the long trip to Montreal and had tea and a bit of pastry in the Faculty Club with Raymond Klibansky. It was obvious that he wasn't particularly glad to see me; as a tenured professor he apparently felt rather uncomfortable in the presence of a quasi-unemployed colleague. We'd agreed to meet around 4:30, and when a bell rang shortly before 6:00, he said, "You must excuse me. Dinner's going to served here now." With that I was dismissed, and set out for home as the dark winter night descended. That experience is engraved on my memory. I guess I shouldn't have expected that someone who'd already found a seat on the train would welcome other passengers. The remarkable part was that he was a successful man who basically had nothing to fear. Everything had worked out for him, and somehow or other his path had always been smoothed. After his emigration he first got an honorary lecturer's position at London University's King's College and was made a fellow of the Warburg Institute, where he had a leading role in the major project on the influence of Platonism in the Middle Ages.[11] As far as I know, he never found himself facing the abyss, or worrying about his professional future. In spite of that, he was extraordinarily ungenerous when he was approached for help by the less fortunate.

There was one other person who I hoped would help me gain entry into the academic world—for it was clear that my position at Dawson College was only temporary, that the college would close at the end of the year, for financial reasons, and that my promised transfer to McGill was down the drain. This person was a Dominican monk, a Père Faribault. In 1935–36 he'd published a major, fifty-page review essay in a Dominican journal, examining my gnosticism book from the Catholic vantage point. The review was not entirely positive, but conveyed intense interest and respect.[12] It was the most thorough review I'd received, not merely because of its length but also because of the painstaking analysis. At the time, the German periodicals had been silent; it was a tricky situation—if they praised my book, it meant praise for the work of a Jewish author, an émigré, while if they criticized it they could be suspected of joining the chorus of anti-Jewish sentiment. Only *Gnomon*, one of the most reputable review journals, asked the famous scholar Arthur Darby Nock of Harvard to review the book. He wrote an intelligent and critical review, for the most part negative, but respectful, focusing primarily on the historical and philological aspects, since he didn't know what to say about my philosophical approach.[13] Other than that there were only a few brief Dutch and French reviews. So now I wrote to the Dominican monastery in Ottawa that was listed as the journal's publisher, and informed Père Faribault that I was in Canada and would like to meet the man who'd given such close and generous attention to my book. I received no answer. Later, when I'd found a job on my own at Carleton College in Ottawa, I phoned the monastery one day. I was connected to the abbot, who said immediately, "Aha, you're Professor Jonas; I'm very familiar with your name. Our Brother Faribault was studying your book intensely. I said, "Yes, that's why I'm calling. I wrote Père Faribault some time ago, but never received an answer. I hope he hasn't died?" "No," said the abbot with some hesitation, "he hasn't died, but he can't write back to you." It turned out that he'd become mentally ill and was living in a Dominican rest home. By the way, every time I tell this story, someone is sure to say, "I hope it wasn't working on your gnosticism book that drove him mad!"

In a sense Dawson College was a dream. We lived in a cozy little world that protected us from the harsh winter outside, a world where we were all comrades in arms. We had about a thousand students. Even though philosophy wasn't a subject in which they could major, only an elective with which they could fulfill their general-education requirements, I had fairly large classes, with eager students who took down every word I said and discussed the material avidly. Our daughter, Ayalah, spent the year between her first and second birthday there. When we first arrived, she wasn't walking yet, and in the morning, when I went to the communal men's bathroom to shave, she would crawl along the corridor with me, saying, "Shave! Shave!" When I shaved, I always put a dot of shaving cream on her nose, and she enjoyed the whole process immensely. During that winter she learned to walk. And then the time came when our son was about to be born. In early May one of the students drove us to the Catholic hospital in St. Jean, near the college. I sat there with the book I'd brought along, remembering that before Ayalah's birth, for which I'd been present in Israel, the labor had gone on all night and into the early hours of the morning. It was a book of stories by Conrad Ferdinand Meyer, and I started reading one of the novellas, *Jörg Jenatsch*, I think. I was still on the first chapter when the doctor came down the hall and said, "It's a boy." His tone was so casual that I said, "What? Mine?" He said, "That I don't know, but it's a boy."

Lore spent a week in that hospital, under the wonderful care of the Catholic nursing sisters, and the entire thing came to only twenty-five dollars. When I brought Lore and little Jonathan home to Ayalah, who'd been alone with her papa the whole time Lore was in the hospital, I gave her a large doll and said, "Mama's back, and she's brought this for you." But suddenly a baby began to cry in the next room, whereupon Ayalah immediately pricked up her ears, dropped the doll, and rushed next door. She understood right away that the baby was a new member of the family.[14] After a few days we had a proper bris. Since out here in the country there was neither a Jewish community nor a synagogue, I had a mohel come from Montreal, and we arranged a little celebration with Jewish friends.

By the time our son was born, I had found a position at Carleton College for the coming year. From Quebec I'd sent out seventy or eighty letters, to all the universities from the Atlantic to the Pacific coast, offering my services. Usually I was told that there was no position available at the moment, but my interesting application would be kept on file for the future. Only Carleton invited me to come to Ottawa, at the college's expense, for an interview with President Maxwell McOdrum. I presented my credentials to him, including a letter from Martin Buber, a letter from Scholem, several reviews of the gnosticism book, and certification from the Hebrew University that I'd been a lecturer there. I hadn't had a distinguished academic career yet, but the name of Martin Buber made a big impression. When McOdrum saw the letter from him, the decision was as good as made.

The college had been founded only a few years earlier and was still in the building-up phase, with philosophy not yet fully staffed. There was one philosopher there already, however, so only a junior position was available. McOdrum said, "You're actually too good for the position I can offer you. But all my budget will allow is an assistant professorship. And I don't know whether you'll find that acceptable." To that I replied, "Mr. President, I realize that as a recent immigrant I have to expect certain disadvantages and pay the price for entering the academic profession in such an irregular way. So I'm prepared to work for a small salary. But the title of assistant professor would destroy my academic career on this continent once and for all. So I must have a different title." He said, "Yes, but I can't make you an associate professor, because that title carries a salary I can't afford." "Maybe a title can be invented," I suggested. "What do you have in mind?" "Perhaps guest professor or visiting professor — something that doesn't indicate a specific rank." To that he said, "Let me check first whether I can do that legally. Excuse me, please." He was gone for five minutes, during which time he phoned the college's legal counsel for advice. When he came back, he said, "Yes, that's something we can do. Choose your title. Which do you prefer — visiting professor or guest professor?" I thought for a moment and picked visiting professor. And that's how I received my first real academic appointment, which was converted in two or three years to an associate professorship. At last I'd gained entrée — that was in May 1950.[15]

As far as my relationship with the students and faculty was concerned, things went very well for me at Carleton College.[16] I wasn't exactly friends with the other philosophy professor, who was considerably younger and somewhat arrogant, having earned his Ph.D. from Princeton, but our collaboration went smoothly. My courses were mainly on the history of philosophy.[17] But more interesting than the small world of the college were the other people I got to know during this period. My most important encounter was with Marta Wassermann, the widow of the German-Jewish novelist Jakob Wassermann. She'd been his second wife, and following his death she'd studied psychology with C. G. Jung. After years of teaching at McGill University, she'd made use of her psychoanalytic training to establish a thriving practice in Ottawa and had become the leading psychoanalyst there.[18] She soon heard that someone new had arrived with whom she could enrich her social life. She had something like a salon, to which we were invited. She made a point of tracking down all the interesting people in the arts or scholarship in Ottawa and inviting them to her gatherings, which always took place on Sundays. One day a strikingly handsome couple appeared at one of her gatherings: a tall, blond man with an aquiline nose, and a long-legged, slim woman. It turned out that this was Prince Yussupov. And who was he? The son of the man who'd murdered Grigori Yefimovich Rasputin! When a small group of nobles decided in 1916 to carry out the assassination, Prince Felix Yussupov had been chosen to do the deed. His son had emigrated to Canada and become a chemist with the National Research Council.

Another interesting friend was Ludwig von Bertalanffy from Vienna, descended from the Hungarian nobility, who'd also come to Canada as a refugee scholar with the support of the Lady Davis Foundation. One time he described his family history and talked about an aunt who'd lived in a castle and owned a gold chamber pot. Gold chamber pots — the idea that something like that even existed we owe exclusively to Ludwig von Bertalanffy. He was an outstanding biologist, and had found a position at the Université d'Ottawa, run by a Catholic order. But he was a reluctant Catholic who now had to toe the line, because the university monitored closely whether its faculty members went to Mass often enough. So he did his part by going to church assiduously. He and his wife became close friends of ours. He was a highly educated man who took a great interest in philosophy. But above all he played an important role in the development of modern theoretical biology. He'd come up with the theory of open systems, and was capable of expressing these new ideas mathematically.[19] An example of an open system, as opposed to a closed system, is the living organism, because it exists, thanks to metabolism, in a reciprocal relationship with its surroundings. That was something I was thinking about myself, in conjunction with my philosophy of the organic, and he'd approached the phenomenon from the biological and mathematical angle. So we exchanged significant ideas on nature, the essence of biological systems, and living organisms' mode of existence. The fact that he'd also written on Nikolaus von Kues shows how multifaceted his interests were.[20] We had a real intellectual friendship, which meant a great deal to me because I hadn't found any philosopher in Ottawa with whom I could have worthwhile discussions.[21] Having a biologist as a friend was a real stroke of luck because at the time I was working out a biological philosophy.

During this period I undertook my first little exploratory trip to the northeastern United States, including New York, also traveling from there by train to Cincinnati, where a cousin of mine from Mönchengladbach was living.[22] Cincinnati was the home of Hebrew Union College–Jewish Institute of Religion, which later gave me an honorary doctorate. It was a Reform rabbinical seminary with outstanding scholars on the faculty.[23] I visited several people whom I knew from before, and as chance would have it I met Leo Baeck at my cousin's house; Baeck was also visiting, giving a series of lectures. He greeted me warmly, not primarily because of my gnosticism book but because of an old connection to the Horowitz family in Krefeld. He asked me, "Do you know that I was present at the death of your grandfather, my friend Jakob Horowitz?" I said, "No, I had no idea. All I know is the circumstances under which my grandfather died." He said, "I can describe the scene exactly, because I was an eyewitness. Your grandfather had retired from his post as head rabbi in Krefeld a little while earlier and had moved to Düsseldorf to spend his retirement with your uncle Leo, the doctor. And your grandfather, who was a brilliant thinker and magnificent speaker, delivered a lecture at the B'nai Brith Lodge in Düsseldorf. I sat in the front row." In those days Leo Baeck was a rabbi in Düsseldorf; his time in Berlin came later.[24] "I no longer recall the subject of his lecture," he continued, "but finally he said, 'And now, ladies and gentlemen, we come to the end.' At that he collapsed backward. His son leaped onto the podium and caught him. And he died there in his son's arms. That was your grandfather's death." I'd already heard this story from Uncle Leo, but now in Cincinnati I'd met the famous and venerable rabbi Leo Baeck, who'd survived Theresienstadt, and heard the tale again. In Cincinnati I also met Eugen Täubler, a professor of ancient history, whom I knew from Berlin as a Prussian Zionist or Zionist Prussian. He said to me (in his typical fashion), "So, you took part in the war, fought against Hitler, and now you have to go looking for a job. That's unconscionable. One should force a university at machine-gun-point to hire you!"

My trip also took me to Chicago, where I renewed my friendship with Leo Strauss, which had been maintained through letters. I'd seen him last in London, where he'd spent the early part of his exile. In the late thirties he'd found his way to America. He offered an amusing account of how he—an incredibly unworldly and anxious person—had prepared for the

Atlantic crossing, as if it were still the time of the Pilgrims. He bought himself a "sou'wester," and appeared on board the modern steamship, as he told me laughing, dressed in a complete sailor's outfit, to defy the Atlantic storms. He'd found his first academic home at the New School for Social Research in New York, and had in the meantime made his way to Chicago.[25] Here I also learned something about the hierarchy among American universities, most of them private institutions, usually established with large endowments and maintained with generous voluntary donations. The University of Chicago is one of the outstanding institutions in the country. Most of the Ivy League universities, so-called because of their ivy-covered old buildings, are located on the East Coast—for instance, Harvard, Yale, or Princeton, or Brown University in Rhode Island. At the beginning of the twentieth century, the immensely rich Rockefeller had offered a large donation to Brown, but when the university wrote back that it didn't want to accept money that had blood clinging to it, he made the same offer to the University of Chicago, which didn't belong to the Ivy League. There people said, "We know the money's dirty, but we'll soon get it clean," and they accepted the donation, which played a major part in the university's expansion.

When I was reunited with Leo Strauss, our meeting opened up the possibility of a teaching position on the East Coast, in Annapolis on the Atlantic. There a German émigré called Jakob Klein, an admirer and friend of Strauss's, had a position. Together with Strauss he'd fostered a politically conservative philosophy among Jewish intellectuals—Strauss had been an early supporter of Mussolini, before he turned antisemitic.[26] The antirevolutionary Strauss was so conservative that when he read my gnosticism book he instinctively sensed that gnosticism contained a revolutionary element, and wrote to me that despite his personal acquaintance with me he hadn't realized that I was a secret revolutionary. Well, this Jakob Klein, who'd made a name for himself with a superb study of Greek mathematics,[27] had become the dean of a small, innovative college, and Strauss wrote to him on my behalf, with the result that I received an invitation. Although Klein was very interested in me, no job was forthcoming, because the school had already hired two Jewish refugee scholars. The president explained to me, "We can't go on this way; otherwise we'll get the reputation of being a reception camp for Jewish refugees." Perhaps this state of affairs was fortunate, because the college was an institution dedicated entirely to classroom teaching, where I would never have had the freedom to work on my own books.

From Ottawa I reestablished contacts with Europe. In 1952 I went to Brussels for an international philosophy conference. That was my first visit to Europe since my time there as a soldier. At the conference I was approached by Hans Blumenberg, a young man who'd come from Kiel, bringing me a message from my old fellow student Walter Bröcker: "He knows your book on gnosticism and has a very high opinion of it. He wants to ask whether you'd consider an offer from the University of Kiel." That was my first such offer from the country I'd fled or left, from which I'd been banished. I said, "All right, I'll think it over." Later a correspondence with Bröcker developed, which finally ended with a "no" from me. I knew from the beginning that I'd reject the offer, but I took my time, so as to be able to show elsewhere that I'd been offered the professorship.

I didn't stay in Brussels but traveled around as well. I remember going to Bruges with Hans Blumenberg and several other young philosophers from Germany to buy lace. And then I went to Germany, to Munich, to be more precise. I'd learned that my old girlfriend, Gertrud Fischer, was living in Munich, and I'd tracked down her address. Hannah Arendt, whom I saw from time to time when I visited New York from Canada, had told me about a lecture she'd given in Munich. "After the lecture someone came to the Green Room to see me — guess who! Your Gertrud Fischer! But now her last name is Kröker. She came in and burst into tears at seeing me again." I'd also heard from my cousin Lisl Haas, the photographer, who was living in Birmingham, that Gertrud was still alive. I wrote and told her I was coming, so we met at the railroad station. In those days — 1952 — much of Munich was still in ruins, and the station, too, was partly destroyed. The reunion with Gertrud was moving. I explained to her why I hadn't visited in 1945 and hadn't even made an attempt to establish contact. The same thing was true for various other people. I didn't know whether I could expect someone who'd lived in Germany and suffered as a result of the bombing to want to meet someone who was happy to see Germany defeated and approved of the destruction of the German cities. She said, "What nonsense! You could have said that to me, because in spite of everything I was on the side of those who were dropping the bombs, not on the side of those who were hit." I knew, of course, that Gertrud had never sympathized with the Nazis. But I thought that when it came to the smashing of her own country, its cities, its churches, its famous buildings, her solidarity might belong to defeated and destroyed Germany. Gertrud had married in the meantime and had a little daughter. We walked to the English Garden, sat down on a bench by the Chinese Tower, and told each other everything we'd experienced in the intervening years. I don't know how many hours we spent on that bench, talking and talking. So that's how our connection was reestablished. A year or two later Lore came to Germany, because in the meantime her parents had moved back from Israel and her father had resumed his practice as a lawyer. He worked for an organization that was handling restitution payments, and eventually settled in Regensburg in a law practice. When her mother became ill, Lore went to Germany for a month to stay with her. But she'd also made up her mind to look up Gertrud—and that's how Lore and Gertrud met behind my back, the two women who had played and still played the main role in my life. Afterward Gertrud wrote me an enthusiastic letter about meeting Lore. That was the beginning of a long friendship.

During my time in Ottawa I decided once and for all not to return to Jerusalem but to seek my future in the United States. In letters to Scholem I'd repeatedly asked about the prospects of getting a chair at the Hebrew University or becoming Hugo Bergman's successor. In 1951, at Scholem's instigation, I received an official letter from the university, offering me one of two full professorships in philosophy. At the same time, Scholem let me know that he'd recommended me when the position opened up. People had promptly asked him, "Will he really come back?" "At that," Scholem wrote, "I took a strong stance and vouched for your willingness to accept an offer." For he knew me as a stalwart old Zionist. Now came my decision, which I reached only after an intense inner struggle. I'd left Israel in response to an opportunity, a step that had given me complete freedom for the future. But I realized that turning down this offer would close this particular door for good. So I weighed the offer very seriously. "I have two small children now, and they should have a chance to grow up in peace, and not be subjected to mortal danger and deprivation, which will be inevitable in Israel for the foreseeable future; resources are scarce and we'd lead a Spartan existence." So there were economic and political considerations. In addition to thinking of my family, I saw other factors that applied specifically to me: "I've finally found a safe harbor, where, even though I don't have any particular attachments, I have peace and quiet at last, and won't be entangled in public controversies and crises. Here I can simply let things take their course. And they run smoothly without me. In Jerusalem I would constantly have something brought to my attention that I couldn't say no to." Furthermore, I was starting to publish in English. In Jerusalem I would again have to face the nightmare of Hebrew, in which I'd never become very fluent. I'd been reduced to stuttering awkwardly, and would have needed a long time to develop a prose style that was appropriate to what I was trying to say and was even halfway respectable. I thought, "For God's sake, I'm forty-nine now, and just starting my academic career. Should I really embark on a major move again? It's too much. Life is too short. When you're faced with absolute necessity, you have no choice, but that isn't the case this time." And finally, I was horrified at the thought that someday I would have to see my son marching off to one of the wars we would have to wage in Israel — and that after I'd seen my brother-in-law killed in one of these struggles. I wanted to live in a peaceful world now. So it was a mixture of sensible and morally correct but also self-centered considerations. I thought, "Not again, not another new beginning."

So I turned down the offer — in a clumsy, undiplomatic letter, for which Lore always reproached me. The clumsiness consisted in my saying the truth, explaining why I couldn't accept.[28] The response was an outraged letter from the secretary to the rector of the university. And Scholem, who'd advocated for me, was completely beside himself and never forgave me for saying no. But Martin Buber, who was more magnanimous than the others in such matters, told me, "I really liked your letter. The others who turn down an offer find all sorts of noble reasons why, to their immense regret, they can't accept the position. And you simply told the truth, which made perfect sense. You also had every right to do so." It's perfectly clear, of course, why the people in Jerusalem responded so indignantly — they saw my action as an act of betrayal by an old Zionist.[29] The Hebrew University subsequently took ample revenge. Imagine this: in 1977 an international conference was to take place in Jerusalem to mark the three-hundredth anniversary of Baruch Spinoza's death. I'd worked and published on Spinoza, and was thus one of the few contemporary philosophers who really took Spinoza seriously and had done substantial research on him.[30] Furthermore, I proposed a paper on a topic no one else had thought of — there would have been nothing else like it on the program — namely, the psychophysical problem as seen by Spinoza and later by Niels Bohr.[31] An interesting idea, in any case. But Nathan Rotenstreich wrote back that unfortunately there was no more room in the program; all the slots had already been assigned, but of course they would be very glad to have me attend the conference — as a member of the audience. The conference was still several months off, and they could easily have rearranged the program to fit me in.

So apparently I didn't belong at a conference put on by the Hebrew University; after all, I'd betrayed it by turning down the position. Contributors who'd never had any dealings with the university, who'd never really lived in Palestine, were treated entirely differently. My later colleague Aron Gurwitsch, for example, had spent only three months in Jerusalem in the 1930s, trying to find a position at the Hebrew University, and had been told with regret, like everyone else, "Sorry — not possible." He'd continued on his journey and finally landed in America. The only real interest he'd shown in the Zionist cause or the Hebrew University was the attempt to find a position there, as a refugee. Later, when a Festschrift was being put together for Hugo Bergman, Aron Gurwitsch was invited to contribute, while I, who was in regular correspondence with Bergman, exchanged articles with him, and knew he was very interested in my work, received no such invitation. When I subsequently visited Bergman, I had to apologize for not being represented in the Festschrift and explain that it hadn't been my choice. He liked me and appreciated my scholarship, having read everything I'd written. In response to one article I sent him, which he thought especially well of, he said, "What a pity it didn't appear in Hebrew." Anyway, that was the university's revenge. I would never be allowed to participate in anything connected with the Hebrew University. It went so far that I was also not invited to contribute to the Festschrift for Scholem, despite the fact that Scholem had quoted me time and again, and my work on gnosticism played a certain role in his own work. The next time I saw Scholem, either in America or Israel, I forget which, I said to him, "Herr Scholem, I'm so sorry that I'm not in your Festschrift. I wasn't invited. I would have been eager to express my admiration for you." To that he responded, "Herr Jonas, my dear Jonas, you shouldn't be surprised, not after you left us in the lurch!" "Hold on, Scholem," I answered. "Tell me this: Would a contribution from me in honor of you have pleased you or not?" At that he came down off his high horse and said, "Of course it would have pleased me."

In spite of everything, it was possible to remain in touch with Scholem. He would scold me now and then, but he was just as invested in the relationship as I was. Occasionally he came to America and would meet with me and visit me at home. Each time he shook his finger at me and said, "Jonas, in Jerusalem they haven't forgiven you for that; they'll never forgive you. And you know what you did to me?" Apparently that was particularly important to him. "I had egg on my face. I said, 'Jonas will come, no doubt about it.' And then you didn't come." And he added, "To this day the humanities faculty hasn't recovered from your rejection. We never found anyone as good as you, anyone who could teach ancient philosophy for us as competently. That's what you did to us." To which I replied, "All right, Scholem, let's get back to what we were talking about." That's how he expressed his anger — together with a great compliment. When I told Ernst Simon about this, he told me, "You see, that's the honest truth. Scholem really thinks very highly of you. And that's one reason he has such a hard time forgiving you for not coming. His anger is really the result of great respect." So even though he never forgave me, Scholem didn't sever relations with me in the radical fashion in which he broke with Hannah Arendt over the Eichmann controversy. Now and then he would also make it plain that he liked me, despite having reason to be angry with me. He still seethed at my letting him down, as he felt compelled to let me know from time to time. And I would say, "All right." This conflicted relationship had nothing to do, by the way, with our possibly having been rivals; his self-esteem was far too robust for that. I don't know whether he regarded anyone as a rival — after all, he was so incredibly convinced of his own importance that self-doubt was utterly foreign to him. And in what respect could I have been his rival? In Judaic scholarship? Obviously there was no question of that. That I understood more of philosophy than he did he would have conceded without hesitation. After all, he didn't have a high enough opinion of philosophy to find my superior knowledge oppressive. Just one example: in 1935 the eight-hundredth birthday of Maimonides was celebrated in Jerusalem, and Julius Guttmann, whom I already knew from Berlin and the Hochschule für die Wissenschaft des Judentums, delivered the keynote address in the Hebrew University's amphitheater on Mount Scopus — so out of doors. And I still recall how dismissively Scholem spoke of the entire occasion and of Maimonides: "His is an alienated and diluted Judaism, bled dry by rationalism and abstraction." The cabbalah, with its myths, as Scholem interpreted them, was flesh and blood, while Maimonides's Aristotelianism was a watered-down form of Judaism on about the same level as the Judaica studies practiced by Abraham Geiger and Leo Baeck. For him that was not the real Judaism.[32]

For many years the rest of us tried to guess whether Scholem himself was a believer, and no one ever found out, not even his closest friends. That also goes for our Pilegesch circle, for George Lichtheim and me. What did he believe, how much did he want to believe, but without being able to? He never said anything you could pin down, so this remains one of the unsolved Scholem puzzles. But he was convinced that if the Jewish religion had anything interesting, powerful, vital, relevant, exciting, and creative to offer, it was to be found in the realm of the Kabbalah, not in Maimonides & Co. He was certainly not devout, but you couldn't be an atheist and teach at the Hebrew University. I recall his asking me after the war, when the matter of my being appointed to a chair came up, whether I believed in God — an inappropriate question, somehow, for one scholar to ask another. He also expressed the opinion that my research on gnosticism was too Christian in spirit; I should make every effort to find another topic. His question was foolish, one of his many faux pas. Scholem had a great talent for faux pas. He could say and do the most impossible things. And if you called him on something, he would either deny it — "Oh, I never said that" — or he would claim, "That was supposed to be a joke." I skirted around the question somehow, and remember it only because I found it so unsuitable, but don't recall my response, which was probably pretty lame.

At any rate, despite my "betrayal," Scholem continued to harbor a suppressed affection for me, as the following incident shows. During one of his visits to America, he told me a story about Jacob Taubes. Scholem felt a deep hatred for Taubes, or at any rate had roundly condemned him — and not without reason. He saw Taubes as a con man and an intellectual fraud.[33] He described the following situation: "Imagine what that man Taubes did in Jerusalem. In my seminar he heard me present a new interpretation of a text, and not a week later he gave a public lecture in Jerusalem in which he offered my interpretation as his discovery! Imagine that!" I said, "Scholem, that goes to show that you can't be mad at him, that he's not a fraud on purpose. To present your interpretation in Jerusalem, under your very nose, to the same people who heard you lay out your idea — that proves that Taubes convinces himself after he's just heard something that he came up with it himself. I'd see this story as excusing him, not damning him." Scholem found my explanation persuasive, and said — and that's why I'm telling this — "Yes, you've always been the knight who comes to the defense of the accused." He'd reproached me in the past, too, in an affectionately critical manner, for my chivalrous nature: "Well, Jonas, you're a real Don Quixote." This situation, and the way he reacted to it, indicated to me that he still liked me and saw something praiseworthy in me.

I'd first encountered this Jacob Taubes in 1949. He'd heard that, in conjunction with the annual meeting in Boston of the American Philosophical Association's eastern division, I intended to visit Karl Löwith in New

York. He wrote to say that my work meant a great deal to him. He said he'd written his doctoral dissertation on occidental eschatology, and it had been decisively influenced by my work on gnosticism and had in the meantime been published.[34] He would be very grateful if we could meet in New York. Before the meeting, I asked Karl Löwith, "Do you happen to know a Jacob Taubes?" "Of course I know him," he replied. "Well, could you tell me something about him? He's sent me a letter. I've never heard of him, but he refers to a book he's written and asks to meet me. Do you know the book?" "Oh, yes," he said, "I know the book." "Well, is it any good?" At that he said, laughing, "Oh, it's a very good book. And that's no accident — half of it's by you, and the other half's by me." Taubes never finished another book, by the way, but his career must be one of the real miracles in the academic world. The greatest, most expensive institutions were taken in by him; he held a professorship at Columbia and later became a full professor at the Free University in Berlin — all on the strength of a dissertation that had appeared in 1947 and was indeed very good. I actually think he was rather gifted and could have accomplished quite a bit if he'd kept to the straight and narrow. But apparently that was too much trouble — or too boring — for him.

There's a delightful story about how Taubes was tripped up at Harvard, where he was trying to land a position, by Arthur D. Nock and the German historian and political scientist Carl J. Friedrich, the son of a professor at Marburg. Friedrich told me this story. Taubes showed up at Harvard, acting immensely self-important, a real know-it-all. No matter what topic came up during a soirée or an intellectual gathering, he always had something to contribute, and it was always original. Some people who'd become suspicious began to be annoyed, and said to themselves, "Let's show him up." So at one of these gatherings, the conversation came around to the psychological theory of Bertram of Hildesheim, a medieval scholastic, whose thinking constituted an interesting hybrid of the Thomistic and Scotistic schools. After the first exchange of views, during which Taubes had listened without commenting, as if he were thoroughly acquainted with the subject, he spoke brilliantly about Bertram of Hildesheim's psychology and astonished those present with his profound and comprehensive knowledge — until he was informed that no such person existed; he'd been invented for the purposes of this discussion. That put an end to Taubes's hopes of a career at Harvard. But time and again he managed to land on his feet, like a cat.

I must add that to a large extent I have Jacob Taubes to thank for the fact that during my time at Carleton College I was encouraged to write an

English version of my gnosticism book. He got the Beacon Press in Boston, owned by the Unitarian Church, to commission me to write a book on gnosticism. Later he said at one point, "Jonas, I know many people have grounds for resenting me. Toward you, however, I really have a clear conscience. I think I have nothing to regret or be ashamed of as far as you're concerned." I agreed, and responded, "Taubes, I have no problem with you." The other person who pushed for an English version of my theories on gnosticism was Philip Rief, Susan Sontag's first husband, an intelligent man who'd thought about psychoanalysis in philosophical terms and written a good book on Freud.[35] He was a fine intellectual, although his wife of course became far more famous. At the time he was an editor at Beacon Press, and Taubes had brought the project to his attention. A person who played an important part in the writing of the book, which appeared in 1958,[36] was Jay Macpherson, with whom I worked on the English text. She became a lifelong friend. I'd noticed her in my lecture course on philosophy, a young girl with black hair pulled back tightly in a bun. She wore a sort of monklike robe, but down below, where you could see her legs, she had on socks in two different colors and unmatched shoes. It was obvious that she paid very little attention to her appearance, but she listened intently, and it soon turned out that she was an extraordinary person. She was a very gifted poet and published a small volume of poetry, followed a few years later by another.[37] She received a national award for poetry. Jay had had a difficult childhood, and in many respects was emotionally traumatized. But in our household she felt especially comfortable, and became very attached to my wife and me. In her I found a master of the English language, who furthermore had an intellectual affinity for gnosticism. Her gift wasn't philosophical, but this mythical realm suited her. Later she discovered an inspiring teacher in an important Canadian literary theoretician, Northrop Frye, the author of an important book on William Blake.[38] She wrote her dissertation under him and then became a professor of English literature at the University of Toronto.

CHAPTER 10

Friendships and Encounters in New York

In 1955 I finally accepted an offer from New York's New School for Social Research. I recall that when I informed President McOdrum of my decision he said, "I can't compete with those American institutions. I'd like to keep you here, but I know I can't offer you as much as the New School." In Ottawa my salary had increased from $2,500 to $5,500. Now I would be receiving $8,000, but it turned out that this amount was worth less than $5,500 in Ottawa. How did I come to be offered the position? The New School had hired me several times to teach in its summer school. I soon realized that this gave them a chance to look me over. They were planning to hire someone, and had heard about me from two sources—from Leo Strauss, who'd taught at the New School but in the meantime had gone to Chicago, and from Karl Löwith, who was leaving for Heidelberg and was slated to be replaced. When I taught there, it was clear to me that the faculty was much more interesting than at my nice Carleton College, and that the students were far more demanding than the industrious and pleasant Canadians.[1] After my two trial appointments, there was a strong Jonas faction at the school. Alfred Schütz, however, who saw himself as the representative of phenomenology,[2] favored filling the professorship vacated by Karl Löwith, which was not yet securely funded, with Aron Gurwitsch, his friend and phenomenological soul brother. Gurwitsch was teaching at the time at Brandeis University, was of Russian Jewish descent, and had studied in Freiburg under Husserl. Later he'd gone to Paris and, at a time when the interest in phenomenology was beginning to take hold, had collaborated with Maurice Merleau-Ponty, among others.[3] As I mentioned earlier, he came to Jerusalem, but when he saw that there was nothing available at the university, he returned to Paris, then made his way to America, where he joined Hannah Arendt's circle of friends. Hannah was tremendously loyal to those she'd known in exile in Paris, those who'd suffered, hoped, and feared with her. So even though philosophically she had little in common with Aron Gurwitsch, who, with his Russian phenomenology and the orthodoxy that accompanied it, was a narrow-minded Husserlian, she had warm personal feelings for him. But it was not until after Schütz's death that Gurwitsch came to the New School, for the Philosophy Department's full professorship was offered to me first.[4] Later we became good colleagues.[5] Some time after that, when we had an opportunity to create a position jointly with the Department of Political Science, and Hannah Arendt's name came up, Gurwitsch was opposed, while I spoke in favor of her appointment. Hannah didn't have a permanent academic position anywhere, because she really wanted to remain a freelance writer. Eventually she accepted a part-time position, which required only half of her time and energy, and allowed her to spend several months with the Committee on Social Thought in Chicago, living in New York the rest of the year.[6]

This Committee on Social Thought, an interdisciplinary program that worked in an unconventional manner, also engaged me from time to time as a guest or part-time professor, and later offered me a full-time position. That was the only time I was strongly tempted to leave the New School. A position at the University of Chicago would have been advantageous for my academic reputation, and I would probably have had even better students there. But by then I was already sixty, and approaching the mandatory retirement age of sixty-five, which Chicago could extend to sixty-eight at the most, by special dispensation. Since I'd entered academic life so late and had had my children when I was already older — in 1955 I'd become a father for the third time at fifty-two — I couldn't afford to retire at sixty-eight. In the negotiations with the University of Chicago, it was thus the question of retirement that tipped the balance. My good friend Adolph Lowe, one of the pillars of the graduate faculty at the New School and ten years my senior, was determined to do everything possible to keep me in New York. He persuaded the administration to make me a special offer. He was retiring just then and had a special professorship, the Alvin Johnson Chair, which wasn't subject to the usual faculty regulations. He suggested that I be made his successor and given the benefits that couldn't be conferred on a regular faculty member. I was promised that I could extend my professorship as long as I wanted, unless a committee of three determined that intellectually I was no longer able to perform my duties. Chicago couldn't match this guarantee, so the decision was made. In the end I didn't retire until 1976, when I was seventy-three, having spent a total of twenty-one years, from January 1955 to the fall of 1976, at the New School for Social Research.[7]

The move to New York meant not only leaving a small provincial city for a metropolis, and a tremendously interesting and turbulent institution, but also a new home for my family. A combination of coincidences resulted in our settling in New Rochelle. In the summer of 1952, when I was going to teach in the summer school, we drove by car from Ottawa to Larchmont in Westchester County, where Karl Löwith had placed his house at our disposal for the summer. From there you could drive or take the train in to Manhattan. Löwith had asked friends to look after us a bit, and in this way we made the acquaintance of two mathematicians, originally from Germany, who in the end were responsible for our deciding to settle in New Rochelle after I took the job at the New School, and also formed the center of our future circle of friends. The first couple we met were Kurt Friedrichs and his wife, Nelly. He'd come from Göttingen, at one time the mecca for mathematicians. In the first four decades of the twentieth century David Hilbert was the mathematical giant there, and he gathered a group of younger mathematicians around him. The director of the Mathematics Department and Hilbert's right-hand man was Richard Courant, of Jewish descent, though he would have preferred to deny it. Courant discovered Friedrichs, who at the time was teaching at a *Gymnasium*, and brought him to Göttingen. Friedrichs did so well that at twenty-eight he became a professor of mathematics at the Braunschweig Technical University. In February 1933 he met Nelly Grün at a university ball, a strikingly beautiful Jewish woman, who'd grown up in Braunschweig but had been born in Lyon. Friedrichs kept asking her to dance with him, and when she finally returned to her table, she said to her friends, "That student just didn't want to stop dancing," whereupon her friends said, "Student? Don't you know who that is? He's the youngest professor here at the university." That evening sealed the fate of these two young people. When Friedrichs asked Nelly to marry him, such a marriage was already considered an act of subversion and "racial misconduct." To the great credit of his Christian family, it received Nelly with open arms and even supported Friedrichs when for her sake he gave up his position as full professor at a German university. As a French citizen, Nelly was able to emigrate without interference. She went to New York, and Friedrichs followed soon after. He found a position in the Math Department at New York University, which Richard Courant had built up. Courant wanted all the mathematicians he hired to move to New Rochelle so he could have company. That was why a considerable number of distinguished Jewish émigré and non-Jewish mathematicians lived in that town.

The circle included Lippman Beers, for example, who came from Riga, had earned his Ph.D. in Prague, spoke fluent Russian, and had a passion for Russian literature. He was an outstanding mathematician and later became president of the American Mathematical Association. At the time he was doing everything he could to rescue scholars from the Eastern Bloc and bring them to America. He made many trips to the Soviet Union to fetch persecuted mathematicians, who, as it turned out, were almost always Jews. He himself was an old leftist. I still remember the time I mentioned that my hero in this century was Winston Churchill, and Beers remarked, "I'm surprised that an intelligent person like you, Hans, can admire someone who's so conservative." As he saw it, a good person had to be a leftist, especially if he was an intellectual. The Jewish religion meant nothing to him; he'd originally belonged to the socialist Bund, which was anti-Zionist.[8] I asked him once, "I know you're an atheist, but doesn't being Jewish mean anything to you?" His reply: "It means everything!" That was a deeply significant moment. His connection to Jewishness was something for which he probably couldn't formulate a theory, simply a fact that rose up from the depths of his being, in defiance of reason. It was ironic that his daughter accompanied him to Jerusalem for a conference and fell in love with an American Jewish mathematician who was highly observant. After returning from Jerusalem, Beers commented, "The God of our fathers has taken revenge on me and given me a son-in-law who's strictly Orthodox."

A couple who became close friends in New Rochelle were Wilhelm and Trude Magnus, whom we met at the Friedrichses' and liked immediately. They hesitated at first to invite us over, because they thought we might have reservations about them, as they were Christians from Germany. Wilhelm Magnus came from a long line of professors. His mother had had close friendships with Jews. In the midthirties he'd been invited to Princeton, where he'd inquired as to his chances of staying in America, because he was firmly opposed to the Nazis. He was told, "Prof. Magnus, you can go back—after all, you're Aryan. You're in no danger. We have to focus on those who must get out." That made sense to him, so he returned to Germany and accepted a professorship in mathematics in Frankfurt, where he'd done his graduate studies and met Max Wertheimer,[9] the cofounder of Gestalt psychology, and others who later emigrated and also ended up at the New School. During the war he had to perform work essential to the war effort at Telefunken, but was spared serving in the military because he'd had TB. All through the war he and his wife said to themselves, "If we survive this, we're going to leave Germany." Shortly after the war Richard Courant brought him to his department, and he ended up in New Rochelle, too.[10] When the question of where we should live came up, it was our warm friendship with the Magnuses above all that persuaded us to buy a house in New Rochelle. From that time on, our entire circle of friends was dominated by mathematicians, which did me immense good, since they all had a strong affinity for the natural sciences. My intense desire to inform myself on current developments in science couldn't have been satisfied better than by my long discussions with Wilhelm Magnus or Kurt Friedrichs, who also had an old affection for philosophy that he'd never had a chance to indulge. He was delighted to have a philosopher turn up and join the circle. With Wilhelm Magnus I even developed a friendship such as I hadn't experienced since my relationships with Günther Stern and Dolf Sternberger in Germany.

In contrast to New Rochelle, in Manhattan we had contact mostly with humanists and social scientists. Among them, in addition to Aron Gurwitsch and his wife, was the old war-horse of the Graduate Faculty for Political and Social Science, Adolph Lowe, who took me under his wing. In America he'd had to transform himself from Löwe to Lowe, the decision made for him by an immigration official who said, "Löwe? I'm going to put that down as Lowe." I'd met him and his wife through Karl Mannheim at the Pension Rosenblüth in London. Before that I'd had essentially no contact with economists other than those who were members of my Zionist organization. But from then on he took a lively interest in me, and always felt responsible for me, seeming never to realize that I was a grown man. "That young Jonas has to be set on the right path — he has all sorts of crazy notions," is what he probably thought. He was always upset that I smoked, insisting I was killing myself. He must have also disapproved of my volunteering for military service; in his opinion I'd had better things to do. The same was true of marrying and having children. So in New York, too, he was also always ready to offer advice and assistance.[11]

During our later years in New York, a friend and conversational partner who turned up from time to time in Hannah Arendt's circle was Paul Tillich. By then he'd become very famous in America as well as in Europe — a tall, handsome goy of impressive spirituality. On New Year's Eve, Hannah always gave a large party for her friends, at which he continued to appear even when he was no longer teaching at Union Theological Seminary but had moved to Chicago and was traveling a great deal around the world and in America — which continued until his death in 1965.

But of course my most important friendship from the New York years was that with Hannah Arendt, with whom I was now able to reconnect. I'd visited her during the war in Paris while I was in London. At the time she was still married to Günther Stern. He'd taken the pseudonym of Günther Anders, because the name Stern immediately identified him as the son of the famous psychologist William Stern.[12] When someone suggested that he adopt a different name, he decided to call himself Anders, which simply means "different" in German. The pseudonym then became his legal name. He and Hannah had married in Heidelberg, but had spent the last years before Hitler's seizure of power in Berlin. They had an intense and amicable collaboration, though Hannah assumed a rather subservient position, helping him with his work while she toiled away behind the scenes at her important study of Rahel Varnhagen.[13] Günther thought he'd found a wonderful assistant, never noticing that intellectually she was outstripping him, in fact leaving him far behind. This shift came to light in Paris, where Hannah was soon a very respected figure among the émigrés. She was working in those days for Jewish organizations that were helping Jews emigrate. For several years she was active with the Youth Aliyah (aliyat ha-noar), chaired by Henrietta Szold.[14] Günther's sister, Eva Michaelis-Stern, moved to London and directed the Youth Aliyah from there, while Hannah was busy with what might be called the Paris subheadquarters. Günther remained somewhat aloof from the organization, and found himself consigned to the role of prince consort, which was almost unbearable to a vain and ambitious man like him. Furthermore, Heinrich Blücher turned up in Paris, a German refugee who'd participated in the Spartacus uprising and been part of the intellectual wing of Berlin's leftist-Marxist movement. He was a very gifted man, self-taught, who'd shaped himself into a highly interesting intellectual.[15] Later Hannah spent several weeks with me in Jerusalem, in conjunction with her Zionist activities. After the great French debacle occurred, I learned that she'd reached America safely with Günther Stern. During the war years we didn't correspond at all. But, in 1949, as soon as I'd arrived in Canada, I went to New York between Christmas and New Year's for a reunion with Hannah and my friend Günther. By then they'd divorced, to Günther's great sorrow. By the way—he was very fond of Hannah. This became apparent when Hannah died. The letters I received from him at that time could have been written by a husband mourning his wife. He was inconsolable. Despite having said hateful, hostile things about her in the meantime, he experienced her death as a terrible blow, the final loss of the woman he'd loved the most in his life.

When I saw Günther in 1949, the old friendship was rekindled immediately. I detected, however, an element that I'd never seen in him earlier

—a streak of bitterness. Everything had supposedly conspired against him. America had treated him badly, and he was alone in every respect. He'd found another partner, but when I visited him in a New York hotel, she wasn't with him. She was probably still in California, from where he'd returned only recently. He'd attempted at first to find a foothold in the academic world, lecturing for a while at the New School, giving docent tours in the Metropolitan Museum, and publishing one or two papers, which I found excellent.[16] But he hadn't succeeded in landing a teaching position anywhere, perhaps because he was intellectually difficult and obstinate. Finally he'd ended up as a factory worker in California. His knowledge of American production techniques was chiefly formed by this experience in industry. He never got past this image of America, which was colored with resentment at the alienated position of the worker in what he saw as a soulless, semi-automated production system, like that depicted in Charlie Chaplin's film *Modern Times*. He never recognized that modern production methods were the same in all Western societies. For him these methods were inextricably bound up with America and his wretched experience during the war.[17] His second wife, who came from Vienna, later persuaded him to settle in Austria. He refused to go back to West Germany, even though he was offered many positions at universities. But Ulbricht's Germany didn't attract him either, so he chose Vienna, where he later separated from his wife.

On that same visit to New York I also saw Hannah again. By now she'd married Heinrich Blücher, who at first glance seemed to be merely a hanger-on. Later, when we moved to New Rochelle, Lore and I also became friends with him—Lore somewhat more than I, because Blücher showered her with attention, I somewhat less, probably out of a certain jealousy. Compared with Günther Anders, he struck me as being not quite top-of-the-line, but over the years I came to understand that he meant a great deal to Hannah; this was a real love match. Hannah spoke to me once about her relationship to Blücher, expressing it this way: "In my whole life I've actually loved only two men—Martin Heidegger and Heinrich Blücher." The breakup with Heidegger had been an outward break; it came about when she decided to go for her Ph.D. and felt she had to end the relationship for moral reasons. With his approval, she went to Heidelberg to write her dissertation under Karl Jaspers; she couldn't very well have her lover as her doctoral supervisor. But her love for him never waned. During the early Hitler years, when she witnessed his behavior, she certainly became inwardly alienated from him—but we never discussed this. All I know is that she forgave him relatively soon after the war.[18] Heidegger came to see her when she was giving a speech in Freiburg early in the postwar period. She was among the first émigrés to visit Germany[19] and received a great deal of attention. In the journal *Wandlung*, founded by Dolf Sternberger, Viktor von Weizsäcker, and Karl Jaspers, she published the first preliminary studies for her later work on the origins of totalitarianism.[20] After her speech in Freiburg, there was a knock on her hotel-room door, and there stood Heidegger, saying, "I've come to turn myself in." But both of them, as she told me freely, were so overwhelmed by their feelings that I doubt she really made him turn himself in. Her good Heinrich had no choice but to accept the situation, for she didn't conceal it from him, the more so since he himself took ample advantage of the modern notion of an open marriage. He could be sure of her love, but from then on the newly resumed relationship with Heidegger was part of her life.

Hannah basically didn't approve of Blücher's libertine ways, for she was a faithful soul—Heidegger being the only exception. Otherwise she never had an affair, though countless men tried to make headway with her. She was greatly admired, and occasionally shared with me humorous accounts of things that had happened. One day, when she'd spoken at the Union Theological Seminary, she drove one of the faculty members home. "Suddenly he threw himself at me and began hugging and kissing me. So I said to him, 'Listen, young man, pull yourself together!'" She'd handled the situation calmly, putting him in his place. When I said, "Come on, don't you think that was a bit much?" she replied, "Well, he had to find some way to express his enthusiasm." When I suggested that there were more acceptable ways to express enthusiasm, she said nothing for a moment, then looked at me coyly, and said, "That's the *only* way!" That was Hannah. She disliked feminism, by the way, and told me one time, "I'm completely against it. I have no desire to give up my privileges"—by which she meant the privileges of a lady who has gentlemen eager to serve her. In one respect she was a feminist, however: she was convinced that women are not only stronger and more vital than men but also more perceptive about human affairs and the world, while blindness, wrongheadedness, or obstinacy are male weaknesses. She had a great fondness for men, but it was always tinged with a certain forbearance: "You have to go easy on them. That's just how they are." In my case she'd developed an understanding for my idiosyncrasies long ago, and sometimes teased me about them. But always very lovingly.

The hub of our social relationships in Manhattan was the circle around Hannah Arendt, to which I was always invited, often with Lore. Hannah and I were very fond of each other. But she was also delighted with Lore and gave me the somewhat dubious honor of assuring me several times, "You were so lucky. Man, were you ever lucky!" Implying that I'd had more luck than I deserved and or could have expected. Long ago she'd sized up, with a tolerance that was partly amused, partly concerned, the women with whom I became infatuated. The woman I'd finally married put her fears to rest. She and her husband liked Lore immensely, and a close friendship resulted. But my wife and Heinrich Blücher both kept themselves somewhat in the background, knowing that Hannah and I liked to be alone together from time to time. Often she would invite me for a cup of tea, and we would talk and talk, just as in the old days.

But then a major crisis occurred. The occasion was her *Eichmann in Jerusalem*, which grew out of a series of articles in the *New Yorker*.[21] In 1961 Hannah was sent as a correspondent to Jerusalem, to report on the trial of Adolf Eichmann. Her reports weren't cabled from Jerusalem and published as daily dispatches, but rather appeared only after her return, in weekly installments that had been polished stylistically. In Jerusalem she'd formed her own view not only of Eichmann as a person and a perpetrator but above all of the entire system by which the Jews were exterminated—as a system that in her view was certainly planned by the Nazis but tolerated to some extent by the Jews or made possible by their forced but sometimes also willing collaboration. When she returned to the States, she said, "I think what I have to report will create quite an uproar in Jewish circles."[22] That was clear to her. When she made that statement, I had no idea what was coming, but I was not to be in the dark for long. From the initial article on, I was shocked—first at the tone she'd adopted, second at the explicitly anti-Zionist tenor, and third at Hannah's ignorance when it came to things Jewish. I was familiar with the latter weakness, for she'd never claimed to be an authority on Jewish matters. In fact, her knowledge of Judaism was minimal. Her awareness of Jewish history didn't go farther back than Moses Mendelssohn. For her, the history of the Jews—of modern, German, assimilated, and emancipated Jews—basically began toward the end of the eighteenth century. Everything before that was surrounded by a general fog, lost in the darkness of the past and the Old Testament, which she didn't know and probably hadn't even read, unlike the New Testament, which she'd studied with Bultmann. Now she expressed views that put me in shock.

First there were Hannah's comments on Zionism. I have to mention here that she'd made a brief guest appearance in Zionism back when Hitler came to power. She recognized then that the only way one could still advocate for the Jewish cause was to take the Zionist position, for everything else — the program of Jewish assimilation, emancipation, merging with the host people, and so on — had ended in catastrophe. In contrast to Günther Stern, who identified himself as a Communist, she saw Zionism as the only effective response to the Nazi situation. Yet she didn't immediately give up her connection to the left in Germany, which had come about originally through her husband. On the contrary: for a short time she harbored Communists on the run in her apartment in Berlin — which greatly alarmed her husband. She was much braver than he. But for her the important factor wasn't that they were Communists but that they were victims of persecution; she felt an obligation to help them, which in this case meant putting them up for the night. Her own political commitment was directed toward Zionism, however. That had little to do with me, who'd never tried to convert her to Zionism, since it was clear to me that she wasn't interested. The real influence on her was Kurt Blumenfeld, the ideological leader of German Zionism.[23] He was a witty and intelligent man who came from her part of Germany, though not from Königsberg itself but rather from Insterburg; so he was also an East Prussian Jew. He'd known her family, including her late father, and he met her through me when he came to Heidelberg to give a lecture. He was one of the many men who fell in love with Hannah Arendt. It was almost to be taken for granted that men of high intelligence and sensibility would be enchanted by Hannah — she was used to that. Often they were older men, which was true of Kurt Blumenfeld. He wasn't the sort of man, however, to give her a pass when it came to Zionism; on the contrary, he worked hard to win her over. But it took Hitler to make her an advocate of Zionism.[24]

I assume it was Blumenfeld who brought her into the new network of Zionist activities. Eventually she ended up in the Youth Aliyah, after she'd taken on duties with the Zionist Union for Germany, which had increasingly become the key organization for all German-Jewish concerns. That was the period in which Hannah called herself a "Zionist." It didn't last long. When she visited me in Jerusalem — it was in 1936, I think — she declared, "I'm a Zionist." But after the end of the war, the first piece of hers that I read was an essay in an American Jewish journal titled "Zionism Reconsidered," in which she was already dissociating herself from the goals of

Zionism.[25] In Palestine, during the years between the end of the war and the United Nations' decision to partition the territory, which was followed by the founding of the state of Israel, we were shocked at the turn in her thinking about things Jewish. It was a rejection of Zionism, for which she gave odd reasons that were appalling to us, the friends who admired her, including Scholem but also a young woman who'd worked with her in the Youth Aliyah. All we could do was shake our heads. But when I saw Hannah again, I didn't bring up the subject.[26]

Zionism had simply been an episode in her life. It was all the more impossible for me to discuss this matter with her because I'd left the Jewish state myself and thus couldn't very well act as a spokesman for Zionism. Not until her articles began to appear in the *New Yorker* did all this begin to be significant in our relationship. I said, "You can't talk about these things this way" — by which I meant her knowledge of Judaism, which was revealing itself once more as extremely skimpy and in part simply wrong, but also the cutting, sarcastic tone in which she spoke of the role played by the Jews and pre-Hitler Zionism. In the very first article, which discussed German Zionism's response at the beginning of the Hitler period, she managed to distort the title of Robert Weltsch's famous article, "Wear It with Pride, the Yellow Spot,"[27] into "Wear It with Pride, the Yellow Star," and to insinuate that Weltsch had given the Nazis the idea for the Jewish star. She didn't even know, or had conveniently forgotten, that the yellow badge had been a medieval invention. To her, Weltsch's article, which had been intended to strengthen the persecuted German Jews' self-confidence, suggested something like agreement with the Nazis on the question of nationalism — as if Zionism and National Socialism had had something in common. When I read that, I immediately phoned her and told her I had to talk to her about the article. I prepared for the discussion by sending her a long letter, in which I quoted passages from her piece and pointed out some of the most glaring errors. But now I discovered that you couldn't talk to Hannah once she'd made up her mind. No argument, no persuasion, no correction of factual mistakes could shake her basic conception or even get her to entertain other possibilities. She was opinionated to a degree that was fatal in this situation. I begged her not to publish further articles in the series, or at least to alter the style and rethink certain facts about Zionism and Jewish history, to inform herself better. I recall saying to her, "Your *am-ha'arazut* [ignorance of things Jewish], which your friends have known about for a long time, is playing dangerous tricks on you." She had the temerity to assert that the theory of eternal antisemitism was a Zionist invention — going no farther back than the end of the nineteenth century.[28] She wasn't even familiar with the Pesach Haggadah, where it says, "In every generation men rise against us to destroy us." She wasn't aware that this understanding had formed an unbroken line in Jewish historical consciousness from the time of the pharaoh. Instead she tried to convince herself and others that the notion of antisemitism's being a natural component of Jewish existence was a Zionist invention and obsession. In short, I was shocked at her lack of knowledge, but above all at the way she made us Jews, and especially the Zionists, partially to blame for the Shoah, instead of portraying our forced participation in our own extermination as tragic and terrible. Unlike Primo Levi, who'd been there himself, Hannah set herself up as a judge of others trapped in this unspeakable situation; she was incredibly sure of herself, and without explicitly saying so, implied that if she'd been there, she would have handled things in an entirely different way. It was less and less possible for me to forgive her, especially when she put forth her thesis of the "banality of evil," as if Eichmann had basically been an innocent fellow who didn't know what he was doing, but simply followed orders. Having been completely taken in by the way he portrayed himself, she said not a word about his fanatical devotion to the Nazi ideology. Yet it was documented, for instance, that Eichmann had continued with the extermination of the Jews in Hungary long after his superiors had called a halt. He wanted to finish the job. He said, "Even if we lose the war, I want to see one thing accomplished: the extermination of the Jews."[29] Hannah presented a terribly distorted picture — of both the Jewish and the Nazi positions.

The moment came when I had to ask mutual friends to inform her that regrettably I had to break off our relationship, because the basis on which we could communicate, the foundation of our friendship, had been destroyed by her Eichmann book. An additional factor was that she refused to listen when others admonished her. Scholem had also written to her, a wonderful letter, to which she responded publicly in a contemptuous tone — she accused him of being a paid spokesman for the Jewish establishment, which had allegedly ordered him to reprimand her in public. Scholem had met Hannah through me when she came to Palestine with a children's transport organized by the Youth Aliyah, and they'd immediately hit it off, even if they never became close friends. But now Scholem also broke with her completely, and even later he could never forgive her for the Eichmann book.[30] But Hannah was obsessed. Anyone who spoke out against her was either stupid or in the pay of the enemy. Suddenly the entire foundation of our trust for one another collapsed, everything that had made it possible for us to be tolerant of each other's views. So often we'd said or thought, "All right, that's your opinion, and I have a different one, but both of us have good reasons for thinking the way we do; we've simply come to different conclusions." That was an attitude I couldn't have anymore, for the way she was behaving didn't deserve respect. I heard that Hannah had confided to someone, "Even Hans Jonas doesn't want to have anything to do with me." Now we were living twenty-five kilometers apart, she in New York City, I in New Rochelle. I came into Manhattan three or four times a week, we had friends and acquaintances in common, but we didn't see each other, didn't exchange a word, a letter, a greeting. It was clear that this was by my choice, not hers.

How long this situation lasted, I don't remember exactly, but I think it was almost two years. Finally Lore put her foot down and said, "Hans, what you're doing is ridiculous. You can't abandon a friendship like the one you've had with Hannah, not even over an extreme disagreement. And it's just a book, after all. You can't cut her out of your life this way. You should get in touch with her again." And that's what I did. I don't remember how— I assume I just phoned her, and Hannah said, "Of course, come by, just stop by." And we got together again, but it was clear to me that I had to give up any thought of talking through our conflict. I'd learned that Hannah never backed down and never recanted. So we had a silent agreement never to bring up the subject. And thus our friendship was soon back to what it had been—though with this gulf, which we avoided speaking of. For the most part all was forgotten, but something in my picture of her had changed. I'd first met her when she was a shy young girl. In the meantime she'd become a tremendously self-confident celebrity who could adopt a very authoritarian tone and above all wasn't willing to let anyone tell her anything. In her personal life she was the same touching, good-hearted friend she'd always been.

My picture of Hannah Arendt includes, along with her loyalty as a friend and her completely unpretentious eagerness to be of help, certain other features that I learned about only later. As I said in my eulogy, she had a genius for friendship.[31] An example from my own experience makes that beautifully clear. A year or two after her death, Lore and I arranged a meeting in Switzerland with her cousin, Ernst Fürst from Königsberg, whom I'd got to know in Marburg. He'd become a lawyer, was living in Tel Aviv, and had been a banker for a time. Since he was the only person in Hannah's family with legal expertise, Hannah had discussed her will with him on numerous occasions, and had changed it from time to time. When we saw each other, Fürst said, "Were you aware that she had you in her will?" I said, "No." "Oh, yes, for quite a long time. She told me she wanted to do something for Hans Jonas. He was married, and had three children, and she was familiar with his circumstances, his salary, especially his inadequate retirement pension, and knew he had to get three children through college. He needed help." So she'd set aside quite a large legacy for me in her will, and I'd had no inkling. Then one day, when she was visiting her cousin in Tel Aviv, she'd said, "We can change that now. It's not necessary anymore. He's been promised a German pension, and I know exactly how much, because I'm getting the same." This pension resulted from a new interpretation by the German constitutional court of the restitution legislation as it applied to academics. It was known to the few who benefited from it as the "Lex Arendt." For Hannah had fought for seven years, with the help of an attorney, to make sure that those of us who'd been about to complete our *Habilitation* when the Nazis came to power would be treated like those who'd already completed it. The change would entitle us to restitution as fired civil servants. She was in this category, along with me and a handful of others. So she knew exactly what the provisions were. But that shows an important side of her nature — her solicitude for others, for those people she cared for. But she'd breathed not a word about any of this.

A second story reveals her humanity even more strikingly. Hannah had a housekeeper, a black woman from New York called Sally. Sally had a son whom she sometimes brought to work with her. Hannah soon discovered that he was a very bright little boy. And she said, "He shouldn't be in public school." And as long as she was alive, she made sure — quite apart from the salary she paid Sally — that the boy went to a private school. At the memorial service, the one who cried most was her Sally. Hannah was an unusual person. But along with her splendid qualities, she had a few weaknesses that were hard to take. They weren't obvious until she became a public figure. The hardest thing for me to forgive was that she doubted the motives of those who contradicted her. She refused to recognize that they might have honest convictions, which in some cases might actually be correct.

PART 2

Philosophy & History

CHAPTER 11

Taking Leave of Heidegger

After the war my work in philosophy was marked initially by my renunciation of Heidegger's existentialism in favor of my philosophy of life. One impetus for this step was certainly my shock at Heidegger's behavior during the Nazi period, including his inaugural address when he was installed as rector of the University of Freiburg on 27 May 1933,[1] and at his shabby and disgraceful treatment of Husserl.[2] During my time in London I'd heard that he'd become a Nazi, and when I asked friends in disbelief how that was possible, someone in the know told me pointedly that I'd merely failed to see that Heidegger was moving in that direction. He asked me, "Why in the world did you go and study with him? I still can't understand that. And why are you so surprised? The signs were all there in Heidegger's thinking. Many of his traits, for instance his blood-and-soil romanticism and the like, predisposed him to greet the 'national awakening' with enthusiasm." Whether my friends were speaking with the benefit of hindsight or whether what they were saying was really true, I can't judge. Given Heidegger's influence on me,[3] his behavior was a cruel and bitter disappointment, not only in him as a person but also in the power of philosophy to arm people against such folly. In the originality of his thought, Heidegger remains a powerful figure in intellectual history, a pathbreaker who opened up new territory. That the most profound thinker of our time fell in with the goose-stepping brown-shirted battalions struck me as a catastrophic failure on the part of philosophy, as a disgraceful moment in world history, as the bankrupting of philosophical thought. At the time I cherished the notion that philosophy could preserve us from such things, could fortify our minds. I was even convinced that dealing with the most lofty and important matters ennobled human beings and improved their souls. And now I realized that philosophy had failed to do this, hadn't protected this mind from the error of paying tribute to Hitler, and apparently, if my friends were right, had even predisposed him to do so. That couldn't be. The behavior of all the fellow travelers, the turncoats, the quislings could be blamed on stupidity, blindness, weakness, cowardice, but that the most important, original philosophical thinker of my era fell into line was an unbelievable blow to me — personally and professionally.

For this reason I made no attempt to get in touch with Heidegger after the war, and I also broke with his philosophy. When I visited Marburg in 1945, I had a brief conversation with Rudolf Bultmann about him. All he said was that since 1933 he'd had no contact with Heidegger. At first this subject hardly came up in our discussions. But it did come up later, in the following context: in 1959–60, when I was spending a sabbatical with my family in Munich but was doing a lot of traveling, lecturing at German universities, I also went to Heidelberg. My lecture there was cosponsored by both the Philosophy and Theology departments, which often happened, because my work on gnosticism had made a name for me among theologians, while as a philosopher I'd by now published on topics that had nothing to do with gnosticism.[4] In the meantime I'd returned to secular philosophy. Among those who welcomed me to Heidelberg was the Protestant theologian Günther Bornkamm, an old colleague from Marburg, who'd also taken courses with Heidegger, but had studied primarily with Bultmann and had written his dissertation under him. We knew each other quite well. In the meantime he'd been offered the chair in New Testament theology at the University of Heidelberg. After my lecture, he came up to me and, after greeting me cordially, said, "I have an important message for you. Two weeks ago Martin Heidegger delivered a lecture here in Heidelberg. I mentioned to him that we were expecting you, and he asked me to give you his best regards. He stressed that I mustn't forget, that it was very important to him. So I promised to pass along his greetings."

That took my breath away, because it came as a complete surprise. After the war I hadn't had the slightest desire to resume contact with Heidegger. Unlike Hannah, I hadn't forgiven him. And now I had to decide on the spur of the moment how to react! I recall that I hesitated for half a minute. Many things went through my head. It was clear to me that this was no superficial gesture along the lines of "Oh, if you see him, say hello to him for me." Heidegger never did anything spontaneously and without premeditation, so he clearly had a reason for sending me greetings. He wanted me to know that he would welcome being in contact with me again. The question was whether I should take this olive branch or not. After considerable reflection, I responded simply, "Thank you." It expressed gratitude to Bornkamm for giving me the message, but also implied "No." But that wasn't the end of the matter. It left me no peace, but kept going around and around in my head. I even began to wonder whether I'd done the right thing. The decision I reached wasn't easy, and much seemed to speak against it; after all, I couldn't deny that Heidegger had been a very significant figure in my life.

So on a later visit to Marburg I posed the question to Bultmann. I described the scene with Bornkamm and said, "Dear friend, what do you think: did I do the right thing? I'd like to have your advice, because I'm feeling unsure of myself." Bultmann replied, "Let me answer with an anecdote. In 1948 or '49, at any rate several years after the war, I went to Zurich. I'd been invited to give several lectures. It was the first trip I'd taken outside the country since the war, and I stayed in a hotel. One afternoon I received a call from the reception desk, telling me, 'There's a Herr Professor Heidegger down here in the lobby asking whether he may come up and see you.'" It turned out that Heidegger was in Zurich at the same time for a lecture and had heard that Bultmann was there. So Bultmann said, "Please send the gentleman up." "That was the first time," Bultmann continued, "that we'd seen each other in fifteen years. We hadn't exchanged a word since 1933, not even in letters. So he came upstairs, and we talked. And after a while I said to him, 'Martin, it's time for you to make a public statement—you can't put it off any longer. That's what we expect of you, and that's what you owe us and yourself. You have to take public responsibility for the positions you took publicly in 1933, and retract them honestly.' And Heidegger promised to do so. My dear Hans, ten years have passed since then, and he hasn't done it. And as long as he hasn't, your reaction is the only right one. That's my response." He also wanted to indicate that my position as a Jew was different from his, and that in my place he would also have refused to reestablish contact. Heidegger hadn't specifically wronged Bultmann, whereas his general assent to the German national awakening, as well as his mistreatment of Husserl and various other things, had contributed to making the Jews pariahs. It was easier for Bultmann to resume relations with him. Later there was a gathering of "old Marburgers": once a year the academics from the twenties came together in Marburg—theologians and philosophers who'd experienced the Heidegger-Bultmann period. Heidegger regularly showed up, as did quite a number of my former fellow students, who in the meantime were well-placed German academics, and Bultmann obviously attended as well, which resulted in their meeting again. It wasn't the old friendship, to be sure, but at least they had a relationship. But Bultmann affirmed that the situation was different for me; I had a right to demand that Heidegger recant before I agreed to see him again.

I followed his advice for many years. Not until Heidegger's eightieth birthday was approaching did I say to myself, "He's not only the most important thinker of our century but also the teacher from whom you learned more than from any other and who helped shape you as a philosopher — an undeniable fact of your existence. Before he dies, it would be good to see him once more." So when I was visiting Germany and Switzerland, I wrote from Berne to him in Freiburg. Soon I received a reply from Zurich, where he happened to be at the time. My letter had begun with the words, "Dear Herr Heidegger, a letter from me can hardly expect a warm reception from you." This formulation alluded to a major critical attack I'd mounted against Heidegger at Drew University in New Jersey. The occasion was a three-day international conference on hermeneutics, especially the impact of Heidegger's recent work on the language of Protestant theology. Heidegger had at first agreed to come, but had then withdrawn, and I'd been invited in his place to give the keynote address — under the mistaken assumption that as an old student of Heidegger and Bultmann I was the ideal person to open the symposium. I accepted the assignment. This was one of the few times when I was less than scrupulously honest, for I did nothing to dispel the impression that my introduction would be friendly and supportive of Heidegger. Perhaps I was thinking, "This is my chance to settle accounts." So I delivered a lecture with the title "Heidegger and Theology."[5] My address caused an uproar. I received standing ovations, and the next day the *New York Times* published a long front-page article, reporting that a single lecture had completely turned the conference around, such that from now on the focus was not so much on Heidegger as on Jonas. The next day I had to give an interview to the *Times*'s religion reporter, which appeared on the first page of the cultural section. The battle lines were drawn — with a big headline. It was a sensation, and a disaster for Heidegger. The Heidegger disciples who'd come from Europe, especially from Germany and Switzerland, were bitterly offended, while the American theologians applauded.

One of the main spokesmen for the German theologians was Heinrich Ott, Karl Barth's successor in the Theology Department at Basel.[6] The question that had been posed was simply this: Does Heidegger's language — not the language of *Being and Time*, of which Bultmann had made extensive use in his interpretive works, but the oracular language of Heidegger in his old age — provide an adequate means of expression for theology? The assumption underlying the symposium had been that it did. The German-speaking theologians, who were at home with philosophy, argued that philosophical thinking offered them an opportunity to articulate their Christian theology not in the archaic language of the New Testament and the Bible but in the language of the latest, most chic philosophy. What Hegel had made possible in his day, Heidegger would make possible today. I laced into this assumption right at the outset, presenting the opposing thesis, namely that Heidegger's philosophy, together with the language it had spawned, was in its essence profoundly pagan, and that these Christian theologians didn't know what they were getting themselves into. I also stressed how paradoxical it was that a Jew, a non-Christian philosopher, should take it upon himself to warn the theologians against entering into a marriage or a bond that could only be pernicious to the cause of Christianity. I illustrated my point with ideas and expressions taken from Heidegger's recent works, which I juxtaposed with the biblical message. "Is theology," I asked my audience, "perhaps lured by [the familiar sounds] onto alien ground made all the more dangerous by the mysterious masking, the inspirational tone, which makes its paganism so much more difficult to discern than that of other straightforward, identifiably secular philosophies?"[7] "My theological friends, my Christian friends," I exclaimed, "don't you see what you are dealing with? Don't you sense, if not see, the profoundly pagan character of Heidegger's thought? . . . That theology can admit this foe — no mean foe, and one from whom it could learn so much about the gulf that separates secular thinking and faith — into its inner sanctum, amazes me. Or, to express myself reverently, it passes my understanding."[8] I also indicated, when speaking of Heidegger's "Call of Being," how ambiguous this call can be: "Heidegger's own answer is, to the shame of philosophy, on record and, I hope, not forgotten."[9] And last but not least I confronted Heidegger's notion of man as the "shepherd of being" with the Bible's simple demand, and the failure of mankind in our time to meet that demand: "Man: the shepherd of being — not, mind you, beings! Apart from the blasphemous ring which the use of this hallowed title must have to Christian and Jewish ears, it is hard to hear man hailed as the shepherd of being when he has just so dismally failed to be his brother's keeper. The latter he is meant to be in the Bible."[10] Rhetorically it was one of my most effective talks, but also one of the most carefully argued.

In the audience at Drew was a Jesuit theologian named William J. Richardson, who had just finished a magnum opus on Heidegger and had reached the opposite conclusion from mine, namely that Heidegger and Christianity were eminently compatible. A famous and massive tome.[11] A little more than a month after the conference, the annual Suarez Lecture was given at Fordham University, where Richardson taught. In connection with the publication of his book, he'd scheduled a lecture on Heidegger in this series, intended, to put it somewhat ironically, to present the Christian appropriateness of Heidegger's late philosophy, his accommodation with the Christian faith. After my lecture he'd sat down and reworked his lecture. I wasn't invited, but I heard about the event and arrived a little late for the Suarez Lecture because I hadn't been able to find a place to park. As I entered the hall with Lore, the first word I heard was "Jonas." Richardson was just explaining what he'd originally intended to say, and then he went on, "But Jonas changed all that." He summarized what had happened recently at Drew, and then he offered his response to my theses. The lecture appeared later in a philosophy journal under the title "Heidegger and God—and Professor Jonas."[12] Never again have I appeared in such distinguished company! He charged that I'd completely misunderstood Heidegger, and that Heidegger, properly understood, was definitely of significance for contemporary theological language. Despite this disagreement, we maintained friendly relations. Having spotted me in the audience, he invited me after the lecture to join him in a small room where we had a glass of wine together. And he asked rather anxiously whether I'd been very angry with him. I said, "Not at all. It was very interesting."

My lecture had even greater resonance in Germany than in America, however. Word of what I'd said spread like wildfire, and German universities wrote to ask whether I'd be willing to come over and give the lecture in German. Soon a plan for a university lecture tour was put together for me. I accepted the invitation, wrote a German version, and set out. Among other places, I went to Frankfurt and Heidelberg, while I of course avoided Freiburg, not wanting to deliver the lecture right under Heidegger's nose. I recall that Theodor Adorno was enthusiastic, while Gadamer seemed agitated but didn't participate in the discussion and told me later, "I didn't want to risk our friendship. That's why I didn't say anything. But in private I have to tell you that your criticism of Heidegger misses the mark." Gadamer wouldn't listen to any challenge to Heidegger. In Tübingen my lecture made possible my first, and unfortunately also my last, meeting with Ernst Bloch, who was seated in the auditorium. He was very much taken with what I had to say, and was glad to hear me say it. The next day he invited me to see him, and I spent an afternoon with him, drinking an excellent wine and having a wonderful conversation. He was an elderly man, very intelligent and with an excellent sense of humor.

All in all, my lecture garnered much applause wherever I went, some of it inspired by gloating. At long last people could give expression to resentment of Heidegger. Now it was permissible and acceptable to oppose him. Heidegger heard about my lecture, of course, because it was reported on in the press. In the fall of that year Richardson returned to America from a visit to Heidegger at his summer house in Todtnauberg—Richardson was welcome there because of his book. He reported to me that Heidegger had complained, "My former student Jonas was here in the spring or summer, going from university to university and attacking me." But his real complaint was this: "And no one got up to defend me." That was an exaggeration, of course, because here and there someone did get up and speak for the Heideggerian position. My lecture tour later resulted in an entire collection of essays on the topic, under the title of my talk, "Heidegger and Theology."[13]

In 1969 a personal encounter with Heidegger came about after all. I allowed it to take place because I wanted to achieve a reconciliation, which is basically what happened. I wrote to Bultmann at the time, "I would like to inform you that I have finally reconciled with Martin Heidegger, now that he is approaching his eightieth birthday, and had a nice conversation with him a few days ago in Zurich."[14] Actually our meeting consisted for the most part of a brief exchange of memories from our time in Marburg, while the matters that were of decisive significance to me weren't mentioned. If I'd hoped that anything would be said about the events after 1933, about the fate of the Jews in Germany, about my mother's death, I was bitterly disappointed again. With this meeting I put to rest my inner struggle over my relationship to Heidegger, but any clarification on his part, let alone a word of regret, was not to be. What had come between us for good would remain shrouded in silence.

CHAPTER 12

On the Value and Dignity of Life

PHILOSOPHY OF THE ORGANIC AND

ETHICS OF RESPONSIBILITY

My first publications in the Anglo-Saxon world—with the exception of the gnosticism book and the appended essay "Gnosticism and Modern Nihilism," in which I called attention to the close relationship between gnosticism in antiquity and the existentialist understanding of the world and of being[1]—dealt with subjects entirely different from those I'd written about in German. The switch to English, for which I'd prepared myself by reading the *London Times* and English philosophical literature, including the writings of David Hume and John Stewart Mill, didn't cause me anything like the problems I'd faced when trying to master Hebrew in Palestine. The tradition of English academic prose proved helpful; it places a far greater value on simplicity and clarity than is the case in German scholarly writing, where a frightfully complex literary style is often mistaken for evidence of profundity. In my writing I now made a much greater effort to express my ideas clearly and succinctly than in my German works, in which I'd felt free to express myself in the jargon of Heidegger or Kant. As for the content, I continued the exploration of the natural sciences that I'd begun during the war. To be specific: I was interested in what science could teach us about the real world, in particular about the nature of being. In Jerusalem I'd already given a series of lectures, sponsored by the British Council, on the relationship between philosophy and science, and had returned from the war with a plan on which I wasn't really able to make much headway during the few tumultuous years before I left Israel. The first article I wrote in English in Canada, where I had peace and quiet, bore the title "Is God a Mathematician?" In it I delved into classical Creation myths, as well as the Judeo-Christian concept of transcendence, and sketched the outline of a philosophical biology. The essay later became an important chapter in my book *The Phenomenon of Life*.[2]

From then on I published essays in various journals, concentrating primarily on the philosophy of the organic. At the international philosophers' conference in Brussels that provided the occasion for my first trip to Europe after 1945, I spoke on "motility and emotion in the animal's soul" — a study of what constitutes animal being, in distinction to that of plants and of humans.[3] An almost Aristotelian topic, and I recall that Nathan Rotenstreich, who'd come from Jerusalem (a typical neo-Kantian and Hugo Bergman's successor at the Hebrew University), asked me, "Why are you interested in the souls of animals? Is that really a philosophical topic?" He saw it as completely irrelevant.

The first paper I read at a conference of the American Philosophical Society, held in Boston, took up the ideas of Alfred North Whitehead, who was becoming increasingly significant for my philosophy. Since at the time I was still naïve and credulous enough to think I had to stick to the stated time limit, I presented a brief, pointedly formulated paper, "Causality and Perception," in which I treated a Kantian problem with the new ontological tools I'd acquired from reading Whitehead, but in a sense I already went beyond his philosophy.[4] The paper had been sent in ahead of time and duplicated, and in the first row, among the twenty or thirty listeners, sat someone who was holding a copy of the text, followed my presentation attentively, and afterward congratulated me. It turned out that this was a student of Whitehead's who was serving at the time as the more or less official representative of the Whitehead school in the United States. Whitehead hadn't achieved national prominence in American philosophy, however, because a man for whom metaphysics was a serious philosophical topic was out of place in the American philosophical climate, which was at once positivist and committed to analytical logic. He was a mighty figure nonetheless, with disciples scattered all over America.[5] In New York I soon became one of the few to offer seminars and courses on Whitehead.

I seized the opportunity to give academic lectures in or outside New York that allowed me to add another piece to the puzzle of my philosophy of the organic. An important turning point came in 1958, when the twenty-fifth anniversary was approaching for the University in Exile, founded in 1933, thanks to the energy and creative vision of Alvin Johnson. Although I'd come to the New School only three years earlier and was thus its newest faculty member, I was asked to deliver the keynote address. It was probably Alfred Schütz, God rest his soul, who had the idea that I should speak on "the practical uses of theory." So the topic hadn't been my idea, but I had no reason to reject it; on the contrary, I thought, "This subject really deserves serious attention." This festive occasion gave me a pretext for developing conceptual clarity on an issue that in a general sense wasn't new to me, but which I'd never thought through or developed conceptually: the radical difference between knowledge [*Erkennen*] in its classical sense and its modern significance. I became aware that the dignity of contemplating being that Aristotle, Plato, and the Stoics had posited had been replaced by something geared toward practical application, specifically control over nature: knowledge of being is no longer directed toward understanding nature and contemplating the timeless order of things, but on the contrary aspires to force nature to do something that nature would never think of, but which one can impose on nature if one has observed how it functions. So I began this address by juxtaposing two quotations. The first came from Thomas Aquinas's commentary on Aristotle's *De anima*, where he says that the activities of man possess varying degrees of worth; some — the practical ones — exist for specific benefits, and the others, the theoretical endeavors, are undertaken for their own sake, for which reason they carry greater worth. I contrasted this statement with one by Francis Bacon, who, three hundred years after Thomas, described and celebrated the purpose of knowledge as granting man insight that would allow him to achieve mastery over nature. But such knowledge can be gained only by watching nature in action, which allows one to conduct experiments that tease out the laws of nature. This process enables man to transcend nature in order to improve the human condition on earth. The actual goal of acquiring knowledge, as Bacon sees it, is not contemplation of the eternal — for Plato the eros of knowing ultimately points beyond the temporal to the eternal — but gaining control over nature. The kingdom of man is one of dominated nature, which enables us to replace the misery of being cast adrift on earth with meager resources with the surplus we can obtain from nature; this power makes the control of human beings by other human beings superfluous, for in the past the goal of such control was always to exclude some from the scarce gifts of nature.

I went on to show why modern science leads to technology, that this is not a question of our being at liberty to apply knowledge to nature; rather the modern knowledge of nature of necessity results in technical applications. Thus for the first time I derived theoretically the essence of modern technology from the essence of modern science, and explained that thereby an inexorable dynamic is set in motion, with the result that we can no longer make out whether — to use an image from antiquity — man is steering the chariot and goading the horses on, or is merely being dragged along by another force. Thus the topic was broached as to the fateful significance and problematics of modern technology in the context of the unique modern perception of nature and knowledge.[6]

This lecture attracted attention. Leo Strauss, who'd come from Chicago for the celebration, told me, "That's the most philosophical observation you've ever offered." "And besides," he added, "it was so dense and concentrated that even I couldn't follow completely. No question, you have to work out these ideas further." This address represented a sort of milestone in my theoretical work. Another important lecture, which I consider one of my most significant pieces, was "The Nobility of Sight: A Study in the Phenomenology of the Senses," which made Aron Gurwitsch happy for a change, because it at least moved in the direction of phenomenology. I pointed out the organic basis of all our intellectual accomplishments and possibilities, the connection between the organism and the most lofty and even the most abstract intellectuality, for in the unique properties of human sight I saw the basis for abstraction and conceptualization, even more than in the senses of taste and hearing.[7] Hannah Arendt, who read the lecture when it was finished, said, "That's beautiful. All your life you've looked and seen and taken pleasure in what your eyes have perceived. And now you've captured in writing what seeing actually is." But Lore, who was well aware that I wanted to write a book on the philosophy of the organic, was dissatisfied with me because I kept writing single essays in which I worked out one aspect of the topic or another instead of bringing everything together in a coherent whole. In the sixties, when I'd finally finished the book manuscript, I sent it to the University of Chicago Press, which proceeded more than carefully and deliberately, soliciting expert readings and taking two years before it finally rejected the book. This rejection wasn't unjustified, as I must admit in retrospect, for the book was unnecessarily difficult, dense in its organization and written in a systematic philosophical language that severely limited the potential readership.

Now that I'd lost so much time, I decided not to revise the book but to take some already written essays that treated separate aspects of my new philosophy, by now rich and complex, and represented the important facets of my theory of the organic; organize them into chapters by subject matter; and publish them under the title *The Phenomenon of Life: Toward a Philosophical Biology*. The book appeared in 1963 in English, but not until 1973 in a German edition.[8] Although the book came into being by way of a literary shortcut rather than being conceived as a whole, I consider it my most important philosophical work, because it contains the elements of a new ontology. In a sense it's motivated by the same ambition as Whitehead's *Process and Reality*,[9] and focuses on the same fundamental themes, going to the heart of things and inquiring into the nature of being. My thesis was that the essence of reality reveals itself most completely in the organic components of the organism—not in the atom, not in the molecule, not in the crystal, also not in the planets, suns, and so forth, but in the living organism, which indubitably is a body, but harbors something more than the silent being of matter. Only from this starting point is it possible to develop a theory of being. Yet it was clear to me that you can't stop there; you must keep asking questions and trace out the consequences. Thus the book ends with an afterword that explains why a philosophy of the organic inevitably leads to an ethics that is already implied and needs to be worked out. That was a sort of pledge that I would next turn my attention to an ethical system based on the organic.[10]

It was another invitation to deliver a lecture that helped me see that this reflection on ethics had to occur in the context of the development of modern technology. In 1967 the American Academy of Arts and Sciences in Boston, at the suggestion of the distinguished legal scholar Paul Freund, who was teaching at Harvard, invited me to speak at a conference on the problems associated with medical and biological experimentation on human beings. My topic was "Philosophical Reflections on Experiments with Human Subjects." So I holed up in the Catskills, where our friends the Magnuses had a summer place, and meditated during long walks in the woods on this new ethical subject that I'd been confronted with. My talk, which appeared not long afterward in *Daedalus*,[11] made an unexpected public splash; several years later I was invited to give the same talk at a medical conference in Heidelberg, where questions of medical ethics were also up for discussion. In my paper I essentially accomplished the transition from my general ontological reflections to a concrete practical ethics. The attention I garnered was due among other things to the publication a few months before the conference of the findings of a special commission set up by the Harvard Medical School and chaired by Henry K. Beecher.[12] The commission had been charged with rethinking the definition of death and clarifying the concept of brain death, which was being proposed as the criterion for determining that a patient in an irreversible coma was dead. The commission argued in its report that a redefinition of death was necessary in light of two considerations: it was problematic that modern medical technology now made it possible to keep patients alive indefinitely through assisted breathing and circulation of the blood, and that the previous ethical standards of medicine, as well as the accepted definition of death, prohibited stopping such treatment and thereby bringing about death. But a redefinition also seemed essential to the commission because of the great demand for human organs, for around this time the technique of organ transplantation was coming into its own. The report proposed that innumerable human lives could be saved if the time of death was defined in such a way that organs could be harvested from comatose patients while they were most viable. In my talk, I deviated from my actual topic to offer a brief polemical comment on the prestigious commission's redefinition of death in terms of brain death. I pointed out that an extrinsic interest — promoting ease of organ transplantation — had influenced the commission's thinking, and I made my objection clear, laying out the possible hidden consequences of such a concept and formulating the rule that there was no more absolute right than the right of a human being to his own body and that no one had any inherent right to another person's organs.

Shortly after the publication of my paper, a group of doctors from San Francisco approached me, asking me to give my philosophical blessing after all for the redefinition of death as brain death, so important for the whole enterprise of organ transplantation. It was a delightful group of doctors who had thought long and hard about medical ethics and were devastated that a philosopher had expressed doubts about something they viewed as major medical progress. My encounter with this circle began with a letter from a fellow émigré from the Hitler period, Otto Gutentag, a philosophically trained and inclined physician, who up to then had embodied a sort of philosophical conscience for this group and now conveyed to me his objections to my arguments. Since they had a great interest in getting me to see the error of my position and in dispelling my doubts, they invited me to San Francisco, where I spent an enormously instructive week at the University of California Medical Center. Not only was I allowed to be present for conversations between doctors and their patients or doctors and organ donors; I also attended, properly disinfected and robed, an open-brain operation — a spooky experience. I also got to meet a famous kidney-transplant expert, Dr. Samuel Kountz, a black man who'd achieved distinction in medicine and academic medicine — a rarity in those days. He let me watch from close up a total kidney transplant. I saw blood begin to circulate through a kidney taken from a deceased donor and flown in. At a certain moment he said, "Okay, I want you to feel this." He took my hand and guided it into the opened-up abdomen, letting me touch the connection between the kidney and the bladder, and said, "See, it's working now!" And in fact I could feel the fluid flowing. We had long discussions, and the doctors went to a great deal of trouble to convince me that what they were doing was right, good, and noble, and deserved my approval. These doctors were dedicated to their profession, and it was important to them that their practice be morally correct and that they not go down the wrong path. Eventually I wrote a further essay titled "Against the Stream," in which I reported on the efforts of this group and me to come to an understanding.[13] There could be no doubt that what they were doing was magnificent, but my essential objection remained intact — the interests of the unconscious patient whom the doctors declared dead needed to be protected.[14]

On the strength of my lecture in Boston, I was made a short while later a founding fellow of the Hastings Center, established in 1969 as an institute for bioethics. The Center would play an important part in my further public activity in America. Thanks to my involvement, I was now part of a public body that for the first time was bringing together reflection on ethics in scientific research and highly practical decision-making on public policy and legislation. The Center's mission was to seek clarity on problems arising from progress in medicine and biology, in other words to work out the ethical consequences for medical practice, the organization of health care, and legislative regulation. The fellows were an interdisciplinary group of biologists, medical doctors, lawyers, sociologists, theologians, and philosophers, who formed task forces to work through specific problems and formulate recommendations. Among them were Paul Freund from Harvard; the theologian Paul Ramsey from Princeton; Robert S. Morison; the Catholic philosopher Daniel Callahan, who assumed the position of director; as well as the president of the Center, the Jewish psychologist and psychoanalyst Willard Gaylin from Columbia University. It was a committed group of self-appointed stakeholders, joined in a significant effort to formulate a humane ethics. For me, who became a zealous member and was considered the spokesman for philosophy in the group, it was love at first sight, evidence that the initiative of individuals can get something under way that can have a profound effect on society. After a while the Hastings Center acquired such an important reputation that certain congressional commissions in Washington couldn't discuss ethical questions without hearing testimony from its fellows. Among the first members, by the way, was Henry K.

Beecher, the chair of that Harvard commission that had called for a redefinition of death, against which I'd spoken out. He was by no means a brazen advocate for medical progress and experimentation but rather a man who'd earned great respect by uncovering abuses in hospital experiments. While he was still alive — he died of cancer shortly after the founding of the Center — a Henry K. Beecher Prize in Medical Ethics was established, and the first recipient after his death was Hans Jonas, who'd attacked the Beecher Report — a fine example of the generous spirit of this institute.

It wasn't until the Hastings Center called my attention to the ethical problems inherent in modern technology that I became fully aware that medicine was one form of technical progress that was concretely and ethically germane to my topic. Many of my later essays on medical ethics were the fruits of my involvement with the Center and appeared in the Hastings Center reports.[15] When I wrote *The Phenomenon of Life*, I'd been unaware of the practical ethical relevance of my philosophy. My lecture and the resulting reactions changed the situation completely. I recall a letter I received from one of my students, who wrote enthusiastically from Chicago to comment on my paper: "This is philosophy as I've always imagined it, philosophy that intercedes in life and provides guidelines for how one should live or what one should do or avoid." So I'd found myself participating in a debate as a result of which, for the first time in my life, philosophy became important in a practical sense. Here a group of people engaged in practical activity saw themselves either affirmed or attacked by philosophy, but at least hoped to receive guidance from philosophy. I never completely abandoned the realm of theoretical reason, but from this time on I entered what Kant would have called the realm of practical reason, and cultivated that field in my own way. At any rate, my concept of the role of philosophy changed fundamentally at this late date in my life. If up to that time, with my philosophy of the organic and in spite of my essay "The Practical Uses of Theory," I'd essentially taken the original philosophical position that philosophy was only for the philosophers, who worked to achieve knowledge for its own sake, now I slid irreversibly into the role of a philosopher who not only commented on current practical questions but sometimes even intervened to prescribe or warn against a course of action.

The Marxist philosophers had always seen things this way, but from my point of view, because of the Marxist concept of the secondary nature of the intellect and of philosophy (as part of the superstructure of practical interests), they weren't sovereign stakeholders in a philosophical claim to leadership. It was clear that for them political decisions came first, and the philosophical justification and articulation were secondary. But in my case there was no commitment to a particular political ideology. Of a believing Catholic or Protestant philosopher one could say that the religious bond implied a certain role. For me what was at issue was a view that had long been viewed as inappropriate, namely that philosophy wasn't simply an expression of a political position, as it was for the Marxist philosophers, but that as a philosopher one had an obligation to make an independent contribution to the things of this world and human affairs. It's in this sense that I view this last phase of my theoretical endeavors as a change in my conception of the role of philosophy in general. Whether my individual conclusions are of lasting value, whether they can be implemented or not, is a separate question; what's decisive for me is that here philosophy acquires a mission that it was long reluctant to claim. Kant was the last to recognize this mission. At stake here is a transformation in philosophy's self-understanding, which I can only hope will be moved forward by better minds than mine.

It's my conviction, and this brings me to a philosophical topic, that ontology necessarily entails a doctrine of obligation. But is that really true? Can an objective perception of being, one whose premises don't point it in a specific direction, but which represents an objective, neutral ontology, yield a doctrine of values or even a doctrine of duties? This key question now became my main subject of philosophical inquiry. Since then I've considered many possible arguments for an ontological basis for ethics. I probably can't hope to have said anything so compelling on the subject that it would convince people that being implies obligation. But at least I've put back on the table a question that seemed to have been answered once and for all, a question that modern analytic-positivist philosophy counts among the errors in thought that made philosophers personae non gratae. But I felt I had to take the risk of suggesting that values were more than a matter of subjective choice, the risk of deriving certain obligations from being, for I'm sure that I'm right about this, even if I haven't succeeded in completely working out the proof that being can tell us something about how we should live, but above all about the responsibilities that we human beings, acting consciously and freely, must fulfill. That this question has now taken on global and planetary dimensions is a result of the expansion of our power. We've become doers, and have incurred responsibility for extremely far-reaching decisions with unpredictable consequences. The philosophical basis of this challenge is not the product of a particular time, however, but consists of a pure ontology, from which a doctrine of "thou shalt" and "thou shalt not" and of "good" and "evil" can be derived. We need a new ethics for the age of technology, one that confronts the challenges of our era. Heidegger, for one, recognized this need, and attempted to take it on, though what he has to say on the subject, his speculations on the fate of the Western mind, which he claims has been moving farther from the actual truth ever since the pre-Socratics, seems to miss the point completely.[16] The only thing that must be recognized is the altered reality for human beings and their relationship to the world around them, including the threat to our future—that's what my outline aims to accomplish. Of course greater minds must come along to create the philosophy that will do justice to this task. My efforts are a first attempt.

While I was working out the philosophical ideas that were to form the theoretical core of my book *The Imperative of Responsibility*, I felt compelled to break the rule Hannah Arendt and I had adopted, which was never to show each other our manuscripts in rough draft but only as finished products. But when I was writing the chapter on the theory of responsibility, in which my discussion of the parent-child relationship brought in the connection between being and obligation, between ontology and ethics, I needed advice.[17] So I gave her the text and said, "I'd like to hear what you think.[18] Then we met one evening at her place, and she made the momentous statement, "Before I take up any details with you, I want to say just one thing: it's clear to me that this is the book the good Lord had in mind for you. And it's beautifully written." That was a wonderful affirmation. Otherwise she had all sorts of objections, which was entirely understandable, given that she was a political philosopher. She absolutely rejected my argument that man's fundamental responsibility could be explained biologically, on the basis of the natural order. In her view, responsibility was a voluntary relationship derived from the polis, from civic or political life, not from the family. And she invoked Aristotle, who distinguished clearly between the private sphere of the family unit and the public sphere of the polis. She stuck to that position and was of the opinion that responsibility for the general welfare was essentially artificial and unnatural, a product of the *contrat social*, according to Western tradition. We agreed that modern technology was becoming a threat to the world and that we humans bore responsibility for the future. But her philosophical justification for this position would have looked very different from mine. We talked about this difference, but she said, "No matter, what you've written is magnificent."

At the time I was already aware that I would be rather isolated in my philosophical position, and that some would probably dismiss it with a smile. "That's so old-fashioned, long since discredited. That's what Aristotle believed—of course, he understood being the same way, and thought there were better and not-so-good forms of being, perfection and imperfection, successful and unsuccessful lives. But the teleological view, according to which nature itself can sometimes reach its goal or not, as the case may be, is passé. And now along comes Jonas—but then anyone can argue for anything nowadays, and why shouldn't there be neo-Aristotelianism if that's what Jonas wants. It's his hobbyhorse." Although Aristotle didn't play much of a role in my thinking, it's undeniable that after my *Imperative of Responsibility* appeared some people told me, "There's an Aristotelian element in your thinking." I should add, purely anecdotally, that one of the first people to express support for my book when it came out in German in 1979 was Gadamer. He sent me quite a long letter, which began with the words, "Dear Herr Jonas, I am writing to identify myself as a grateful reader of your book." And elsewhere in the letter he writes, "Your work has made it clear to me that these days Aristotle has been becoming increasingly important for us." There's certainly some truth to that, and after Robert Spaemann, a Catholic philosopher with clear Aristotelian tendencies, as the book he wrote with Reinhard Löw, *Die Frage Wozu?* [The Question What For?],[19] clearly shows, praised my work, there was little I could do to keep myself from being classified as a neo-Aristotelian. I wouldn't have classified myself that way, but it's hard to defend yourself against others' views. At any rate, I wasn't in bad company. One result, however, has been that those who consider themselves members of the Frankfurt School see me as conservative, the more so because I can't be assigned to any of the current camps in German philosophy and thus seem to be an outsider. That becomes visible symbolically in the fact that Jürgen Habermas, who's well-disposed toward me and views me with a certain respect, blocked me from receiving the Adorno Prize, as he told me himself, but was much taken with the notion that I should receive the Sophie and Hans Scholl Prize, and at a dinner at his house said, "Yes, that fits. Given the conservative spirit you represent."

The Imperative of Responsibility owes its tremendous influence, if I'm not mistaken, not to its philosophical framework but rather to the general recognition, which even then relatively attentive observers could less and less ignore, that something could go wrong with the human race, that it was even on the verge of putting its own existence in jeopardy through ever-increasing technical interventions in nature. By now word has got around that we are well on our way to destroying our biosphere, as acid rain, the greenhouse effect, the contamination of rivers, and so many other dangerous developments show. I have the impression that the newly awakening and highly justified fear of such threats accounts for the success of my book, while I doubt my ontological philosophy has much effect. In the book I clearly and unmistakably invoke this fear; I am even at pains to formulate a "heuristics of fear."[20] To be sure, fear is not one of the prized human emotions, but it is essential that we experience appropriate anxiety and fear and open ourselves up to them. I think the fact that so many people felt that the book spoke to them results from certain anxieties that humanity has been experiencing at the spectacle of its own power since World War II. After all, the postwar period began with the shock of the atom bombs dropped over Hiroshima and Nagasaki. But I still don't understand why my book wasn't too late on the scene already when it appeared in 1979, because any intelligent person could have seen ten years earlier in what direction things were headed. I recall one of the first comments I received, from a friend in New Rochelle, who said, "Too bad this didn't come out ten years ago!" She was right; conditions were already ripe then, and you wouldn't have had to be a prophet to see how things stood and to write such a book. But at the time I wasn't ready. The aspect of the book that caught on was what was in the air, while the parts that were truly original and intended to bring about certain philosophical changes received little attention.

I wrote *The Imperative of Responsibility* mostly in German, but I included several portions originally written in English, which I revised and turned into chapters. I decided in favor of German because I knew it would take me two or three times longer to write material of equal quality in my adopted language. I didn't want to submit an unsuitable manuscript, as I'd done with the book on my philosophy of the organic. I'd recently had my sixty-ninth birthday, and didn't know how much time I had left. For that reason I chose the course of least resistance, thinking the ideas would flow more readily in German. Nonetheless the writing took me almost seven years. In 1972 I had my first real summer off, and went to Israel, which I'd picked as a place where I could have peace and quiet. I'd been invited to stay in a villa where there would be household help and I could live out in the country, completely undisturbed. Besides, it was far from America and New York, where I was constantly being called upon to do things. The owner of the villa was Gertrud Feuerring—a wealthy lady and the widow of a man whose first name had been given to the town: Bet Jizchak. This Jizchak Feuerring had been the owner of large ore deposits in Sweden, and his wife had inherited his fortune. She was a good businesswoman and a major philanthropist. She'd built a guesthouse for intellectuals — artists and scholars who wanted to devote themselves to their work undisturbed. She'd met me through Gershom Scholem and invited me to come for the summer. I began to write there, but I needed several more retreats for writing, in Israel and Switzerland, before the manuscript was finished.

And then, in 1978, came the momentous seventieth birthday of my friend Dolf Sternberger, a rather large celebratory gathering at an inn on an estate in Neu-Isenburg, near Frankfurt. The event took place outdoors, and Dolf introduced me to one of the guests: "This is my publisher, Siegfried Unseld, and this is my friend Hans Jonas. You should publish something of his someday." Whereupon Unseld asked me, "Are you working on something at the moment?" I replied, "Actually I am. I'm writing about technology and ethics." To that he responded, "That would be of interest to me." And a month later, when I returned from my summer trip, I wrote him a letter, reminding him of our meeting and letting him know that I was now in a position to send him one or two chapters and an outline of the entire book. He asked me to do so, and then I had a chance to see what goes into being an enterprising entrepreneur, for within a week I had his answer: "Yes, I'll take the book." He was fascinated by it immediately. The man was no philosopher, but he had a very good nose. And not only Unseld but also his staff at Suhrkamp were quite excited about my book. When I visited for the first time, the book was already in press. Unseld had invited us, and put us up in the Frankfurter Hof — a very expensive hotel. He had a highly competent editor for philosophical texts, whom I heard saying to Unseld, "This is our ethics for the rest of the century. We have to make a special effort with this book." I don't know whether he was referring to the speed of production or the size of the print run, but I thought, "Well, well, that's quite a mouthful."

On this occasion Unseld drove Lore and me through Frankfurt in his Jaguar to show us the sights, among them St. Paul's Church. As we passed, he said, "That's where the Peace Prize of the German book industry is conferred every year." We knew about the prize, because our friend Paul Tillich had received it there, and when it was conferred on Karl Jaspers, Hannah Arendt flew over to deliver the laudation, and afterward gave me a full account. Unseld commented, "You're going to speak there, too!" We returned to the hotel, and after he'd said good-bye, Lore turned to me and said, "Did you hear what he said at St. Paul's?" And my answer, of course, was, "Oh, that's just talk." But what does God do in his inscrutable ways? Unseld turned out to be right—if not about St. Paul's, then certainly about the Peace Prize of the German book industry.[21]

In connection with my receiving this prize on 11 October 1987, when Robert Spaemann delivered the laudation and I spoke on the subject of man's global responsibility, titling my talk "Technology, Freedom, and Duty,"[22] I accepted an invitation from the town of Mönchengladbach to visit my old *Gymnasium*. There I was honored extravagantly, and it made me very happy when they handed me the essay I'd written for my university qualifying exam back in 1921, which they'd dug out of the archives. It had survived the Hitler period and all the bombing. In my handwriting! It was still there! Along with the teacher's comments and the final grade of "very good." I recalled that I'd written a really good essay. The topic was: "You long to wander far and wide and are preparing yourself for a speedy flight; be true to yourself and true to others; then even narrow confines will be wide enough"—Johann Wolfgang von Goethe. I'd packed into the essay everything I'd absorbed in the way of philosophy, including Arthur Schopenhauer, but above all Kant. My entire line of thought was developed around a longish quotation from Goethe: the speech of Faust, old and blind, about the new territory he is creating, the very quotation with which I'd begun my speech at the Peace Prize ceremony! And at its heart was the responsibility that man takes on as master of the earth:

> A veritable Eden here inside,
> Although the flood foam at the brink outside!
> If a crack appearing, the sea pours in, then each
> By common impulse race to repair the breach.
> Yes, I believe, uphold as my fixed faith
> As the ultimate truth we human beings know:
> He only earns his freedom, life itself,
> Who daily strives to conquer it anew.
> So, so we'd pass, amid the dangers here
> As child, grown man, and graybeard, the busy year.
> To see such life, such glad activity!
> To stand with free men upon ground that's free!
> Then, then I might say to the passing moment,

"Linger awhile, you are so fair!
The footprints of my earthly passage cannot
Even after eons disappear."[23]

Even back then I'd emphasized the concept of responsibility, even back then I'd known this rather long passage about Faust's technical success by heart. In my essay for the exam I'd offered an interpretation quite different from the one we'd discussed in class. Not only had I commented on the anxieties about the crises to which this mastery of nature could lead—the fundamental topic of *The Imperative of Responsibility*; I'd also introduced the notion that human beings are saddled with an immense responsibility. I was somewhat shocked to discover that after sixty-six years I'd gone back to those same ideas, and I said to Lore, "My God, have I been at a standstill? Have I made no progress in all these decades? I had it all worked out back then?"

I should add that not all the reactions to *The Imperative of Responsibility* were positive. In retrospect, I would say that the political implications of my thinking—the renunciation of utopias as well as the skepticism toward democracy's ability to meet the challenges of the future—were probably the most controversial.[24] In this connection I should also say something about the relationship between philosophy and politics. Philosophy has probably always aspired to have a political impact (since politics is the realm, after all, in which ideas are converted into practice), and thereby to affect the human condition, to the extent this condition is shaped by the provisions of communal life. As we know, this was Plato's dream, even though he was also exceedingly doubtful that anything could come of it. But his own attempt to implement this idea is famous. He undertook it when he was educating a young Sicilian, the tyrant Dionysos of Syracuse, which gave him an opportunity to translate some of his ideas into political power. The attempt failed in classic fashion. Indirectly philosophy has influenced the course of politics time and again, of course. There was even a philosopher on the emperor's throne: Marcus Aurelius, a Stoic, who, however, didn't represent any particular political philosophy other than the noble ideal of doing one's duty. His is a highly personal philosophy, as the title of his surviving work expresses: *Eis emauton*.[25] He meditated on the condition of the human soul, as well as on the idea that among the human being's duties is responsibility for the community; he recognized that he himself bore a huge responsibility for the greatest political entity in the world, the Imperium Romanum.

His is an impressive work, but you can't say that in it he outlines a political philosophy. His abstract reflections emerged from his sense of morality, and from the moral standards he derived from stoicism, which imposed certain duties.

But reflections on the best form for human communal living — democracy, tyranny, or monarchy — can't be found in *Eis emauton*. How the secret effects of philosophy on the practice of government manifest themselves is hard for me to judge, but even without having studied political philosophy in detail I know that since the Renaissance philosophy has repeatedly chimed in when it was a question of identifying the best form of government. Although philosophy has never exerted direct influence, at least it has shaped outcomes through the aftereffects of its ideas. Niccolò Machiavelli on the one hand, Jean-Jacques Rousseau on the other — there's a long history of philosophers' taking an interest in politics, while real politicians or rulers in general show no interest whatsoever in thinkers.

But in the history of philosophy there have always been voices speaking out against Plato's idea that the real power should be placed in the hands of philosophers. There's a saying of Kant's on the subject that deserves close attention, and it begins something like this: One shouldn't expect kings to become philosophers or philosophers to become rulers, but the latter is specifically not desirable, for possession of power necessarily corrupts, and that's something the philosopher should be warned against. That there should be communities in which philosophers can live and in which philosophy is possible is highly desirable, on the other hand. That was more or less a declaration of renunciation.[26] Hegel had somewhat different notions,[27] but de facto only the French Revolution and the history of the Marxist movement offer examples in modern times of invoking philosophers or of certain philosophical ideas gaining influence on the thinking of those actively engaged in politics and thereby playing a decisive role in history.

In the context of this long history, most of which inspires melancholy thoughts, something quite remarkable has happened to me. Of neither Rousseau nor Marx can it be said that their political effect was unintentional. For Marx the political is primary in any case, and when it comes to Rousseau, you can also say that the notion that the expectation his ideas would influence reality was a fundamental component of his thinking. The question was always: What is the best form for a state? What are the best laws? What is the best form of government? But those philosophies were primarily concerned with the question as to how human beings should live with each other, whether they be philosophers or ordinary citizens or subjects. The question never arose as to how the human being should behave toward nature. From the blossoming of the Mediterranean cultures in early antiquity to the threshold of modern times, this was a question that was alien to philosophy. How human beings should behave toward one another was the focus of individual ethics, and in a sense also became a question for a collective ethics, specifically by way of utilitarian reflection on the form of government and social organization that should be considered most beneficial to the human being.

In my book I also devoted quite a bit of thought to the question of political systems.[28] But in one respect my book introduces a new element into political philosophy: it leaves aside the question as to which of the various political ideologies and programs is inherently best for human beings and their future. Instead I assert that that question is not significant; the key question is now which offers the greatest likelihood of meeting successfully the completely new challenge confronting human society: how we can live with nature — or how nature can survive together with us. The focal point of my book is no longer primarily relationships among human beings but this new horizon for ethical reflection. Not that this was my discovery, for I was only one among many who were beginning to think about such matters. But as it turned out, my book was apparently the first to pose this question explicitly and precisely. One result of my discussion of the relative virtues and opportunities presented by authoritarian and democratic systems, of Marxism and the free market economy, of capitalism and communism, was that each side accused me of being a spokesman for the other. In particular I was castigated for seriously considering that Marxism might be the better choice as a champion of humanity's future — not in perfecting the "new man," but in a much more modest, defensive sense: preserving humanity from catastrophe. That became my criterion, while the utopian question or the question of intrinsic value, which Plato had of course posed, as had Kant and every other philosopher interested in politics, was of secondary importance.

To be sure, Aristotle was enough of a realist to ask, when it came to discussing the various types of state, which was the most durable or which should be preferred to another according to various criteria. But among the criteria he mentioned, this completely new question never appeared: Which among the various types of states, ideologies, societal designs, or existing social systems offers the greatest likelihood that for the sake of preserving life, which is threatened, we will be willing to undergo the painful process of saying no to the development of all possible technologies? In advocating for this approach, I didn't consider political philosophy according to its own criteria, but placed the emphasis on this extrinsic criterion alone: Which type of state offers the best prospects from this new point of view? And I left the question open! It seems obvious that a dictatorial system is in a far better position to impose on its citizens the sacrifices we must make. But at the same time, we've experienced the other things a dictatorship can be expected — and feared — to bring about, the more so because the basic question remained: Do those in power perceive the situation correctly?[29] Suddenly philosophy's new assignment became one that had to be undertaken together with biologists, physicists, and theoretical economists — for the sake of saving life on earth. Well, that was my position, and the only form of political philosophy that I really rejected was utopianism. We can't afford a utopian notion of individual fulfillment, of achieving an ideal society; it's simply too dangerous. First of all, such a goal is overreaching, and second, under current conditions it can lead straight to destruction — by raising people's expectations instead of moderating them. This was my objection to Ernst Bloch's *Principle of Hope.*[30]

My book achieved overwhelming success in Germany, while in America it had nowhere near the same resonance. That has to do in part with the receptivity in Germany to philosophical works and the philosophical approach to topics, something that's rare in America, with its pragmatic and positivist climate. In America philosophy tends to concern itself more with linguistic analysis and formal epistemology, leaving the world and its conditions to the scientists. Jo Greenbaum, dean of the graduate faculty at the New School, told me one time that he'd asked colleagues at the University of Chicago what people there thought of Hannah Arendt's and my approach to philosophy. One of those whom he asked remarked that what we did wasn't philosophy at all; philosophy was a positive discipline, with a precisely formulated set of questions — he meant linguistic analysis and formal logic — and neither of us thought along such lines. "It's not philosophy," this man said; "it's interesting, also good to have, and there should be departments that work on such things. I'm in favor of that. But the name for it has yet to be invented. I wouldn't know what it should be called. I do know it's not philosophy." I burst out laughing when I heard that — priceless! So there were still some fossils around who were pursuing the kind of work for which the concept of philosophy was originally created — by the

Pythagoreans! And now this ancient philosophy was so out of style that those of us who worked in it had the amusing chore of inventing a suitable designation for what we were trying to do! But this comical response certainly has its symbolic seriousness as well: in America people don't really believe in philosophy in the sense in which it's pursued in France or Germany. At any rate, I was taken less seriously by the professional philosophers in America than in Germany. Another factor may be that although ecological topics are discussed in America, they're apparently far less prominent than in Europe—and in the political arena least of all.

The experience that surprised me most in connection with *The Imperative of Responsibility* was that almost the first positive reactions to the book came from the political side. It was politicians like Helmut Schmidt and Hans-Dietrich Genscher who soon made their views known in public. One day I received a call from Bonn, asking whether I'd be willing to see Egon Bahr. I had no idea who he was, since I wasn't following the political scene in West Germany. He came to see me and spent the first half hour talking about himself, so as to introduce himself to me, and I found out that in Bundestag debates my name was being invoked by members of all parties, and that the Christian Democrats and Social Democrats were determined not to let each other lay exclusive claim to Hans Jonas. I'm under no illusions when it comes to the question of whether my book actually had political consequences. But as far as lip service goes, the remarkable thing was that suddenly a philosophical book was not merely being discussed by philosophers and sparking agreement, disagreement, or head shaking in lecture halls and seminar rooms, but was also present in the real public sphere. Entirely unexpectedly I found myself in a position that every philosopher must naturally wish for, namely a position to gain influence, by means of certain insights the philosopher considers important, on those in power—of whom the philosopher should never be one; in that I agree completely with Kant. This was something I'd never counted on.[31] I'm not so vain as to think that an idea acquires force from being much discussed, but this much is clear: if it's not discussed, it will certainly acquire no force. If it's spoken of by many, at least the possibility exists that it can have an effect. To that extent I'm very happy about my "growing fame"—quite apart from any considerations of vanity, which it would be foolish to deny. This turn of events gives me grounds to hope that *The Imperative of Responsibility* hasn't remained a mere exercise in philosophy, but instead has found an echo and perhaps made some people more willing to pay attention to my theses and to incorporate them into their regular thinking. Much is accomplished thereby for the cause, even if I myself have a skeptical, sometimes even pessimistic response when I ask myself whether the system that's enabled the Western world to flourish so dramatically is appropriate for meeting the threats of the future.

Of course I've stepped on some toes, because I've stated unambiguously that certain limitations on freedom are going to be essential if we're to survive. To illustrate with one example: we can't afford to let the population continue to grow on this planet as it has done in the last centuries and continues to do today at a statistically measurable rate. On the contrary, overpopulation — from the ecological standpoint — already represents too great a burden on the biosphere. To regulate human procreation, the political system must intervene in this most private and personal sphere. If that isn't a limitation on freedom! But if you assert openly that democracy and individualism aren't the most suitable forms of government and life for facing the challenges of the future, you lay yourself open to suspicion in the West of supporting either fascist/dictatorial or authoritarian/hierarchical positions — something of which no less a thinker than Karl Popper has publicly accused me.[32]

CHAPTER 13

"All this is mere stammering"

AUSCHWITZ AND GOD'S IMPOTENCE

From the time I first started to think for myself, my relationship to Judaism had that dichotomous character that is probably fairly typical for a modern Jew of our era when it comes to the Jewish heritage, at least if you don't simply turn your back on it and forget it.[1] Although I was deeply moved by the Bible, I wasn't a believer. I no longer had the belief in that personal God, creator of heaven and earth, who parted the Red Sea and spoke in thunder from Mt. Sinai. But I found that certain parts of the Bible contained something tremendously important for human beings, something with which I felt connected because it was my heritage. Central to this message was the discovery of the ethos articulated by the Prophets. To me they are the true embodiment of the Jewish message, which always addresses the present, whatever it may hold, and almost always in opposition to the prevailing notions. In this respect Judaism has made a great contribution to religious consciousness, and this aspect has a future, while I go woozy at the thought that the new orthodoxy's fundamentalism, which we see raising its head, might prove victorious. So I was well acquainted with the biblical tradition, and I was quite well informed on the intellectual development of post-biblical Judaism. But I never seriously studied the Talmud, and what I knew about Jewish thought during the long history of the Diaspora was fairly meager and general. I was somewhat more knowledgeable about philosophical developments in medieval Judaism — in the work of Maimonides, Juda Halevi, Salomo ibn Gabirol — and of course the history of modern Judaism: a history of emancipation, assimilation, and absorption of modern culture, which also meant rejecting the old. My Zionist commitment preserved me from taking that step. Although my Zionism was primarily political, for me it always included the obligation to hold fast to the Jewish heritage. Thus it was self-evident that I would have my little son circumcised. Also we always assumed that we would have our children grow up aware of being Jewish, and that as much as possible we would make sure they learned about their heritage.

To what extent this sense of belonging forms part of my general view of the world has always been somewhat unclear to me, however. On the one hand I took in what modern science had to say about the world, while on the other I was more and more convinced of the inescapable bond that the fate of the Jews represented. But both things existed simultaneously. The *shma Israel*, the "Hear ye, O Israel," always had a magical force for me. I recall an interconfessional conversation in New York in which the "God is dead" theology current in Protestantism was discussed,[2] and I said, "When I hear the *shma* being recited, it always sends shivers up and down my spine." Yet I couldn't have stated whom I felt obligated toward. I couldn't really identify with the personal notion of "the God of our fathers" — invoking the faith of our ancestors didn't do anything for me. Instead there's something about the phenomenon itself: I always saw some unique, puzzling, mysterious, and binding quality in Jewish history and the accidental belonging of Hans Jonas, born in 1903 in an industrial town on the Rhine, to this history — something even more profound and definitive than my Zionist commitment. I could imagine revising my Zionism, but rejecting the *brit* — the bond between God and Israel — is unthinkable to me, even if my image of the divine partner in this bond has remained completely nebulous. There's a mystery that holds us in thrall, regardless of any temporally determined, private, personal positions we may embrace intellectually and consciously.

Hannah Arendt also felt this bond, by the way. Once, when we were speaking about it, she said, "How odd. I can't imagine a world without Jews. Of course, if we're Jews, we'll continue to be Jews." Being a Jew as a sort of *character indelibilis* that none of us would want to shake off. She had grave doubts as to whether the state of Israel would survive, but she quoted to me something that David Ben Gurion had allegedly said: "Even if everything we've established is smashed again — and it's in grave danger — I'm convinced that the further existence of Jewry is assured for the next thousand years by what happens here." She quoted that approvingly, and exclaimed, "A people with such a memory." So she considered herself part of that people.[3] Then there was a conversation at her apartment that I'll never forget. Lore and I were there for the evening, along with Mary McCarthy and a friend of hers who lived in Rome and, as it soon turned out, was a devout Catholic. She took a lively interest in me, and drew me out by asking: "Do you believe in God?" I'd never been asked that so directly, and by someone who was almost a stranger at that! I looked at her dumbfounded, then thought for a moment and said — to my own surprise, "Yes." Hannah was startled — I can still see the shocked look she gave me. "Really?" the woman asked. And I replied, "Yes. In the final analysis, yes. Whatever it means, the answer 'yes' comes closer to the truth than 'no.'" Not long after this I was alone with Hannah, and the question of God came up again. She said, "I never doubted that there was a personal God." To which I replied, "But Hannah, I never knew that! And if that's the case, why did you act so shocked at what I said the other day?" And she responded, "I was shaken to hear that coming from your mouth, because I'd never thought you felt that way." So we'd surprised each other with this confession.

One day I received an assignment that almost forced me to take a theological position. In 1961 I was invited to give the annual Ingersoll Lecture at the Harvard Divinity School. This was a famous lecture series in which someone spoke on the topic of "immortality" — whether from a historical, theological, or philosophical point of view. Paul Tillich, Alfred North Whitehead, and many other prominent personalities had spoken in this series, and it was a great honor to be asked. Well, it's obvious that the question of immortality is inseparable from the question of God. So I sat down and wrote a text in which I first expressed the philosophical perplexity over this question that wasn't mine alone, then resorted to a means of reflection and expression that Plato pointed us toward: to myth. When it comes to certain questions, Plato tells us, philosophical Logos has nothing to say, while myth has the ability to speak of them metaphorically. My experience with gnostic mythology had prepared me well for expressing a truth that couldn't be spoken of directly. So for my lecture I came up with the myth of a God who, in the course of the Creation, has stripped himself of his own power and rediscovers himself in the affairs of the world, a doctrine of a God who, in the experiment of the Creation, has given up absolute power and essentially placed himself in the hands of the evolving world. This adventure can end with God's enjoying an enriched being, but it can also end in failure. So I approached the question of immortality by way of the theological construction of a God who voluntarily becomes powerless, who expects that the world will honor this great risk, assuming responsibility for his fate and that of his creation. "Although neither eternal life awaits us," I concluded at the time, "nor an eternal return of the here-and-now, immortality can still be present to our senses when, during our short time on earth, we attend to our threatened mortal affairs and act as helpers to our suffering, eternal God."[4] Rudolf Bultmann was fascinated by my lecture,[5] by the way, and Hugo Bergman wrote in an enthusiastic letter, "Too bad it wasn't said in Hebrew!"

In my Ingersoll Lecture I'd already brought in Auschwitz, suggesting that God himself was wounded by what had happened there, that because of the murder of Europe's Jews "there was weeping in the heights at the waste and despoilment of humanity. . . ."[6] But it wasn't until much later, when I was awarded the Leopold Lucas Prize in 1984 by the University of Tübingen, that I returned in my lecture, "The Concept of God after Auschwitz," to the myth I'd created and the connection to the Shoah.[7] Now, I must explain that when I indulged in these "excurses," leaving the proper realm of philosophy, Lore was almost always dismayed, because it made her uneasy to see me venturing into this completely uncontrollable area of theological speculation. She considered it improper and somehow irresponsible of me to express myself publicly in an area where no one could challenge my reasoning. While I was writing the Ingersoll Lecture she'd already allied herself with our friend Adolph Lowe to dissuade me from dragging Auschwitz into the discussion of immortality. Now, when I very deliberately chose this topic, it made her extremely nervous; she thought it was all right to think about it in private but not in public. And in fact it isn't appropriate for a philosopher! For that reason, in my lecture I left open the question as to whether it was fitting for a philosopher. The hundreds who'd come to hear my talk sat there in the Tübingen auditorium as if transfixed, as I could feel while I was speaking. But the colleague who'd recommended me for the prize, a talented younger philosopher named Rüdiger Bubner, was appalled, and whispered to my wife, "This I hadn't expected. No. It's not at all what I had in mind." He'd recommended me as a philosopher, and here I was explicating this concept of God! And I recall that two or three years later this same Bubner was present when I gave a lecture on philosophical anthropology in Salzburg,[8] and turned to Lore, saying, "Now *that* was a good lecture!" To which she replied, "In contrast to the one in Tübingen, you mean!"

As a result of my public confession in Tübingen I essentially lost any chance of dodging the question, "Where do you stand on the matter of God?" I had to face the music, for I was so brash as to think I could reconcile the profound longing to believe in God, or in the presence of the divine in the world, with my philosophical insights and convictions. Just as I ended my lecture with the sentence, "Ladies and gentlemen, all this is mere stammering," later on, when people challenged me to defend my position, I always replied, "I have no desire to convince anyone or to represent a theological theory that I would have to defend." I'm not even sure that I convinced myself. But that's the absolute maximum, and it's modest enough, of what I can still accept in the way of the divine — which in earlier times used to illuminate everything but today is becoming increasingly difficult to believe in — in conjunction with the sum total of things, including my scholarly knowledge of the world, the universe, and life on earth. Yet I'm profoundly convinced that pure atheism is wrong, that there's something more, some-thing we can perhaps articulate only with the help of metaphors but with-out which being in all its facets would be incomprehensible. Although it seems to me that a philosophical metaphysics can't develop a concept of God directly, that this pathway has been closed to us ever since Kant's cri-tique of reason — hence my resorting to myth — I also believe that a rational or philosophical metaphysics isn't prohibited from formulating "supposi-tions" about the presence of the divine in the world.[9] It seems to me, rather, that philosophical ontology is allowed to leave room for the divine. It's a questionable, groping attempt, for which I've never claimed a monopoly on truth, and which owes its validity only to the fact that it doesn't simply deny what once exercised such a powerful influence within human history and in which, in the words of the Prophets, for instance, inspiration came from a source that is more than merely the world and nature. Myth also tries to develop a concept of God that makes bearable that which otherwise couldn't be borne.

Even without Auschwitz my reflection on the concept of God would have come to this conclusion, but perhaps it would have lacked the urgency and intensity that characterized the question of whether belief in God could coexist with what happened in the Shoah. Bultmann had always struggled with the question of how to reconcile belief in God with the findings of modern science, and I'd tried in my eulogy for him to suggest ways to do that. Yet I also argued that while we couldn't speak of direct intervention by God, in the sense of a miracle, intervention by way of the soul was think-able: God's voice, as testified to by the Prophets — "Thus spake the Lord to me" — could awaken souls, and that's the only form of divine intervention in the world that's consistent with the strictly scientific explanation for the material course of events.[10] Altogether we must avoid seeing any events in the world as a sign from God. One example: I remember that a great Ital-ian steamship sank near the American coast. A woman told me the story of a friend who hadn't been able to sleep that night and had gone up on deck, with the result that he was rescued. If he'd stayed in his cabin, he would have drowned with the others. She asked, "Can't that be seen as God's intervention?" My response was, "And that same intervening God let the others drown?" We have to be careful not to interpret events that seem like miraculous rescues in moments of greatest need as acts of God. It's another matter to theorize that God can make himself heard in the world. That's different from steering the world, which is possible only for human beings, who are physical organisms and thus able to move things in the world. God can work only through the human spirit. Through this spirit God can regain power, just as he can fail when human beings fail. There's no saying that God will find a hearing in people's souls and that the prophets whom he inspires will prevail — especially since Auschwitz that's become another, far more disturbing, question of consistency than the one with which Bultmann struggled. But fundamentally there is this opening through which the supernatural can influence the natural world — the only causality I still concede to God. If you observe the history of the Prophets, however, you see that it's no mean feat to influence the world this way. I know, of course, that people like my old friend, the atheist Günther Anders, find it obscene even to speak of the existence of God after Auschwitz.[11] Yet even he confessed to me in a letter that my speculations had fascinated him somehow. That may be the only way we still have for broaching such things — suggesting, without claiming to know the truth, yet leaving room for the supernatural in the world. That there is indeed a supernatural element in human affairs — for this the human spirit seems to offer evidence.

CHAPTER 14

Didactic Letters to Lore Jonas, 1944–45

TRANSLATED BY AMMON ALLRED

Nr. I January 3, 1944 (PAL/8119 BDQ Jonas M)
No 35 Ist PAL LAA BTY R.A> M.F.F.

Your "philosophically unschooled mind" has made quite a valid philo-sophical objection. You object to the proposition that the world requires the human being to be watchful for it, to reflect it and, in that reflection, acquire a new existence for it. Rather, it seems to you that this claim is itself something the human being inherently postulates of his relationship to the world—a demand with which the human furnishes the world and which returns to the human from it: to a certain extent, as you express it, a "doubled reflecting." Taken on its own terms, this is perfectly correct, and I would not hesitate to employ it as a description of the human side of the way things are, were it not opposed as an alternative to those other ideas. This exclu-sionary *ausschließenden* meaning of your interpretation is founded upon the common assumption which has, over several centuries, become habit-ual to philosophical thought, that something like a "claim" can simply go out from the human I. This leads well beyond the immanent description of human phenomena and brings up the ontological question of the human in the being of the collective world. On this, the following remarks.

Idealism, which ties everything to consciousness and makes the subject the foundation of the world, at least insofar as it gives meaning to it, has for some time ceased having the final word for me. But, if one does not want to get oneself mixed up with dualism, the reality of the world requires credit to be given to matter[1] for the accomplishment of having generated from itself: life in its ascending rank, the operation of the senses, human beings, and also therefore the intentionality of their consciousness of it—the world—itself. That hierarchical order of life leading up to human beings can be interpreted precisely according to grades of world-lightening, ever increas-ing world perception, and finally the most free and therefore the most faith-ful, most comprehensive objectivation [*Objektivation*]. In this process, the "reflecting" of the world becomes ever more complete, beginning with a most obscure sense perception somewhere in the lower reaches of the animal kingdom, indeed in the most primitive sensation of stimuli, in which world and object are already somehow experienced, i.e. made subjective. Such a continuous process, each time reaching itself higher, cannot possibly have gone forth blindly, the result of mechanical permutations of material elements, generated out of manifold substrates as an accidental by-product to which subjective appearances are attached. Furthermore, if matter has organized itself in this fashion and with this direction, then it is necessary to ascribe this possibility to it primarily and likewise to include in it the concept of world-substance as the governing, dynamic (teleological) motivator in the concept of world-causality. This transforms the whole of ontology. If substance has organized itself in this direction, then one should not avoid making the inference that it organized itself *with* this orientation, i.e. that the goal was contained within it and belonged to it, i.e. that the "possibility" [*Möglichkeit*] is a positive and productive characteristic of it, i.e. that life, sensation, perception, thought are intended in it; i.e. that through the human being's objectivation of substance, an original tendency is fulfilled, i.e.—since the human being is substance's own product—that it itself fulfills itself in that objectivation. Notice now that it indeed makes sense (and is not *just* anthropomorphism) to say that the world requires the human being . . . but reason still requires a more essential completion in order to justify the concept of a claim, even if one already admits the possibility of fulfillment or realization. But back to that later. (More follows.)

Nr. II. February 25, 1944 PAL/8119 Jonas H
No 40 I Pal L.A.A. BTY R.A.

When the infusorium[2] touches up against another body, it is not merely affected in a mechanical sense, but also in terms of sensation, and correspondingly its reaction is not physical, but rather biological, or some such behavior. In this respect every external (mechanical) cause-effect relationship between bodies or forces is fundamentally surpassed. In sensation the "something" that affects is co-represented. In this way, a new existence for it as an object is opened in the tiniest fissure on the horizon, dawning in the subjective reflex, in the experience of touch. The affected thing also feels itself in the stimulus. In stimulus and reaction, approaching or withdrawing, accepting or rejecting, its self is activated, like a point against the environs of the not-self. This also reveals the polarity of the relationship of life in embryo. The premise of these phenomena is that the living substance, organism, or smallest individual has originally individuated itself from and against the world and has made itself independent by setting itself against matter. The individuation shows that although the living being is itself a piece of the world, as far as it is concerned all that remains of the world is other, exterior, encroaching on the organism from without or escaping within, in the singular encounter with the foreign body (expanded or restricted as such), in the totality and as the horizon of the external world. The external world is only considered in terms of the organism's overwhelming interest in its own life-process, which has to assert itself in the external world and is by constitution egoistic. But this is already an appearance of an elementary ground on which all later characteristics of life are ultimately based and whose entrance into the cosmos marks an ontological revolution, recurring once again with the entrance of spirit:[3] this is the way it is for freedom in opposition to matter.

The essence of life, which exists as a determinate agglomeration of matter, is not identical with the matter of which it consists. It is not captured through identity to matter but is rather an organizing form which has itself for a goal and which maintains its independence from a material existence to the degree to which it constantly changes its existence. Indeed, without exception, the organizing form only preserves itself through this variation. With this wondrous state of affairs a principle enters into the world without parallel in the physical world of mere matter.

This is the being of the simple, immediate identity of the in-itself. Each exists in its place in space-time as a determinate particle of mass, which it is, quite simply, apart from its own doing, in the empty self-identity of a category of substance: its duration is mere continuance, its selfhood is therefore a function of the continuity of the dimensions of space and time, its form an accident clinging onto matter, lacking authentic reality. It is this thing and not that thing, because *it* is here now and that thing is over there right now; it remains this thing, i.e. is the same at a later point in time, because the continuous succession of all intermediate states leads from its present place to its new one. This succession sort of passes it from one state to the next, not loosening its grip for a single moment. The discontinuity of sub-atomic processes as taught by modern physics does not annul the possibility of identifying touching substrates in a technical sense but rather places this possibility outside the extension of the concept of identity as the condition of its adaptability to what is nonliving: it does not satisfy the constancy of the form of development, in which variations happen. Particles of mass have no other principle of identity than this external principle, which could either grant or deny to them the *principia individuationis* (space and time). This means that for matter identity is as much an external characteristic as individuation. This characteristic belongs to unities on the basis of the totality of the physical world, whose parts they are, and this characteristic is determined by this totality.

The identity of the living being, however, is its own incessant production, the result of the active self-founding self-constitution and self-renewal of its form.

Its existence is a function and not a substance; its duration a happening and therefore not just continuance, whereas what merely continues is constantly left behind in the process of the living being's self-foundation. Should it ever become what merely continues, it would cease to be. The fixed, material identity of particles of mass stands against the dynamic, functional identity of what is living. Happening, to which fixed identity is subjected (what happens to it), is the proper element of the dynamic.

Consequently the existence of the living being is not given in itself, as is that of matter, but is rather its own creation in each of its moments. Admittedly, on account of its bodily presence, it is a concrete product of matter in each of its temporal cross-sections and on that side a thing among things: but its being is not the presence of the product that it is at each of these moments, but rather ultimately is itself only its ongoing self-creation. It is nothing else apart from this production: thus it gives itself over to itself entirely and is set upon itself. It sinks back into the being of the in-itself or the indifference of the substrate of the merely present when its production ceases.

Being as production demands a center, from out of which it can produce, a manifold, in which it produces, and a limit, up to which it produces — its unity constitutes these from without (its difference from the world) and inwardly everything — a finite quantity — each according to its component-function, is an agent of production. The principle of the organism is given in this elementary organization (which is present in the nucleus, protoplasm, and cellular membrane of the most primitive creatures). The indifferent contiguity of particles of mass is annulled in this organization and replaced by the differentiation of the organic form, which is founded on the residual indifference of the former as an entirely new plane of being, with its own categories of unity and variation. Without the fixed identity of substrates having changed themselves as such, they have become subordinated in their arrangement to an organizational principle, as parts of the living substance, the organism, which disposes of them according to the laws of its dynamic identity, in the service of developing higher forms. As an organic product, such is the being of the organizing form.

Form, then — and I mean by this independent, self-actualizing form — is an essential characteristic of life. With it the difference between form and matter, which is a purely abstract difference in the case of the dead, emerges as a real difference. Indeed this marks a total reversal of the ontological relation: form has become the essence and matter the accident. Expressed ontologically: in organic configuration, the material element ceases to be the substance (which it still is on its own plane) and is now only the substrate.

The self-sufficiency of the living form shows itself primarily in that it does not have its material constitution once and for all time, but rather interchanges it with the surrounding world in ceaseless appropriation and expropriation — and that's how it remains itself. This means that its material constitution is concurrent, and this concurrence is its proper function. Seen from the perspective of the fixed identity of matter, the living form is only a transitory point for matter, through which it passes according to its own law, and its apparent unity nothing other than a constitutive state of its diversity. But in actuality [*Wirklichkeit*], from the standpoint of life taken as a new categorical plane, the form is what is actual in the relation: it does not simply passively allow world-material to flow through it, but rather it itself is that which actively draws material into itself and pushes it out of itself and builds itself from it. For the lifeless, the form is nothing but a varying condition of the underlying matter. For the living, active, organizing form, varying material contents are conversely conditions of its underlying identical being. Matter's diversity itself is the extent of the actuality of form's unity. Instead of saying that the form of life is a transitory point for matter, it is more correct to say that the succession of material constitutions, which are constituted concurrently, are transitory phases for the process of the being of the form.

In the material universe, in its immeasurable, mute, indifferent-quantitative history, which is a history of atoms and their bonds, life is naturally also a "state" of matter, and a very ephemeral state at that: but also a paradoxical state, in which matter itself makes itself into the state of something different, which is founded upon it — the living form — and makes room for a qualitative principle, which it puts in control of its quantitative being: in short, a state, in which it transcends itself. The fact that the indifferent being of matter has produced this from its womb shows that principles are concealed within it, principles we are not in the habit of connecting with their concept, but which we must incorporate into the most thoroughgoing interpretation.

The independence of form does not signify a separated being: the concurrent, concrete unity of matter and form, which is a universal, ineffaceable characteristic of the world, naturally exists here also, namely in the co-occurrence of form with its material basis at each moment. The organism is always at the same time the form of a determinate manifold of matter. But while in the sphere of matter, as we have said, the separation of form and matter and the self-positing of form are abstractions accruing to substance from the accidental being of the form, on the ontological plane of life, conversely, the difference between both is concrete, and their concurrent equality, which can really be produced in the cross-section of each moment, is only an abstraction when regarded from the form of the totality of life: since even an individual cross-section of existence's course of time is itself a mere abstraction from the perspective of the living being. The actuality of its form is in the succession of its momentary materialities, which it makes into its duration. This alone is the concretion of its unity, where unity is taken not as a logical attribute, but rather as a productive completion. Although the now-point of a material totality—each now-point—gives the same completion and, as a theoretical index, can be replaced by any other, the organism's cross-sectional now, which is material and still complete in that way, gives each apart from what is proper, life, the form of which can only be found temporally and in its functional totality. Temporality, not simultaneous space, is the medium of the totality of the form of the living being; and this temporality is not the indifferent being-apart that time is for the movement of matter and for the succession of its contents, but rather the qualitative element of the presentation of the form of life itself, as it were the means for binding its unity with the diversity of its substrates. Indeed, this binding is life in its dynamic progress.

As much as an error as it is to be misled by the ability to abstract the material form from matter to hypostasize its form as being in itself, i.e. to forget its elementary dependence and to reinterpret abstract moments as concrete entities (an ontological misunderstanding at the root of much philosophy)—conversely, it would be equally wrong to understand the concurrent coincidence of form with its material substrate as an identity. But self-identity, which is merely a logical attribute for the dead being, the expression of which does not go beyond tautology, is ontologically richer for the living being, in its proper function as material otherness rather than a constant, achieved characteristic.

If one takes the heretofore described structures together and recognizes the heretofore observed reversal of ontological relationships as opposed to those of the general substance of the world, at least in its given form, as matter, to whose region life *with* these reversals still necessarily belongs, then one is entitled to speak of an ontological revolution, which has happened in the history of matter with the appearance of this new material form of being, "life." The principle of this revolution is the rendering of "form" as intelligible within matter, the enabling of a specific independence of form which, in accordance with all merely material structures of the world, is "impossible." The description of its characteristic traits, instruments, and varieties is the task of biology. And the development and progression of its independence is the principle of the whole history of the development of life, which occasions further revolutions as it proceeds, each a new step in the direction life has set out upon.

Emancipation of form from the immediate identity of matter, emancipation from the fixed self-identity of matter, dynamic self-actualization of form in matter and against matter: a principle of *freedom* lights up for the first time in the monstrous bondage of the physical world, arrested within itself. In the blind impulses of primordial organic substance, a freedom, alien to the suns, planets, and atoms — and its original, elementary expression is the variation of matter.

(More follows.)

Number III
March 31, 1944 (no 52.)
On the anniversary of the first half-year of our marriage, my love. May the following be as blessed!

With the concept of freedom, we have a guiding concept for the interpretation of life. The mystery of becoming is impenetrable for us: Thus it remains a supposition — for me personally a strong hypothesis — that the founding principle for the transition from lifeless to living substance was itself already a tendency designated for this purpose within the depths of being. But it is certain that this concept is already in place in the description of the elementary structures of life.[4] In this descriptive sense, freedom is therefore an ontological, foundational character of life as such; it also shows itself to be the thoroughgoing principle—at the very least, the result each time—of its progress to higher forms of matter, in which each time freedom builds itself to freedom, the higher on the lower, the more complex on the more simple: at both extremes of the concept of freedom the whole of development allows for this interpretation (a schematic example of which should be given later). Within the constellation of life, the polar pairs are, as already indicated, form and matter (onto which secondary polarities will later be superimposed), and its entire operation at first consists in the variation of matter.

This, however, is the same as discovering that freedom is dialectical and has its other side constitutively. We observed that the independence of form did not signify separate being, nor did its nonidentity with its substrate signify immateriality (which applies universally across the whole scale of foundation, on which it is a matter of grade within world-substance of more functional freedom; nowhere will a pure separation be encountered; there the lower basis, however much it has been outstripped, nonetheless remains the basis). The living form, existing temporally, is at each moment materially concrete—but it cannot remain in the concretion of one time, i.e. in co-incidence with its determinate amount of matter. It cannot: thus its "freedom" is a necessity, its "can" a "must," its performance the exclusive mode of its "being:" therefore at the same time as the variation of matter, its characteristic possibility, gives the living form sovereign primacy in the world of matter, it is also an insurmountable imposition. This is the antinomy of the freedom of life at its root and in its most elementary form. To recap: the freedom that manifests itself in the form of life is the faculty to vary its matter—"it can vary"; but insofar as it is, it cannot not vary. It must perform its ability in order to be, indeed this is its being. A freedom to act, but not to fail to act.

In order to be able to vary its matter, it must have, find, and obtain matter. The existence of the life-form demands ceaseless access to new matter, matter not associated with it [*die nicht mit ihr gegeben ift*], but lying in the foreign world. Therefore it is bound to the world and reliant on it in a particular way. Relying on the world in its need, it is oriented toward it; oriented (opened facing it), it is related to it; related to it, it is ready for encounter; ready for encounter, it is capable of experience. In its active self-concern for its being, primarily in busying itself with supplying matter, which it provides for itself by constant encounter, it actualizes the possibility of experience. Through experience it "has" a "world." Having a world, the transcendence [*Transzendenz*] of life, in which it is necessarily reaching out beyond itself and widening its being into a horizon, is already given as a tendency along with its organic dependence on matter, which for matter's part grounds life's formative freedom from matter. Thus, the dialectic of the fact of life proceeds from the fundamental positivity of ontological freedom (form-matter) to the negativity of biological necessity (variation of matter) and beyond that again to the higher positivity of transcendence, which unifies both, and in which freedom has taken possession of necessity and sublated it into the faculty of having a world.

Let us remain for the time being with the moment of necessity, which is particular to life and which bears its inimitable character as much as freedom does. Reliance on matter outside itself is the flip side of the ontological freedom of life. This reliance is no less novel a phenomenon in its physical being than is that freedom itself. In itself, matter has not known it. The individual material entity, however, persists in its simple self-identity and is sufficient in its being. That it is and what it is may indeed by a function of this material totality, which conditions each as a part of the cosmic whole. Thus, its isolablity may only be a temporary abstraction: but within this universal conditionality, its particular existence is self-sufficient and without need of foreign matter, preserving its difference from its neighbors through all activities of variation. In contrast, the neediness of life goes out beyond its own material constitution and relates itself to the foreign as potentially its own, only possessing what is its own as potentially foreign. The intrinsic transcendence of all life, which is grounded in this self-transcendence through neediness, discloses in its higher stages an ever wider world to the self. Reliance refers to the field of its possible fulfillments and thus institutes intentionality as a foundational character of all life. We will return later to the analysis of this transcendence.

Henceforth, we will see the antinomies that are determined in the dialectic of the freedom of life as a form-matter relationship. These antinomies give that relationship a deeply paradoxical being. They are combined in the following way:

The constitutive neediness of life is given as one with the emancipation of form. Together, they constitute an indivisible existence. Freedom in relation to matter, which busies itself in the matter-varying being of form, at the same time signifies *ipso facto* reliance on matter. In fact it is precisely the other side of the index of its ontological freedom, according to the measure of the exchange-dynamic of form. On its positive side nonidentity with its own matter is the difference of the form existing in itself; on its negative side it is the insufficiency of each simultaneous materiality to the same. This nonidentity lets life coincide with ever more matter over time: therefore it does not decrease, but rather, on balance increases the materiality of the form that has been loosened from its fixed identity with matter, and as such "made free." Emerging from the sureness (unquestionableness) of physical identity into the venture of difference and freedom, the life-form is superior to matter and at the same time exposed to all matter. Since this emergence sacrifices simultaneous completeness for successive actualization, its relationship to matter becomes transitory, accidental at each moment — but for this reason it is also necessarily expanded: multiplying itself in time through its succession of materializations, broadening itself in each. Now by appending the horizon of potentials to actual matter, which is now required of it, intensifying in quality from indifferent having to having-to-get. All genuine characteristics of life through whose concepts we always explicate the state of affairs are similarly two-sided. We always highlight this aspect within life. Thus life has won independence from nature and, with the self-causality of the organism, it has asserted an extramechanical autonomy, the exact price of this autonomy being an existential dependence, necessarily foreign to the stable being of lifeless matter. Again: What is internally the self-closure of the functional totality is, in the performance of its functionality, itself a correlative openness to the world. The self of individual life is opposed to everything else as the external world or the foreign — yet even this opposition actualizes itself through "transcendence" (which rests upon opposition and draws this relationship of opposition from out of itself) as absorption of the external qua external into the internal or as the being-outside-of-itself of the internal in the external. The unity of life is isolated as an individual from the coherent web of the world — yet this isolation precisely signifies the capacity to make contact with a variety of others. Indeed, it signifies both in direct proportion: the more decisively individuality, i.e. isolation, develops itself in the progress of forms of life, the more, and in the same relation, the radius of its potential contacts grows, in both expanse and variety. This also means that the more centralized and punctual the Life-I, the broader its periphery, and *vice-versa*, the more nested it is in the whole of nature, the more indeterminate in its difference and the more blurred in its centrality, so much the smaller is its periphery of world-contacts [*Weltkontakten*]. Life has a fundamental spacing from the world, from whose homogeneity the form particularizes itself and draws back into its peculiarity: but even this spacing offers a dimension for relating to the world. This relationship roots itself in those necessary real-relations already identified. But it does not cover itself with these relations. Rather, it can surpass them toward universality.

In the end, the frailty of this existence is the very flip side of the sovereignty of its self-foundation: precisely because from moment to moment it is a functional product and not a lasting state, its self-constituting identity is of a precarious, refutable duration; the creativity with which it challenges its continuance constantly evades extinction. The form, which is free in its orientation toward matter but not free of matter, is preserved only through constant renewal. It stands from the beginning under the sign of transience, annihilability [*Vernichtbarkeit*], and death. That life is mortal is indeed its fundamental contradiction, but this also belongs inseparably to its essence. Life cannot at any time be imagined apart from its mortality. Life is not mortal although it is life, but rather because it is life. This is in accordance with its most original constitution, since the relationship of form and matter, upon which life is based, is of such a revocable nature, one that cannot be vouchsafed. Its actuality, a paradoxical and constant contradiction of mechanical nature, is at bottom a constant crisis, which it never securely copes with, each time only as the continuation of its crisis. Given over to itself, and standing entirely on its own production, but dependent for its fulfillment on conditions over which it has no power and which might fail it; dependent consequently on the favor and disfavor of external reality; exposed to the world, against which, and at the same time through which, it must assert itself; having become independent of and yet subjected to its causality; emerging from identity with matter, but in need of it; free, but dependent; isolated, but in necessary contact; seeking contact, but destructible because of it: conversely, no less threatened by want of contact: endangered thus on both sides, by both the tremendous power and brittleness of the world, and standing on the narrow ridge between; capable of disruption in its process, which ought not be interrupted; vulnerable in its organized partitioning of functions, which is only effective as a totality; capable of encountering death in its center, capable of being ended at each moment in its temporality — thus the living form pursues its unmeasured existence as a particularity within matter, paradoxical, labile, unsure, threatened, finite, and closely related to death. The adventurousness of this existence, full of anxiety for death, places the original venture of freedom, undertaken by substance by becoming organic, in a garish light. The daunting price of anxiety, which from the beginning of life had to be reckoned with and which increased in direct proportion to life's higher development, is that the question concerning the meaning of this venture cannot be brought to rest. It is only in this human being's question, curious about the substance that has attempted to gain form since the dawn of life, that the original questionability of life considered in itself gains, after millions of years, speech.

(More follows.)

Nr. 4

December 30, 1944 PAL/8119 BRD JONAS

No. 120 P BTy., The Jewish Field Reft. R.A.C.M.F.

My love, letter 120: If I'm not mistaken, this makes some 30 letters over two months that we've been separated. I find that great. And you? And tomorrow evening is the New Year, the departure of 1944, which still owes us a good deal. I will not write about 1945—we both know what we wish of it. This time, I believe, it will be fulfilled. Still, I add one wish of my own to it: that my mother lives and sees her son again. Mönchengladbach has been heavily bombarded again. For the moment at least, the German offensive has been brought to a standstill. 1918 was more difficult still. Nothing to report about me right now. Tomorrow, another excursion, upon which I hope to reach a particular destination.

So: spirit and matters of fact, and spirit and the organic. I unfortunately cannot find your letter [concerning this]. You write: only spirit is the particular, the animal is the general. And only spirit is interesting: matters of fact are at most worthy of remark and meaningless in themselves, or superfluous. "From this point of view even my own existence is superfluous. My only justification is that I love the spiritual. . . ." The matters of fact not worthy of remark include, for example, the teething of a child — in this case, the jointure between "matters of fact" and the "animal." You are naturally right, that in the region of the human, spirit is individual in a higher grade than its animal subject. And let it be said of the isolated individual that — according to human standards of measurement — it only becomes individual through spirit. But in the region of life, the peculiar organic development "human being" is something quite particular; and in the region of being, the matter of fact of "life" is in turn another unique exception, so to speak, the extreme of improbability as compared to the innumerable probabilities of mechanical nature. The qualitative as compared to the merely quantitative. And it is individual in its essence: the fundamental structure of life is that it is organized into self-centered unities. Life only exists in the form of individuals, in the primitive as well as the most highly developed: each involves the concept of the "organic." I speak of the organic individual, not of the spiritual. But the former is the preliminary stage of the latter, the latter the superstructure of the former. And in the region of being, in which life is embedded and from which it has particularized itself so extremely and exceptionally — the region of matter? Again, how rich in particularity, and a great particularization of the whole, if we regard the mere fact of the difference and of the uncanny tensions between isolated elementary unities, considered as improbable compared to the general neutralization of "entropy." If one thinks this through to its end, one comes to the conclusion that the wholly nonparticular, the simply universal is actually only undifferentiated, hypothetical ur-substance,[5] or the nothing. And that could not persist in its indifference, as the matter of fact of being, i.e. the world, proves. The sheer multitude of particularizations of elementary matter here ought not lead us astray. Granted, the multitude of fundamental unities, the endless repetition, recognizable solely as self-sameness, makes the material world something paradigmatically quantitative for our observation. But I am convinced that the individual electron, or whatever the most elementary unity is, presents an eminently qualitative state of affairs in the constant preservation of its particularity again the leveling powers of energy. Only it is totally withdrawn from us. Ultimately, its existence is a robbery within the uniform expanse, the result of which remains behind as the immense extension of empty space between individual, and thus uncanny, peculiar intensifications. Its enormous sheer quantity obscures this. But we now hit upon this interesting consequence: that this quantity decreases with higher particularity, which is more complex organization at the same time, that the more individual is also the more peculiar: all the millions of bacteria are numerically nil compared with the atoms or molecules or other formations of dead nature; all multicellular organisms, in all their innumerablity, nil compared with them; all mammals nil compared with these; and all spiritual or intellectual individuals . . . factually, the quantity, which rules, all withdraws in the higher expressions of the qualitative — partly, therefore, because here more quantity is required for the expression of the individual case (thus higher qualitative organizations are subordinated) — and there is comprised a progressive coherent context between individuality and peculiarity. To the same degree, its formations also become more accessible, more penetrable — "more interesting."

Now, as to the relation of spirit to this—and since the organic is only a special case of being, we want to place the question in its generality: the relationship of spirit to the matter-of-factual. Now, the fundamental truth is that spirit is at first and at last concerned with matters of fact. With all matters of fact? With more than all: as cognitive it is concerned with the contents of their existence, as creative it is concerned with those yet to be created. With all the contents of existence? Yes, but not to the same degree (on this later). Only with matters of fact. At first and at last with them, i.e. it must get out from them and always arrive at them again: it stretches between these points the span of its own ideal realm, a new matter of fact, but not an arbitrary ordering, since it aims at cognition or at the presentation of being, and employs its abstract and metaphorical symbols toward this goal. It must always return to matters of fact, in order not to lose itself in idle play. Are the primary data, matters of fact of the first order, the only kinds of data given? No, since when the confrontation of matter with these givens is up and running, the sum of its mirrorings reflecting into one another constitutes a secondary stratum—and in what ensues, stratum upon stratum is layered over the original. This is a reality, which immediately becomes an object of spirit. Spirit encounters itself, and spirit prefers primarily to tarry in it as the medium of its own, intimately familiar nature. The more it does so, the more this region between the constant growth of new strata, in which this self-relatedness plays a part, increases in its variety of figures, in its entwinements and in its extension. But spirit ought not to forget in its concern with its spellbound interest in its own figures that "matters of fact" are the first and authentic objects, actuality of the first order: i.e. it ought not forget that they are not primarily objects, but rather are the having-of-objects or the for-the-sake-of-objects. The entire stratum is intentional and the large number of strata, as they are transparent to one another, are such that the earlier shine through the later. It must be transparent to its base object throughout, right up to the last stratum. If it loses this transparency (if it conceals rather than remaining opened, as often has happened and still happens), or if spirit forgets this about its object, then it has replaced the object entirely and cares no more for the matters of fact themselves—thus it loses the relationship to truth, to the thing; it becomes scholastic or purely aesthetic. And thus the truth—the authentic meaning—of the formation itself with which it is in love also escapes it. This is because spirit ultimately wants to be measured by things, by the actuality of being. All that it is comes from matters of fact: even the most cunning visions of the mystic and the most abstract speculations of the metaphysician want to express the matters of fact of being itself, the true actuality — the "world" — in its possible delimitation. If people were persuaded that their orders of angels, their region of heaven, were the pure fantasy of their own spirit — they would lose any interest in it and their preoccupation with it would appear as empty mischief. And what does it mean to us, that we have come to know most or much of it as mere fantasy? Returned in this way to its reflections and attempts at truth, has it become a worthless trinket for us? No, it remains still a testament and key to another actuality: that of the human being and his spirit — itself one of the most great matters of fact and probably the most interesting, which only discloses itself functionally, in its manifestations: a piece of the world itself, but at the same time possessing all the world, including itself, as objects and endlessly retrieving these objects through its rapprochements and refractions. This process is for itself the theme of all themes. But, as we also accompany spirit in its far-ranging attempt at interpretation (objectivation), experiencing it along with it, and as we also only understand this as its self-attestation, thus as we tarry in the ideal, we are nonetheless directed toward truth and reality: toward the cognition of the matter of fact of the human being, his nature, his essence, and his actuality. We again are dealing with matters of fact — in this case in three entwined strata: the matter of fact of this testament, which can stand powerfully on its own as it attends to great works; the matter of fact of what it deals with, its "theme," the intention whose terminus is always the world as actuality of the first order; and the matter of fact of the historicality of the human being, which stands behind him. This latter matter of fact is a thing that demands of its apprehension the widest and most attentive relationship to things of them all, since all the others reflect themselves in it — appear to it and come to the visible surface in it. It intends them in all its refractions and comprehends them in its interpretive or reproductive activity with varying luck. Historicality is for us a door and often a labyrinthine path *to the world*. Its being a door, taken together with its errors, belongs to the essence of spirit. If we want to arrive from there at the truth of the subject qua subject, i.e. at the correct cognition, the cognition which is faithful to the facts, then we ought not remain in an aesthetic intuition or a mere retrospective appreciation of historicality's creations. Even less ought we confine ourselves in our treatment of it to a psychological "understanding" of the mechanism of its functioning, the concealed drive of its production (this would be to disregard its own purpose, and we would indeed—in our ultimately unserious curiosity—have "seen through" it, but its claim would have withdrawn; we would surely have been unjust to it). Even more: *to* the truth of the human being belongs, as we must now discover forthwith, *his relation to truth*—thus *the things themselves*. This must be our guiding thread in our wanderings throughout the formations of spirit. They form an interpretive stratum over being, which is itself a great actuality for itself: But along with *what* they want to interpret, objective being, it must also still be important to the spirit that interprets *them* how it has been important to them.

What, then, can "to love the spiritual" (or to love spirit) mean other than: to love being? And what does this mean other than: being interested in matters of fact, i.e. finding value in paying attention to them? What does this mean other than: taking those details as important, holding in reverence those things which sink into themselves? All this is attached to the command to let actuality come into its justification. For its sake is spirit such as to be for its own sake. Neither of these facts should be avoided.

But the shortcut that only loves the spiritual and builds itself into its creations, too proud for the tedious, meandering path of actuality, is a dainty thing, too highbrow for the reverse prejudice of being involved with the material (or the animal) but also somehow immoral—and *not* a vindication, which spirit also required of it: spirit finds itself in its measure with actuality, in the faithful. But, concerning this tediousness, later.

In fact, all progress and all renewal of spirit on earth grows from new discovery or recovery of the world, of nature. Only from contact with his mother does this titan, after all his storming of the heavens, in all his wandering, ever win new power—and truth. That is the meaning of the renaissance—of every "renaissance." Discovery, observation, and penetration of actuality, in the great as well as the small. Science makes use of this. But art also: how deep the intuition of detail in a Homeric description. How much patient study of the human form, of its anatomy and of its mimetic expression in the Moses of Michelangelo. How great the cognizance with matter in every aesthetic transposition. In what great detail did Leonardo, at the infancy of both the new art and the new science, devote himself to the observation, the optical and functional study of nature in the myriad ways it surrounds us, particularly to the organic—not sparing his great genius from being "fragmented" into the many "unimportant" small things, as you would say. But for greatness the small is never too small. That is one of its secrets, and its name is originality. (And certainly, with all of his incomplete beginnings, Leonardo was greater than the scholastic or Aristotelian of his time, who could build a completed system of the world from his finished categories, something at which Leonardo, the observer of matters of fact, never succeeded.) "Objectivity" is the law of all spiritual deeds. Only music constitutes an exception to this: *it* is solely the free creation of the human being; it has nothing to do with objects and truth; it is, so to speak, the pure sovereign figuration of the dimension of time without space, therefore without the world.

In this infinite task, which spirit takes upon itself over against reality, the human being attains one of his determinations, if not his determination. Spirit is prepared for this from its depths in the history of being and becomes visible for the first time in the appearance of life, when matter for the first time feels itself in the most dark sensation of stimuli of living substance. I have begun to treat of this in my philosophy. The result, present in human spirit, is expressed most fully by Spinoza: the *amor dei intellectualis*, the intellectual intuition of being, is a part of the inf[inite] love with which the divine loves itself. Through this, a meaning of existence, of substance, is executed by itself, since we come from it and are a part of it.

First, therefore to attain being and to intuit; then to fathom and love it; finally to reflect and testify: that is the whole of wisdom: "everything else is commentary." How to carry this out? It is no objection to say that not everyone can do it—and that only a very few can do so fully. It is an ideal—the anthropological imperative. But virtually everyone can attain the first part. The capacity for this belongs to the generic equipment of *Homo sapiens*. The second could be regarded as a genuine endeavor by far more than try it—if "fathom" does not necessarily include only independent discovery but also learning what has already been thought, going down a greater or lesser part of the way. The third part is for the chosen, those who witness for humanity, which makes it also the most difficult. But is it a fault for an ethics to contain a goal for the elite, as small as this elite may be? The true must reach the peaks within this ethics.

How, then, to carry out the first part. It is the fundament of everything. I will turn back to the undertaking of the beginning.

(More follows.)

Dearest love, I have now arrived at the 12th of January. With a great interruption: I write under extremely unfavorable conditions, and at the moment also under the weight of news that is without joy for me personally. But none of that touches on the center of existence, which remains free for the free one to do his own doing.

Kisses from deep within

Your

Hans

Nr. V

January 26, 1945 PAL/8119 BDR. JONAS H

No. 134 B-Troop, P-Battery

The Jewish Field Regt. R. A.

C.M.F.

My love, today I would like to further develop the undertaking of letter 120.

All being, as we saw, is particular. It therefore provides matter to intuition and is — in and for itself — of value to intuition. But here is where the phenomenon of the order of magnitude and quantity makes its entrance. In order of magnitude, the elementary unities of being lie far below the threshold of our sensibility and can therefore never be immediate objects. At the same time, they are of such quantity that we simply could not linger with them as individuals. For both reasons, we can only observe their behavior *en masse*. This means we can only grasp their external reciprocal action statistically, following the law of large numbers, not their inner being. For us, they have no individuality and no difference. Granted, the elementary particle certainly has its inner qualitative essence, as mentioned at the start. If we could penetrate into it and conceptualize its action and reaction from within, then, in the intuition of the individual electron, we would most likely have the key to the mystery of being at our disposal and would require neither detour nor the feeble external compensation of the statistical sample. But we cannot do that and must content ourselves with measurable behavior. Admittedly, with the living being, the observation of visible behavior (which, however, goes far from the merely measurable), often leads to an understanding of the inner law of its life — since we possess the key to it from our own, more or less similar being. In contrast, we do not possess this key for atoms.

Atoms enter into the order of magnitude of our sensory-world only through the figure of tremendously numerous associations, in those characteristic agglomerations which are for us the whole of elementary things:

grains of sand, stones, drops of water, clouds . . . again so numerous and similar in form that we do no perceive them as individuals but only whole large groups of them as units. (This perception is also conditioned partly by their sensory—if not also their physical—smallness.) But they also enter into the sensory world with significant qualitative generic differences between these large groupings, which are grouped according to their similarity—the whole wealth of matter and its elementary forms of appearance in nature. And here the form, in many cases, begins to lift itself out of a generic likeness, as something particular. The particular figure, coloring and veining of a stone, the purity of a crystal, the form and luminescence of a cloud, the movement and play of colors of the sea beneath the sky—they all can draw our attention to themselves and grip our sensibility, hungry for form and quality. In particular, it is here that there are pluralities of delimited sets in characteristic compositions of "groups," which present intuition with quasi-individual unities from out of the generically alike many. And they join themselves together with other constellations similarly characteristic in type, forming an ensemble of a whole subsection of nature—a complete piece of the world with an individual physiognomy. These groups are, for example, brush, a forest, a mountain chain. This ensemble, which can be surveyed and whose elements work in concert, forms a landscape. Its space encompasses an infinite swarm of smaller, more individual forms and actual individuals, each of which is for itself an independent and completely valid object of intuition, but which is taken by the observation of the larger only as part of the whole and not for itself. But such is the case for the focus of vision, the lens-width of attention, so to speak, which can at each moment direct itself to an individual from its survey of the wider field of vision, so that it immediately becomes available to attention as a whole with many individuals in itself. And from being one of the general components in a homogeneous plurality, it immediately goes to being an individual for itself. A forest is certainly a whole in a broader fashion that, as it were, absorbs its constituent parts, the individual trees, into itself. But it does not cancel or sublate the individuality of the tree, which only dives beneath the surface of the seemingly identical repetition of the plurality. In the "whole" they actually only function with their likeness and not with their individuality, so that they can be interchanged and even eliminated, so to speak, without altering the character of the whole. But if we direct ourselves to the individual tree, then *it* has the character. The forest retreats into general background, and it, the single tree, now appears as the complete individual, with the total inexhaustibility of the same, which is based in the infinitude of aspect of each sensory thing and in the simultaneously typical and unique configuration of its great plurality of parts, variable within the limits of the typical. This individuality is easily visible in the tree that stands alone, and we confer upon it its own perceived meaning. The forest makes us forget it, so that instead of "not seeing the forest for the trees," the proverb ought to say "not seeing the trees for the forest." In the plurality of parts of the tree, regarded in its full individuality, the leaves are the identically formed universal that constitutes the particular whole, not in their unity, but rather in their multitude. But for itself, the individual leaf, in its form, color, veining, etc., is again a small, sensuous cosmos and the whole of many parts. And on it goes. This means: Each object of our attention in the world of composition is essentially accentuated (or: integrated) — as a part of the greater or the whole of the smaller — as the erstwhile particular between two horizons of adumbration into the universal: above, the horizon of the encompassing group, from which the focus of regard of the directly viewed single instance does not appear as a concrete individual but as the indifferent swarm-cloud, continuing to even higher frames of being; below, the horizon of its own formative parts, which once again do not appear for themselves, but as identically formed general building-material, themselves continuing into even smaller subparts. This integration of the individual from the two dimensions of the universal is continually (if not also exclusively, as we will see later) a function of the morphology of our attentiveness, i.e. a phenomenological characteristic of consciousness, a correlate of the configuration of the structure of actuality: attention's line of sight wanders from point to point, where it encounters, objectivates, and *makes* into concrete individuals, while at its edges it disappears into the cloud of the half-exposed and unexposed, and from there the universal.

This manifold, intertwined stratification of whole and parts, and of individuality and universality, at each time determined relative to observation, extends across the width of the whole order of magnitude of our sensuous world, retrieves itself from step to step of the complex, and disappears first across the threshold of the microscopically small into the indistinguishable likeness of the elementary. This is the lower limit.

Up above, our world concludes at the macrocosm, which through its tremendous spatial, temporal, and quantitative measurements transcends our receptivity, no less than did the world of the elementary, small things.

Because of a significant paradox of sensibility, the world of the immediately large appears from the perspective of an equally immense distance in the figure of the infinitely small unities of intuition: stars, mere points of light almost devoid of matter. A grain of dust gives more material to intuition. In comparison to the large, the relationship to the tiny, to which it so to speak dialectically reverts, repeats itself: the phenomenon of enormous quantity and of likeness in form. Correspondingly, we do not busy ourselves with a singular sun (taken as our own), as awesome and overpowering a reality as it also is in itself, but rather with classes of suns — blue, white, yellow, red — with enormous and typical agglomerations of them — star clusters, spiral nebulas, and galaxies. Only in this way do we get the better of the oversized measure of that world, like the infinitesimal measure of the smallest. Thus again, almost the same as in the atomic world, we ignore the apprehension of the single case, we abstain from individuation and content ourselves with the mechanisms of the crowd, the results of the external statistical integration of large numbers, speaking of stars as though they were specks of dust, even atoms. And the same also applies here: If we had the breadth of intuition and of duration to track the life of even a single one of these suns, if we could penetrate into its insides and make its processes and dynamics present to us with the resources of representation — by grasping *one* star in all the phases of its existence *and* in its inner laws (in which naturally the whole co-existing totality of stars co-operates, therefore also co-appears), we would probably have the key to the mystery of everything. We would not need the denaturing of the large number. . . . But here, as there, we cannot do it. And yet: the combination of both statistical methods of dealing with large magnitudes at opposite limits of the expanse of being, the lower and the upper, each of which must for itself give up on individual objectivation or unity — the combination of atomic physics and astrophysics — allows us to unexpectedly penetrate into the "life" of the stars and for the first time gives the surface of astronomical quantitative measurement the relief of depth, cutting it to the fit of cognition. Thus the one most universal apprehension of being completes the other — but both together, like each itself, remain in the realm of the purely quantitative, nonqualitative, and merely measurable. Only the manifold twinkling of the starry night sky remains to us as the object of qualitative intuition.

Now, between these extremes, between the submicrocosm and the macrocosm, a small subsection of the indifference of countless being, lies the

world of earthly form, the realm of our actual intuition, the only morphological being.

More later. For now, a thousand kisses.

With love

Your

Hans

Nr. VI
III.

The earthly world is our world. Although quantitatively it is only a tiny subsection of the whole of being, although our size-relationships, our duration
of time, and our sense-capacity ban us to this vanishing corner and fleeting moment of the all and withhold all small elements and motions within
it from us, although we live screened off in this way from the higher and
the lower, except insofar as instruments and abstractions do not expand the
limits for us without, however, being able to provide us with the full objectivity of intuition; although our dealings with the small world, which for
its part consists less of atoms than of shimmering accidents of one atom
of the large world, are therefore only the most coarse, summary integra-
tions of masses — yet, in this way perception and spirit or intellect find in
this world of ours their genuine inexhaustible theme. And in fact we do
not have any loss to mourn. In fact, this earthly world, in its multiplicity
of forms, in its differentiation of self-expressions of matter, places under
its shadow every thing in the immeasurable width of world-space with its
immeasurable quantities that can be exhibited as a rule. The result of the
most uncanny cosmic accidents, this peculiar, world-accidental earth is the
scene for the accident of all accidents. All three physical states of matter are
realized and co-exist in it thanks to a temperature span of barely more than
100 degrees centigrade around the freezing point of water (a priceless subsection of the universal) and are thus capable of affecting one another and
bringing the diversity of elements to appear in significantly distinct formations, formations which are not betrayed in the raw physical state of these
elements in the glowing mass of the sun — an infinite fullness of qualities
and figures in constancy and variation, where the difference is little more
than a spectral line that points to the cosmic fog of the potential manifold:
actually our world is *the* morphological world pure and simple, an accidental manifestation of matter, in which the monotony of the quantitative and

mixed is penetrated and broken into specific partitions and singular com-
pactions — we call this "nature."

This is just another way of saying that our world, the earthly one, is a
world of things. With this, the individual enters into the scheme. Alongside the multiplicity of genera of matter, taken in themselves, and alongside
matter's compounds, we already have in nature an unanticipated diversity
of outlines, each self-individuating agglomerations, in ephemeral or durable form, barely repeatable in their singularity, and then occurring simply
once in the spatiotemporal configuration of earthly nature, taken in a nar-
rower or wider context. And this onceness is once more raised to higher
powers through the infinitude of poss(ible) [*mögl(ichen)*] aspects (per-
spectives), each a onceness made possible by what happens just once. (This
potentiality is added to nature through the sensuousness of the being that is
essentially percipient.) All this is full of individuality.

But this individuality does not come from itself. It is for an observer.
Earlier I said of the "integration of the individual out of the universal" that
it is — largely — a function of morphological attention. This applies to all
merely morphological individuality (differentiation of form). Diversity is
not in itself individuality. Lifeless nature, with its richness of differences,
merely offers the substrate for it: the auth(entic) integration to individual
unity is prepared by the observer, ratcheting sense-perception up; it is not
a property of the thing itself, no *factor* of its being or becoming, only a
resort of its mat(erial) fate encountering a look (although in crystals, nature
already comes hard against the limit of the self-accomplishing form of
unity). In other words: we have been dealing up to now with the *phenomenological* concept of the individual (integration through the subject). For
this, the differentiating look of an observer is an essential condition.

But now something new appears in the region of nature, in which the
world-accident of the earth is driven to its climax, a climax that could not
have been anticipated or imagined in the least: unities of the many not by
virtue of intuition but by virtue of themselves; things, whose thing-being
[*Dingsein*] and this-being [*Diessein*] lie within them and are continually
sustained by them (*entelecheia*);[6] forms, which are not the conclusion, but
rather the original cause (*arche*) of determinate agglomerations of matter — self-positing unity, self-integrating form: living organisms. This *self-
integration* of life in its support for singularities first yields the ontological
concept of the individual as opposed to the merely phenomenological concept. As a self-centered unity whose being is its own function and already

in accordance with its original essence, in and for itself, every living being is not first an individual after the resultant form — an individual in the onto-logical and not just the phenomenological sense. This means nothing other than that life has introduced individuality into the cosmos for the first time, that a) only living beings are genuinely individuals, and b) that all living beings are such individuals.

As if to demonstrate the obviousness of this, ontological individuality, the realm of life in the unfolding of its forms, brings an uncanny enrich-ment of morphological individuality into the world: The multiplicity of fig-ures of life places lifeless nature into the shadows to such an extent that, in comparison, we can only find the proper articulation and richness of struc-ture of the forms there. And while the richness of structure in each singular life-form has for itself its basis, as product — and indicator — of its ontolog-ical individuality, the fantastic diversity of forms which manifests itself in the *kinds* of life, constitutes an abundance of morphological individuality of mediate rank, which substitutes the species for the bearer of singular traits. It is here where morphological intuition most strongly senses the differen-tiation of life and has enough to do in apprehending the expressions charac-teristic of the type: the ontological individual does not step as such into the line of sight, particularly where, for observation, the smallness and abun-dance of number subject it to the equalization of large numbers. When we consider that there are some 50,000 different kinds of ants, which organize socially into cohabitations each time consisting of many thousands, some-times hundreds of thousands, of individuals, whose singular individuality is difficult for our sight to distinguish and in whose behavior only that which is strongly typical of the kind is cognizable, then it becomes clear that here the "specificity" of nature is essentially or exclusively our object. But the plurality of the same specificity is so inexhaustible that the typical becomes for us the individual, in that in its own differentiation it more than satisfies our regard for individuality.

It is an unprovable, but probable, supposition that this does not just reflect the limitations of our intuition and our capacity for differences, but rather also reflects an objective state of affairs, insofar as the behavior typi-cal of the kind so dominates on the lower steps of life, that the "personal" element of individual behavior possesses no significance as a quality of its own. In any case, the wide distance that separates our order of life from that of the ants makes it absolutely inaccessible to us, and no similarity of form (mimicry), which only has a place in close biological relations, makes possible a communication of understanding. But the closer we come up the steps of life leading to our own order of life — to characterize it more precisely: in the regions of higher mammals — the more we are able to fasten onto the appearance and behavior of the singular being and to identify ourselves with it. This could also be expressed by saying that for us the ontological individual increasingly coincides with the phenomenological individual.

If our earlier supposition was correct, this subjective rapprochement of both these individualities parallels a factual, objective accumulative development of individuality on the rising steps of life. One who deals with horses or dogs knows that within their traits typical of the kind, they have individuality in the sense of pers(onal) characteristics, and I accept that each animal handler can say the same of his animals.

If we make this state of affairs clear, then we see that yet one more new — third — concept of individuality has turned up unnoticed here: In the ontological sense a slipper animalcule is no less an animal than the most developed vertebrate — this concept is not fit for gradation: it is based in the organized being of life and not in the possession of "individual properties." These latter are suitable for an individuality that constructs itself progressively in the differentiation and development of higher forms of life, perhaps as a simple consequence of greater compounding, and finally arrives at a "personal" level of behavior in the human being — and even there to unlike degrees — where it finds its full actualization. We could name this individuality prior to reaching the level of the spiritual or intellectual level the "characterological" and save the concept of "personal individuality" for human beings at the level of spiritual and intellectual consciousness.

These further developments of the concept of individuality all fall naturally under the *ontological concept*: They bear the fact of ontological individuality in general, which is present in the organism in itself, as the higher steps of its fundamental possibility. But these steps have their reflex also in a more marked phenomenological individuality. The unmistakable self-containment in look and habit, which determines the appearance of a certain individual within the kind, makes it distinguishable and recognizable, is the manifest testimony of that developed individuality of the higher step, which itself lies in an inner ontological principle.

Finally, there is yet a third connection between life and individuality, in which both the others are profoundly intertwined. Not only has life first introduced ontological individuality along with itself, and not only has it accordingly enriched the wealth of forms of possible phenomenological individuality: It is also that for which phenomenology exclusively is, and therefore also that for which phenomenological individuality is. It could probably be rigorously demonstrated that the perception of individuality by the living being is intertwined with the original state of affairs in the most basic foundation, and consequently from the very beginning, that the living being itself qua living being *is* the ontological *individual*. Without here analyzing the context any more precisely, let me briefly outline this demonstration: that the self-centered unity of the living It is the condition of the "thisness" [*Diesheit*] of its receptivity to external stimuli, i.e. its concentration into deposited unities from out of the diffuse horizon of world matter (or world energy), which exerts an influence from all sides. This is roughly what the diffuse stimulus draws from the expansive and sensitive surface of the life-complex toward the center and what gets combined to an analogical thickness there through a kind of refraction. In the last analysis, this is nothing other than the projection or reflection of the received It. This is in its way a universal law, that the degree of distinctiveness and thingliness [*Dinglichkeit*] of the impression of the external world stands in direct proportion to the development of a central selfhood, which the subject of such objectivity has to be. Up the long stepladder of freely moving animals gifted with special senses (both the attributes characterize the correlation of both these sides: greater constitution of selfhood = greater distinctiveness of perception; or: more individuality = more individualization of objectivity), as the heretofore most complete actualization of ontological individuality, this correlation in human spirit leads to what Kant called the "transcendental (or: 'synthetic') unity of apperception," the subjective correlate of the fully crystallized "object" of human world-sight. The paradox that this all-crystallizing objectivity pairs the highest individualization of world-sight with the capacity for higher universalization is an index for the additional elements that spirit has introduced into the process over and beyond the most complete sensuousness. But we should keep sight of the fact that the human being, with his transcendental faculty of objectivity, no less than with his extreme self-individuation, has before him the heritage of the whole development of life and still receives in surpassing what began darkly eons earlier and has itself, through the infinitely difficult self-effort of organized matter, brought its own stem to him, right up to the threshold. No inheritance imposes a greater duty on us.

AFTERWORD

"BUT FOR ME THE WORLD WAS

NEVER A HOSTILE PLACE"

Christian Wiese

❦

*This book, let it be said in advance, is not an autobiography. Originating in
conversation, it aims to capture memories of historical events and situations
that are particularly vivid to me and of which I was often merely a witness.
In other words: these are supposed to be memorabilia in the original sense
of the term. Quite a bit is anecdotal in character, recording entertaining
or interesting episodes. I am guided not by any systematic intention or
consistent theme; I simply narrate what comes to mind. And maybe
that can be organized somehow. But I'd like to say that the
unplanned quality is part of the plan.*

With these words Hans Jonas began the conversation that Rachel Salamander describes so compellingly in her foreword, and which resulted, ten
years after his death on 5 February 1993, in the German edition of this wonderful work. The rich memories that come alive in these pages mirror the
depth of Jonas's thinking and his remarkable capacity for recollection, qualities that enabled him to conjure up with brilliant clarity personal situations, stories, and philosophical insights. If one listens to the tapes, they
confirm what his many published interviews and conversations revealed:
Hans Jonas was a splendid storyteller, capable of recalling intricate autobiographical details and expressing all his knowledge, the most complicated
connections, in clear and aesthetically appealing language. He spoke, with
a charming sense of humor, in a voice that cast a spell over the listener.
The conversations did indeed yield "memorabilia" that conjured up a world
eminently worth remembering. It is the world of a philosopher, born in
Germany and driven into exile, who endured a number of serious reverses
in his life before his books and ideas eventually found an audience in Germany. His reminiscences, formulated in his mother tongue, appeared, in
time for the one-hundredth anniversary of his birth, in the country that had
shaped him most profoundly and at the same time had wounded him most

grievously. That they are now being published in his adopted home, the United States, provides evidence that Jonas's thinking is finally receiving the attention in the English-speaking world that it has enjoyed since the 1980s in Europe and even in Asia. It is.to be hoped that the special character of these memoirs will give readers insight into the historical context in which Jonas's work as a philosopher should be understood, in all its facets.

The worlds this book conjures up are those of Germany's Jews before the Nazi period, of the émigrés who evaded the Nazis by going to Palestine, and of the intellectuals in exile in New York — distant worlds of which younger generations can now catch a glimpse only through the vivid stories and analyses offered by eyewitnesses like Hans Jonas. For that reason alone these "memorabilia" are precious. But they are also valuable for the variety of genres that come together here to form a fascinating counterpoint: autobiography, exile literature, love story, history of philosophy, historical reflection, and philosophy in action.

One of the most riveting features of Hans Jonas's memoirs is the manner in which he speaks of other people; it is incisive and frank, sometimes ironic or critical, but above all loving. His narrative not only mirrors his own rich personality; it also conjures up vibrant images of all the figures who were important in his life — evidence of the attentiveness and perspicacity with which he interacted with them, without denying their weaknesses. His most significant friendships, in the context of the German-Jewish emigration, were those with Hannah Arendt and Gershom Scholem. These friendships were not free from dramatic crises; the passages about these crises reveal him as a person with a real gift for friendship, but also as a man who did not shy away from conflict when it was a question of remaining true to himself and his convictions. His passionate but ambivalent friendship with Scholem, overshadowed by what his friends in Jerusalem considered Jonas's "betrayal of Zionism," and by growing differences of opinion on scholarly matters — resulting from the clash of two strong personalities — certainly constitutes one of the most exciting components in those passages in which Jonas describes his personal relationships.[1] As for the long, heartfelt friendship that linked Hans Jonas with Hannah Arendt, starting during their time in Marburg, "under the spell of Heidegger," it would be difficult to surpass Jonas's own account — affectionate, sometimes lovingly critical, respectful of Arendt's intimate relationship with Heidegger and the rapidity with which she forgave him after 1945, full of admiration for her humane qualities and sensibility, for her own gift for friendship, and generous in acknowledging the richness of her thought and her work.[2] It is characteristic of the absolute honesty that was his hallmark that Jonas did not refrain from recounting the dramatic clash that might have destroyed their friendship, had that friendship not been far too deeply rooted. The memoirs speak of this painful episode in detail and with a lucidity that requires no further interpretation.[3] It is precisely the stories of his friendships or his love affair with his wife that draw the reader into the world of his relationships and reveal the philosopher as a person of great humanity and emotional integrity; it is to be hoped that this image will keep the memory of him alive for many years to come.

Although Jonas asserted that in the conversations on which this book was based he consciously took an unsystematic, associative approach, trusting that another hand would "perhaps organize it all," that assertion should be recognized as something of an exaggeration. Guided by the questions posed to him by Rachel Salamander and Stephan Sattler, he actually followed a very clear narrative line. But Jonas's comment suggests that the project of turning the spoken word into a book, of shaping this wealth of memories into a coherent text — without destroying its spoken quality — struck me at first as a truly Herculean task. At the same time, Jonas's statement justified my making a considerable number of editorial changes — from judicious cutting and editing to dividing the text into focused, chronologically ordered chapters. That process necessitated several interventions, from relocating certain narrative passages to interpolating material from other sources, for instance where, in the "Taking Leave of Heidegger" chapter, the tape had failed to record and the text had to be augmented from other conversations and essays. One gap in Jonas's narrative was filled from a different source entirely: the passage in chapter 9 about the Jonases' life as a young married couple in the Arab village of Isawiya before the outbreak of the 1948 War of Independence. That account draws on an autobiographical piece by Lore Jonas.[4] In addition, extensive notes were provided to give the reader more context, to point in the direction of further reading, and to make available obscure biographical archival material. Many texts by and about Hans Jonas, hitherto largely or completely unknown, have been integrated into the book, some from archives, some from Lore Jonas's private collection.[5] Prominent among them are the wonderful poems from the Pilegesh circle, Hans Jonas's appeal to the youth of Palestine to join the fight against Nazi Germany, and numerous letters that illustrate and add depth to his stories. The same is true of the remarkable "didactic letters," published here for the first time, that the soldier sent his wife in Jerusalem in 1944–45. They offer an intimate look at a decisive turning point in his thinking — the first expression of his "new ideas" about a "philosophy of the organic." Similarly, Franz Rosenzweig began drafting his *Star of Redemption* in letters written during the last months of the First World War, while he was serving on the Macedonian front.

The German edition of these memoirs contains a lengthy afterword that undertakes to connect the many and varied facets of Jonas's thought with the narrative of his life and to provide a detailed interpretation. The essay emphasizes the Jewish aspects of Jonas's biography and work, many of which appear in a new light when viewed against the background of his account. Now that I have published my monograph, *The Life and Thought of Hans Jonas: Jewish Dimensions*, which offers a thorough commentary on Jonas's memoirs, the reader can be referred to that work. The following brief observations are intended merely to stress that Jonas's intellectual contributions as a historian of religion, a philosopher, and an ethicist should, in the future, never be viewed separately from his own biographical awareness, rooted in his quintessentially Jewish twentieth-century experience. To be sure, his prolific work is not dedicated to an interpretation of Judaism as a purely religious phenomenon, nor would he have wanted to be characterized as a Jewish philosopher. Rather he was convinced that his most important mission, that of formulating an ethics of human responsibility for preserving life on this planet, had to be undertaken, in a period devoid of consensus on theological and religious principles, without reference to such categories. Such an ethics had to be universally applicable, lest it appear dogmatic or irrelevant. The tense relationship between his Jewish identity and his universal aspirations as a historian of religion and a philosopher, which manifests itself in his reflections on his relationship to the Jewish tradition, was expressed most saliently by Jonas himself when he confronted his deep personal attachment to Judaism with the ethos of a philosopher committed to pure reason.[6]

In light of the connection between existential experience and philosophy to which Jonas repeatedly called attention,[7] the biographical elements acquire decisive significance for illuminating the Jewish dimensions of his work. The intellectual direction of his philosophical thinking, with its discontinuities but also its fundamental consistency, which can be found in the central motif of human beings' responsibility for the life of the world, understood as the "Creation," cannot be appreciated fully unless one recognizes his origins as a German Jew and his fate as an émigré. Part of Jonas's life experience is his decision to embrace Zionism, brought about by his early encounters with antisemitism and his sense of being a stranger in Germany. Another essential part of his experience is his life in Palestine in the 1930s and his personal involvement in the struggle against Nazi Germany, of which his far-sighted appeal to Jewish men offers moving evidence, as well as the discovery of his mother's tragic fate in Auschwitz. Jonas's account of his determined opposition to the "National Socialist principle" and of the shattering experience of the extermination of Europe's Jews, which occupies a good deal of space in his memoirs, is a stirring *document humain*, without which the further development of his philosophy after the war cannot be fully appreciated. This account leaves no doubt as to the significance of Jonas's Jewish identity for his life's work.

Awareness of his Jewishness acquired a profoundly existential significance for Jonas during the struggle against Nazi Germany and after 1945, when the full dimensions of the extermination of Europe's Jews became known. This awareness began to take shape as a result of Jonas's emigration, when his research on religious history and his academic career were rudely interrupted. It grew during his military service, in the course of which he formulated, in his "didactic letters" to his wife, the core of his new philosophy of life. It was intensified by the painful discovery that his beloved mother had perished in Auschwitz, and it was to her that he dedicated his essay "The Concept of God after Auschwitz," written almost forty years later. As his memoirs show, the intellectual insights derived from Jonas's wartime experiences inspired his lifelong confrontation with nihilism and his philosophical affirmation of the value of human life, however vulnerable, imperfect, and transitory that life might be. The ideas snatched from the experience of inhumanity were to issue in Jonas's fervent plea for an ethics of responsibility in the face of the threats posed by modern technology. Jonas's antinihilist position and the philosophical passion with which he defended the life of all human and other beings clearly originated in the confrontation with the Shoah and the Nazis' utter disregard for all humane values. Even in his last speech, delivered in Udine on 30 January 1993, a few days before his death, Jonas reminded his audience that it had been in "one of the heartlands of our vaunted culture" that that "hellish revelation" had occurred that more than any previous event "calls into question man's right to be seen as created in God's image."[8] It is characteristic of Jonas's thought and of his entire work that in this speech he associates the Nazis' disregard for human life in the past with current and future threats to life on earth brought about by humans' technological hubris.

These memoirs mirror the development of Jonas's thought with remarkable clarity. His scholarly involvement with the phenomenon of gnosticism in antiquity, a phenomenon in which he saw important parallels to modern nihilism; his realization of the political affinity of his teacher Martin Heidegger to Nazism, which Jonas perceived as a catastrophic failure of philosophy;[9] and his commitment to a "philosophy of the organic" after 1945 all resulted in his recognition that human beings should not view the world as an inhospitable place but should accept it and take responsibility for making it a place where all organic life can survive. Jonas's positive orientation toward life finds particularly compelling expression in the passage in the memoirs where he measures the light and darkness in his life and comes to the conclusion that for all the horrors he has experienced, particularly the loss of his mother, he has never seen the world as a hostile place. This moving confession points beyond the purely autobiographical to one of the underlying motifs of his philosophy: the affirmation of life in the face of death.

In the final chapter of his memoirs, chapter 13 of this book, Jonas expounds on his ambivalent relationship to religion and his understanding of Judaism. Here we see the powerful connection between his philosophy, his ethical approach to ecology and bioethics, and his ideas on religion. Despite the secular basis of his ethical theory in *The Imperative of Responsibility*, elements of Jewish tradition play a major part in the articulation of that theory, above all the motif of the Creation. That motif includes the implicit respect for preserving the Creation that is incumbent upon one of its creatures, the human being. In the essay "Matter, Mind and Creation," Jonas points to the liturgical epithet for God as *rotseh ba-hayim* — the "one desirous of life" — as a driving, if not explicit factor in his philosophical thinking. The human counterpart to that divine characteristic is the freedom and the responsibility to respect the dignity and autonomy of each and every life.[10] He understands this traditional element, which was taken up and passed on to Western philosophy by Christianity, as Judaism's most valuable legacy to the modern era, marked by technological and ecological crisis.

Jonas's philosophical reflections on the ethical relevance of the Jewish tradition and the Jewish existential experience acquire their greatest force where he undertakes to justify his struggle to understand God and the nature of the human being in the context not only of the modern skepticism toward all metaphysics but also of the experience of the Shoah. The philosopher's memoirs allow us to witness his decades-long struggle to find an interpretation that would satisfy him — a deviation, as he admits, from what is usually considered legitimate territory for philosophy. His essay "The Concept of God after Auschwitz: A Jewish Voice" offers a unique contribution to the many voices involved in theological and philosophical discussion of post-Auschwitz Jewish faith. The fascinating aspect of Jonas's reflections, which he puts forward "with fear and trembling,"[11] can be found in the combination of profound existential shock at God's silence in the face of a genocide of unparalleled dimensions, philosophical rigor when it comes to rejecting the concept of God as an omnipotent ruler over history, and the beauty and depth with which he presents his "hypothetical myth" of an evolving, suffering God who shed his divinity when he created life, placing the world and his own divinity in the hands of a fully autonomous mankind. According to Jonas, God kept silent at Auschwitz because he had relinquished his power, precisely in order to give mankind the freedom to act responsibly. That an era of genocide and potentially devastating technological development places God himself at risk emerges as a secret leitmotif in Jonas's cosmogonic "speculations." The ultimate goal of these speculations is to express Jonas's passionate opposition to any devaluation of human life and to fatalism, which he views as a betrayal of the responsibility God conferred on man when he made man in his image.

Jonas's memoirs, as well as his writings, reveal the way in which he tried to remain true to both Judaism and philosophy, not in the sense of reconciling them but of allowing them to resonate with one another in his thinking and his emotions. The counterpoint between these two elements in his work testifies not to a purely personal commitment to a religious tradition but to Jonas's conviction that in a period when human life itself is in grave danger, Judaism possesses the theological and ethical force to articulate and galvanize the human sense of responsibility. The life-affirming tone of the memoirs is echoed in Jonas's writings and public appearances, especially toward the end of his life. As Jonas said in his speech when he received the Peace Prize of the German publishing industry in 1987, "To be aware of the cloud hanging over us . . . paradoxically allows us to glimpse the light of hope. . . . This light does not glow like that of Utopia, but its warning illuminates our path — together with the belief in freedom and reason. In the end, the principle of responsibility thus joins the principle of hope—no longer an extravagant hope for an earthly paradise but a more modest hope that the earth may continue to be habitable and may permit our race an existence worthy of it. . . . This is the card on which I wish to wager."[12]

CHRONOLOGY

1903   Hans Jonas is born in Mönchengladbach on May 10, the son of the textile manufacturer Gustav Jonas and Rosa Horowitz.

1916   The death of Jonas's younger brother, Ludwig. Bar mitzvah.

1918   The November revolution in Germany. Jonas becomes interested in Zionism and, to the dismay of his father, joins a Zionist circle in Mönchengladbach.

1921   School-leaving examination. Jonas begins his study of philosophy and art history in the summer semester at the University of Freiburg, taking courses with Edmund Husserl, Martin Heidegger, and Jonas Cohn. Meets Karl Löwith. Joins the Zionist student organization IVRIA.

1921   Moves to Berlin for the winter semester, where he studies philosophy at the Friedrich-Wilhelm University until 1923 (with professors Eduard Spranger, Ernst Troeltsch, Hugo Gressmann, Ernst Sellin, and Eduard Meyer, among others) and Judaica at the Hochschule für die Wissenschaft des Judentums (with professors Julius Gutmann, Harry Torczyner, Eduard Baneth, et al). Friendship with Leo Strauss and Günther Stern (Anders). Involvement with the Zionist organization Makkabäa and the Cartel of Jewish Associations (KJV).

1923   March–October agricultural training (Hachshara) in Wolfenbüttel as preparation for emigration to Palestine. Decision to continue his studies in Germany. Academic year 1923–24 in Freiburg.

1924   Move to Marburg University for the winter semester. Studies with Martin Heidegger and Rudolf Bultmann. Beginning of friendship with Hannah Arendt. Together with Gerhard Nebel, Karl Löwith, Gerhard Krüger, Günther Stern, et al. forms the circle of philosophy students around Heidegger. First studies of gnosticism. After the decision to pursue the doctorate, intermittent studies in Heidelberg, Bonn, and Frankfurt am Main.

1928   Return to Marburg. Completion of the doctorate with Martin Heidegger with dissertation "The Concept of Gnosticism." Winter semester 1928–29 in Paris at the Sorbonne.

1929   Beginning of love relationship with Gertrud Fischer.

1930   Publication of *Augustin und das paulinische Freiheitsproblem*.
Until 1933 private studies in Frankfurt am Main and Heidelberg.
A member of the group around the sociologist Karl Mannheim.
Friendship with Dolf Sternberger. Plan to write a *Habilitation*
(second dissertation, qualifying for a professorship), and
preparation for teaching as an instructor.

1933   Hitler's "seizure of power." In response to the anti-Jewish boycott,
Jonas decides to leave Germany. Emigrates to London at the end of
August and works on revising his gnosticism study for publication.
Trips to Holland, Switzerland, and to Paris, where Hannah Arendt
and Günther Anders are in exile.

1934   Part I of *Gnosis und spätantiker Geist* published by Vandenhoeck &
Ruprecht in Göttingen.

1935   Arrival in Palestine for Passover. Beginning of friendship with
Gershom Scholem, Hans Lewy, Hans-Jakob Polotsky, George
Lichtheim, and Shmuel Sambursky. Formation of the Pilegesh
circle.

1936   Visit of Jonas's parents to Jerusalem for Passover. Beginning of the
Arabs' uprisings against the Zionist settlement program. Jonas
volunteers for the self-defense organization Haganah.

1937   At Purim, Jonas meets Lore Weiner. In the fall goes to the island of
Rhodes to work on part 2 of the gnosticism study.

1938   In January, news of the death of his father. Return to Jerusalem.
After the Night of Broken Glass in November, Rosa Jonas turns
over her immigration certificate for Palestine to her son Georg,
who is imprisoned in Dachau. In 1939, new restrictions on
emigration to Palestine, imposed by the British, prevent Jonas's
mother from leaving Germany. Jonas receives teaching assignments
at the Hebrew University. After the death of Edmund Husserl, Jonas
eulogizes him at the university.

1939   Immediately following the outbreak of war on 1 September, Jonas
pens the appeal "Our Part in This War: A Word to Jewish Men,"
and volunteers for the British army.

1940   Basic training at the British camp in Sarafant. Member of the
British army's First Palestine Anti-Aircraft Battery. Deployed to
Haifa to counter aerial attacks from Damascus and Beirut.

1942   Deportation of Jonas's mother to the ghetto in Łódź, later to
Auschwitz, where she is murdered.

1943   Marriage to Lore Weiner in Haifa.

1944   Jonas becomes a member of the newly formed Jewish Brigade Group. Training in Alexandria and elsewhere. Deployed to southern Italy. During this time writes "didactic letters" to his wife, discussing his new ideas on philosophy.

1945   In July Jonas travels through Germany with his unit. Stationed in Venlo, visits to Mönchengladbach. Here Jonas learns of his mother's death. Trips to Göttingen, Marburg, and Heidelberg. Reunions with Karl Jaspers and Rudolf Bultmann. In November returns to Palestine.

1946   Living in the Arab village of Isawiya. Instructor at the Hebrew University in Jerusalem and teaching appointment at the British Council.

1948   Declaration of the independent state of Israel and outbreak of war. The Jonases move to Alfasi Street in Jerusalem. Jonas is drafted as an artillery officer by the Israeli army. Death of Lore's brother, Franz, in Jenin. Birth of daughter, Ayalah.

1949   Discharge from the army. Move to Canada as a fellow of the Lady Davis Foundation at Montreal's McGill University. Teaching philosophy at McGill's Dawson College.

1950–51

     Guest professor, then associate professor of philosophy at Carleton College, Ottawa. Birth of son, Jonathan. Friendship with Ludwig von Bertalanffy. During this period, trips to New York, Chicago, and Cincinnati. Reunion with Hannah Arendt, Günther Anders, and Karl Löwith.

1952   Jonas declines offer of professorship of philosophy at the Hebrew University. Quarrel with Gershom Scholem over his "betrayal of Zionism." First postwar trip to Europe, for the International Congress for Philosophy in Brussels. Side trip to Munich and meeting with Gertrud Fischer. Declines a professorship in Kiel.

1954   *Gnosis und spätantiker Geist*, second volume, published.

1955   Birth of daughter, Gabrielle. Named professor at the New School for Social Research in New York (where Jonas remains until 1976; in the meantime, visiting professorships at Princeton, Columbia, and the University of Chicago). Purchase of house in New Rochelle. Friendship there with Kurt and Nelly Friedrichs and with Wilhelm and Trude Magnus. In New York, part of the circle of friends around Hannah Arendt and Heinrich Blücher, which includes Adolph Lowe, Aron Gurwitsch, and Paul Tillich.

1958   Publication of *The Gnostic Religion: The Message of the Alien God and the Beginnings of Christianity.* Academic convocation lecture "The Practical Uses of Theory." Beginning of intensive thinking about modern technology.

1959–60

Jonas spends his sabbatical in Munich. Lecture tours in Germany.

1961   Ingersoll Lecture at the Harvard Divinity School, "Immortality and the Modern Temper."

1963   Break with Hannah Arendt over her book on the Eichmann trial in Jerusalem; almost two years pass before they reconcile.

1964   Jonas's lecture "Heidegger and Theology" at Drew University in New Jersey creates an uproar. Lecture tour to Germany. Not until 1969 does Jonas have a brief personal encounter with Heidegger, in Zurich.

1966   Publication of *The Phenomenon of Life: Toward a Philosophical Biology.*

1967   "Philosophical Reflections on Experiments with Human Subjects" lecture delivered to the American Academy of Arts and Sciences in Boston. Focus on concrete ethical problems in biology and medicine, such as brain death and organ transplantation.

1969   Founding fellow of the interdisciplinary Hastings Center.

1973   *Organismus und Freiheit* published.

1974   *Philosophical Essays: From Ancient Creed to Technological Man* published.

1976   Speech at the memorial service for Rudolf Bultmann in Marburg. Retires from teaching.

1978   Publication of *On Faith, Reason, and Responsibility: Six Essays.*

1979   *Das Prinzip Verantwortung: Versuch einer Ethik für die technologische Zivilisation* becomes an overwhelming success in Germany.

1982–83

Eric Voegelin guest professorship at the University of Munich.

1984   Jonas receives the Leopold Lukas Prize of the Protestant Theological Faculty at the University of Tübingen. Acceptance speech "Der Gottesbegriff nach Auschwitz: Eine jüdische Stimme."

1985   Publication of *Technik, Medizin und Ethik: Zur Praxis des Prinzips Verantwortung.*

1987   Jonas receives the Peace Prize of the German publishing industry. Acceptance speech "Technik, Freiheit und Pflicht." Receives the Medal of Honor from the Federal Republic of Germany and is made an honorary citizen of the town of Mönchengladbach.

1988   Publication of *Materie, Geist und Schöpfung: Kosmologischer Befund und kosmogonische Vermutung.*

1991   Honorary doctorate from the University of Konstanz.

1992   Honorary doctorate from the Free University, Berlin.

1992   Publication of *Philosophische Untersuchungen und metaphysische Vermutungen.*

1993   Publication of *Philosophie: Rückschau und Vorschau am Ende des Jahrhunderts.* On 30 January receipt of the Premio Nonino in Urbino, Italy. On 5 February Hans Jonas dies in New Rochelle. He is buried in the Jewish section of the multifaith cemetery in Hastings-on-Hudson.

NOTES

Chapter 1. Youth in Mönchengladbach during Wartime

(pp. 3–21)

1. On the situation of the Jewish community on the eve of the First World War and on its attitude in 1914, see Egmont Zechlin, *Die deutsche Politik und die Juden im Ersten Weltkrieg* (Göttingen, 1969), especially 86–100. On the attitude of Jewish intellectuals toward the war, see Ulrich Sieg, *Jüdische Intellektuelle im Ersten Weltkrieg: Kriegserfahrungen, weltanschauliche Debatten und kulturelle Neuentwicklung* (Berlin, 2001).

2. On the antisemitically motivated "Jewish census" of 1916, which was based on the charge that a smaller percentage of Jews had volunteered, and the effect of this census on the Jewish community, see Zechlin, *Die deutsche Politik*, 516–567.

3. On Jakob Horowitz, see *Krefelder Juden* (Krefelder Studien, vol. 2), issued by the Krefeld City Archives. On the tradition of the Breslau Seminar, see Guido Kisch, *Das Breslauer Seminar (Jüdisch-Theologisches Seminar, Fraenckel'scher Stiftung) in Breslau 1824–1938: Gedächtnisschrift* (Tübingen, 1963) (Horowitz bibliography, 169). See also Eleonore Stockhausen, "Zur Geschichte der jüdischen Gemeinde Krefelds im 19. Jahrhundert," in *Krefelder Juden* (Bonn, 1981), 63–65.

4. On the Jewish community in Borken, see *Leben und Schicksal der Juden in Borken: Eine Dokumentation aus Anlass der Ausstellung im Stadtmuseum Borken vom 9. bis 27. November 1987*, issued by the Arbeitsgemeinschaft "Jüdisches Leben in Borken und Gemen" (Borken, 1989).

5. From the turn of the century on, mixed marriages became increasingly common. According to Monika Richartz in *Jüdisches Leben in Deutschland*, vol. 2 (Stuttgart, 1979), between 1901 and 1905 18% of all Jewish marriages were mixed; between 1906 and 1910, the number increased to 23.7%; from 1911 on, 38 Jewish marriages out of 100 were mixed (17). Between 1911 and 1915, 22% of Jewish men and 13% of Jewish women married non-Jews. On Jewish views of mixed marriages and on the social history of Christian-Jewish mixed marriages, see Kerstin Meiring, *Die christlich-jüdische Mischehe in Deutschland 1840–1933* (Hamburg, 1998).

6. A vivid picture of the way of life and the self-image of assimilated middle-class Jewish families at this time can be found in Gershom Scholem's "Zur Sozialpsychologie der Juden in Deutschland 1900–1930," in Reinhold von Thadden, ed., *Die Krise des Liberalismus zwischen den Weltkriegen* (Göttingen, 1978), 256–277.

7. See Gerhart Hermann Mostar, *Friederike Kempner, der schlesische Schwan: Das Genie der unfreiwilligen Komik* (Munich, 1980).

8. Friederike Kempner, *Dichterleben, Himmelsgabe: Sämtliche Gedichte* (Berlin, 1989), 193–196.

9. See Friederike Kempner, *Gegen die Einzelhaft oder das Zellengefängnis* (1869). She developed a comprehensive program for social policy in her *Büchlein von der Menschheit* (1885).

10. On the ideology of the pan-German movement, see Alfred Kruck, *Geschichte des Alldeutschen Verbandes 1890–1939* (Wiesbaden, 1954).

11. See Heinrich Lersch, *Ausgewählte Werke*, vol. 1 (poems) (Jena, 1965), 56.

12. Lersch, *Aufglühe dein Blut* (Jena, 1918); *Deutschland! Lieder und Gesänge von Volk und Vaterland* (Jena, 1918). On Lersch's later affinity to National Socialism, see his *Deutschland muss leben* (Jena, 1935). On his biography, see Fritz Hüser, ed., *Heinrich Lersch, Kesselschmid und Dichter 1889–1936* (Dortmund, 1959).

13. See Lersch, *Ausgewählte Werke*, vol. 1, 127f.

14. Kurt Pinthus, *Menschheitsdämmerung: Symphonie jüngster Dichtung* (Berlin, 1920). On this anthology, see Horst Denkler, *Gedichte der "Menschheitsdämmerung": Interpretationen expressionistischer Lyrik* (Munich, 1971).

15. The poem referred to is "Noëmi" in Pinthus, *Menschheitsdämmerung*, 306–310. See Margret A. Parmée, *Ivan Goll: The Development of His Poetic Themes and Their Imagery* (Bonn, 1981).

16. On Buber's Zionist speeches and his influence on the Jewish youth movement, see Klaus Dawidowicz, "Martin Buber und der deutsche Zionismus," *Kairos* 34–35 (1992–93), 192–217; Maurice Friedman, *Begegnung auf dem schmalen Grat: Martin Buber—Ein Leben* (Münster, 1999), 47–66; and the introduction by Robert Weltsch to Martin Buber, *Der Jude und sein Judentum: Gesammelte Aufsätze und Reden* (Darmstadt, 1992), xiii–xl. See also Eleonore Lappin, *Der Jude 1916–1928: Jüdische Moderne zwischen Universalismus und Partikularismus* (Tübingen, 2000).

Chapter 2. Dreams of Glory: The Road to Zionism
(pp. 22–38)

1. Felix Dahn, *Der Kampf um Rom: Historischer Roman* (1867).

2. Edward Gibbon, *The History of the Decline and Fall of the Roman Empire*. 6 vols. (1776–88).

3. Presumably Wilhelm Gottlieb Soldan, *Geschichte der Hexenprozesse: An den Quellen dargestellt* (1843, 3rd ed. 1911).

4. On Rathenau as a representative of assimilated Jewry in Germany, see Peter Berglar, *Walther Rathenau: Ein Leben zwischen Philosophie und Politik* (Graz, Vienna, Cologne, 1987).

5. On the congregation in Mönchengladbach, see Günther Erckens, *Juden in Mönchengladbach: Jüdisches Leben in den früheren Gemeinden M. Gladbach, Rheydt,*

Odenkirchen, Giesenkirchen-Schelsen, Rheindahlen, Wickrath und Wanlo, 2 vols. (Mönchengladbach, 1988–89).

6. On the synagogue, see Michael Brocke, ed., *Feuer an Dein Heiligtum gelegt: Zerstörte Synagogen 1938 Nordrhein-Westfalen* (Bochum, 1999), 381ff.

7. On the characterization of German-Jewish orthodoxy in this period, see Mordechai Breuer, *Jüdische Orthodoxie im Deutschen Reich 1871–1918: Die Sozialgeschichte einer religiösen Minderheit* (Frankfurt/Main, 1986); on Westfalen, see Thomas Kollatz, "Westfälisches Judentum zwischen Reform und Orthodoxie im 19. Jahrhundert," in Kirsten Menneken and Andrea Zupancic, eds., *Jüdisches Leben in Westfalen* (Essen, 1998), 98–108.

8. Carsten Colpe, *Die religionsgeschichtliche Schule* (Göttingen, 1961); Gerd Lüdemann, "Die religionsgeschichtliche Schule," in Bernd Möller, ed., *Theologie in Göttingen: Eine Vorlesungsreihe* (Göttingen, 1987), 325–361; Lüdemann and Martin Schröder, *Die Religionsgeschichtliche Schule in Göttingen: Eine Dokumentation* (Göttingen, 1987). On the dispute between Jewish scholars and the School of Religious History, see Christian Wiese, *Wissenschaft des Judentums und protestantische Theologie im Wilhelminischen Deutschland: Ein "Schrei ins Leere"?* (Tübingen, 1999), 140–172.

9. The reference is to the *Handkommentar zum Alten Testament*.

10. On the significance of prophecy for Jonas's interpretation of Zionism, see Hans Jonas, "Die Idee der Zerstreuung und Wiedersammlung bei den Propheten," *Der Jüdische Student* 4 (1922), 30–43.

11. Martin Buber, *Die Legende des Baalschem* (Zurich, 1993) and "Drei Reden über das Judentum," in *Der Jude und sein Judentum*, 3–140.

12. On the affinity of Jewish intellectuals in the nineteenth and twentieth centuries for Kant, see Julius Guttmann, *Kant und das Judentum* (Leipzig, 1908); Hans Mosche Graupe, "Kant und das Judentum," *Zeitschrift für Religions- und Geistesgeschichte* 13 (1966), 308–333. In a passage in the interviews on which these memoirs are based, Jonas replies, when asked whether Kant or Plato is more important to him, as follows: "The answer is: Plato — of course. In some respects, Kant has things to say to us that are far more relevant, for he was a man of the eighteenth century, and in Kant the connection between the critique of epistemology and moral philosophy is much more accessible for us. You can cite him directly. With Plato, however, you have to go back a much greater distance to make him applicable to the present. But of course Plato is the greater one, the one we have to study again and again from scratch, the one we must discover, whereas we can get to know Kant thoroughly. With Plato, you're never finished. That's the great foundation for all of Western philosophy."

13. Immanuel Kant, *Grundlegung zur Metaphysik der Sitten*, ed. Bernd Kraft and Dieter Schönecker (Hamburg, 1999), 11.

14. See for instance Werner Jochmann, "Die Ausbreitung des Antisemitismus," in

Werner E. Mosse and Arnold Paucker, eds., *Deutsches Judentum in Krieg und Revolution 1916–1932* (Tübingen, 1971), 409–509.

15. See Ernest Hamburger, "Hugo Preuss: Scholar and Statesman," *Leo Baeck Institute Year Book* 20 (1975), 179–206.

16. On the phenomenon of intensified "postassimilationist" Zionism resulting from antisemitism, see Jehuda Reinharz, "The Zionist Response to Antisemitism in Germany," *Leo Baeck Institute Year Book* 30 (1985), 105–140.

17. On the Centralverein and its ideology, see Abraham Barkei, *"Wehr Dich!" Der Centralverein deutscher Staatsbürger jüdischen Glaubens (C.V.) 1893–1938* (Munich, 2002); Jehuda Reinharz, *Fatherland or Promised Land: The Dilemma of the German Jew, 1893–1914* (Ann Arbor, Mich., 1975); on the Zionist approach to this concept of identity, see Reinharz, *The German Zionist Challenge to the Faith in Emancipation, 1897–1914*, Spiegel Lectures in European Jewish History (Tel Aviv, 1982).

18. Franz Werfel, *Das lyrische Werk* (Frankfurt/Main, 1967), 86f.

19. *Im deutschen Reich: Zeitschrift des Centralvereins deutscher Staatsbürger jüdischen Glaubens* 1–28 (1895–1922).

20. Julius Berger (1883–1948) played a leading role in Keren Hajessod's work in Central Europe, and moved to Palestine in 1924.

21. Cf. Adolph Asch and Johanna Philippson, "Self-Defence at the Turn of the Century: The Emergence of the K.C.," *Leo Baeck Institute Year Book* 3 (1958), 122–139.

22. On German Zionism and its primarily philanthropic focus, see Yehuda Eloni, *Zionismus in Deutschland: Von den Anfängen bis 1914* (Gerlingen, 1987) (on the ZVfD, 73–219); Jehuda Reinharz, ed., *Dokumente zur Geschichte des deutschen Zionismus 1882–1933* (Tübingen, 1981), especially the introduction (xix–il).

23. Theodor Herzl, *Der Judenstaat: Versuch einer modernen Lösung der Judenfrage* (1896).

24. Leon Pinsker, *"Autoemanzipation!" Mahnruf an seine Stammesgenossen von einem russischen Juden* (Berlin, 1882).

25. Achad-Haam, *Am Scheidewege*, 2 vols. (Berlin, 1913); see Steven Zipperstein, *Elusive Prophet: Ahad Ha'am and the Origins of Zionism* (London, 1993).

26. Georg Landauer (1895–1954), Zionist leader, director from 1929 on of the Palestine Bureau in Berlin, moved to Palestine in 1934 and became director of the Jerusalem Jewish Agency's Central Bureau for the Resettlement of German Jews in Palestine; see Georg Landauer, *Der Zionismus im Wandel dreier Jahrzehnte*, ed. Max Kreutzberger (Tel Aviv, 1957).

27. In Hebrew: "The Young Worker"—a Jewish socialist, non-Marxist workers' party founded in 1906 in Palestine; its mission was to settle Jewish workers in Palestine as farmers, a profession from which Jews had been alienated as a result of conditions in the Diaspora. Through the "conquest of work," these workers were to experience moral

renewal. The movement was active in Germany starting in 1917 and exerted a strong influence on German Zionism.

28. See Yosef Gorny, *Zionism and the Arabs, 1882–1948: A Study of Ideology* (Oxford, 1987), and Gideon Shimoni, *The Zionist Ideology* (Hanover, N.H., 1995).

29. On the effect of the bloody struggles that took place in Palestine in 1929 on German Zionism, see Jehuda Reinharz, ed., *Dokumente zur Geschichte des deutschen Zionismus*, 424–492.

30. Here Jonas is probably referring to an entry Lasalle made in his diary on 2 February 1840. See Lasalle, *Tagebuch*, ed. Friedrich Hertneck (Berlin, n.d.), 31: "Indeed I believe I am one of the best Jews there are, without attending to the ceremonial laws. I could lay my life on the line . . . to rescue the Jews from their current oppression. I would not even fear the gallows if I could make them a respected people once again. Oh, when I indulge myself in my childish dreams, it is always my fondest idea to make the Jews independent, with me leading them, weapon in hand."

31. See Sigmund Freud, *Die Traumdeutung* (Studienausgabe, vol. II) (Frankfurt/Main, 1972), 207f.: "When . . . the first understanding arose for the consequences of being descended from a foreign race, and the manifestations of anti-Semitism among my classmates impelled me to take a stand, the figure of the Semitic general assumed even greater stature in my eyes." In reference to an antisemitic incident described by his father, to which his father claimed to have responded calmly, Freud writes of his reaction as a child: "I countered this situation, which did not satisfy me, with the image of another, which corresponded better to my feelings, the scene in which Hannibal's father, Hamilkar Barkas, insisted that his son swear before the household altar to take revenge on the Romans. From that time on, Hannibal occupied a place in my fantasies."

Chapter 3. Between Philosophy and Zion: Freiburg – Berlin – Wolfenbüttel (pp. 39–58)

1. On neo-Kantianism in Marburg and Cohen's role, see Ulrich Sieg, *Aufstieg und Niedergang des Marburger Neukantianismus: Die Geschichte einer philosophischen Schulgemeinschaft* (Würzburg, 1994).

2. On the Zionist organization in Freiburg, see Ruben Frankenstein, "Zionismus in Freiburg im Breisgau," in Heiko Haumann et al., eds., *Der Erste Zionistenkongress von 1897: Ursachen, Bedeutung, Aktualität* (Basel, 1997), 239–242.

3. See Rudolf Bernet, *Edmund Husserl: Darstellung seines Denkens* (Hamburg, 1996); Dermot Moran, *Edmund Husserl* (Oxford, 2002); Friedrich Wilhelm von Hermann, *Hermeneutik und Reflexion: Der Begriff der Phänomenologie bei Heidegger und Husserl* (Frankfurt/Main, 2000).

4. See the description in Jonas's unpublished lecture "Husserl and Heidegger" (Leo

Baeck Institute Archives, New York, AR 2241/MS75): "The impression Husserl made as a teacher was powerful, but . . . with certain comical traits. May I say first that Husserl was the quintessential German professor. His teaching was monologic in nature. His truth was firmly established, and from the moment he had found it, a genuine exchange with others had become completely uninteresting to him. This wholly one-sided, unwavering concentration on the one truth he had to offer was his strength and his weakness, an almost solipsistic characteristic that he shared with a number of German philosophers, but which in his case derived a kind of coolness from the moral pathos with which his belief in his own truth was combined. Certain traits, which conferred on him a kind of orthodoxy, something Jewish in his complete remove from everything Jewish, was unmistakable. In his Göttingen period, which preceded his time in Freiburg, he was dubbed by his students 'the rabbi of Göttingen.' . . . A German full professor had mandatory courses to teach, sometimes on topics he would not have chosen himself. One such mandatory course was on the history of modern philosophy. Nothing was farther from Husserl's real interests than the history of philosophy, for the truth is of course not interested in the errors of the past. But his course on philosophy since Descartes was extraordinarily dramatic, and unforgettable to me. His treatment of each of these philosophers . . . ended with the formulaic sentence, 'Only modern phenomenology has found the real answer to this question.' . . . He was completely naïve in this belief. It was the naïveté of complete certainty and conviction, complete disregard for everything else, and complete unworldliness."

5. Edmund Husserl, *Logische Untersuchungen*, 2 vols., facsimile edition of the second, partly revised edition (The Hague, 1993).

6. Aristotle, *On the Soul*.

7. See Martin Heidegger, "Augustinus und der Neuplatonismus" (summer semester 1921), in *Gesamtausgabe, II. Abteilung: Vorlesungen 1919–1944*, vol. 60, *Phänomenologie des religiösen Lebens* (Frankfurt/Main, 1995), 160–199.

8. See Karl Löwith, *Mein Leben in Deutschland vor und nach 1933: Ein Bericht* (Stuttgart, 1986), 1ff.

9. See Margret Heitmann, *Jonas Cohn (1869–1947): Das Problem der unendlichen Aufgabe in Wissenschaft und Religion* (Hildesheim, 1999), and "Jonas Cohn: Philosoph, Pädagoge und Jude: Gedanken zur Werdegang und Schicksal des Freiburger Neukantianers und seiner Philosophie," in Walter Grab and Julius H. Schoeps, eds., *Juden in der Weimarer Republik* (Stuttgart, 1986), 179–199.

10. On Husserl's relationship to Judaism, see Karl Schumann, "Edmund Husserl (1859–1938)," in Hans Erler, Ernst L. Ehrlich, and Ludger Heid, eds., *"Meinetwegen ist die Welt erschaffen!" Das intellektuelle Vermächtnis des deutschsprachigen Judentums* (Frankfurt/Main, 1997), 112–117.

11. See Marvin Farber, ed., *Philosophical Essays in Memory of Edmund Husserl*

(Cambridge, Mass., 1940), and *The Foundation of Phenomenology* (Cambridge, Mass., 1943).

12. See Hans Jonas's lecture "Husserl und Heidegger" (see note 4 above). Jonas describes how Husserl reacted to a student's reports on nightlife in Berlin, in which "prostitution was also mentioned." According to him, Husserl exclaimed, "But not in the city of Hegel and Schleiermacher!" Referring to Husserl's characterization of Paris as a "disreputable city," Jonas continues, "But Berlin was the city of Hegel and Schleiermacher, in which there wouldn't be any prostitution. All this innocence and childish naiveté and remoteness from reality existed side by side with great purity, with genuine purity and devotion to the idea of thought. It was a combination that is probably not possible anywhere else, and probably will not be possible again. Such ignorance and innocence can probably no longer be maintained even when a theoretician closes himself off as much as possible from outside interference."

13. Marianne Awerbuch, "Die Hochschule für die Wissenschaft des Judentums," in Rainer Hansen and Wolfgang Ribbe, eds., *Geschichtswissenschaft in Berlin im 19. und 20. Jahrhundert: Persönlichkeiten und Institutionen*, Veröffentlichungen der Historischen Kommission zu Berlin (Berlin and New York, 1992), 517–552; Heinz Hermann Völker, "Die Hochschule für die Wissenschaft des Judentums in Berlin 1900–1942," in Hartmut Walravens, ed., *Bibliographie und Berichte: Festschrift für Werner Schochow* (Munich, 1990), 196–230.

14. The instructor in the Talmud and rabbinical matters at the institute was Eduard Baneth (1855–1930).

15. Judah Halevi, *Der Kusari*, new, completely revised edition of this work published in 1853 in German translation (Zurich, 1990).

16. See Julius Guttmann, *Die Philosophie des Judentums*, with an assessment by Esther Seidel and a biographical introduction by Fritz Bamberger (Berlin, 2000).

17. See the portrayal of the theology of these two scholars in Ulrich Kusche, *Die unterlegene Religion: Das Judentum im Urteil deutscher Alttestamentler* (Berlin, 1991).

18. See Eduard Meyer, *Ursprünge und Anfänge des Christentums*, 3 vols. (Stuttgart and Berlin, 1921–23). On Meyer's portrayal of the Jews, see Christhard Hoffmann, *Juden und Judentum im Werk deutscher Althistoriker des 19. und 20. Jahrhunderts* (Leyden, 1988), 133–188, and "Classical Scholarship, Modern Anti-Semitism, and the Zionist Project: The Historian Eduard Meyer in Palestine (1926)," *Studies in Zionism* 13 (1992), 133–146.

19. See Hoffmann, *Juden und Judentum*, 200–245; David N. Meyers, "Eugen Täubler: The Personification of Judaism as Tragic Existence," *Leo Baeck Institute Year Book* 39 (1944), 131–150.

20. On the Jewish youth movement and its organizations, see Yehuda Eloni, *Zionismus in Deutschland*, 405–459 (on the Blau-Weiss, founded in 1912 by Felix

Rosenblüth, 449–459). See also Chaim Schatzker, "The Jewish Youth Movement in Germany, 1900 to 1933" [in Hebrew], Ph.D. dissertation, Hebrew University, Jerusalem, 1969; Michael Brenner, "Turning Inward: Jewish Youth in Weimar Germany," in Brenner and Derek Penslar, eds., *In Search of Jewish Community: Jewish Identities in Germany and Austria, 1918–1933* (Bloomington, Ind., 1998), 56–73.

21. Ernst Toller, *Man and the Masses: A Play of the Social Revolution in Seven Scenes*, trans. Louis Untermeyer (Garden City, N.Y., 1924).

22. At the time Strauss saw himself as a "political Zionist" and supporter of the "revisionist" movement of Vladimir Jabotinsky; see Leo Strauss, "Why We Remain Jews: Can Jewish Faith and History Still Speak to Us?" in *Jewish Philosophy and the Crisis of Modernity: Essays and Lectures in Modern Jewish Thought*, ed. Kenneth Hart Green (New York, 1997), 311–356, especially 319f. On Strauss's biographical development, see Green, "Leo Strauss as a Modern Jewish Thinker," in ibid., 1–84, especially 3ff.

23. Leo Strauss, "Das Problem der Erkenntnis in F. H. Jacobis philosophischer Lehre," Ph.D. dissertation, University of Hamburg, 1922.

24. See David N. Myers, "The Fall and Rise of Jewish Historicism: The Evolution of the Akademie für die Wissenschaft des Judentums (1919–1934)," *Hebrew Union College Annual* 63 (1992), 107–144.

25. A group of the non-Zionist "comrades" even called themselves "the black horde." See Stefanie Schüler-Springorum, "Jugendbewegung und Politik: Die deutsch-jüdische Jugendgruppe 'Schwarzer Haufen,'" *Tel Aviver Jahrbuch für deutsche Geschichte* 28 (1999), 159–209.

26. On the songs of the Jewish youth movement, see Max Matter, "'. . . Stolz wollen wir aufrecht schreiten, in Treue für Juda streiten . . .' Jüdische Jugendbewegungen und ihre Lieder," in Freddy Raphael, ed., "*. . . Das Flüstern eines leisen Wehens . . .": Beiträge zu Kultur und Lebenswelt europäischer Juden* (Konstanz, 2001), 133–148.

27. See Michael Bühler, *Erziehung zur Tradition — Erziehung zum Widerstand: Ernst Simon und die jüdische Erwachsenenbildung in Deutschland* (Berlin, 1986); Ernst Simon, *Entscheidung zum Judentum: Essays und Vorträge* (Frankfurt/Main, 1980), and *Sechzig Jahre gegen den Strom: Briefe von 1917–1984* (Tübingen, 1998).

28. While still a schoolboy and already a member of a small group of Jewish youths ("Jung-Juda"), Scholem had protested vehemently in 1914 against the lack of Jewish substance in Blue and White; see Gershom Scholem, *Von Berlin nach Jerusalem: Jugenderinnerungen* (Frankfurt/Main, 1977), 59–63. See also Scholem, "Jugendbewegung," in *Die blauweisse Brille* no. 1 (1914), Erich Brauer and Gerhard Scholem, eds. (quoted in Yehuda Eloni, *Zionismus in Deutschland*, 455).

29. See Martin Buber, *Der Weg des Menschen nach der chassidischen Lehre* (Gütersloh, 1999).

30. Franz Rosenzweig, *Der Stern der Erlösung* (Frankfurt/Main, 1988 [1921]); see

Stéphane Mosès, *System und Offenbarung: Die Philosophie Franz Rosenzweigs* (Munich, 1985), and *Der Engel der Geschichte: Franz Rosenzweig, Walter Benjamin, Gershom Scholem* (Frankfurt/Main, 1994).

31. Ernst Bloch, *The Spirit of Utopia*, trans. Anthony Nassar (Palo Alto, 2000). On Bloch, see Arno Münster, *Ernst Bloch: Eine Biographie* (Frankfurt/Main, 2003).

32. On the Jewish Lehrhaus, see Michael Brenner, *Jüdische Kultur in der Weimarer Republik* (Munich, 2000), 81–113.

33. See, for instance, Leo Strauss, "Franz Rosenzweig und die Akademie für die Wissenschaft des Judentums," in *Jüdische Wochenzeitung für Kassel, Hessen und Waldeck* 13 (December 1929).

34. Felix A. Theilhaber, *Der Untergang der deutschen Juden: Eine volkswirtschaftliche Studie* (Berlin, 1921).

35. See Scholem's characterization of this translation as a "gift that the German Jews were able to leave the German people in a symbolic act of gratitude as they departed." From the historical point of view, Scholem goes on to say, after Auschwitz the translation was no longer a gift but "the grave marker for a relationship that was obliterated by unspeakable horrors": "The Jews who undertook the translation are no more. The children of those who escaped these horrors will no longer read German. The German language itself has changed radically in this generation." See Gershom Scholem, "An einem denkwürdigen Tage," in *Judaica 1* (Frankfurt/Main, 1981), 207–215.

36. See Steven E. Aschheim, *Brothers and Strangers: The East European Jews in German and German-Jewish Consciousness, 1800–1923* (Madison, Wis., 1982); Trude Maurer, *Ostjuden in Deutschland 1918–1933* (Hamburg, 1986).

37. See Sammy Gronemann, *Howdoloh und Zapfenstreich: Erinnerungen an die ostjüdische Etappe 1916–1918* (Leipzig, 2000), and *Erinnerungen* (Berlin, 2002).

38. See Peter A. Degen, "Albert Einstein: Ein deutsch-jüdischer Physiker zwischen Assimilation und Zionismus," in Ulrich Lilienthal and Lothar Striehm, eds., *Den Menschen zugewandt: Festschrift für Werner Licharz* (Osnabrück, 1999), 147–158.

39. Karl Kraus, *Die letzten Tage der Menschheit: Tragödie in 5 Akten mit Vorspiel und Epilog* (Vienna, 1919).

40. See Sander Gilman, *Jewish Self-Hatred: Anti-Semitism and the Hidden Language of the Jews* (Baltimore, 1986); on Kraus, see Robert S. Wistrich, "Karl Kraus: Jewish Prophet or Renegade," *European Judaism* 9 (1975), 32–38.

41. See Karl Kraus, "Der Neger," in *Grimassen: Ausgewählte Werke*, vol. 1 (1902–14) (Berlin, 1971), 537ff.

42. Karl Kraus, *Gedichte* (Frankfurt/Main, 1989), 267f. The quotation from Kant to which the poem refers goes as follows: "At the sad spectacle not so much of the evils that assail the human race as a result of natural causes but of those that human beings perpetrate on one another, one's spirit is cheered by the prospect that things may yet

improve; and this cheering occurs with unselfish benevolence, for we ourselves shall be in the grave long since, and will never harvest ourselves the fruits that we have in part sown" (quoted in *Grimassen*, 267).

Chapter 4. Marburg: Under the Spell of Heidegger and Gnosticism
(pp. 59–72)

1. Thomas von Aquin, *Über Seiendes und Wesenheit* (Latin and German), ed. Horst Seidl (Hamburg, 1988).

2. See for instance Martin Heidegger, "Das Rektorat 1933/34—Tatsachen und Gedanken (1945)," in *Gesamtausgabe*, vol. 16: *Reden und andere Zeugnisse eines Lebensweges* (1910–76) (Frankfurt/Main, 2000), 372–391. See also George Leaman, "Das politische Denken Martin Heideggers," in Leaman, ed., *Heidegger im Kontext: Gesamtüberblick zum NS-Engagement der Universitätsphilosophen* (Hamburg, 1993), 109–150; Gerhard Schmidt, "Heideggers philosophische Politik," in Gottfried Schramm, ed., *Martin Heidegger: Ein Philosoph und die Politik* (Freiburg, 2001), 217–236.

3. See Elisabeth Young-Bruehl, *Hannah Arendt: For Love of the World* (New Haven, Conn., 1982); Elzbieta Ettinger, *Hannah Arendt, Martin Heidegger: Eine Geschichte* (Munich, 1995).

4. See Hans Jonas, *Wissenschaft als persönliches Erlebnis* (Göttingen, 1987), 16ff. On Jonas's contribution to scholarship on gnosticism, see Christian Wiese, "Revolte wider die Weltflucht," afterword to Jonas, *Gnosis: Die Botschaft des fremden Gottes* (Frankfurt/Main, 1999), 401–429, and Walter Betz, "Der Religionswissenschaftler Hans Jonas," *Zeitschrift für Religions- und Geistesgeschichte* 48 (1996), 68–80.

5. See Jonas, "Gnosticism and Modern Nihilism," *Social Research* 19 (1952), 430–452. See the interpretation by Micha Brumlik, *Die Gnostiker: Der Traum von der Selbsterlösung des Menschen* (Berlin, 2000), 252–294.

6. Jonas, *Wissenschaft als persönliches Erlebnis*, 14–19.

7. See the text of the recommendation in Martin Heidegger, *Gesamtausgabe*, vol. 16, 89.

8. See the contributions by Günther Anders in *Über Heidegger*, ed. Gerhard Oberschlick. (Munich, 2001).

9. See Young-Bruehl, *Hannah Arendt*.

10. On Arendt's later political thought, see Dana Villa, *Politics, Philosophy, Terror: Essays on the Thought of Hannah Arendt* (Princeton, N.J., 1999).

11. Hannah Arendt, *Der Liebesbegriff bei Augustin* (Berlin, 1919). See Ronald Beiner, "Love and Worldliness: Hannah Arendt's Reading of Saint Augustine," in Larry May and Jerome Kohn, eds., *Hannah Arendt: Twenty Years Later* (Cambridge, Mass., 1997), 269–284.

12. Max Weber, *The Protestant Ethic and the Spirit of Capitalism* (1905).

13. Max Weber, *Gesammelte Aufsätze zur Religionssoziologie*, 3 vols. (Tübingen, 1988).

14. See Hans Jonas, "Karl Mannheims Soziologie des Geistes," *Schriften der deutschen Gesellschaft für Soziologie* 1 (1929), 111–114.

15. See Blomert, *Intellektuelle im Aufbruch: Karl Mannheim, Alfred Weber, Norbert Elias und die Heidelberger Sozialwissenschaften der Zwischenkriegszeit* (Munich, 1999).

16. *Briefwechsel zwischen Wilhelm Dilthey und dem Grafen Paul Yorck von Wartenburg 1877–1897* (Halle, 1923). See Karlfried Gründer, *Zur Philosophie des Grafen Paul Yorck von Wartenburg: Aspekte und neue Quellen* (Göttingen, 1970).

17. See Marion Yorck von Wartenburg, *Die Stärke der Stille: Erzählung eines Lebens aus dem deutschen Widerstand* (Munich, 1995).

Chapter 5. Emigration, Refuge, and Friends in Jerusalem
(pp. 73–94)

1. On the situation of the Jewish community in Germany during this phase of the Weimar Republic, see George L. Mosse and Arnold Paucker, eds., *Entscheidungsjahr 1932: Zur Judenfrage in der Endphase der Weimarer Republik*, 2nd rev. edition (Tübingen, 1966). On the causes for the Jewish community's slowness to recognize, even after 1933, the threat it was facing, see Marion Kaplan, *Der Mut zum Überleben: Jüdische Frauen und ihre Familien in Nazideutschland* (Berlin, 2001), 11–15.

2. On the beginning of the persecution, see the relevant essays in Wolfgang Benz, ed., *Die Juden in Deutschland 1933–45: Leben unter nationalsozialistischer Herrschaft* (Munich, 1988); Arnold Paucker, *Die Juden im nationalsozialistischen Deutschland/The Jews in Nazi Germany, 1933–1943* (Tübingen, 1986).

3. Hans Jonas, *Gnosis und spätantiker Geist, Erster Teil: Die mythologische Gnosis* (Göttingen, 1934); 2nd edition, 1954; 3rd edition, revised and expanded, 1964.

4. See chap. 8.

5. See Kaplan, *Der Mut zum Überleben*, 187–298.

6. On Jewish-Arab violence and the role of the British, see Anita Shapira, *Land and Power: The Zionist Resort to Force, 1881–1948* (Oxford, 1992).

7. See Yaacov Shavit, *Jabotinsky and the Revisionist Movement, 1925–1948* (London, 1988); Joseph B. Schechtman, *The Life and Times of Vladimir Jabotinsky* (Silver Spring, Md., 1986).

8. The reference is to Richard Lichtheim, *Das Programm des Zionismus* (Berlin, 1911).

9. See Richard Lichtheim, *Rückkehr: Lebenserinnerungen aus der Frühzeit des Zionismus* (Stuttgart, 1970) (on Turkey, 215–334).

10. On his research on Marxism, see George Lichtheim, *Ursprünge des Sozialismus* (Gütersloh, 1969), and *Kurze Geschichte des Sozialismus* (Munich, 1975).

11. See Miriam Lichtheim, *Ancient Egyptian Literature: A Book of Readings* (Berkeley, Calif., 1973), and *Moral Values in Ancient Egypt* (Fribourg, 1997).

12. See Ruth Bondy, "Der Dornenweg deutscher Zionisten in der Politik: Felix Rosenblüth in Tel Aviv," *Menora* 9 (1998), 297–314.

13. See Eli Shai, "Samuel Hugo Bergman: A Partial Portrait," *Ariel* 57 (1984), 25–36; William Kluback, *Courageous Universality: The Work of Shmuel Hugo Bergman* (Atlanta, 1992); Hugo S. Bergman, *Jawne und Jerusalem: Gesammelte Aufsätze* (Königstein, 1981), and *Tagebücher und Briefe*, 2 vols. (Berlin, 1985).

14. Carl Schmidt, *Ein Mani-Fund in Ägypten: Originalschriften des Mani und seiner Schüler* (Berlin, 1933).

15. See Hans Jakob Polotsky, *Manichäische Handschriften der Sammlung A. Chester Beatty*, vol. 1 (1934), and "Manichäismus," in August F. Pauly and Georg Wissowa, eds., *Real-Enzylopädie der klassischen Altertumswissenschaft*, supp. 2 (Stuttgart, 1935), 240–271. See also Marcel Erdal, "Hans Jakob Polotsky (1905–1991): An Appreciation," *Mediterranean Review* 8 (1994), 1–9.

16. As he made clear in a letter written to Gershom Scholem on 25 June 1938, Jonas was personally as well as philosophically impressed by Buber: "Buber's lecture was brilliant, a real pleasure in both content and form. The man himself makes a stronger impression on me than I had imagined from a distance, probably because I knew him before this almost only from his public demeanor, which after all always has its dubious aspects, whereas in private conversation, when one is alone with him, every disturbing element disappears, and his uncommonly positive qualities come to the fore. I am surprised at the development in his thinking that this sixty-year-old manifests, to say nothing of the remarkable breadth of his knowledge. He has philosophical force and depth. Besides, in him I have found a really active supporter, whose willingness to intercede for me I can count on (Scholem papers, Jewish National University Library [hereafter cited as JNUL], 4°1599).

17. Oswald Spengler, *Der Untergang des Abendlandes: Umrisse einer Morphologie der Weltgeschichte* (Vienna, 1918).

18. Hans Lewy, *Chaldean Oracles and Theurgy: Mysticism, Magic, and Platonism in the Later Roman Empire* (Paris, 1978).

19. See Hans Jonas, "Husserl and the Problem of Ontology" (in Hebrew), *Mosnajim* 7 (1938), 581–589. In the same 1938 letter to Scholem quoted in note 17, Jonas offers a vivid picture of the difficulty he had preparing a lecture at the university (and a radio lecture on Husserl): "I had . . . my 'debut' at the university and shortly before that my first radio lecture in Hebrew . . . for all of this a great deal of preparation, both of the content and the language—the latter something I never had to contend with before. But giving my maiden lecture and doing it in Hebrew at the same time is a lot to take on. I began my preparation—when Bergman shared with me an invitation to

a memorial lecture on Husserl at the university—by going through Husserl's entire collected works in the space of ten days. Then I wrote and discarded several drafts, finally typed up a text in German that bore no resemblance to any of them, and then sweated it out for a week with Jernensky [his Hebrew teacher, C.W.] to get the lecture into Hebrew. The result surpassed my expectations, to the extent that such a thing can be assessed from the immediate success of a lecture, and gave me some good cards to play in the game here, which I can certainly use. I anticipate further positive repercussions, though I am clear as to the limitations on what I can reasonably hope for." The radio address appeared in Hebrew under the title "In Memoriam Edmund Husserl" in *Turim* (1938), and began with the following words: "At the beginning of May, Edmund Husserl, one of the great philosophers of our time, died in Freiburg. He had been active as a teacher and scholar at the university there until his retirement in 1929, the leading figure in a school of philosophy to which students flocked and which exercised a profound influence on Germany's philosophical life. He taught a generation to think, experienced fame, and then died in obscurity, the world around him transformed and no longer willing to eulogize him. In the face of this silence in the country to which he gave so much, we are honor-bound to remember him here. He himself, who had turned his back on Judaism as a young man, who was a German professor and saw himself entirely as a servant of European learning, as a guardian of the European cultural heritage, would certainly never have envisaged that what was neglected in Freiburg would be done in Jerusalem. The fact that today a student who sat at his feet years ago is allowed to memorialize him on Jerusalem radio in Hebrew is itself emblematic of our time."

20. George Lichtheim, *Marxism in Modern France* (New York, 1968).

21. Martin Jay, "The Loss of George Lichtheim," *Midstream* 19 (1973), 41–49.

Chapter 6. Love in Times of War
(pp. 95–109)

1. In a letter dated 25 July 1938 to Gershom Scholem, Jonas describes a violent incident in Jerusalem: "Last month I witnessed an incident in Jerusalem that has shaken me to the core. You have no doubt heard about 'bloody Tuesday.' One of the bloody deeds took place right below my window, around 5:30 in the morning. I immediately went to the window and the next moment ran outside and dragged a mortally wounded Arab to the Hadassah. I assure you, it is hard to imagine anything more terrible" (Scholem papers, JNUL, 4°1599).

2. Despite his participation in the Jewish self-defense force, Jonas, like some of his friends in Jerusalem, including Gershom Scholem, was also a member of the peace group Brith Shalom, which was advocating for a fair settlement with Arab interests. On this organization and its German-Jewish origins, see Hagit Lavsky,

"German Zionists and the Emergence of Brith Shalom," in Jehuda Reinharz and Anita Shapira, eds., *Essential Papers on Zionism* (New York, 1996), 648–670; Shalom Ratzabi, *Between Zionism and Judaism: The Radical Circle in Brith Shalom, 1925–1933* (Leyden, 2002).

3. On this subject, see the correspondence between Scholem and his mother, in which deliveries of chocolates and marzipan from Germany to Palestine play a not inconsiderable role: *Betty Scholem–Gershom Scholem: Mutter und Sohn im Briefwechsel, 1917–1946*, ed. Itta Shedletzky with Thomas Sparr (Munich, 1989).

4. Hans Jonas, "The Nobility of Sight: A Study in the Phenomenology of the Senses," *Philosophy and Phenomenological Research* 14 (1953–54), 507–519.

5. See Lore Jonas, "Mein Vater Siegfried Weiner (1886–1963)," in *Regensburger Almanach* 1989, 49.

Chapter 7. A "Bellum Judaicum" in the Truest Sense of the Word
(pp. 110–130)

1. Drafts of this document that can be found in the Hans Jonas papers in the Philosophical Archives of the University of Konstanz (handwritten draft HJ 5–9–332; typescripts HJ 5–9–1/2/3) provide insight into the stages of its genesis. Originally the appeal began with the words "When, on 3 September, England and France declared war on Hitler's Germany, Jews all over the world immediately had the thought: This war — whatever else it may always mean for those involved — is also *our* war. Whatever else this hour holds in the way of world and individual peoples' guilt — Jewish fate stamps it as *our* hour. Our feeling unmistakably recognizes it as such: political judgment confirms this and demands our complete participation in this war. We must view it as the Jewish people's cause, to be waged in its name. Let us account to ourselves for the prerequisites for and results of this attitude." A copy of the final version is also deposited in the Konstanz archives (HJ 5–9–40) and at the Leo Baeck Institute in New York (AR 2241 addenda). It was published in the *Jüdischer Almanach 2001/5761 des Leo Baeck Instituts* (Frankfurt/Main, 2000), 79–91. Cf. the interpretation by Christian Wiese, "Ein Bellum judaicum in des Wortes tiefster Bedeutung: Hans Jonas' Kriegsausruf 1939 im Kontext seiner Biographie und seines philosophischen Denkens," ibid., 92–107.

2. Included were numerous important figures in German Zionism, e.g., Gershom Scholem, Sally Hirsch, Benno Cohn, Alfred Berger, Georg Landauer, Walter Gross, Max Kreutzberger, Robert Weltsch, and Moshe Smoira.

3. Cf. Elias Gilner, *War and Hope: A History of the Jewish Legion* (New York, 1969); Matityahu Mintz, "Pinchas Rutenberg and the Establishment of the Jewish Legion in 1914," *Studies in Zionism* 6 (1985), 15–26.

4. On Britain's policy in Palestine during the war, see Bernard Wasserstein, *Britain*

and the Jews of Europe, 1939–1945 (Oxford, 1979); Ronald W. Zweig, *Britain and Palestine during the Second World War* (London, 1986).

5. On the motivation of these émigrés, see Yoav Gelber, "Central European Jews from Palestine in the British Forces," *Leo Baeck Institute Year Book* 35 (1990), 321–332. The decisive element was the determination to be among the liberators of the surviving remnant (321).

6. Michael Evanari, *Und die Erde trage Frucht: Ein Lebensbericht* (Gerlingen, 1987).

7. On the prehistory and the genesis of the Jewish Brigade Group, see Yoav Gelber, *Jewish Volunteers from Palestine in the British Army during the Second World War* (in Hebrew), vol. 1 (Jerusalem 1979) and vol. 2 (Jerusalem 1981). On the history of the brigade, see Morris Beckman, *The Jewish Brigade: An Army with Two Masters, 1944–45* (Staplehurst, 1998). On Churchill's role in the British change of attitude, see especially 42–50.

8. On Enzo Sereni and the development of his thought, see Ruth Bondy, *The Emissary: A Life of Enzo Sereni* (Boston, 1977); Evelyn Wilcock, *Pacifism and the Jews* (Gloucestershire, 1994), 61–71.

9. The "Didactic Letters" written in 1944 are printed here for the first time; see chap. 14.

10. In a letter to Scholem, Lore Jonas wrote on 12 March 1945, "Otherwise he is doing well. He is near Rome. Goes into the city every week and is of course thrilled. His letters (among other things) are hymns to Michelangelo on the one hand and the Quattrocento on the other. Weren't you the one who once accused him of being a sybarite for his preoccupation with art? I think it's something he has a right to indulge, don't you?" Scholem papers, JNUL, 4°1599.

11. In his last speech, given on the occasion of his receiving the Premio Nonino on 30 January 1993 in Udine, Jonas recalled his encounters in Italy and emphasized that he had carried these stories with him ever since, "like a sacred gift that had been entrusted to me." See Hans Jonas, "Rassismus im Lichte der Menschheitsbedrohung," in Dietrich Böhler, ed., *Ethik für die Zukunft: Im Diskurs mit Hans Jonas* (Munich, 1994), 21–29.

Chapter 8. Travels through a Germany in Ruins
(pp. 131–148)

1. Primo Levi, *The Drowned and the Saved* (New York, 1988). See Alksandar Tisma, *Kapo* (Munich, 1999).

2. Lore Beyerlein, ed., *Von drei Reichen: Briefe des Malers Kurt Beyerlein aus den Jahren 1941–1945* (Reinbek, 1947).

3. Hans Jonas, "Origenes' Peri Archon: ein System patristischer Gnosis," *Theolo-*

gische Zeitschrift 5 (1949), 101–119, and "Die origenistische Spekulation und die Mystik," *Theologische Zeitschrift* 5 (1949), 24–45.

4. Not until 1954 did the second part of *Gnosis und spätantiker Geist* appear with Vandenhoeck & Ruprecht, under the title *Von der Mythologie zur Mystischen Philosophie*, dedicated "To the Memory of my Mother. Auschwitz 1942." Jonas dedicated a later edition of volume 1 to the memory of his father.

5. Rudolf Bultmann, *Das Evangelium des Johannes* (Göttingen, 1941).

6. Erich Dinkler, "Die christliche Wahrheitsfrage und die Unabgeschlossenheit der Theologie als Wissenschaft," in Otto Kaiser, ed., *Gedenken an Rudolf Bultmann* (Tübingen, 1977), 15–40.

7. Hans Jonas, "Im Kampf um die Möglichkeit des Glaubens: Erinnerungen an Rudolf Bultmann und Betrachtungen zum philosophischen Aspekt seines Werkes," in Kaiser, *Gedenken*, 41–70. Jonas offered a moving retrospective look at Bultmann's personality and his "dialogue with him, that of philosopher with theologian, of Jew with Christian, but above all, of friend with friend." "I would give a great deal to be able to continue this conversation begun so long ago with the living man, but now can do so only with his dear shadow. A man of the most impressive purity has left us, a completed life, always at one with himself. He is not to be pitied, but once again the world has been robbed of one of those people who enable us to restore our wavering faith that it is "worth the trouble to be a human being" (70).

8. Bultmann expresses his hope "that the meanwhile matured skill of the author will win over the reader," and stresses that he himself has devoted years of his life to the study of gnosticism, but has never learned as much from any of the previous works on the subject as from this one, indeed that here "the full significance of the phenomenon was first revealed" to him. He specifically approves of the use of existentialist analysis and asserts his confidence "that this work will prove fruitful in several respects to research on intellectual history, not least of all to the interpretation of the New Testament" (foreword to Jonas, *Gnosis und spätantiker Geist*, pt. I, 1934). In a recommendation that Rudolf Bultmann wrote on 12 December 1933 to help Jonas's career as an émigré, he says, among other things, "Herr Dr. Jonas is a scholar of outstanding talent. He combines the ability to engage in systematic thought with a gift for historical research, and is thus particularly well equipped for the analysis and portrayal of phenomena germane to intellectual history. . . . As a result of his thorough education, he is equally familiar with the intellectual tradition of the Old Testament, of Judaism, and of the New Testament, as well as with the intellectual tradition of Greek antiquity. . . . I consider [the gnosticism book] a brilliant accomplishment. Research on gnosticism was first limited to what was seen merely as a phenomenon in the history of the church and of dogma, then as a phenomenon in Hellenistic religious history, with interest focusing primarily on the mythological tradition as absorbed and adapted by gnosti-

cism. Herr Dr. Jonas shows here for the first time what significance gnosticism holds in the context of the entire intellectual history of the West, how in gnosticism the ancient understanding of God and the world is reshaped, under the influence of oriental tradition as well as with the effects of the general historical conditions at the end of classical antiquity, and reshaped in a way that is of fundamental importance for the conceptual development of Christianity and at the same time for the entire post-antiquity Western intellectual history. The book will prove unusually fruitful. It is my heartfelt wish that Herr Dr. Jonas may have an opportunity to continue his scholarly work; that is all the more my wish inasmuch as I have also come to respect and value Herr J. as a human being" (Scholem papers, JNUL, 4°1599).

9. Hans Jonas, *Augustin und das paulinische Freiheitsproblem: Ein Beitrag zur Entstehung des christlich-abendländischen Freiheitsbegriffs* (Göttingen, 1930).

10. See Hans Schmidt, *Jonah: Eine Untersuchung zur vergleichenden Religionsgeschichte* (Göttingen, 1907).

11. Wilhelm Bousset, *Hauptprobleme der Gnosis* (Göttingen, 1907).

12. Hugo Koch in *Theologische Literaturzeitung* 55 (1930), no. 2, col. 266. "What Jonas inflicts on the reader in the way of excessive use of foreign terms, noun pile-ups, abstractions, longwindedness, stiltedness, and pomposity is altogether too much. . . . The work is dedicated to Herr Professor Bultmann, and he may enjoy such language. Others rightfully see it as the kind of sheer nonsense with which German scholars make a mockery of themselves and of German scholarship in the eyes of the rest of the world. . . . If the content matches in quality the incomprehensibility of its style, it must be absolutely outstanding. But I have no desire to translate this gibberish into German and render it understandable."

13. Julius Ebbinghaus, *Zu Deutschlands Schicksalswende* (Frankfurt/Main, 1946), 45f.

Chapter 9. From Israel to the New World: Launching an Academic Career
(pp. 149–169)

1. This interlude in Isawiya was not described in the interviews but has been based on an article by Eleanore Jonas, "Two Years in an Arab Village: Peace and Neighborly Contact during the British Mandate," *Aufbau* 2000, no. 25 (14 December 2000).

2. See Hans Jonas, "Yiscor: To the Memory of Franz Joseph Weiner," *The Chicago Jewish Forum* 9/1 (1950), 1–8.

3. A letter written in 1949 by Lore Jonas to Fania and Gershom Scholem conveys a vivid picture of the family's first experiences in Montreal: "We think of you often and speak of you and miss you. This new, large country is also a very foreign country; and once the first excitement of arrival has passed and one comes to one's senses a bit, one feels very much alone. There are a good many Jews, of course — 75,000 —

and those we have met thus far are all very nice and friendly (and rich), but not quite what we are looking for. At a recent party the following exchange took place: Mrs. X: 'What does your husband do?' I, embarrassed: 'Philosophy.' Mrs. X: 'He will not make much money on that.' I: 'Quite.' Hans has hardly met any colleagues because they are all on vacation. The way we were received, by the way, was overwhelming by Palestinian standards. We were picked up at the station in a car and taken to a three-room apartment that had been rented for us in advance. Frigidaire, gas stove, telephone all included, of course. In addition, they had sent us a crib as a housewarming present. And stocked the refrigerator with butter and eggs. Hans is working a lot, and I am very happy that after so many interruptions he has got back to it. But that means he's not much company. But after all, that's the reason for our being here" (Scholem papers, JNUL, 4ᶜ1599).

4. See the biography by Michael R. Marrus, *Samuel Bronfman: The Life and Times of Seagram's Mr. Sam* (Toronto, 1991).

5. See Edgar Bronfman's autobiography, *The Making of a Jew* (New York, 1996). On his father, see 1–16.

6. See Jonas's letter to Scholem, 1 September 1949: "My fellowship is actually an 'individual fellowship,' i.e., not connected with a university position or a specific university. Rather it is left up to me to establish contacts and eventually 'climb aboard' a university.' . . . McGill is a good hub from which one can establish connections. But the Department of Philosophy here seems to be fairly completely staffed, and besides, one of the full professors is . . . Raymond Klibansky, so they already have a German Jew" (Scholem papers, JNUL, 4°1599).

7. See the description by Lore Jonas in a letter to the Scholem family dated 1 December 1949: "Here at Dawson we are living in a sort of glorified kibbutz, eating in the common room, but with four rooms to ourselves rather than one, and shared washrooms, or, as Hans puts it, 'It's like a monastery, but with nuns.' We are far from the city and its temptations (25 miles), and the local temptations are so slight — a snack bar and the Faculty Club — that there is simply nothing left to do but work, which we divide up in such a way that I do the laundry and Hans writes philosophical essays. . . . The first thing we bought here was a desk, so Hans has no excuse for not working, and because it was very expensive, he wants to amortize it and is making very good use of it. You can see, everything is turning out very well. Dear Fania, the lot of the woman is the same everywhere — ironing, the aforementioned laundry, darning socks, etc. That has to be done in Canada just as it does in Jerusalem. The achievement of this country that I like best is the washing machine, if I may be so unsophisticated as to say so. The people here, the married couples among whom we live, are nice, usually simple and uncomplicated. Altogether I like them much better than the representatives of the Jewish bourgeoisie whom we met in Montreal. Our Jews in Israel

have more in common with these goyim than with the golus Jews" (Scholem papers, JNUL, 4°1599).

8. See Lore Jonas's letter to the Scholem family, dated 1 December 1949: "In the meantime the infamous Canadian winter has set in, and we are already freezing our toes off, but those in the know assure us that this is nothing — the marrow in our bones will be frozen before this is over. In retrospect a little *chamsin* [hot desert wind] was very nice, but you never appreciate such things until you don't have them anymore" (Scholem papers, JNUL, 4°1599).

9. See Cusanus texts I, *Predigten: Dies Santificatus*, ed. Raymond Klibansky (Heidelberg, 1929); *Magistri Eckardi Opera Latina*, Dasc. I, *Super oratione dominica* (Leipzig, 1934); *Magistri Eckardi Opera Latina*, fasc. XII, *Quaestiones Parisienses* (Leipzig, 1936).

10. See Raymond Klibansky, *Erinnerung an ein Jahrhundert: Gespräche mit Georges Leroux* (Frankfurt/Main, Leipzig, 2001).

11. See Raymond Klibansky, *The Continuity of the Platonic Tradition* (London, 1939), and Klibansky, ed., *Corpus Platonicum Medii Aevi*.

12. Père Faribault, "Un livre de Jonas: Gnosis und spätantiker Geist," *Études et Recherches* 2 (1937), I–II,1.

13. Arthur Darby Nock in *Gnomon* 3 (1936), 605–612.

14. On 28 July 1950, Jonas wrote to Scholem, "Things are going well for us; we are spending a quiet summer (to the extent such a thing is possible with a growing family). . . . Ayalah plays in the garden, is cheerful and very actively interested in the world around her, but is not speaking yet. Since she has not read Freud, she is very tender to her little brother, kisses his little hands, strokes his head (something we have never done in her presence), and wants to give him his bottle; and feels immensely superior. Jonathan is quieter than she is — he's no Sabra, after all" (Scholem papers, JNUL, 4°1599).

15. See Jonas's letter to Scholem dated 24 April 1950: "Carleton College is a nondenominational English-language institution founded to compete with the French-language clerical University of Ottawa; it is not even ten years old, and has large ambitions. Actually the plan had been to have only one new philosophy instructor, and when I appeared on the market, as a sort of bargain, but of course not for a junior position, they made an extra effort. . . . So it was worthwhile that in my very first year here I took on the servitude of teaching, although I occasionally felt it was disrupting my own work" (Scholem papers, JNUL, 4°1599).

16. See the letter from Jonas to Scholem dated 18 February 1951: "Things continue to go well with us, materially considerably better than an Israeli deserves in the third year of the Jewish state's existence. . . . My relationship with my colleagues is excellent, if not overstimulating. . . . The students are puzzled by philosophy, *not* made easy for

them, un-American, and welcome the unaccustomed effort as 'something different,' apart from success (which is questionable). It is just becoming clear to me that I represent something entirely new and exceptional in the education offered here — my most intelligent students have indicated as much indirectly, and some of them very directly. When in one of my classes I said 'Yes' in response to being asked whether I would be here next year, a chorus of 'Ah!' was heard. Two or three real intellects have risen above the stereotypical crowd, making it worthwhile to present material that goes over the heads of the others. This 'response experience' provides great satisfaction" (Scholem papers, JNUL, 4°1599).

17. During his first semester at Carleton, Jonas offered History of Ancient Philosophy up to Aristotle, History of Modern Philosophy from Descartes to Kant, and Philosophy of Religion (see letter to Scholem, 28 July 1950, JNUL, 4°1599).

18. Marta Karlweis Wassermann (1889–1965) had published several novels of her own, as well as her travel account, *Eine Frau reist durch Amerika* (Berlin, 1922), and a biography of her husband, *Jakob Wassermann: Bild, Kampf und Werk* (Amsterdam, 1935).

19. See Ludwig von Bertalanffy, *Theoretische Biologie*, vol. I (Berlin, 1932), and *Biophysik des Fliessgleichgewichts: Einführung in die Physik offener Systeme und ihre Anwendung in der Biologie* (Braunschweig, 1953). See Lima Takao, *Der Begriff der Ganzheit und seine Anwendung bei Ludwig von Bertalanffy* (Kiel, 2001). For a biographical portrayal, see Gerhard Nierhaus, *Ludwig von Bertalanffy: 1901–1972* (n.p., n.d. [1979]).

20. Ludwig von Bertalanffy, *Nikolaus von Kues* (Munich, 1928).

21. See Jonas's letter to Scholem, dated 5 November 1950: "Here I have only one colleague with whom I can debate philosophical questions, Prof. Ludwig von Bertalanffy (from Vienna), a biologist who thinks like a philosopher . . . with whom I have formed a close drinking and arguing friendship. He calls me an 'old Aristotelian,' for which I have not yet found a suitable riposte" (Scholem papers, JNUL, 4°1599).

22. Letters to Scholem reveal that Jonas was hoping during this period to find a permanent position at the liberal Hebrew Union College in Cincinnati or at the conservative Jewish Theological Seminary in New York (see letter of 1 September 1949). Lore Jonas wrote on 1 December 1949 about this trip: "We must take a look at this much-praised America. Canada is not quite the same" (Scholem papers, JNUL, 4°1599).

23. See Samuel E. Karff, ed., *Hebrew Union College: Jewish Institute of Religion at One Hundred Years* (Cincinnati, 1976).

24. On Baeck's significance for German Jewry before the Shoah, see among others the essays in Georg Heuberger and Fritz Backhaus, eds., *Leo Baeck 1873–1956: Aus dem Stamme von Rabbinern* (Frankfurt/Main, 2001).

25. On the intellectual development of Leo Strauss as an émigré, see Peter Graf

Kielmansegg et al., eds., *Hannah Arendt and Leo Strauss: German Emigrés and American Political Thought after World War II* (Cambridge and New York, 1995).

26. There is a wealth of literature on Strauss's political thought. See in particular Kenneth L. Deutsch, *Leo Strauss: Political Philosopher and Jewish Thinker* (Lanham, Md., 1994); Shadia B. Drury, *Strauss and the American Right* (Basingstoke, 1999); Harald Bluhm, *Die Ordnung der Ordnung: Das politische Philosophieren von Leo Strauss* (Berlin, 2002).

27. Jakob Klein, *Die griechische Logistik und die Entwicklung der Algebra*, 2 vols. (Berlin, 1934 and 1936).

28. The actual letter, written in Hebrew to the rector of the Hebrew University, begins as follows: "The delay in my response to your letter of 3 September 1951 has to do with the fact that I had to consider my response for rather a long time. The offer from the university, which represents the fulfillment of an old wish of mine, comes at a time that confronts me with questions that lie outside the academic realm and affect others besides me. When Prof. Bergmann [*sic*] asked me in the summer of 1950 whether I was prepared to be a candidate for a position in philosophy, I answered — without hesitation — in accordance with this wish. Yet it was clear to me that accepting the position would require major sacrifices on the part of those whose fate depends on my decision . . ." (copy in Scholem papers, from JNUL, 4º1599).

29. On the Zionist character of the Hebrew University in Jerusalem, see David N. Myers, *Re-inventing the Jewish Past: The European Jewish Intellectuals' Zionist Return to History* (New York, 1995).

30. See for instance Hans Jonas, "Spinoza and the Theory of Organism," *Journal of the History of Philosophy* 3 (1965), 43–57.

31. See Hans Jonas, "Parallelism and Complementarity: The Psycho-Physical Problem in Spinoza and the Succession of Niels Bohr," in Richard Kennington, ed., *The Philosophy of Baruch de Spinoza* (Washington, D.C., 1980), 121–130.

32. See Gershom Scholem, *Die Wissenschaft vom Judentum* (Frankfurt/Main, 1997).

33. On the substantive reasons for the later break between the two thinkers, see Thomas H. Macho, "Zur Frage nach dem Preis des Messianismus: Der intellektuelle Bruch zwischen Gershom Scholem und Jacob Taubes als Erinnerung ungelöster Probleme des Messianismus," in Stéphane Mosès and Sigrid Weigel, eds., *Gershom Scholem: Literatur und Rhetorik* (Cologne, 2000), 133–152.

34. Jacob Taubes, *Abendländische Eschatologie* (Bern, 1947). See Richard Faber, ed., *Abendländische Eschatologie: ad Taubes* (Würzburg, 2001).

35. Philip Rief, *Freud: The Mind of the Moralist* (New York, 1959).

36. Hans Jonas, *The Gnostic Religion: The Message of the Alien God and the Beginnings of Christianity* (Boston, 1958). The German edition appeared in 1999.

37. See Jay Macpherson, *O Earth Return* (Toronto, 1954), *The Boatman* (Oxford, 1957), and *Welcoming Disaster* (Toronto, 1974). See also Lorraine Weir, *Jay Macpherson and Her Works* (Toronto, 1989–90).

38. Northrop Frye, *Fearful Symmetry: A Study of William Blake* (Princeton, N.J., 1947).

Chapter 10. Friendships and Encounters in New York
(pp. 170–183)

1. See Jonas's letter to Scholem of 10 October 1951: "During the summer I was a visiting professor in the graduate faculty of the New School for Social Research in New York, teaching a course on 'The Organism in the Theory of Being since Descartes,' which, to my great surprise, was very well received. I myself was pleasantly impressed and stimulated by the maturity and interest of my students, among them a number of very serious Ph.D. candidates. Ottawa does not provide such intellectually alert students" (Scholem papers, JNUL, 4°1599).

2. See Michael Hanke, *Alfred Schütz: Einführung* (Vienna, 2002); Alfred Schütz, *Gesammelte Aufsätze*, 3 vols. (The Hague, 1971–72).

3. See Ulrich Melle, *Das Wahrnehmungsproblem und seine Verwandlung in phänomenologischer Einstellung: Untersuchungen zu der phänomenologischen Wahrnehmungstheorie von Husserl, Gurwitsch und Merleau-Ponty* (The Hague, 1983).

4. See Richard Grathoff, ed., *Alfred Schütz–Aron Gurwitsch: Briefwechsel 1939–1959* (Munich, 1985). In a letter dated 21 January 1954 Schütz writes to his friend Gurwitsch, "Yesterday we had a committee meeting and a faculty meeting, and contrary to my expectations there was a vote. Unfortunately we lost, honorably . . . Jonas had powerful support from Leo Strauss and his clique. What tipped the balance was that I of course had to point out that you were willing to come only on the condition that you would receive tenure, while this is not the case with Jonas. After an hour and a half of debate, a secret ballot was held, and you received 7 votes, while Jonas had 9. . . . In my opinion, the result was due purely to the aforementioned circumstance. I do not know Jonas personally, and hope it will be possible to work with him. As I recall, you have said very positive things about him" (347f). In a letter dated 1 May 1956, Schütz comments that he is "not on good terms personally" with Jonas (390).

5. See Jonas, "Aron Gurwitsch," *Social Research* 40 (1973), 567–569.

6. The Committee on Social Thought, established in 1941 by the historian John U. Nef (1899–1988) and others, is an interdisciplinary institute for intellectual history at the University of Chicago, in which philosophers, historians, literary scholars, sociologists, political scientists, and scholars of religion work together.

7. Unfortunately Hans Jonas did not address the interesting story of his time at the New School. For a history of that institution, see Peter M. Rutkoff, *New School: A His-*

tory of the New School for Social Research (New York, 1986); Claus-Dieter Krohn, *Wissenschaft im Exil: Deutsche Sozial- und Wirtschaftswissenschaftler in den USA und der New School for Social Research* (Frankfurt/Main, 1987).

8. The Bund was a movement that aimed for the integration of Jews into a socialist society while preserving their cultural uniqueness. See Zvi A. Gitelman, "A Centenary of Jewish Politics in Eastern Europe: The Legacy of the Bund and the Zionist Movements," *East European Politics and Societies* 11 (1997), 543–559.

9. See Viktor Sarris, "Reflexionen über den Gestaltpsychologen Max Wertheimer und sein Werk: Vergessenes und wieder Erinnertes," in Marianne Hassler and Jürgen Werthheimer, eds., *Der Exodus aus Nazideutschland und die Folgen: Jüdische Wissenschaftler im Exil* (Tübingen, 1997), 177–190.

10. On Magnus's work, see William Abikoff, *The Mathematical Legacy of Wilhelm Magnus: Groups, Geometry, and Special Functions* (Providence, R.I., 1994).

11. See Claus-Dieter Krohn, *Die philosophische Ökonomie: Zur intellektuellen Biographie Adolph Lowes* (Marburg, 1996).

12. On Stern, see Werner Deutsch, "Im Mittelpunkt die Person: Der Psychologe und Philosoph William Stern (1871–1938)," in Hassler and Wertheimer, eds., *Der Exodus aus Nazideutschland*, 73–90.

13. Hannah Arendt, *Rahel Varnhagen: The Life of a Jewish Woman*, trans. Richard and Clara Winston (New York, 1974), reprinted as *Rahel Varnhagen: The Life of a Jewess*, ed. Liliane Weisberg (Baltimore, Md., 1997).

14. See Eva Michaelis-Stern, "Zu Henrietta Szolds 25. Todestag," *Das Neue Israel* 33 (1980), 288–291; on the Youth Aliyah, see Yoav Gelber, "The Origins of Youth Aliya," *Studies in Zionism* 9 (1988), 147–171; and Sara Kadosh, "Youth Aliya Policies and the Rescue of Children from Europe, 1939–1942," in *Twelfth World Congress of Jewish Studies* (Jerusalem, 2001), 95–103.

15. See Bernd Neumann, *Hannah Arendt und Heinrich Blücher: Ein deutsch-jüdisches Gespräch* (Berlin, 1988).

16. For instance, Günther Stern, "On the Pseudo-Concreteness of Heidegger's Philosophy," *Philosophy and Phenomenological Research* 3 (1948), 337ff. See the bibliography in Konrad Paul Liessmann, *Günther Anders* (Munich, 2002), 203–207. On Anders's biography and philosophy, see also Gabriele Althaus, *Leben zwischen Sein und Nichts: Drei Studien zu Günther Anders* (Berlin, 1989); Margret Lohmann, *Philosophieren in der Endzeit: Zur Gegenwartsanalyse von Günther Anders* (Munich, 1996).

17. See Konrad Paul Liessmann, *Günther Anders*, 53–78; Günther Anders, *Die Antiquiertheit des Menschen: Über die Seele im Zeitalter der zweiten industriellen Revolution*, vol. 1 (Munich, 1956); Helmut Hildebrandt, *Weltzustand Technik: Ein Vergleich der Technikphilosophien von Günther Anders und Martin Heidegger* (Berlin, 1990).

18. On the controversial discussion of the human and philosophical relationship

between Hannah Arendt and Martin Heidegger, see for instance Ingeborg Nordmann, " 'Gegen Philosophie hilft nur Philosophie. Und ich habe keine eigene auf Lager': Hannah Arendts Auseinandersetzung mit Martin Heidegger," in Jutta Dick and Barbara Hahn, eds., *Von einer Welt in die andere: Jüdinnen im 19. und 20. Jahrhundert* (Vienna, 1993), 266–285; Dana Villa, *Arendt and Heidegger: The Fate of the Political* (Princeton, N.J., 1996); Reinhard Mehring, "Zwischen Philosophie und Politik: Hannah Arendts Verhältnis zu Heidegger," *Zeitschrift für Religions- und Geistesgeschichte* 53 (2001), 256–273.

19. See Arendt, *Besuch in Deutschland* (Berlin, 1993).

20. See Arendt, "Konzentrationslager," *Die Wandlung* 3 (1948), 309–330; "Parteien und Bewegungen," *Die Wandlung* 4 (1949), 459–473; *Elemente und Ursprünge totaler Herrschaft* (Frankfurt/Main, 1955); *The Origins of Totalitarianism* (New York, 1958).

21. Arendt, "Eichmann in Jerusalem," *New Yorker* (February–March 1963).

22. Documentation of the controversy can be found in Friedrich Arnold Krummacher, *Die Kontroverse Hannah Arendt, Eichmann und die Juden* (Munich, 1964). Among the many works on the controversy, see Dana Villa, "The Banality of Philosophy: Arendt on Heidegger and Eichmann," in May and Kohn, eds., *Twenty Years Later*, 179–196; Richard Bernstein, "Did Hannah Arendt Change Her Mind? From Radical Evil to the Banality of Evil," in May and Kohn, eds., *Twenty Years Later*, 127–146; Richard Wolin, "The Ambivalence of German-Jewish Identity: Hannah Arendt in Jerusalem," *History and Memory* 8 (1996), 9–34; Gary Smith, ed., *Hannah Arendt Revisited: "Eichmann in Jerusalem" und die Folgen* (Frankfurt, 2000); Steven E. Aschheim, ed., *Hannah Arendt in Jerusalem* (Berkeley, Los Angeles, London, 2001).

23. On Blumenfeld, see Kurt Blumenfeld, *Erlebte Judenfrage: Ein Vierteljahrhundert Deutscher Zionismus* (Stuttgart, 1962); Jochanan Ginat, "Kurt Blumenfeld und der deutsche Zionismus," in Blumenfeld, *Im Kampf um den Zionismus: Briefe aus fünf Jahrzehnten*, ed. M. Sambursky and Jochanan Ginat (Stuttgart, 1976), 7–36 (see also the letters to Hannah Arendt).

24. See Ingeborg Nordmann, "Zwischen Paria und Zionist: Die Freundschaft zwischen Hannah Arendt und Kurt Blumenfeld," *Babylon* 15 (1995), 86–98.

25. Hannah Arendt, "Zionism Reconsidered," *Menorah-Journal* 33 (1945), 162–196. See Richard J. Bernstein, "Hannah Arendt's Zionism?" in Aschheim, ed., *Hannah Arendt in Jerusalem*, 194–202; Moshe Zimmermann, "Hannah Arendt: The Early Post-Zionism," in Aschheim, ed., *Hannah Arendt in Jerusalem*, 181–193.

26. That Jonas held a critical opinion of Arendt's work even before the quarrel over the Eichmann book can be seen from the following passage in a letter to Scholem of 10 October 1951: "Many people I would have liked to meet were of course away from New York in midsummer. But Hannah was there, and our friendship was renewed after a 15-year interruption. It was unclouded, although I had to contradict in vigorous terms—

without success — her portrayal of the Jewish problem in her most recent, very clever, but still by no means correct book, 'The Origins of Totalitarianism'" (Scholem papers, JNUL, 4°1599).

27. Robert Weltsch, *Tragt ihn mit Stolz, den gelben Fleck: Eine Aufsatzreihe der "Jüdischen Rundschau" zur Lage der deutschen Juden* (Nordlingen, 1988). On Weltsch, see Herbert A. Strauss, "Zum zeitgeschichtlichen Hintergrund zionistischer Kultur-kritik: Scholem, Weltsch und die Jüdische Rundschau," in Peter Freimark and Alice Jankowsky, eds., *Juden in Deutschland: Emanzipation, Integration, Verfolgung und Ver-nichtung* (Hamburg, 1991), 375–389.

28. Arendt, *Origins of Totalitarianism*.

29. On Eichmann's historical role, see Hans Safrian, *Eichmann und seine Gehilfen* (Frankfurt/Main, 1997).

30. For the correspondence between Scholem and Arendt on the Eichmann book, see Scholem, *Briefe*, vol. 2 (1948–1970), ed. Thomas Sparr (Munich, 1995), 95–111. On its interpretation, see Stéphane Mosès, "Das Recht zu urteilen: Hannah Arendt, Gershom Scholem und der Eichmann-Prozess," in Gary Smith, ed., *Hannah Arendt Revisited*, 78–92.

31. See Hans Jonas, "Hannah Arendt, 1906–1975," *Social Research* 43 (1976), 3–5, and "Acting, Knowing, Thinking: Gleanings from Hannah Arendt's Philosophical Work," *Social Research* 44 (1977), 24–43.

Chapter 11. Taking Leave of Heidegger
(pp. 187–193)

1. Martin Heidegger, "Die Selbstbehauptung der deutschen Universität" (1933), in *Gesamtausgabe*, vol. 16, 107–117. For an interpretation of the installation speech and its repercussions, see, among others, Victor Farías, *Heidegger und der Nationalsozia-lismus* (Frankfurt/Main, 1987), 151–168. There is an extensive literature on Heidegger's relationship to Nazism; see, for instance, Bernd Martin, "Universität im Umbruch: Das Rektorat Heidegger," in Eckard John, ed., *Die Freiburger Universität in der Zeit des Nationalsozialismus* (Freiburg, 1991), 9–24; John, ed., *Martin Heidegger und das "Dritte Reich": Ein Kompendium* (Darmstadt, 1989); Rüdiger Safranski, *Ein Meister aus Deutschland: Heidegger und seine Zeit* (Frankfurt/Main, 1998).

2. See Jonas's account in his lecture "Husserl und Heidegger" (Leo Baeck Insti-tute Archives, New York, AR 2241/MS 75): "As far as his relationship to his teacher is concerned, the venerable and elderly Husserl, who had brought him to this chair as his successor, from the moment of the Nazi seizure of power Heidegger did not see Husserl, did not greet him on the street, did not communicate with him, in fact let him live alone and die equally alone in 1938, in Freiburg, this city that Husserl had made famous for philosophy. Among the files from his time as rector was an edict

that forbade Husserl and other non-Aryans to enter university buildings and use the library. To be precise, because powerful accusations are being expressed here, Heidegger later characterized this as an act that was carried out by underlings using his signature stamp, an act of which he was unaware. That is possible. The fact remains that in 1938 Husserl became terminally ill. Characteristically it was Frau Heidegger, originally a convinced Nazi, who told her husband, 'Martin, you must go to the old man — he's sick and is going to die.' And Heidegger, Martin, took refuge in illness. He developed a fever and stayed in bed until Husserl had died and the burial was over. And from the philosophical rostrum of Freiburg University the reigning philosopher, Husserl's student and successor, said not a word about the fact that the most significant figure in the philosophical life of the previous generation in Germany had passed away. These are tragic facts."

3. See Richard Wolin, *Heidegger's Children: Hannah Arendt, Karl Löwith, Hans Jonas, and Herbert Marcuse* (Princeton, N.J., 2001), 101–133.

4. See chap. 12 for a thorough treatment.

5. Hans Jonas, "Heidegger and Theology," *Review of Metaphysics* 18 (1964), 20–233.

6. See Heinrich Ott, *Der Weg Martin Heideggers und der Weg der Theologie* (Zollikon, 1959).

7. Jonas, "Heidegger and Theology," 211.

8. Ibid., 219f.

9. Ibid., 218.

10. Ibid., 229.

11. William J. Richardson, *Heidegger: Through Phenomenology to Thought* (The Hague, 1963).

12. Richardson, "Heidegger and God — and Professor Jonas," *Thought* 40 (1965), 13–40.

13. Gerhard Noller, ed., *Heidegger und die Theologie: Beginn und Fortgang der Diskussion* (Munich, 1967) (Jonas's essay, 316–340). For a new treatment of the topic, see Pero Brkic, *Martin Heidegger und die Theologie: Ein Thema in dreifacher Fragestellung* (Mainz, 1994).

14. Letter from Hans Jonas to Bultmann dated 19 November 1969 (Bultmann papers, Tübingen University Library). Hannah Arendt wrote on 8 August 1969 in a letter to Jonas, "I had a brief message from Heidegger: 'The conversation with Jonas was very gratifying'" (General Correspondence, 1938–1976, Hannah Arendt Papers, Manuscript Division, Library of Congress, Washington, D.C.). In Heidegger's original letter (2 August 1969) to Arendt, the statement continued, "He has apparently got away from theology altogether" — presumably an allusion to Jonas's lecture, "Heidegger and Theology." Arendt replied on 8 August 1969, "Jonas was here — ecstatic about the

meeting in Zurich, which he described very thoroughly, as is his way. He has 'got away altogether' from much more than just theology" (Hannah Arendt–Martin Heidegger, *Briefe 1925–1975 und andere Zeugnisse* [Frankfurt/Main, 1998], 178).

Chapter 12. On the Value and Dignity of Life:
Philosophy of the Organic and Ethics of Responsibility
(pp. 194–213)

1. Hans Jonas, "Gnosticism and Modern Nihilism," *Social Research* 19 (1952), 430–452.

2. Hans Jonas, "Is God a Mathematician?" *Measure* 2 (1951), 404–426.

3. Hans Jonas, "Motility and Emotion: An Essay on Philosophical Biology," in *Proceedings of the XIth International Conference of Philosophy*, vol. 5 (Amsterdam and Louvain, 1953), 117–122.

4. Hans Jonas, "Causality and Perception" *Journal of Philosophy* 47 (1950), 319–324.

5. See Ivor Leclerc, ed., *The Relevance of Whitehead: Philosophical Essays in Commemoration of the Birth of Alfred North Whitehead* (London, 1961).

6. Hans Jonas, "The Practical Uses of Theory," *Social Research* 26 (1959), 127–166.

7. Hans Jonas, "The Nobility of Sight: A Study in the Phenomenology of the Senses," *Philosophy and Phenomenological Research* 14 (1953–54), 507–519.

8. Hans Jonas, *The Phenomenon of Life: Toward a Philosophical Biology* (New York, 1963).

9. Alfred North Whitehead, *Process and Reality: An Essay in Cosmology* (New York, 1929).

10. See Jonas's afterword to *Das Prinzip Leben* (Frankfurt/Main, 1994), 401–403, under the title of "Natur und Ethik."

11. Hans Jonas, "Philosophical Reflections on Experiments with Human Subjects," *Daedalus* 98 (1969), 219–247.

12. "A Definition of Irreversible Coma," Report of the Ad Hoc Committee of the Harvard Medical School to Examine the Definition of Brain Death, *Journal of the American Medical Association* 205, no. 6 (5 August 1968), 337–340.

13. Hans Jonas, "Against the Stream: Comments on the Definition and Redefinition of Death," in Jonas, *Philosophical Essays: From Ancient Creed to Technological Man* (Chicago and London, 1974), 132–140.

14. See the later essay "Techniken des Todesaufschubs und das Recht zu sterben" in Jonas, *Technik, Medizin und Ethik* (Frankfurt/Main, 1985), 242–268.

15. See, in the bibliography of this volume, the list of Jonas's publications. On the significance of Jonas to the Hastings Center, see the special issue of the *Hastings Center Report* 25 (1995), no. 7, "The Legacy of Hans Jonas."

16. On Heidegger's and Jonas's differing views on technological civilization, see Erik Jacob, *Martin Heidegger und Hans Jonas: Die Metaphysik der Subjektivität und die Krise der technologischen Zivilisation* (Tübingen, 1955).

17. See Hans Jonas, *Das Prinzip Verantwortung: Versuch einer Ethik für die technologische Zivilisation* (Frankfurt/Main, 1983), 153–241. For a commentary, see Vittorio Hösle, "Ontologie und Ethik bei Hans Jonas," in Dietrich Böhler, ed., *Ethik für die Zukunft: Im Diskurs mit Hans Jonas* (Munich, 1994), 103–125, and Bernd Wille, *Ontologie und Ethik bei Hans Jonas* (Dettelbach, 1996).

18. See the letter to Hannah Arendt of 23 July 1972: "Dear Hannah, Welcome! I am happy that you are here, and we are both counting on seeing you! The enclosed is just in case you have time between projects or can't sleep at night. The first two chapters of my 'Tractatus Ethico-Politicus' (strictly private title), on which I am working here feverishly. A first reaction from you would be tremendously important to me. No one has seen it yet, and I have been alone with this crazy attempt for three months now. I need an answering voice—yours" (General Correspondence, 1938–1976, Hannah Arendt Papers, Manuscript Division, Library of Congress, Washington, D.C.)

19. Robert Spaemann and Reinhard Löw, *Die Frage Wozu? Geschichte und Wiederentdeckung des teleologischen Denkens* (Munich, 1981).

20. Jonas, *Das Prinzip Verantwortung*, 61–83, and "The Heuristics of Fear," in Melvin Kranzberg, ed., *Ethics in an Age of Pervasive Technology* (Boulder, 1980), 213–221.

21. St. Paul's Church was being renovated and was not available for the prize ceremony.

22. Hans Jonas, "Technik, Freiheit und Pflicht: Dankesrede anlässlich der Verleihung des Friedenspreises des Deutschen Buchhandels am 11. Oktober 1987 in Frankfurt am Main," in Jonas, *Wissenschaft als persönliches Erlebnis* (Göttingen, 1987), 32–46.

23. Johann Wolfgang von Goethe, *Faust Part Two*, trans. Martin Greenberg (New Haven and London, 1998), 227.

24. In later conversations, Jonas expanded upon and differentiated his comments on both aspects—his skepticism vis-à-vis the power of mass democracy to develop an ethic of renunciation, as well as his objection to Ernst Bloch's utopian thinking. See the audio book version, "Revolte wider die Weltflucht: Reden und Gespräche," ed. Christian Wiese (Munich, 2000), including the discussion between Jonas and Ingo Hermann.

25. Marcus Aurelius, *Meditations* (New York, 2002).

26. Immanuel Kant, "Zum ewigen Frieden," in *Werke in sechs Bänden*, vol. VI (Darmstadt, 1983), 195.

27. Cf. Gonzalo Portales, *Hegels frühe Idee der Philosophie: Zum Verhältnis von Politik, Religion, Geschichte und Philosophie in seinen Manuskripten von 1785–1800* (Stuttgart and Bad Cannstatt, 1994).

28. See Jonas, *Das Prinzip Verantwortung*, 214–233 and 256–310.

29. See Jonas's reflections on the demoralizing effect of despotism, ibid., 298ff.

30. Ernst Bloch, *The Principle of Hope*, 3 vols., trans. Neville Plaice, Stephen Plaice, and Paul Knight (Cambridge, Mass., 1986); Jonas, *Das Prinzip Verantwortung*, 313–393 (chap. 6). See Horst Gronke, "Epoché der Utopie: Verteidigung des 'Prinzips Verantwortung' gegen seine liberalen Kritiker, seine konservativen Bewunderer und Hans Jonas selbst," in Dietrich Böhler, ed., *Ethik für die Zukunft*, 407–427.

31. On the causes of the book's resonance, see Christian Schütze, "The Political and Intellectual Influence of Hans Jonas," *Hastings Center Report* 25 (1995), no. 7 (special issue), 40–44.

32. Interview with Karl Popper in *Die Welt*, 8 July 1987. On the relationship between Jonas and Popper, see Walter Szostak, *Teleologie des Lebendigen: Zu Karl Poppers und Hans Jonas' Philosophie des Geistes* (Frankfurt/Main, 1997).

Chapter 13. *"All this is mere stammering"*: *Auschwitz and God's Impotence* (pp. 214–219)

1. See the impressive reflection on the tension in Jonas between philosophical thinking and Jewish existence in Hans Jonas, "Interview," in Herlinde Koelbl, *Jüdische Portraits: Fotografien und Interviews* (Frankfurt/Main, 1998), 168ff. See also the interpretation by Christian Wiese, "'Dass man zusammen Philosoph und Jude ist . . .': Zur Dimension des Jüdischen in Hans Jonas' philosophischer Ethik der Bewahrung der Schöpfung," in Johannes Valentin and Saskia Wendel, eds., *Jüdische Traditionen in der Philosophie des 20. Jahrhunderts* (Darmstadt, 2000), 131–147.

2. On the God-is-dead theology of the sixties, see among others Thomas J. J. Altizer and William Hamilton, eds., *Radical Theology and the Death of God* (Indianapolis, 1966); Klaus Rohmann, *Vollendung im Nichts? Eine Dokumentation der amerikanischen Gott-ist-tot Theologie* (Cologne and Zurich, 1977); on the connection between this phenomenon and the challenge of the Shoah, see Stephen R. Haynes and John K. Roth, eds., *The Death of God Movement and the Holocaust* (Westport, Conn., and London, 1999) (including various Jewish responses to this Christian interpretation of faith after Auschwitz). On Jewish attempts to formulate an understanding of God and the world after the Shoah, see Christoph Münz, *Der Welt ein Gedächtnis geben: Geschichtstheologisches Denken im Judentum nach Auschwitz* (Gütersloh, 1995). For a sourcebook on the sixties, see Albert Friedlander, ed., *Out of the Whirlwind: A Reader of Holocaust Literature* (New York, 1968), which contains a contribution by Hans Jonas, "The Concept of God after Auschwitz," 465–476.

3. See Edna Brocke, "'Treue als Zeichen der Wahrheit': Hannah Arendts Weg als Jüdin," *Kirche und Israel* 11 (1996), 136–156.

4. Hans Jonas, "Immortality and the Modern Temper," *Harvard Theological Review* 55 (1962), 1–20.

5. See the interesting correspondence between Jonas and Bultmann, partly reproduced in the appendix to *Zwischen Nichts und Ewigkeit* (Göttingen, 1963), 63–72.

6. Jonas, "Immortality and the Modern Temper," 19.

7. Hans Jonas, *Der Gottesbegriff nach Auschwitz: Eine jüdische Stimme* (Frankfurt/Main, 1987).

8. Hans Jonas, "Werkzeug, Bild und Grab: Vom Transanimalischen im Menschen," *Scheidewege* 15 (1985–86), 47–58, reprinted in *Philosophische Untersuchungen und metaphysische Vermutungen* (Frankfurt/Main, 1992), 34–49.

9. Hans Jonas, *Materie, Geist und Schöpfung: Kosmologischer Befund und kosmogonische Vermutung* (Frankfurt/Main, 1988), reprinted in *Philosophische Untersuchungen*, 209–255. See Theodor Schieder, *Weltabenteuer Gottes: Die Gottesfrage bei Hans Jonas* (Paderborn, 1998).

10. Jonas speaks of "transcendence breaking into immanence" in the case of the Prophets: "Those who experienced and spoke of such a thing were not discovering a hidden God but hearing a God who wanted to announce himself and make himself known to all the world through them. The initiative is his (if we do not wish to know better than they), and that is predicated on the following: the *will* of him who reveals himself (and therefore a temporal element in him!) and the *power* to reveal himself, i.e., to act on the world, specifically by way of the human soul" ("Im Kampf um die Möglichkeit des Glaubens," 67).

11. On his interpretation of the *condition humaine* after Auschwitz, see Günther Anders, *Besuch im Hades: Auschwitz und Breslau 1966. Nach 'Holocaust' 1979* (Munich, 1979); on the theodicy question, see Anders, *Ketzereien* (Munich, 1982), especially 103ff; Anders, *Die Antiquiertheit des Menschen*, vol. II: *Über die Zerstörung des Lebens im Zeitalter der dritten industriellen Revolution* (Munich, 1980), 385. On his relationship to Jewry, see "Mein Judentum" in Hans Jürgen Schulz, *Mein Judentum* (Stuttgart, 1978), 58–76, and Evelyn Adunka, "Günther Anders und das jüdische Erbe," in Konrad Paul Liessmann, ed., *Günther Anders kontrovers* (Munich, 1992), 72–80.

Chapter 14. Didactic Letters to Lore Jonas, 1944–45
(pp. 220–245)

1. Jonas sometimes (as here) uses "*Materie*" for "matter," but more often uses the less technical "*Stoff*" (whose broader meanings beyond the philosophical notion of matter are suggested by the English word "stuff"). Although the two terms need not be synonymous, Jonas uses them more or less interchangeably here, and there is no clear systematic difference that would justify using different terms in English. Consequently, I have translated both as "matter"—A.A.

2. "Infusoria, n. A class of Protozoa, comprising ciliated, tentaculate, and flagellate animalcula, essentially unicellular, free-swimming, or sedentary; so called because

found in infusions of decaying animal or vegetable matter." *The Oxford English Dictionary*, 2nd ed., 1989, *OED Online*, Oxford University Press, 5 September 2007, <http://dictionary.oed.com/cgi/entry/50116632>.

3. The German word "*Geist*" can be translated as "spirit," "mind," or "intellect." In order to highlight Jonas's critique of German Idealism, I have translated *Geist* as "spirit" throughout or sometimes as "spirit or intellect," when Jonas is emphasizing that *Geist* is a property of certain living organisms—A.A.

4. It is a venture of speculation to conclude that this has etiological validity as well as descriptive validity. We will be pushed into making this move if—as we must—we have already made room in the principle's first undeveloped manifestations for the overwhelming continuity with which it furthers its development into increasingly intelligent figures, figures that present it ever more fully. We will be pushed into making this move if we also therefore retrospectively connect this development to its antecedent moments, which must contain the whole: the productive, visible striving for a goal, which spans the whole process, makes a pure "heterogeny of purposes" at the beginning extremely unlikely. Thus, with the ontological concept of freedom, we find ourselves pointed toward matter, in which purposes are not visible, but which reveals its hidden potentiality in the curious adventure of life. Just as matter's fixed, unfree self-identity is not the last word of being after the testament of life, this fixed, unfree self-identity also need not be its first word. A metaphorical history of "substance" may transcend it on both sides . . . hence we are unavoidably restricted to a speculative interpretation of being in which matter finds itself as a mode or state of itself, as an ontological phase. Thus far, we concern ourselves with it as part of a strict phenomenology of life.

5. The "ur" in "ur-substance" refers to fundamentality, primordiality, or primacy —A.A.

6. "Entelechy, n. In Aristotle's use: The realization or complete expression of some function; the condition in which a potentiality has become an actuality." *The Oxford English Dictionary*, 2nd ed., 1989, *OED Online*, Oxford University Press, 5 September 2007, <http://dictionary.oed.com/cgi/entry/50076087>.

Afterword
(pp. 246–253)

1. See Christian Wiese, "'For a Time I Was Privileged to Enjoy His Friendship . . .': The Ambivalent Relationship between Hans Jonas and Gershom Scholem," *Leo Baeck Institute Year Book* 49 (2004), 25–58, and *The Life and Thought of Hans Jonas: Jewish Dimensions* (Hanover, N.H., 2007), 34–68.

2. Jonas's words at his friend's grave express his feelings with great profundity. See Hans Jonas, "Hannah Arendt, 1906–1975," *Social Research* 43 (1976), 3–5.

3. See Christian Wiese, "Mysterium jüdischer Existenz und umstrittene Erinnerung: Hans Jonas und Hannah Arendt — Impressionen einer Freundschaft," in Birgit Klein and Christiane E. Müller, eds., *Memoria: Wege jüdischen Erinnerns — Festschrift für Michael Brocke* (Berlin, 2005), 733–752. See also Wiese, *The Life and Thought of Hans Jonas*, 68–86.

4. See Eleonore Jonas, "Two Years in an Arab Village: Peace and Neighborly Contact during the British Mandate," *Aufbau* 2000, no. 25 (14 December 2000).

5. Here I must express my gratitude to Lore Jonas not only for placing some of these valuable materials at my disposal but above all for the great confidence she expressed in allowing me to serve as the editor of this volume; I can only hope that I have proved worthy of her confidence. I am grateful for the many conversations we had, and for the great patience with which she answered my questions. When I told her how happy it made me to work on her husband's memoirs, she replied, "Yes, he was a wonderful person, wasn't he?" I owe much as well to Rachel Salamander and Stephan Sattler, without whose friendship with Hans Jonas this project would not have been possible. Their knowledgeable, focused, and sensitive questions, although now invisible, elicited and inspired each of Jonas's accounts.

6. See the interview with Hans Jonas in Herlinde Koelbl, *Jüdische Portraits: Fotografien und Interviews* (Frankfurt/Main, 1998), 168–171.

7. See Hans Jonas, *Wissenschaft als persönliches Erlebnis* (Göttingen, 1987).

8. Hans Jonas, "Rassismus im Lichte der Menschheitsbedrohung," Dietrich Böhler, ed., *Ethik für die Zukunft: Im Diskurs mit Hans Jonas* (Munich, 1994), 19–29.

9. See Wiese, *The Life and Thought of Hans Jonas*, 87–98.

10. Jonas, "Matter, Mind and Creation: Cosmological Evidence and Cosmogonic Speculation," in Lawrence Vogel, ed., *Mortality and Morality: A Search for the Good after Auschwitz* (Evanston, Ill., 1996), 190.

11. Jonas, "The Concept of God after Auschwitz: A Jewish Voice," *Mortality and Morality*, 131.

12. Hans Jonas, "Technik, Freiheit und Pflicht," in Jonas, *Wissenschaft als persönliches Erlebnis*, 46.

BIBLIOGRAPHY

I. WORKS BY HANS JONAS IN ENGLISH AND GERMAN

A. *Books and Monographs (by year of publication)*

Augustin und das paulinische Freiheitsproblem: Ein philosophischer Beitrag zur Genesis der christlich-abendländischen Freiheitsidee. Göttingen, 1930. 2nd edition, expanded, with an introduction by James M. Robinson: *Augustin und das paulinische Freiheitsproblem: Eine philosophische Studie zum pelagianischen Streit,* Göttingen, 1965.

Der Begriff der Gnosis: Inaugural-Dissertation zur Erlangung der Doktorwürde der Hohen Philosophischen Fakultät der Philipps-Universität zu Marburg. Göttingen, 1930 (abridged).

Gnosis und spätantiker Geist. Erster Teil: Die mythologische Gnosis. Göttingen, 1934. 2nd edition, 1954. 3rd edition, corrected and expanded, 1964.

Gnosis und spätantiker Geist. Teil II. 1. Von der Mythologie zur mystischen Philosophie. Göttingen, 1954. 2nd edition, revised, Göttingen, 1966.

The Gnostic Religion: The Message of the Alien God and the Beginnings of Christianity. Boston, 1958. 2nd edition, revised and expanded, Boston, 1966.

Zwischen Nichts und Ewigkeit: Zur Lehre vom Menschen. Göttingen, 1963. 2nd edition, 1987.

The Phenomenon of Life: Toward a Philosophical Biology. New York, 1966. 2nd edition, Chicago, 1982. Further editions: New York, 1968; Westport, Conn., 1972; Chicago and London, 1982.

Wandel und Bestand: Vom Grunde der Verstehbarkeit des Geschichtlichen. Frankfurt/Main, 1970. Simultaneously in Vittorio Klostermann, ed., *Durchblicke: Martin Heidegger zum 80. Geburtstag,* Frankfurt/Main, 1970. English translation in *Social Research* 38 (1971), 498–528.

Organismus und Freiheit: Ansätze zu einer philosophischen Biologie. Göttingen, 1973.

Philosophical Essays: From Ancient Creed to Technological Man. Englewood Cliffs, N.J., 1974. Reissued, Chicago and London, 1980.

On Faith, Reason, and Responsibility: Six Essays. San Francisco, 1978. Reissued, Los Angeles, 1981.

Das Prinzip Verantwortung: Versuch einer Ethik für die technologische Zivilisation. Frankfurt/Main, 1979. Paperback edition, Frankfurt/Main, 1984.

Macht oder Ohnmacht der Subjektivität? Das Leib-Seele Problem im Vorfeld des Prinzips Verantwortung. Frankfurt/Main, 1981. English original, "On the Power or

Impotence of Subjectivity," in Stuart F. Spicker and H. Tristram Engelhard, eds., *Philosophical Dimensions of the Neuro-Medical Sciences*, 143–161, Boston, 1976.

The Imperative of Responsibility: In Search of an Ethics for the Technological Age. Chicago, 1984.

Technik, Medizin und Ethik: Zur Praxis des Prinzips Verantwortung. Frankfurt/Main, 1985. 2nd edition, 1987.

Der Gottesbegriff nach Auschwitz: Eine jüdische Stimme. Frankfurt/Main, 1987. English original in *Harvard Theological Review* 55 (1962), 1–20. Republished in *The Phenomenon of Life*, 1966.

Was für morgen lebenswichtig ist: Unentdeckte Zukunftswerte. With Dietmar Mieth. Freiburg, Basel, and Vienna, 1987. Reprinted in *Technik, Medizin und Ethik*. Frankfurt/Main, 1985.

Wissenschaft als persönliches Erlebnis: Drei Reden. Göttingen, 1987.

Materie, Geist und Schöpfung: Kosmologischer Befund und kosmogonische Vermutung. Frankfurt/Main, 1988. Reprinted in *Philosophische Untersuchungen und metaphysische Vermutungen*, 1992.

Philosophische Untersuchungen und metaphysische Vermutungen. Frankfurt/Main, 1992.

Dem bösen Ende näher: Gespräche über das Verhältnis des Menschen zur Natur. Ed. Wolfgang Schneider. Frankfurt/Main, 1993.

Philosophie: Rückschau und Vorschau am Ende des Jahrhunderts. Frankfurt/Main, 1993.

Gedanken über Gott: Drei Versuche. Frankfurt/Main, 1994.

Das Prinzip Leben: Ansätze zu einer philosophischen Biologie. Frankfurt/Main, 1994. New edition of *Organismus und Freiheit*.

Mortality and Morality: A Search for the Good After Auschwitz. Ed. Lawrence Vogel. Evanston, Ill., 1996.

Die gnostische Religion: Die Botschaft des fremden Gottes. Ed. with an afterword by Christian Wiese. Frankfurt/Main, 1999.

B. *Publications in Journals, Newspapers, and Anthologies (by year)*

"Die Idee der Zerstreuung und Wiedersammlung bei den Propheten." *Der Jüdische Student* 4 (1922), 30–43.

"Karl Mannheims Soziologie des Geistes." *Schriften der Deutschen Gesellschaft für Soziologie* 1 (1929), 111–114.

"Husserl and the Problem of Ontology" (in Hebrew). *Mosnajim* 7 (1938), 581–589.

"In Memoriam Edmund Husserl" (in Hebrew). *Turim* (1938).

Review of Karl Barth, *Eine Schweizer Stimme*. *Yedioth* 38 (Tel Aviv, n.d.), 5f.

"Die origenistische Spekulation und die Mystik." *Theologische Zeitschrift* 5 (1949), 24–25.

"Origines' Peri Archon: ein System patristischer Gnosis." *Theologische Zeitschrift* 5 (1949), 101–119.

"Problems of 'Knowing God' in Philo Judaeus." In *Sefer Jochanan Lewy*, 64–84. Jerusalem, 1949.

"Causality and Perception." *Journal of Philosophy* 47 (1950), 319–324. Expanded version in *The Phenomenon of Life*, 1966.

"Yiscor: To the Memory of Franz Joseph Weiner." *Chicago Jewish Forum* 9/1 (1950), 1–8.

"Comment on Bertalanffy's General System Theory." *Human Biology* 23 (1951), 404–426.

"Is God a Mathematician?" *Measure* 2 (1951), 404–426. Final version in *The Phenomenon of Life*, 1966.

"Materialism and the Theory of Organism." *University of Toronto Quarterly* 21 (1951), 39–52.

"Gnosticism and Modern Nihilism." *Social Research* 19 (1952), 430–452.

"A Critique of Cybernetics." *Social Research* 230 (1953), 172–192. Final version in *The Phenomenon of Life*, 1966.

"Motility and Emotion: An Essay on Philosophical Biology." In *Proceedings of the XIth International Congress of Philosophy*, vol. 5, 117–122. Amsterdam and Louvain, 1953. Final version in *The Phenomenon of Life*, 1966.

"The Nobility of Sight: A Study in the Phenomenology of the Senses." *Philosophy and Phenomenological Research* 14 (1953–54), 507–519. Final version in *The Phenomenon of Life*, 1966.

Review of Leon Roth, *Jewish Thought as a Factor in Civilization. Review: UNESCO Publications Committee* 3 (1954), 6f.

"Bemerkungen zum Systembegriff und seiner Anwendung auf Lebendiges." *Studium Generale* 10 (1957), 8–94. Reprinted in *Organismus und Freiheit*, 1973.

"Gnosticism." In *A Handbook of Christian Theology*, 144–147. New York, 1958.

"In Memoriam: Alfred Schutz, 1899–1959." *Social Research* 26 (1959), 471–474.

"Kurt Goldstein and Philosophy." *American Journal of Psychoanalysis* 19 (1959), 161–164. Reprinted in *Social Research* 32 (1965), 351–356.

"The Practical Uses of Theory." *Social Research* 26 (1959), 127–166. Final version in *The Phenomenon of Life*, 1966.

"Gnosis und moderner Nihilismus." *Kerygma und Dogma* 6 (1960), 155–171. Final version in *Zwischen Nichts und Ewigkeit*, 1963.

Review of Michel Malinine, Henri-Charles Puech, and Gilles Quispel, eds., *Evangelium Veritatis. Gnomon* 32 (1960), 327–336.

"Homo pictor und die differentia des Menschen." *Zeitschrift für Philosophische Forschung* 15 (1961), 161–176. Final version in *Zwischen Nichts und Ewigkeit*, 1963. English version in *Social Research* 29 (1962), 201–220. Final version in *The Phenomenon of Life*, 1966.

"Evangelium Veritatis and the Valentinian Speculation." In Frank L. Cross, ed., *Studia Patristica* VI, 96–111. Berlin, 1962.

"Immortality and the Modern Temper." *Harvard Theological Review* 55 (1962), 1–20. Final version in *The Phenomenon of Life*, 1966.

"Plotin über Zeit und Ewigkeit." In Alois Dempf et al., eds., *Politische Ordnung und menschliche Existenz: Festgabe für Eric Voegelin*, 295–319. Munich, 1962.

"The Anthropological Foundation of the Experience of Truth." In *Memorias del XIII Congreso Internacional de Filosofía*, vol. 5, 507–517. Mexico, 1964. Expanded version in *The Phenomenon of Life*, 1966.

"Heidegger and Theology." *Review of Metaphysics* 18 (1964), 207–233.

"Philosophische Meditation über Paulus, Römerbrief, Kapitel 7." In Erich Dinkler, ed., *Zeit und Geschichte: Dankesgabe an Rudolf Bultmann zum 80. Geburtstag*, 557–570. Tübingen, 1964.

"Plotins Tugendlehre: Analyse und Kritik." In Frank Wiedmann, ed., *Epimeleia: Die Sorge der Philosophie um den Menschen. Festschrift für Helmut Kuhn*, 143–173. Munich, 1964.

"Life, Death, and the Body in the Theory of Being." *Review of Metaphysics* 19 (1965), 1–23. Final version in *The Phenomenon of Life*, 1966.

"Response to G. Quispel's 'Gnosticism and the New Testament.'" In J. Philip Hyatt, ed., *The Bible in Modern Scholarship*, 279–293. Nashville, Tenn., 1965. Final version in *Philosophical Essays*, 1974.

"Spinoza and the Theory of Organism." *Journal of the History of Philosophy* 3 (1965), 43–57. Also in Stuart F. Spicker, ed., *The Philosophy of the Body*, Chicago, 1970, and Marjorie Grene, ed., *Spinoza: A Collection of Critical Essays*, Garden City, N.Y., 1973.

"Delimitation of the Gnostic Phenomenon: Typological and Historical." In Ugo Bianchi, ed., *Le Origini dello Gnosticismo*. Leyden, 1967.

"Judaism and Christianity in the Western Tradition." *Commentary* 44 (Nov. 1967), 61–68. Expanded final version in *Philosophical Essays*, 1974.

"Biological Foundation of Individuality." *International Philosophical Quarterly* 8 (1968), 231–251.

"The Concept of God after Auschwitz." In Albert H. Friedlander, ed., *Out of the Whirlwind*, 465–476. New York, 1968. Also in *On Faith, Reason and Responsibility*, 1978.

"Contemporary Problems in Ethics from a Jewish Perspective." *Central Conference of*

American Rabbis Journal (January 1968), 27–39. Revised version in *CCAR Journal Anthology on Judaism and Ethics* (1969). Final version in *Philosophical Essays*, 1974.

"Economic Knowledge and the Critique of Goals." In Robert L. Heilbroner, ed., *Economic Means and Social Ends*, 67–88. New York, 1969. Final version in *Philosophical Essays*, 1974.

"Myth and Mysticism: A Study of Objectification and Interiorization in Religious Thought." *Journal of Religion* 49 (1969), 315–329. Also in *Philosophical Essays*, 1974.

"Origen's Metaphysics of Free Will, Fall and Redemption: A 'Divine Comedy' of the Universe." *Journal of the Universalist Historical Society* 8 (1969–70), 3–24. Also in *Philosophical Essays*, 1974.

"Philosophical Reflections on Experiments with Human Subjects." *Daedalus* 98 (1969), 219–247. Revised version in Paul Freund, ed., *Experimentation with Human Subjects*. New York, 1970. Final version in *Philosophical Essays*, 1974.

"Change and Permanence: On the Possibility of Understanding History." *Social Research* 38 (1971), 498–528.

"On the Meaning of the Scientific and Technological Revolution." *Philosophy Today* 15 (1971), 76–101.

"Philosophical Meditation on the Seventh Chapter of Paul's Epistle to the Romans." In James Robinson, ed., *The Future of Our Religious Past: Essays in Honor of Rudolf Bultmann*, 45–53. New York et al., 1971. Also in *Philosophical Essays*, 1974.

"The Soul in Gnosticism and Plotinus." In *Le Néoplatonisme*, 45–53. Paris, 1971. Also in *Philosophical Essays*, 1974.

"Aron Gurwitsch." *Social Research* 40 (1973), 567–569.

"Technology and Responsibility: Reflections on the New Tasks of Ethics." *Social Research* 40 (1973), 31–54. Also in *Philosophical Essays*, 1974.

"Freedom of Scientific Inquiry and the Public Interest: The Accountability of Science as an Agent of Social Action." *Hastings Center Report* 6 (1976). Also in *Biomedical Research and the Public. Prepared for the Subcommittee on Health and Scientific Research of the Committee on Human Resources*, 33–38, Washington D.C., 1977.

"Hannah Arendt, 1906–1975." *Social Research* 43 (1976), 3–5.

"Hannah Arendt in memoriam. Handeln, Erkennen, Denken: Aus Hannah Arendts philosophischem Werk." *Merkur* 30, no. 10 (1976), 921–935. English version: "Acting, Knowing, Thinking: Gleanings from Hannah Arendt's Philosophical Work." *Social Research* 44 (1977), 24–43.

"On the Power of Impotence of Subjectivity." In Stuart F. Spicker and H. Tristam Engelhardt, eds., *Philosophical Dimensions of the Neuro-Medical Sciences*, Dordrecht and Boston, 1976. Expanded version in *On Faith, Reason and Responsibility*, 1978.

"Responsibility Today: The Ethics of an Endangered Future." *Social Research* 43 (1976), 77–97.

"The Concept of Responsibility: An Inquiry into the Foundations of an Ethics for Our Age." In H. Tristam Engelhardt and Daniel Callahan, eds., *Knowledge, Value, and Belief*, 1–15. Hastings-on-Hudson, 1977. Reprinted in *On Faith, Reason and Responsibility*, 1978.

"Im Kampf um die Möglichkeit des Glaubens: Erinnerungen an Rudolf Bultmann und Betrachtungen zum philosophischen Aspekt seines Werkes." In Otto Kaiser, ed., *Gedenken an Rudolf Bultmann*, 41–77. Tübingen, 1977. English version: "Is Faith Still Possible? Memories of Rudolf Bultmann and Reflections on the Philosophical Aspects of His Work," *Harvard Theological Review* 75 (1982), 1–23.

"A Retrospective View." In Geo Widengren, ed., *Proceedings of the International Colloquium on Gnosticism (Stockholm, August 1973)*, 1–15. Stockholm and Leyden, 1977. Reprinted in *On Faith, Reason and Responsibility*, 1978.

"The Right to Die." *Hastings Center Report* 8, no. 4 (1978), 31–36.

"Straddling the Boundaries of Theory and Practice: Recombinant DNA Research as a Case of Action in the Process of Inquiry." In John Richards, ed., *Recombinant DNA: Science, Ethics and Politics*, 253–271. New York, San Francisco, London, 1978.

"Toward a Philosophy of Technology." *Hastings Center Report* 9 (1979), 34–43.

"The Heuristics of Fear." In Melvin Kranzberg, ed., *Ethics in an Age of Pervasive Technology*, 213–221. Boulder, 1980.

"Parallelism and Complementarity: The Psycho-Physical Problem in Spinoza and the Succession of Niels Bohr." In Richard Kennington, ed., *The Philosophy of Baruch de Spinoza*. Washington, D.C., 1980.

"Response to James N. Gustavson." In H. Tristam Engelhardt and Daniel Callahan, eds., *Knowing and Valuing: The Search for Common Roots*, 203–217. Hastings-on-Hudson, 1980.

"Im Zweifel für die Freiheit?" *Nachrichten aus Chemie, Technik und Laboratorium* 29 (1981). Reprinted in *Technik, Medizin und Ethik*, 1985.

"Reflections on Technology, Progress and Utopia." *Social Research* 48 (1981), 411–455.

"Lasst uns einen Menschen klonieren: Betrachtungen zur Aussicht genetischer Versuche mit uns selbst." *Scheidewege* 12 (1982). Reprinted in *Technik, Medizin und Ethik*, 1985.

"Technology as a Subject for Ethics." *Social Research* 49 (1982), 891–898.

"Ärztliche Kunst und menschliche Verantwortung." *Renovatio* 39 (1983). Reprinted in *Technik, Medizin und Ethik*, 1985.

"Evolution und Freiheit." *Scheidewege* 13 (1983–84), 85–102. Reprinted in *Philosophische Untersuchungen*, 1992.

"Forschung und Verantwortung." St. Gallen, 1983. Reprinted in *Technik, Medizin und Ethik*, 1985.

"Ontological Grounding of a Political Ethics: On the Metaphysics of Commitment to the Future of Man." *Graduate Faculty Philosophical Journal* 10 (1984), 47–62.

"Technik, Ethik und biogenetische Kunst: Betrachtungen zur neuen Schöpferrolle des Menschen." *Communio* XII, no. 6/84 (1984), 501–517. Reprinted in *Technik, Medizin und Ethik*, 1985.

"Warum wir heute eine Ethik der Selbstbeschränkung brauchen." In Elisabeth Ströker, ed., *Ethik der Wissenschaften? Philosophische Fragen*, 75–86. Munich, 1984.

"Ethics and Biogenetic Arts." *Social Research* 52 (1985), 491–504.

"Werkzeug, Bild und Grab: Vom Transanimalischen im Menschen." *Scheidewege* 15 (1985–86), 47–58. Reprinted in *Philosophische Untersuchungen*, 1992.

"Prinzip Verantwortung: Zur Grundlegung einer Zukunftsethik." In Thomas Meyer and Susanne Miller, eds., *Zukunftsethik und Industriegesellschaft*, 3–14. Frankfurt/Main and Munich, 1986.

"The Concept of God after Auschwitz: A Jewish Voice." *Journal of Religion* 67 (1987), 1–13.

"Technik, Freiheit und Pflicht." *Frankfurter Rundschau* no. 236, 12 October 1987. Reprinted in *Wissenschaft als persönliches Erlebnis*, 1987.

"Warum unsere Technik ein vordringliches Thema für die Ethik geworden ist." In Horst Krautkrämer, ed., *Ethische Fragen an die modernen Naturwissenschaften*, 6–21. Frankfurt/Main, 1987.

"Geist, Natur und Schöpfung: Kosmologischer Befund und kosmologische Vermutung." *Scheidewege* 18 (1988–89), 17–33. Expanded version in *Philosophische Untersuchungen*, 1988.

"Heideggers Entschlossenheit und Entschluss." In Günther Neske and Emil Kettering, eds., *Antwort: Martin Heidegger im Gespräch*, 221–229. Pfullingen, 1988.

"Warum die Technik ein Gegenstand der Ethik ist: Fünf Gründe." In Hans Lenk, ed., *Technik und Ethik*, 81–91. Stuttgart, 1989.

"Vergangenheit und Wahrheit: Ein später Nachtrag zu den sogenannten Gottesbeweisen." *Scheidewege* 20 (1990–91), 1–13. Reprinted in *Philosophische Untersuchungen*, 1992.

"Last und Segen der Sterblichkeit." *Scheidewege* 21 (1991–92), 26–40. Reprinted in *Philosophische Untersuchungen*, 1992. "The Burden and Blessing of Mortality." *Hastings Center Report* 22 (January 1992), 34–40.

"The Consumer's Responsibility." In Audun Øfsti, ed., *Ecology and Ethics: A Report from the Melba Conference, 18–23 July 1990*, 215–218. Trondheim, 1992.

"Fatalismus wäre Totsünde." *Freie Universität — Info* no. 7 (1992), 2–3. Reprinted in Dietrich Böhler and Rudi Neuberth, eds., *Herausforderung*

Zukunftsverantwortung: Hans Jonas zu Ehren, 49–51. Münster and Hamburg, 2nd expanded edition, 1993.

"Interview: Der ethischen Perspektive muss eine neue Dimension hinzugefügt werden." *Deutsche Zeitschrift für Philosophie* 41 (1993), 91–99.

"Aktuelle ethische Probleme aus jüdischer Sicht." *Scheidewege* 24 (1994–95), 3–15.

"Philosophy at the End of the Century: A Survey of Its Past and Future." *Social Research* 61 (1994), 812–832.

"Rassismus im Lichte der Menschheitsbedrohung." In Dietrich Böhler, ed., *Ethik für die Zukunft: Im Diskurs mit Hans Jonas*, 19–29. Munich, 1994.

"Not Compassion Alone: On Euthanasia and Ethics." *Hastings Center Report* 25 (1995), 44–45. Special edition on the legacy of Hans Jonas.

"Interview." In Herlinde Koelbl, ed., *Jüdische Portraits: Fotografien und Interviews*, 168–171. Frankfurt/Main, 1998.

"Unsere Teilnahme an diesem Kriege: Ein Wort an jüdische Männer" (September 1939). In *Jüdischer Almanach 2001*, 79–91. Frankfurt/Main, 2000.

II. SELECTED WORKS ON HANS JONAS

Aland, Barbara, ed. *Gnosis: Festschrift für Hans Jonas*. Göttingen, 1978.

Albert, Claudia. "Jonas, Hans." In Bernd Lutz, ed., *Metzler-Philosophen-Lexikon*, 399–403. Stuttgart, 1989.

Apel, Karl-Otto. "Verantwortung heute — nur noch ein Prinzip der Bewahrung und Selbstbeschränkung oder immer noch der Befreiung und Verwirklichung von Humanität?" In Thomas Meyer and Susanne Miller, eds., *Zukunftsethik und Industriegesellschaft*, 15–40. Frankfurt/Main and Munich, 1986.

Apel, Karl-Otto. "The Problem of Macroethics of Responsibility to the Future in the Crisis of Technological Civilization: An Attempt to Come to Terms with Hans Jonas' 'Principle of Responsibility.'" *Man and World* 20 (1987), 3–40.

Baum, Wolfgang. *Gnostische Elemente im Denken Martin Heideggers? Eine Studie auf der Grundlage der Religionsphilosophie von Hans Jonas*. Neuwied, 1997.

Bernstein, Richard J. *Radical Evil: A Philosophical Interrogation*. Cambridge and Oxford, 2002.

Betz, Walter. "Hans Jonas, der Religionswissenschaftler." *Zeitschrift für Religions- und Geistesgeschichte* 47 (1995), 68–80.

Böhler, Dietrich, ed. *Ethik für die Zukunft: Im Diskurs mit Hans Jonas*. Munich, 1994.

Böhler, Dietrich, and Andreas Frewer, eds. *Verantwortung für das Menschliche: Hans Jonas und die Ethik in der Medizin*. Erlangen and Jena, 1998.

Böhler, Dietrich, and Rudi Neuberth, eds. *Herausforderung Zukunftsverantwortung: Hans Jonas zu Ehren*. Münster and Hamburg, 1993.

Culianu, Ion Petru. *Gnosticismo e pensiero moderno: Hans Jonas.* Rome, 1985.

Depré, Olivier. "Philosophie de la nature et écologie: A propos de Hans Jonas." *Études Phénoménologiques* 10 (1994), 85–108.

Dewitte, Jacques. "Préservation de l'humanité et image de l'homme." *Études Phénoménologiques* 4 (1988), 33–68.

Donneley, Strachan. "Whitehead and Hans Jonas: Organism, Causality, and Perspective. *International Philosophical Quarterly* 19 (1979), 301–315.

Donneley, Strachan. "Hans Jonas, la philosophie de la nature et l'éthique de la responsabilité." *Études Phénoménologiques* 4 (1988), 69–90.

Fleischer, Margot. "Verantwortung und Sinnbewahrung: Zur Zukunftsethik von Hans Jonas." In Carl F. Gethmann and Peter L. Oestreich, eds., *Person und Sinnerfahrung: Philosophische Grundlagen und interdisziplinäre Perspektiven. Festschrift für Georg Scherer zum 65. Geburtstag,* 149–169. Darmstadt, 1993.

Foppa, Carlo. "L'analyse philosophique jonassienne de la théorie de l'évolution: Aspects problematiques." *Laval théologique et philosophique* 50 (1994), 575–593.

Frogneux, Nathalie. *Hans Jonas ou de la vie dans le monde.* Brussels, 2000.

Gethmann-Siefert, Annemarie. "Ethos und metaphysisches Erbe: Zu den Grundlagen von Hans Jonas' Ethik." In Herbert Schnädelbach and Geert Keil, eds., *Philosophie der Gegenwart — Gegenwart der Philosophie,* 171–215. Hamburg, 1993.

Goldberg, Arnold. "Ist Gott allmächtig? Was die Rabbiner Hans Jonas entgegnen würden." *Judaica* 47 (1991), 51–58.

Hans Jonas: Ansprachen aus Anlass der Verleihung (Friedenspreis des Deutschen Buchhandels). Frankfurt/Main, 1987.

Hans Jonas zu Ehren: Reden aus Anlass seiner Ehrenpromotion durch die Philosophische Fakultät der Universität Konstanz am 2. Juli 1991. Konstanz, 1992.

Henrix, Hans Hermann. "Machtentsagung Gottes? Ein Gespräch mit Hans Jonas im Kontext der Theodizeefrage." In Johann Baptist Metz, ed., *Landschaft aus Schreien: Zur Dramatik der Theodizeefrage,* 118–143. Mainz, 1996.

Hermann, Ingo, ed. *Hans Jonas: Erkenntnis und Verantwortung.* Göttingen, 1991.

Hirsch Hadorn, Gertrude. *Umwelt, Natur und Moral: Eine Kritik an Hans Jonas, Vittorio Hösle und Georg Picht.* Freiburg and Munich, 2000.

Hösle, Vittorio. *Die Krise der Gegenwart und die Verantwortung der Philosophie.* Munich, 1990.

Hösle, Vittorio. *Philosophie der ökologischen Krise.* Munich, 1991.

Hottois, Gilbert. *Aux fondements d'une éthique contemporaine: H. Jonas et H. T. Engelhardt en perspective.* Paris, 1993.

Hottois, Gilbert, and Marie-Geneviève Pinsart, eds. *Hans Jonas: Nature et responsabilité.* Paris, 1993.

Jakob, Eric. *Martin Heidegger und Hans Jonas: Die Metaphysik der Subjektivität und die Krise der technologischen Zivilisation.* Tübingen and Basel, 1996.

Jüngel, Eberhard. "Gottes ursprüngliches Anfangen als schöpferische Selbstbegrenzung: Ein Beitrag zum Gespräch mit Hans Jonas über den 'Gottesbegriff nach Auschwitz.'" In Hermann Deuser, ed. *Gottes Zukunft— Zukunft der Welt: Festschrift für Jürgen Moltmann zum 60. Geburtstag,* 265–275. Munich, 1986.

Kajon, Irene. "Hans Jonas and Jewish Post-Auschwitz Thought." *Journal of Jewish Thought and Philosophy* 8 (1998), 67–80.

Kettner, Matthias. "Verantwortung als Moralprinzip? Eine kritische Betrachtung der Verantwortungsethik von Hans Jonas." *Bijtragen* 51 (1990), 418–439.

Lesch, Walter. "Ethische Argumentation im jüdischen Kontext: Zum Verständnis von Ethik bei Emmanuel Levinas und Hans Jonas." *Freiburger Zeitschrift für Theologie und Philosophie* 38 (1991), 443–469.

Levy, David J. "Politics, Nature and Freedom: On the Natural Foundation of the Political Condition." *Journal of the British Society for Phenomenology* 15 (1984), 286–300.

Levy, David. *Hans Jonas: The Integrity of Thinking.* Columbia, Mo., and London, 2002.

Löw, Reinhard. "Jonas, Hans." In Walter Killy, ed., *Literaturlexikon: Autoren und Werke deutscher Sprache,* vol. 6, 128–142. Gütersloh, 1990.

Marzahn, Christian, ed. *Wissenschaft und Verantwortung: Hans Jonas im Gespräch mit Rainer Hegselmann u.a.* Bremen, 1991.

Matheis, Alfons. *Diskurs als Grundlage der politischen Gestaltung: Das politisch-verantwortungsethische Modell der Diskursethik als Erbe der moralischen Implikationen der kritischen Theorie Max Horkheimers im Vergleich mit dem Prinzip Verantwortung von Hans Jonas.* St. Ingbert, 1996.

Monaldi, Marcello. *Tecnica, vita, responsabilità: Qualche riflessione su Hans Jonas.* Naples, 2000.

Mucci, Giandomenico. "Dopo Auschwitz: Il Dio impotente di Hans Jonas." *Viviltà Cattolica* 3587 (1999), 425–438.

Müller, Dennis, and Bernard Baertschi, eds. *Nature et descendence: Hans Jonas et le principe "responsabilité."* Geneva, 1993.

Müller, Wolfgang E. *Der Begriff der Verantwortung bei Hans Jonas.* Frankfurt/Main, 1988.

Müller, Wolfgang E. "Zur Problematik des Verantwortungsbegriffs bei Hans Jonas." *Zeitschrift für evangelische Ethik* 33 (1989), 204–216.

Müller, Wolfgang E. "Weltverantwortung und Schöpfungsglaube: Zur theologischen Auseinandersetzung mit Hans Jonas." *Evangelische Kommentare* 23 (1990), 396–399.

Müller, Wolfgang E., ed. *Hans Jonas: Von der Gnosisforschung zur Verantwortungsethik*. Stuttgart, 2003.

Niggemeier, Frank. *Pflicht zur Behutsamkeit? Hans Jonas' naturphilosophische Ethik für die technologische Zivilisation*. Würzburg, 2002.

Oelmüller, Willi. "Hans Jonas: Mythos — Gnosis — Prinzip Verantwortung." *Stimmen der Zeit* 206 (1988), 343–351.

Poliwoda, Sebastian. "Versorgung von Sein: Die philosophischen Grundlagen der Bioethik bei Hans Jonas." PhD dissertation, University of Munich, 1993.

Prieri, Alberto. *Hans Jonas*. Florence, 1998.

Rath, Matthias. *Intuition und Modell: Hans Jonas' 'Prinzip Verantwortung' und die Frage nach einer Ethik für das wissenschaftliche Zeitalter*. Frankfurt/Main, Berne, New York, 1988.

Redeker, Robert. "Dieu après Auschwitz: La théodicée faible de Hans Jonas." *Les Temps Modernes* 582 (1995), 134–150.

Richardson, William J. "Heidegger and God — and Professor Jonas." *Thought* 40 (1965), 13–40.

Ricoeur, Paul. "La responsabilité et la fragilité de la vie: Ethique et philosophie de la biologie chez Hans Jonas." *Le messager européen* 5 (1992), 203–218.

Ricot, Jacques. "Vulnérabilité du monde, vulnérabilité de Dieu selon Hans Jonas." *Sens* 50 (1998), 163–178.

Roser, Andreas. "'Das Prinzip Verantwortung' und seine Probleme: Kritische Anmerkungen zum Entwurf einer Zukunftsethik." *Prima Philosophia*, special edition 1 (1990), 25–52.

Rubinoff, Leon. "Perception, Self-Making and Transcendence." *Philosophical Quarterly* 7 (1967), 511–527.

Schieder, Thomas. *Weltabenteuer Gottes: Die Gottesfrage bei Hans Jonas*. Paderborn, 1998.

Schubert, Jörg. *Das 'Prinzip Verantwortung' als verfassungsrechtliches Rechtsprinzip: Rechtsphilosophische und verfassungsrechtliche Betrachtungen zur Verantwortungsethik von Hans Jonas*. Baden-Baden, 1998.

Scott, Charles E. "Heidegger Reconsidered: A Response to Professor Jonas." *Harvard Theological Review* 59 (1966), 175–185.

Sève, Bernard. "Hans Jonas et l'éthique de la responsabilité." *Esprit* 10 (1990), 72–87.

Sikora, Jürgen. *Hans Jonas, Vittorio Hösle und die Grundlagen normativer Pädagogik*. Eitorf, 1999.

Simon, René. *Ethique de la responsabilité*. Paris, 1993.

Song, Ahn-Jung. *Organismustheorie im ethischen Diskurs: Eine Untersuchung zur Philosophie des Lebens bei Hans Jonas*. Munich, 2000.

Spicker, Stewart F., ed. *Organism, Medicine and Metaphysics: Essays in Honor of Hans Jonas*. Dordrecht and Boston, 1978.

Szostak, Walter. *Teleologie des Lebendigen: Zu Karl Poppers und Hans Jonas' Philosophie des Lebendigen*. Frankfurt/Main, 1995.

Theis, Robert. "Dieu éclaté: Hans Jonas et les dimensions d'une théologie philosophique après Auschwitz." *Révue Philosophique de Louvain* 98 (2000), 341–357.

Tönnies, Sabine. "Hans Jonas zwischen Sein und Sollen." *Rechtstheorie* 22 (1991), 370–381.

Vogel, Lawrence. "Hans Jonas' Exodus: From German Existentialism to Post-Holocaust Theology." In Hans Jonas, *Mortality and Morality: A Search for the Good after Auschwitz*, ed. Lawrence Vogel, 30–36. Evanston, Ill., 1996.

Wendnagel, Johannes. *Ethische Neubesinnung als Ausweg aus der Weltkrise? Ein Gespräch mit dem "Prinzip Verantwortung" von Hans Jonas*. Würzburg, 1990.

Wetz, Franz Josef. *Hans Jonas zur Einführung*. Hamburg, 1964.

Wetz, Franz Josef. "Hans Jonas (1903–1993)." In Hans Erler, Ernst Ludwig Ehrlich, and Ludger Heid, eds., *"Meinetwegen ist die Welt erschaffen." Das intellektuelle Vermächtnis des deutschsprachigen Judentums*, 78–83. Frankfurt/Main, 1997.

Weyemberg, Maurice. "La critique de l'utopie technique chez J. Ellul et H. Jonas." *Tijdschrift voor de Studie van de Verlichting en van Het Verije denken* 17 (1989), 63–136.

Wiese, Christian. "Revolte wider die Weltflucht." In Hans Jonas, *Die gnostische Religion: Die Botschaft des fremden Gottes*, ed. Christian Wiese, 401–429. Frankfurt/Main, 1999.

Wiese, Christian. "'Dass man zusammen Philosoph und Jude ist . . .': Zur Dimension des Jüdischen in Hans Jonas' philosophischer Ethik der Bewahrung der 'Schöpfung.'" In Joachim Valentin and Saskia Wendel, eds., *Jüdische Traditionen in der Philosophie des 20. Jahrhunderts*, 131–147. Darmstadt, 2000.

Wiese, Christian. "Ein 'Bellum Judaicum' in des Wortes tiefster Bedeutung: Hans Jonas' Kriegsaufruf 1939 im Kontext seine Biographie und seines philosophischen Denkens." In *LBI-Almanach 2001*, 92–107. Frankfurt/Main, 2000.

Wiese, Christian. *Hans Jonas: Revolte wider die Weltflucht. Reden und Gespräche*. Munich, 2000. Audiobook

Wiese, Christian. *Hans Jonas — "Zusammen Philosoph und Jude."* Frankfurt/Main, 2003.

Wiese, Christian. *The Life and Thought of Hans Jonas*. Trans. Jeffrey Grossman and Christian Wiese. Dartmouth, N.H., and Waltham, Mass., 2007.

Wiese, Christian, and Eric Jacobson, eds. *Weiterwohnlichkeit der Welt: Neue Perspektiven zu Hans Jonas*. Berlin, 2003.

Wille. *Ontologie und Ethik bei Hans Jonas*. Dettelbach, 1996.

Wolf, Jean-Claude. "Hans Jonas: Eine naturphilosophische Begründung der Ethik." In Anton Hügli and Paul Lübcke, eds., *Philosophie im 20. Jahrhundert*, vol. 1, 214–236. Reinbek, 1992.

Wolin, Richard. *Heidegger's Children: Hannah Arendt, Karl Löwith, Hans Jonas, and Herbert Marcuse*. Princeton, N.J., 2001.

Index

INDEX OF NAMES